Deaths Abstracted from

THE CAMP POINT JOURNAL

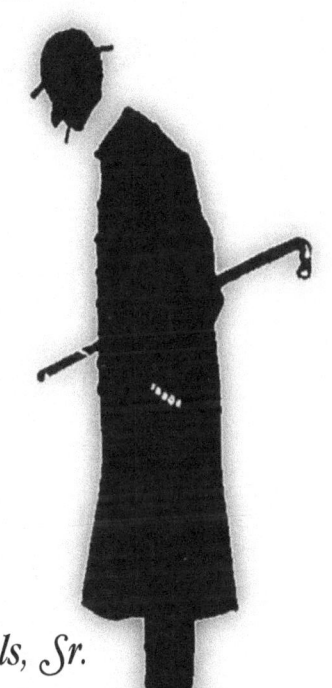

1893–1903

Camp Point

Adams County
Illinois

Mrs. Joseph J. Beals, Sr.
and *Mrs. Sandy Kirchner*

HERITAGE BOOKS
2020

HERITAGE BOOKS

AN IMPRINT OF HERITAGE BOOKS, INC.

Books, CDs, and more—Worldwide

For our listing of thousands of titles see our website
at
www.HeritageBooks.com

Published 2020 by
HERITAGE BOOKS, INC.
Publishing Division
5810 Ruatan Street
Berwyn Heights, Md. 20740

International Standard Book Numbers
Paperbound: 978-0-7884-0908-0
Clothbound: 978-0-7884-6377-8

Table of Contents

ADAMS COUNTY

Illinois

1872

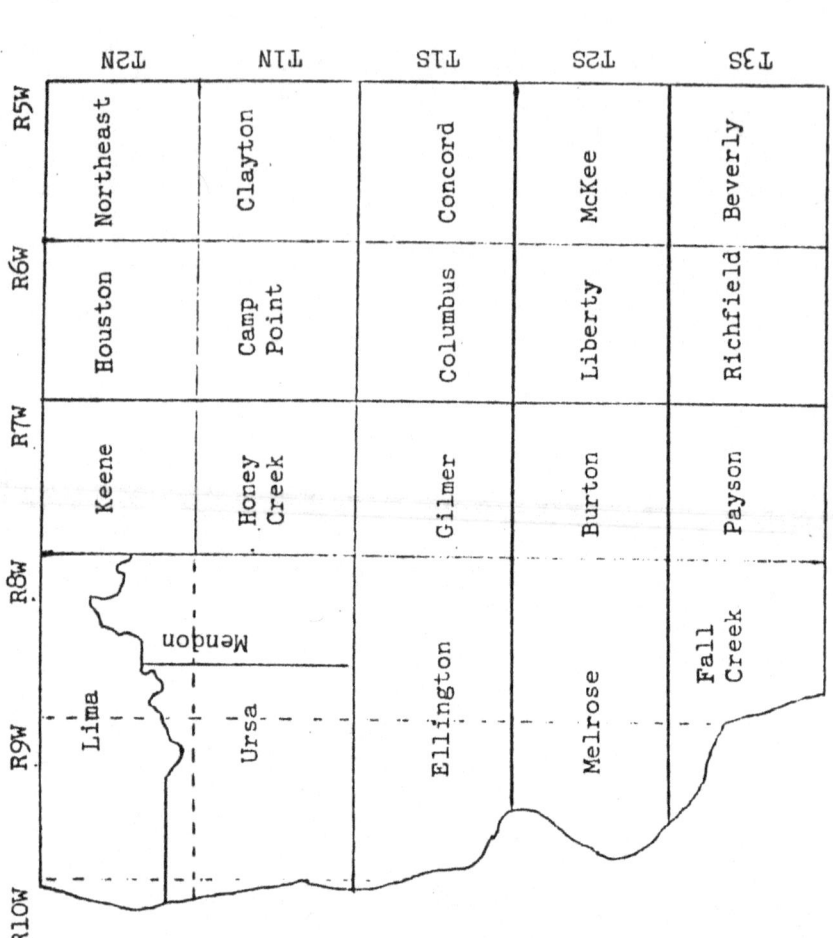

The death related items in this book were abstracted from The Camp Point Journal newspaper of Camp Point, Adams County Illinois. These papers were dated from 1893 through 1903. In the early 1960's while doing research on my own genealogy in Camp Point Journal, we found so much valuable information that we decided to start writing it all on 3" x 5" index cards. We wrote down any items that mentioned a family name. Although this book consists of death related announcements our collection of index cards includes information from advertisements, jury lists, criminal courts and letter remaining at the post office. We hope to prepare these remaining items for publication as time permits. A cross reference in this book contains an additional list of names.

The town of Camp Point was laid off on February 16, 1854 by the order of P.B. Garrett, Benj. Booth, Wm Farlow and Thomas Bailey. It is situated on a beautiful, high, rolling prairie and is at the junction of the C.B. & Q and T.W. and W. Railroads.

In April of 1855 what is known as the original survey of Camp Point was laid out. The following summer James A. Roth came from Quincy and built a store and house, the store is gone and the house was rebuilt by his son John.

In 1856 the Francis Hotel was built by Thos. Ensminger. At about the same time Moses Bryant erected a part of what is now the Omer House

Mrs Joseph J. Beals Sr.
Mrs Sandy Kirchner
P.O. Box 279
Cherokee, IA   51012

AADAMS, LOTTIE - "Mother kills babe" -Apr 15,
1903 - Lottie Aadams of Marshall, Mo. age 19
attending school in Quincy gave birth to a babe
Thursday night and threw it out of the window
on the brick walk below, where it lay until
Friday A.M. When it was found alive the girl
and baby were taken to Blessing Hospital where
the babe died in a few hours. It is possible
the girl is insane.

AARON, JOHN - Death of John Aaron - Jan 27,
1897 - Died-John Aaron, Friday at the home of
his daughter, Mrs J.J. Lusk, Quincy in his 79th
year. Emigrated from Deleware to Adams Co. and
lived here since, except for 13 years spent in
Pike Co. Lived many years near Cliola where
his son Charles was murdered by the negro
Jamison. Mrs Aaron died about 2 years ago.
Leaves 3 children- Will Aaron of Hays City, KS
Mrs S.A. Hull of Denver and Mrs J.J. Lusk of
Quincy.

AARON, JOHN - Co. Seat - Feb 3, 1897 - Will of
John Aaron mentions his daughter Mrs Sallie
Hull- his son, William L. Aaron-his daughter,
Mrs J.J. Lusk-his sister, Martha Aaron and
grandchildren. John C. Broady appt., Ex.

AARON, MRS REMEMBER (JOHN) - Death - Jul 20,
1893 - Mrs Remember Aaron, wife of John Aaron
died at the family home in Quincy Saturday from
effects of a cancer she had had several years.
Remember Hull was born at Kaskaskia, Mar 28,
1819 and came to Quincy in 1849 where she
married John Aaron and spent the rest of her
life in this and Pike Co.'s. Leaves husband
and 2 children-Will Aaron of Hays City, Ks and
Mrs Mary E. Lusk of Quincy. Funeral at the
family residence Sunday.

ACHELPOHL, AUGUST H. - Quincy - Nov 26, 1902
August H. Achelpohl, a native of Germany and a
resident of this city for a half century, died
Thursday, age 60 years.

ACHELPOHL, J.H. - Quincy - Dec 10, 1902 - J.H.
Achelpohl died from a stroke of paralysis on

Wednesday, age 68 years.

ACKLAM, FRANCIS - Wants a Home - Apr 15, 1903
Co. Judge McCrory wants a home for a strong
healthy, 12 year old boy, the same being
Francis Acklam, of Camp Point who was found to
be a dependant boy. His mother died about a
year ago. His parents were seperated some 8 or
10 years ago. Father had remarried and the boy
has been living with his grandmother, who is
too old and poor to look after him. "Whig"

ACKLAM, GEORGE W. - Death - Dec 30, 1903 -
George W. Acklam was born in England Dec 27,
1840. Died Camp Point Dec 23, 1903, almost 63
years old. Son of the late Welbourn Acklam and
came to U.S. in early childhood. Enlisted in
1861 in Co. E, 50th Ill. and served 4 years.
Was taken prisoner at Shiloh and soon after
paroled. Married Jan. 1864 to Mrs Abby Demoss,
who with 2 children survive him. Children are-
Mrs Mary Felsman and Charles Acklam. Also 2
step sons, Oliver and Henry Demoss, and 1
brother, 2 sisters. Funeral Friday P.M. at
Christian Church by Rev. W.H. Applegate.
Buried Village Cemetery.

ACKLAM, MRS WELBOURN - Death of Mrs Acklam- May
8, 1894 - Died, Mrs Welbourn Acklam Sat. A.M.
Funeral Sunday P.M. from Methodist Church.
Maria Hudson was born Aug 5, 1818 in Hamilton
Co. Ohio. Married William Horner on 1835, had
8 children - 6 daughters, 2 sons. Two
daughters died in infancy. Moved with her
family to Adams Co. Ill 1849. Mr H. died 1853
and in 1859 she married Welbourne Acklam who
died in 1889. She died May 5, 1894 at 9:30
A.M. Services by Rev A.N. Simmons Sun. at 3
P.M.

ACKLAM, MARION W. - Death Record - Nov 3, 1897
Died- Marion W. Acklam, son of Benjamin and
Martha E. Acklam at his home in Camp Point Oct
20, 1897. Born Columbus twp Aug 9, 1875.
Services at Pleasant View Church Oct 31 at 3
P.M. by Elder O. Dilley. Buried Pleasant View
Cemetery.

ADAMS, CATHERINE - Quincy - Feb 5, 1902
Catherine Adams who had conducted a grocery
store in this city since 1860 died Wed., age 65
years.

ADAMS, GEORGE - Ancient History - Mar 23, 1894
March 17, 1876 George Adams beat Anna Ferris
to death with a hammer in Quincy.

ADAMS, GEORGE - Local - Feb 9, 1893 - George
Adams, a pioneer citizen of Quincy died at
Pratt, Ks. Friday A.M. lacking only 11 days of
being 79 years old. Remains brought to Quincy
and buried from Vermont St. Methodist Church
Tuesday.

ADCOX, CHARLES - Quincy - Jul 7, 1897 - Charles
Adcox age 45 was killed by a locomotive on the
O.K. track Monday night. Adcox was a drinking
man and it is supposed he was drunk at the
time.

AKERS, J.G. - Probate Notice - Jun 11, 1902
J.G. Akers, deceased 1st Mon. of August 1902
(4th) Thomas O. Sparks, adm.

AKERS, JEREMIAH G. - Death - May 7, 1902
Jeremiah G. Akers died at his home in Columbus
twp near Union Church, Mon. night, after a
brief illness, age 71 years. Was justice for
20 years. Leaves aged wife, 2 sons and 2
daughters. Funeral at Union Church at 2 P.M.

ALBERG, CARL - Local - Apr 20, 1893 - Carl
Alberg, of Kansas city fell dead on the streets
of Quincy Wednesday from hemmorrhage of the
lungs.

ALDEN, MRS JULIA SWEET - Quincy - Jul 19, 1895
Mrs Julia Sweet Alden formerly of this city
died in Centerville, IA and buried here Monday
afternoon.

ALEXANDER, DR WILLIAM R. - Quincy - Oct 20,
1897 - Dr William R. Alexander, formerly of
this city died last week in Chicago.

ALLEN, GEORGE W. - May 4, 1893 - List of
soldiers buried in Camp Point Cemetery. Was in
the Ind. Infantry.

ALTMIX, JOHN - Co. Seat - Nov 11, 1896 - John
Altmix age 71 years and Robert Stewart age 70
years, both residents of this city died Tuesday
afternoon.

ANDERS, JOHN - Ancient History - Apr 6, 1894
Apr 7, 1881 John Anders died on the 4th.

ANDERSON, MISS CORNELIA - Ancient History - Jul
14, 1897 - Sept 1880, Miss Cornelia Anderson
died on the 13th.

ANDERSON, EDGAR - Drowned at Clayton - Jun 15,
1894 - Edgar Anderson age 18, living in Clayton
went to the Wabash reservoir with Fred
Ellerbrock Wed. Anderson was wading when he
stepped in a hole and was unable to swim. Was
son of Prof. H.M. Anderson.

ANDERSON, MRS REV EDWARD - Local - Feb 6, 1894
Died, wife of Rev Edward Anderson at Danville,
Conn. last week. Mr A. was a few years ago
pastor of the Cong. Church Quincy.

ANDERSON, ROBERT - Died - Nov 24, 1897 - At
Pawnee, Neb. Nov 14th Robert, the 4 year old
son of Mr and Mrs C.N. Anderson. Parents have
many friends in this vicinity.

ANDERSON, WILLARD - Found dying in a field -
Jul 6, 1894 - A fatal accident befell Willard
Anderson, a farmer living NW of Tennessee Sat.
A.M. It is supposed he was kicked by a horse.
He was a son in law of Cornelius Falder of
Macomb. "Macomb Bystander"

ANDERSON, WILLIAM W. - Death of W.W. Anderson
Feb 17, 1897 - William W. Anderson was
prostrated with a stroke of paralysis last
Tuesday and died Feb 15th. Born Beaufort Co.
Tenn. Dec 6, 1821. Came to Ill. 1840. Married
Sarah Scott at Beardstown Dec 10, 1847 and came
Adams Co. 1857 where he lived since except for

5 years spent in Hancock Co. Lived Camp Point
since 1862. Father of 10 children-3 sons and 2
daughters survive him. Funeral at family home
Tuesday P.M. by Rev A.N. Simmons and Rev W.M.
Reed. Buried village Cemetery.

ANDREWS, WM - Local - Nov 26, 1895 - Wm
Andrews, a prosperous farmer of Mendon died
Saturday from diabetes, 46 years old. Leaves
wife and 2 children.

ANDRUS, CHARLES W. AND JULIA - Local - Oct 25,
1895 - Charles W. and Julia Andrus, son and
daughter in law of Wm P. Andrus who have been
indicted for the murder of the last named by
the Hancock Co. grand jury. Wm P. Andrus died
near Warsaw on Feb 3, 2 years ago and nearly a
month later was buried in an orchard on the
farm, the body in the meantime being kept in
the old smokehouse. Charles left for Nebr. by
wagon, but Mrs A. was arrested and in custody.

APPLEBY, EDWIN - Killed - Jan 18, 1895 - Edwin
Appleby in company with his 2 brothers and
young Shane went to Golden Tuesday night on the
freight intending to return on Passenger #11.
When the boys got to Golden and climbed on the
passenger they missed Edwin and went back
looking for him. He was found near the
crossing at Emminga's Warehouse with his head
crushed and dead. He had probably fallen off.
Body taken to Earls undertaking rooms at Camp
Point. Funeral at Ebenezer Cemetery in Houston
Thursday. Was 15 years old, son of Mr and Mrs
Wesley Appleby of Camp Point. Had 2 older
brothers and 1 sister.

ARGAST, MRS ED - Local - Dec 17, 1902 - Mrs Ed
Argast, mother of the editor of the Nauvoo
Rustler is dead.

ARING, JOHN - Coatsburg - Dec 11, 1894 - Died-
John Aring, an insane inmate of the Adams Co.
insane asylum died of consumption Wednesday.
Taken to Quincy for burial by his mother and
brother Thursday.

ARNING, GOTTLIEB - Quincy - Oct 25, 1895
Gottlieb Arning, one of the early settlers of
Quincy, died Sunday, 86 years old.

ARNOLD, NICHOLAS - Quincy - Nov 2, 1894
Nicholas Arnold who lived at 223 Maiden Lane
was found dead in bed Wednesday A.M. Daughter
found him. Caused by rheumatism of the heart.

ARNTZEN, HON. BERNARD - Died - Nov 5, 1895
Hon Bernard Arntzen died Saturday at Duluth.
Remains brought to Quincy for burial today.
Born Prussia 1834. Came to U.S. 1849 located
in Quincy where he studies law and was admitted
to bar. Leaves 2 sons and a daughter.

ARNTZEN, BERNARD - Quincy - Nov 15, 1895 - The
will of ex-state Senator Bernard Arntzen
admitted to probate Monday gives 1/2 of
property to Mr and Mrs John M. Cabbell and
other 1/2 to be divided equally between son,
John B. Arntzen and daughter, Mrs Myra
Thompson. Mrs J.M. Cabbell, sister of deceased
is appointed executrix.

ARONSON, RACHEL B. - Quincy - Jul 7, 1897
Rachel B. Aronson, a young lady prominent in
the Jewish circles died suddenly from heart
failure on Thursday.

ARROWSMITH, MRS ELIZA - Quincy - Feb 24, 1897
Died-Mrs Eliza Arrowsmith, one of the early
settlers of the city, died Thursday night, age
76 years.

ASBURY, HENRY - Recent Deaths - Nov 25, 1896
Died the venerable Henry Asbury at the home of
his daughter, Mrs Abbott in Chicago Thursday
night, age 86 years. Was one of the pioneers
of Quincy. Buried Quincy Saturday in Woodland
Cemetery with masonic honors.

ASHCRAFT, CHARLES W. - A Fatal Error - Nov 18,
1896 - Accidental poisoning in this city
Thursday eve. Charles W. Ashcraft age 21 years
lost his life. His father lives on the Seckman
place 3 miles NE of town. "Mt Sterling"

Democrat Message"

ASHCRAFT, JAMES - Local - Apr 3, 1894 - Died,
James Ashcraft at his home in Columbus Saturday
of consumption, 30 years old. Funeral Monday
by Columbus lodge of Odd Fellows.

ASHCRAFT, JAMES - Columbus - Apr 6, 1894 - Died
Saturday at 10 P.M. March 31st, 1894, James
Ashcraft in his 29th year. Leaves a widow and
infant daughter, father, mother, 1 brother, 3
sisters. Services by Rev A. White of the ME
Church. Burial services by Odd Fellows in
village cemetery.

ASHER, BARTLET - Death of B. Asher - Feb 5,
1896   Died-Bartlet Asher Monday night after
illness of several weeks, 86 years old. Native
of Kentucky. Came to Ind. at an early day and
to Ill. 1836 where he lived most of time since,
except few years in Mo. Father of several
children most passed on before him. Buried
today at Coatsburg.

ASHER, BARTLETT - Obituary - Mar 12, 1896
Bartlett Asher born Jefferson Co. Ken. Aug 5,
1810. Came to Owen Co. Ind. when a small boy
lived there until 1844 when he came to Ill.
Died Camp Point Feb 3, 1896. Buried Feb 5th in
Coatsburg Cemetery. Was 85 years 6 mo. old.
Married twice, had 12 children-3 oldest of whom
are living: Jasper and Nancy here and Thomas B.
in Oklahoma. Also leaves 1 sister, Mrs A.
Johnson in Coatsburg. Enlisted in Co. H 39th
Reg. Ill. Volunteers under Capt Wm Downs Mar 3,
1865 discharged because of disability Nov 22,
1865 at Norfolk, VA. Also had 4 sons in Union
Army. Thanks by Jasper Asher   Nancy C. Rader

ASHER, FRANCES - Probate Notice - Apr 1, 1896
Frances Asher, deceased   1st Monday of May 1896
(4th) William J. Adams, adm.

ASHER, MRS FRANCES - Local - May 3, 1895 - Mrs
Frances Asher died at 11 PM Thursday after an
illness of 6 or 7 weeks. Funeral tomorrow at
10 from the home.

ASHER, MRS FRANCES - Death - May 3, 1895 - Mrs Frances Asher, wife of Bartlet Asher died May 1st, age 66 years 1 mon. 25 days. Born near Nashville, Tenn. Married 1845 to Isaac B. Adams who died 1863. They came to Ill. 1854 and lived near Camp Point since, 1872 she married Bartlet Asher who survives her. Leaves 4 sons, 3 living in Camp Point and 1 in Pike Co. Funeral Sat. May 4th from the home by Elder O. Dilley. Buried Village Cemetery.

ASHER, HENRY - Coatsburg - Mar 12, 1902 - A.K. Bailey, P.M. at Meadville, MO is here to attend the funeral of his brother in law, Henry Asher. He was welcomed by old friends.

ASHER, HENRY - Local - Mar 5, 1902 - Fred Frike adm. of the estate of Henry Asher will sell his property next Tuesday.

ASHER, HENRY - Found dead in wagon - Mar 5, 1902 - Coroner Lummus was called to Coatsburg Thursday night to hold inquest over the remains of Henry Asher, a farmer, found dead in his wagon Thusday afternoon. Verdict returned, he had died of apoplexy. He had been living with an unmarried daughter about 3 miles N of Coatsburg and was moving to his married daughters Mrs Fred White who lives mile and 1/2 from town when death claimed him. About 65 years old and a widower.

ASHER, HENRY - Death - Mar 12, 1902 - Henry Asher born Sep 6, 1840 died Feb 28th, 1902, age 61 years 5 mon. 22 days. Married Susan White Aug 25, 1862, they had 12 children-5 died before him-surviving is Warren of Big Neck, Mrs Ettie White of LaPrairie, Mrs Fred White of Coatsburg, John of Paloma, Mrs Cal Upchurch of Augusta, Mrs Lee Davis of Augusta and Minnie Asher of Coatsburg-all at the funeral.

ASHER, JAMES W. - May 4, 1893 - Soldiers buried in Camp Point Cemetery. Listed in Co. E 16th Ill. infantry.

ASHER, PRESTON - Local - Jun 22, 1893 - Preston

Asher, who was formerly a resident of Camp
Point and Columbus died on the 8th inst. at
Albion, Idaho, age 75 years. He was the father
of Mrs G.B. Adams and Mrs Jacob Omer, of Camp
Point. He was taken off with an attack of
typhoid fever.

ASKEW, ARCHIBALD - Kingston Tragedy - Jul 22,
1896 - Tragedy in Kingston Saturday A.M.
Archibald Askew shot his uncle Arthur Callahan
then himself. Mr and Mrs Callahan had been
keeping Emma Askew daughter of Archibald Askew
since the death of his wife 8 years. Emma is
16 years old. Mr Askew also has a younger son
at Slater, Saline Co. MO. Shot Mrs Callahan
while she was sitting with grand daughter and
Emma. Mr Callahan will live. Mr Callahan is
about 65 years old, is an uncle of J.A. and
M.W. Callahan of this ville. Mr Askew died.

ASPEY, GEORGE - Death - Apr 30, 1895 - George
Aspey of Golden died Sunday after illness of
several weeks. Born Penn. Came to Ill. 1866
and has lived in Houston twp, Camp Point and
last fall went to Golden. Leaves a wife, no
children. Services at Ebenezer Church in
Houston twp, Monday afternoon. Was 72 years
old.

ASPEY, GEORGE - Primrose - May 7, 1895 - Remains of George Aspey of Golden formerly of Big
Neck were buried at Ebenezer Monday P.M. of
last week.

ASPEY, GEORGE - Obituary - May 24, 1895 - Died
in Golden after illness of 14 months Mr George
Aspey age 72 years 4 mon. 6 days. Born
Westmoreland Co. Penn. Dec 18, 1822. Married
Miss Drucilla J. Foltz June 13, 1853. 1866 he
and family came west to Missouri for 1 year
then to Big Neck, Ill. where except for 4 years
lived since. Leaves wife and daughter Mrs E.
Nelson. Services by his pastor Rev Royce of
Camp Point Presby. Church. Buried Ebenezer
Cemetery.

ASPEY, GEORGE - Quincy - Jun 4, 1895 - Will of

George Aspey of Houston was filed Saturday.
Leaves all of his estate to wife Drusilla Aspey
for life and at her death 300 to Catherine A.
Foltz, 100 to Maria Aspey, etc. Rest to
Drusilla Hawkins Aspey and children of
Salathiel Aspey and A.M. Foltz.

ASPEY, GEORGE - Probate Notice - Jul 9, 1895
George Aspey, deceased 1st Monday of Sept
(2nd) Jacob Groves and Drusilla J. Aspey,
Ex.'s

ASPEY, GEORGE - Local - May 26, 1897 - Jacob
Groves sold the land belonging to the George
Aspey estate in front of the post office in
Golden to Mrs Catherine A. Foltz.

ASPEY, GEORGE - Ex's Sale of Real Estate - Apr
14, 1897 Of George Aspey, deceased, against
Drusilla J. Aspey, individually, Allison Aspey,
Clara Aspey, Serena Aspey, Ewell Aspey, Burt
Aspey, Viola Aspey, Orton Aspey, Lannis Aspey,
Mariah Aspey, David Aspey, Elizabeth Aspey,
Joseph Aspey, Ezra Aspey, Elias Aspey, Gideon
Aspey, Rachel Aspey, Wesley Aspey, Angie
Troxel, Nancy Troxel, Harriet Troxel, Almeda
Troxel, Isiah Troxel, William Troxel, Urbanus
Hubbs, Rachel Hough, Nancy Hough, Elizabeth
Hough, Agilla Hough, Keziah Hough, Michael
Hough, John Reynolds, Michael H. Reynolds,
Harriet H. Reynolds, Harris A. Reynolds,
Drusilla Nelson, Edith Foltz, Elva Foltz, Noah
Foltz, Catherine A. Foltz, and individually and
as guardian of Elva Foltz and Noah Foltz,
charitable aid and hospital assoc., a corp.,
Orphans home of Council Bluffs, IA will sell
May 15th, 1897. Signed Jacob Groves and
Drusilla J. Aspey. Ex.'s

AULL, JAMES - Ancient History - Aug 9, 1895
August 1878 James Aull died at the home of his
grandson, Joseph Aull, age 86 years.

AUSMUS, GEORGE W. - Death - Sep 13, 1895
George W. Ausmus died at his home in Clayton
Tuesday afternoon, age 59 years. Sick 4 weeks
with cancer of the stomach. He moved to

Clayton from Brown Co. about 6 years ago.
Leaves a wife, the daughter of Henry C. Craig
and a son 20 years old. Two daughters who
attended Maplewood School died before him.

AUSMUS, GEORGE - Quincy - Sep 27, 1895 - Will
of George Ausmus admitted to probate leaves
$1,000 to his son George and $100 to his
grandson, G.E. Lucas. Rest of estate goes to
his widow who is also executor.

AUSMUS, MRS MARGARET - Death Record - Mar 31,
1897 - Died, Mrs Margaret Ausmus at her home in
Clayton on the 25th of brain trouble. Was
daughter of Henry C. Craig. Had been a widow
20 years and childless. Funeral Sat. A.M.

AUSTIN, STRONG - Quincy - Jun 25, 1902 - Strong
Austin, one of the early settlers of Augusta
died during the past week, age 93 years.

AVISE, WILLIAM E. - Death of W.E. Avise - Feb
19, 1896 Died, William E. Avise in Quincy
Friday, age 60 years.

BACON, ROBERT H. - Local - Oct 22, 1902 Robert
H. Bacon, on the pioneer merchants of LaPrairie
died Sunday at an advanced age.

BACON, ROBERT H. - Quincy - Dec 24, 1902 - Will
of Robert H. Bacon was filed for probate last
week. Estate worth $20,000 and is divided among
the children in equal shares. Edward H. Bacon
and Luther E. Thomas are named as exec.'s.

BAEDER, MRS MARY - Co. Seat - Apr 1, 1896
Died, Mrs Mary Baeder, a resident of this city
for nearly a half century died at Coatsburg,
age 68 years.

BAGBY, JUDGE JOHN C. - Deaths this Week - Apr
8, 1896 - Died, Judge John C. Bagby at his home
in Rushville Sat. night. Had been failing in
health for years and only Thursday had returned
from San Diego, Calif. where he had spent the
winter. Born Glasgow, KY Jan 24, 1819.
Graduated from Bacon College in Georgetown, KY

as a civil engineer and admitted to the bar
1845. Located in Rushville 1846. Oct 1, 1850
he married Miss Mary Agnes Scripps who still
lives together with 5 children, one of his
sons, Morris Bagby is a well known pianist.

BAGBY, THOMAS M. - Obituary - Jun 22, 1893
Thomas M. Bagby, an old veteran of Capt. M.G.
Tousley's Co. E 84th Ill. Inf. died at Newtown
in Burton twp June 1st, age 57 years. Born
Felicity, Clermont Co. Ohio Nov 2, 1835. Came
to Adams Co. Dec. 1856 and joined Free Will
Baptist Church in March 1860. Enlisted in
military service at the Livingston school house
Aug 5, 1852. Leaves 3 sisters, 3 brothers and
a wife. Service by Rev Royce of Payson.

BAHR, MRS FLORA - Columbus - Mar 23, 1894
Died, Mrs Flora Bahr (nee Jester) at her home
in Kansas the latter part of Feb. with
pneumonia. Was raised in Columbus. About 40
years old. About 12 years since she and
husband left for the west. Leaves husband and
4 children.

BAILEY, MRS REBECCA - Funeral - Apr 23, 1895
The funeral of Mrs Rebecca Bailey was held at
the family home Friday 2 P.M. Services by Rev
William Stewart, of Quincy an old time friend
of the family. Buried village cemetery in
family lot.

BAILEY, MRS THOMAS - Death - Apr 19, 1895 - Mrs
Thomas Bailey died Apr 17th at her home in Camp
Point after illness of about a week. Mr and
Mrs B. had spent the winter in Calif. and
arrived home on the 20th inst. Mrs Rebecca
Bailey was daughter of Richard and Eleanor
Seaton. Born Jefferson Co. KY Jun 19, 1824.
Came with parents to Camp Point twp Oct 1835.
Married Mr B. Mar 13, 1845, had 1 daughter,
Eleanor, who married A.B. Kelley and died in
the fall of 1882. Leaves a husband of nearly
50 years. Two brothers John S. and Richard
Seaton and an adopted daughter, Mrs Maggie Kay.
Funeral at the house 2 PM today.

BAIRD, BERYL - Died - Jul 15, 1896 Beryl,
infant daughter of Mr and Mrs James Baird died
on the 9th of cholera infantum, age 2 years 11
months. Funeral Saturday afternoon.

BAIRD, CHARLES W. - Death - Jan 14, 1903
Charles W. Baird was born in Pickaway Co. Ohio,
Feb 4, 1822 and died at his home in Camp Point
Jan 7, 1903. Lived Ohio till 1844 when his
father came to Ill. and settled near Barry.
Following year he went to Missouri and Sept 21,
1845 married Miss Christina Harsha who survives
him. They had 6 children-4 sons, 2 daughters;
2 youngest boys are dead. 1847 he returned to
Pike Co. and in 1862 enlisted in 99th Ill. Inf.
until injured which later caused blindness.
Came with family over 30 years ago to Camp
Point. Was blind 17 years. Services at
Methodist Church Friday P.M. by Rev E.A.
Hedges. Buried village cemetery.

BAIRD, JOHN - May 4, 1893 - Soldiers buried in
Camp Point cemetery. Listed in Co. B 7th Ken.
Inf.

BAKER, B.M. - Elm Grove - Mar 23, 1893 - Mr
B.M. Baker died of paralysis last Thursday
night. He lived near N.E. corner of Clayton twp
and was somewhat advanced in years. Leaves a
wife and several children.

BAKER, CALOT E. - Local - Dep 9, 1903 - Calot
E. Baker, a well known Quincy grocer died
Monday after illness of several weeks.

BAKER, CHARLES H. - Dropped Dead - Aug 16, 1895
Charles H. Baker, an old resident of Galesburg
dropped dead at 2 P.M. Monday at his home
there. 70 years old. Lived Galesburg most of
his life. Leaves a wife and 4 children, Harry,
Millie and Will and a younger brother. Had
been baggage master on C.B. & Q and late years
carried mail between Post Office and depots.

BAKER, FRANK - Death Record - Mar 24, 1897
Died, President Baker's, Chaddock College
Quincy, son Frank died Monday, 8 years old.

BAKER, GEORGE - Elm Grove - Nov 1, 1895 George
Baker, who about this time last year was
reported to have killed a young girl in
Missouri near Sedalia and afterwards committed
suicide has materialized to refute the false
report and he is husking corn for Fleming
Tenhaeff.

BAKER, GEORGE - Elm Grove - Nov 30, 1893
Report received that George Baker was recently
found dead in a corn field in some locality in
Missouri, after having poisoned a young lady of
the locality who would not marry him. We do
not vouch for the truth of the report.

BAKER, HARRY EDWARD - Clayton - Feb 22, 1895
Harry Edward Baker age 11 years, son of Elmer
O. Baker died Tuesday A.M. of inflamation of
the bowels.

BAKER, MISS LOIS - Miss Lois Baker Dead - Feb
3, 1897 - Died, Miss Lois Baker, daughter of
Rev B.W. Baker, Pres. of Chaddock College.
Died Saturday of pneumonia, 17 years old.
Funeral Sunday at 3 P.M. Body taken to
Matamora for burial.

BAKER, ORA - Killed - Aug 10, 1893 - George
Baker of Elkhorn twp and daughter Ora started
for the train to go to Minnesota to visit
George's father when the pony ran away and drug
Ora, was dead when pony stopped. Threw Mr B.
out, but he was not serious. She was 15 years
old. "Mt Sterling Examiner"

BAKER, WILLIAM L. - Q. Brakeman Killed - Sep
16, 1903 William L. Baker, a Q brakeman was
killed at Macomb Sunday A.M. by falling under
his train. He formerly lived Clayton.

BALDWIN, FRANK - His Head Blown Off - Mar 25,
1896 Pittsfield, Ill. Mar 19th a accident
yesterday about 9 A.M. which resulted in death
of Frank Baldwin, a farm hand and the injury of
his employer, J. A. Farrand. Was about 23
years old lived Griggsville.

BALDWIN, MR AND MRS SANFORD - Shoots Wife and Himself - Oct 23, 1894 - A report from Hannibal-Sanford Baldwin shot himself and wife after a quarrel yesterday A.M.

BALFOUR, NIXON - Golden - Sep 15, 1897 - Died, Nixon Balfour of Augusta, but formerly of LaPrairie died Friday at 3:30 P.M. Was made a mason in LaPrairie Lodge #267, A.F. & A.M. Sep 26, 1863 and member of it until his death.

BALLARD, MRS ELIZABETH - 20 Years Ago - Feb 16, 1893 - Mrs Elizabeth Ballard died in Camp Point.

BALLARD, JERRY - Ancient History - Mar 26, 1895 March 1880 Jerry Ballard, a well known hotel man of Quincy died.

BALLOW, MRS CHARLES - Death Record - Mar 3, 1897 - Died, Mrs Charles Ballow at Clayton Sunday. Mr Ballow is very feeble and his wife's death may cause his.

BALTHROPE, J. ED. - Quincy - Apr 16, 1895 - J. Ed Balthrope, a promising young lawyer of this city died suddenly in Missouri last week. Buried at Canton, MO.

BALTHROPE, J.M. - Co. Seat - May 6, 1896 Died, J.M. Balthrope, the attorney died Monday A.M. of apoplexy. Born West Virginia. Lived many years in Knox Co. MO. Was about 55 years old. Leaves a wife and 4 children.

BANBOUR, DR W.J. - 20 Years Ago - Apr 6, 1893 Dr W.J. Banbour died in Columbus.

BANE, COL. MOSES M. - Obituary - Apr 7, 1897 Died last week Col. Moses M. Bane at Washington D.C. on the 30th ult. Born Ohio in 1825. Came to Payson 1844 and practiced medicine many years. Was married 3 times. His last wife being a resident of Washington when married. Was member of 50th Reg. Ill. Vol. Lived Camp Point

BANKS, HENRY - Local - Jul 6, 1894 - Died,
Henry Banks, a well known brakeman on the
Wabash. Died suddenly while alone in the car
at Jacksonville. His home was in Mt Sterling
where he was taken and buried Wednesday.

BANKS, JAMES - Death Record - Aug 11, 1897
James Banks a widely known Wabash brakeman died
at Mt Sterling on the 3rd inst. Worked Wabash
many years, but recently was running on the
Chicago & Alton.

BANTON, J. - May 26, 1897 - Soldiers buried in
Pleasant View Cemetery. Listed in Co. G 119th
Ill. Inf.

BANTON, MRS JAMES - Ancient History - Nov 11,
1903 - Nov. 1893 Mrs James Banton died on the
19th.

BANTON, MRS SUSAN - Local - Nov 23, 1893 - Mrs
Susan Banton, living in Concord twp, died
Sunday A.M. of pneumonia. Was 56 years old.
Funeral at Pleasant View Monday afternoon.

BANTON, SUSAN E. - Probate Notice - Jan 5, 1894
Susan E. Banton, deceased 1st Mon. of Feb,
1894 (5th) R.A. Wallace, adm.

BARBER, MRS A.D. - Death - Nov 25, 1903 - Mrs
A.D. Barber died at Hamilton Saturday of
paralysis. Was daughter of Elder Steers, a
noted preacher at Pittsfield. Husband and 3
sons survive her.

BARBER, WILLIAM A. - Dead in Bed - Nov 26, 1895
William A. Barber was found dead in bed near
Ursa Sat. A.M. Working for Mr Flack on a farm
4 miles west of Ursa and slept in a log cabin
there with 2 other men. 57 years old. Came
here 3 weeks ago from Denver where his wife is
now. Two daughters live in Quincy, a son is a
street car conductor in St Louis. Coroner
inquest Sat. returned verdict of heart disease.

BARBOUR, DR W.J. - Ancient History - Mar 25,
1903--Mar 27, 1873 Dr W.J. Barbour, of

Columbus, died in Quincy on the 21st.

BARLOW, JOSEPH C. - Quincy - May 31, 1895
Joseph C. Barlow, pres. of the Barlow
Cornplanter Co. Quincy died Thursday 59 years
old. Leaves wife, 2 sons and 2 daughters.

BARLOW, PERRY - Coatsburg - Dec 11, 1894 -
Died, Perry Barlow Sat. night at 11 at his home
in Coatsburg. Has lived here about a 1/2
century. Was about 67 years old and leaves a
wife, 3 daughters and 1 son.

BARLOW, PERRY - Death of Perry Barlow - Dec 14,
1894 Died, Perry Barlow a resident of Adams
Co. for 50 years. Died at his home in
Coatsburg Dec 8th. Born in Pulaski Co. KY. Oct
28, 1826. The son of Wesley and Mary Barlow.
Married Sarah J. Demoss Jul 8, 1852 and had 11
children. Mother and 4 children survive him.
Services from Christian Church by Elder O.
Dilley. Buried village cemetery.

BARNES, CHARLIE - Local - Jan 15, 1895 - A sad
case of hydrophobia recently at Raritan.
Charlie, 8 year old son of E.L. Barnes, editor
of the Raritan Reporter was bitten by a dog in
Oct. Died 6 P.M. last Thursday.

BARNET, MRS JANE D. - Death of Mrs Barnet - Aug
5, 1896 - Died, Mrs Jane D. Barnet Thursday
July 30th at the home of her daughter, Mrs
Vincent Francis, age 76 years. Funeral Friday
at Methodist Church and buried Sat. in Mendon.
Leaves 4 daughters, Mrs V. Francis, Camp Point-
Mrs Benson, Mendon- Mesdames Simmonds & Mann of
Denver, Colo.

BARRELL, CAPT. GEORGE - Local - Jan 16, 1894
Died, Capt. George Barrell, father of Mrs J.N.
Carter. Died at his daughters home in Quincy
Sat., age 85 years. He followed the sea for 30
years.

BARROWS, MRS MARY - A Mt Sterling Tragedy - Dec
2, 1903 - Mrs Martha Fowler, age 65, attacked,
Mrs Mary Barrows, age 66 in Mt Sterling Monday

A.M. with a hatchet which caused her death.
Mrs F. was suffering an attack of acute
dementia.   Mrs Fowler is in jail.

BARRY, DR. BERT - Local - Feb 19, 1902 - Dr
Bert Barry was found dead in his bed in Mt
Sterling Sat. A.M. was 31 years old and a
accomplished dentist.

BARRY, DANIEL - Quincy - Jun 4, 1902 - Daniel
Barry, a well known grocery merchant, died at
St Mary's hospital on Thursday, age 41 years.

BARRY, JIMMIE - Obituary - Jan 19, 1894 Died,
little Jimmie Barry, 13 year old son of Mr and
Mrs Jas. Barry of Coatsburg Jan 12th 1894.
Services by Elder O. Dilley.   Buried village
cemetery.

BARRY, OWEN - Quincy - Jun 11, 1895 - Owen
Barry of Melrose twp well known in the city, a
native of Ireland, died Saturday.

BARTHOLMEW, WILLIAM - Quincy - Sep 13, 1895
William Bartholmew, age 31 of Springfield, OH
who was visiting friends in this city died of a
complication of diseases Monday A.M.

BARTON, MARGARET - Obituary - Nov 22, 1895
Margaret Barton born Belvidere, New Jersey Oct
15, 1818.   Parents were Presbyterians and she
united same church early in life.   Married
Joseph B. Christie 1841 and moved to Ill. in
1842 living at Columbus until 1868 when they
moved to Camp Point.   Mr Christie died in 1883
and since she has lived with her children.
Mother of 5 children-1 daughter, Mrs Effie
Stone died several years ago.   2 sons and 2
daughters are living - George Christie in
Meadville, MO., Jerome O. Christie in Quincy,
Mrs T.A. Lyon in Camp Point and Mrs Rev. Patch
in Cleveland, OH.   While living at Columbus she
joined Methodist Church and was a member to her
death when she died at the home of her son in
Quincy Tues. eve, Nov 19th.   Remains will
arrive from Quincy Sat. afternoon and funeral
at Methodist Church 2:30 P.M.

BARTON, WILLIAM - Local - Aug 13, 1902 -
William Barton, formerly a well known resident
of this city died at Palmyra on Thursday, age
33 years.

BASSFORD, JOHN - Quincy - Dec 15, 1897 - John
Bassford who was treated in Blessing Hospital
for pneumonia and fever went home in his night
clothes and died a few hours later from
exposure.

BASTERT, HENRY C. - Local - Jan 9, 1894 - Died,
Henry C. Bastert, a german citizen of Quincy
last Thursday age 78 years. Came to Quincy
1845. Was uncle of Henry Bastert of Camp Point
twp.

BASTERT, HENRY C. - Local - Jan 9, 1894 - Died,
Henry C. Bastert, a prominent german citizen of
Quincy died last Thursday age 78 years. Came
to Quincy in 1845. Was an uncle of Henry
Bastert of Camp Point twp.

BATES, THOS. J. - Local - Dec 11, 1894 - Thos.
J. Bates of Galesburg was here to attend the
funeral of his brother in law, James Sharp. He
moved from here nearly 3 years ago.

BATTELL, MRS ELIZA A. - Death of Mrs Battell -
Jul 22, 1896 - Died, Mrs Eliza A. Battell Sat.
at the home of her brother, A.L. Harrington,
Auburn, NE. Remains brought to Bushnell for
burial Mon. She was widow of the late John F.
Battell. Spent most of her life in Adams Co.
After death of Mr B. she lived with her sister
Mrs G.O. Pond of Camp Point. Went to NE. to
live with brother after the death of her
sister. About 75 years old.

BATTELL, JOHN F. - Battell Estate - Feb 17,
1897 - In the estate of John F. Battell, who
died in 1868 there are claimants from all parts
of the country and Cuba. He left a widow Eliza
Battell and at her death land was to go to the
heirs of the sisters of John F. Battell. She
died last June in NE. Heirs live in Trinidad.
"Macomb Journal" Mrs Battell made her home in

Camp Point for more than 25 years with her
sister Mrs G.O. Pond.

BAUGHMAN, GEORGE - Obituary - Jan 16, 1894
Died, Jan 12th one of the pioneers of Quincy,
George Baughman age 80 years. Was native of
Maryland. Came to Quincy 1832. Married Sarah
Kreis 1838. Had 4 sons, 2 daughters who
survive him. They are Sam K. of Camp Point,
Henry of Colorado, William of Calif., Charles
of Colorado, Mrs Clark of Chicago and Mrs King
of Quincy.

BAUGHMAN, GEORGE - Quincy - Jan 30, 1894 - Will
of the late George Baughman was admitted to
probate Friday. Leaves all his estate real and
personal to his widow Sarah Baughman for her
use, after death divided among her 6 children-
Samuel K., Henry J., Emily K., William E.J.,
Charles E. and Mrs Lizzie Clark and
grandaughter Laura C. Barton share and share
alike. Widow and son Samuel K. Baughman
appointed exec.'s.

BAUMAN, MRS ANNA - Local - Nov 12, 1895 - Mrs
Anna Bauman died at Leadville, Colo. Sat. Was
mother of Mrs Will Reynolds with whom she was
spending the summer.

BAUMAN, MISS CATHERINE - Death Record - Dec 8,
1897 Died Miss Catherine Bauman in Leadville,
Colo. on the 4th inst. age 35 years. Born Camp
Point and lived here till 3 years ago when she
went to Colo. to live with her sister, Mrs Will
Reynolds. Remains brought to Camp Point in
company with those of her mother who died there
2 years ago. Services Tuesday. Buried village
cemetery. Deceased leaves a brother and 3
sisters.

BAUMAN, MRS TRACY - Coatsburg - Nov 13, 1894
Died on Tues. the 6th inst, Mrs Tracy Bauman
(Nee Hammer). Buried Coatsburg Cemetery on the
8th. Husband died about 6 months ago. Had 3
small children, born and raised here. She was
about 27 years old. Also leaves 2 brothers-
Fred and Antone Hammer.

BAVERLY, VICTOR - Local - Oct 19, 1893 - A boy
named Victor Baverly, of Elvaston was thrown
from a road cart and his gun discharged into
his left side. Died within a few hours.
Accident occurred in the bottoms on Lima twp.
Was about 17 years old.

BAYLESS, RALPH - Heartbreaking - Oct 4, 1895
Ralph, son of Mr and Mrs Jeff Bayless was given
carbolic acid by mistake by his mother died
Tuesday A.M. was 2 years old. They had moved
to Macomb about 4 years age and he worked at
one of the potteries.

BEAN, GARRET - Local - Apr 13, 1893 - Garret
Bean, one of the oldest citizens of Hancock Co.
died Apr 8th at his home north of Loraine in
Hancock Co. Came to Ill. from KY in 1827 and
settled in Hancock Co. 1836 on the farm where
he died.

BEATTY, ISAAC C. - Quincy - Mar 11, 1903
Remains of Isaac C. Beatty who died in Good
Samaritan hospital of St Louis, were buried
here on Wed. afternoon.

BEAVER, MRS ANNA - Co. Seat - Jan 22, 1896
Died-Mrs Anna Beaver of LaGrange, MO. age 41
years died at St Mary's Hospital Wed.

BECHERMEYER, HENRY - Local - Apr 6, 1893
Henry Bechermeyer committed suicide in Woodland
Cemetery, Quincy, Friday by shooting himself in
the head.

BECK, WILLIAM - Local - Feb 10, 1897 - William
Beck, living in Ellington was tossed over the
fence by a steer nearly 2 weeks ago died
Thursday from his injuries, 38 years old.
Leaves a wife and 1 child.

BECKER, MRS LUCINA - Quincy - Jul 23, 1902
Will of Mrs Lucina Becker was filed for probate
Tuesday. Leaves homestead to her daughter, Mrs
Mary Blocker and her grandson, Edward Bonner
and all her personal property to her daughter,
Katie Becker and Mrs Lucy Soule. H.B. Dines

named exec.

BECKERDITE, MRS ELIZABETH - Elm Grove - Mar 16,
1894 - Mrs Steed with her family attended the
funeral of her mother, Mrs Elizabeth Beckerdite
age 84 years. Her home was in the neighborhood
of Huntsville.

BECKET, LUKE - Ancient History - Jul 16, 1895
July 1877 Luke Becket was run over and killed
by a passenger train on the Omer farm N.E. of
town.

BECKETT, CORNELIUS O. - Obituary - Aug 13, 1893
Cornelius O., son of Rezin and Sarah J. Beckett
was born Dec 18, 1872 and died at his home near
Hebron Church Aug 18, 1893 and buried at Hebron
on the 20th.

BECKETT, JAMES M. - May 26, 1897 - Soldiers
buried in Hebron Cemetery. Listed in Co. G,
78th Ill. Inf.

BECKETT, JOHN D. - May 26, 1897 - Soldiers
buried in Hebron Cemetery. Listed in Co. G,
78th Ill. Inf.

BECKETT, JOSEPH S. - Ancient History - Nov 2,
1894 - Nov 1, 1878 Joseph S. Beckett died Oct
19th.

BECKETT, JOSEPH S. - Ancient History - Mar 24,
1897--Oct 1878 Joseph S. Beckett died.

BECKETT, LUKE - Ancient History - Nov 25, 1896
July 1877 Luke Beckett, an old citizen was run
over by the evening Q passenger, about a mile
north of town and instantly killed.

BECKETT, MRS MARY DOWNING - Obituary - Apr 8,
1903 - Mary Downing was born Cumberland Co.
Virignia Mar 4, 1813. When 10 years old came
with parents to Clark Co. Ind. Married Robert
A. Beckett Feb 27, 1834 in her 21st year. Next
year they came to Adams Co. Ill to Hebron
vicinity where they assisted forming the Hebron
Methodist Episcopal Church. She had 12

children-7 sons and 5 daughters, 5 sons and 2
daughters survive her, Joseph, of Stronghurst,
Ill., James A. and Rezin D. and Harriet
Bottorff live in Golden, Robert A and Cornelius
L. live Deerfield, Kan., Mary Nevius lives
Burlington, Ia. Moved to Golden in 1887. Mr
B. died 1892. She was taken sick while
visiting granddaughter, Mrs Robert J. McCray of
Golden. Died March 24th. Services at
Methodist Episcopal Church in Golden, Ill.
Tuesday 1 P.M. by Rev E. Hale Fuller, her
pastor. Buried family plot Hebron Cemetery.

BECKETT, MRS POLLY - Death - Mar 25, 1903 -Mrs
Polly Beckett died at her home in Golden
Tuesday A.M., 90 years old. Was daughter of
the late Rezin Downing and was born in
Virginia. Family lived a number of years in
Ind. where she was married to Robert A. Beckett
and they came to Ill. in the 30's and settled
west side of Clayton twp. Few years ago they
moved to Golden. Mr B. died a number of years
ago. Surviving are 5 sons--Joseph, of
Henderson Co., James A. and Rezin of Golden,
Robert A. and Cornelius of Deerfield, Kan. Two
daughters--Mrs I.A. Bottorff of Golden and Mrs
Nevius of Burlington, IA. Two sisters--Mrs
Nancy Hughes and Mrs Harriet Garner and 1
brother, William Downing also survive.

BECKETT, MR AND MRS W.T. - Local - Aug 28, 1894
The little babe of Mr and Mrs W.T. Beckett died
Saturday night.

BECKETT, MR AND MRS W.T. - Local - Jan 19, 1894
Died, little babe of Mr and Mrs W.T. Beckett
Tuesday eve. Funeral Wednesday.

BECKETT, WM - May 26, 1897 - Soldiers buried in
Hebron Cemetery. Listed in Co. G. 78th Ill.
Inf.

BECKMAN, HENRY - Local - Jul 27, 1893 - A child
of Henry Beckman's of Concord twp was buried in
the village cemetery Monday P.M.

BECKMAN, JOSEPH - Quincy - Jun 21, 1895 -

Joseph Beckman died Wednesday eve.   Funeral
will be Friday.

BECKMAN, JOSEPH - Local - Jun 21, 1895 - Joseph
Beckman who was so seriously hurt near Quincy
Monday and died from effects Wed. eve is an
uncle of Henry Beckman of Concord twp.

BECKMAN, MINA - Died - Jul 27, 1893 - Sunday
A.M. the 23rd inst, Mina, infant daughter of Mr
and Mrs Henry Beckman, age 2 months 11 days of
pneumonia.

BECKMEYER, GOTTLIEB - Quincy - Jun 28, 1895
The will of Gottlieb Beckmeyer was admitted to
probate. With the exception of $5.00 given to
an adopted son, the estate to be equally
divided among his 6 children.

BECKNER, GEORGE W. - May 4, 1893 - Soldiers
buried in Camp Point Cemetery. Listed in Co.
M.--11th Ind. Cavalry.

BECKSTEIN, ANNIE - Coatsburg - Jul 27, 1893
Since our last, the remains of Annie Beckstein,
of the poor farm community was laid to rest in
the Yellow Hill Cemetery at the west end of the
poor farm.

BEDEWEG, JOHN G.H. - Local - Mar 30, 1893
John G.H. Bedeweg, a wealthy German citizen of
Quincy, died Sat. night. He had lived in
Quincy about 50 years. He was a brother in law
to Frank Warmker and related to Fred
Mensendike, of Camp Point.

BEHAN, MRS MARGARET - Found Dead - May 19, 1897
Mrs Margaret Behan was found dead in her bed
Fri. A.M. Cause was old age. Husband died
about 25 years ago and had since lived with her
son John. Buried Catholic Cemetery in Quincy.

BEHAN, MR AND MRS MICHAEL - Local - Feb 12,
1895 - A son was born to Mr and Mrs Michael
Behan Friday night and died Monday.

BELKNAP, E.H. - Death of E.H. Belknap - Nov 4,

1896 - Word received Sat. that E.H. Belknap for
many years one of the well known conductors on
the Burlington died at his home in Galesburg
Friday. Retired 6 years ago from railroad.

BELL, CHARLIE - Clayton - Oct 12, 1894
Charlie Bell was injured while playing ball and
questionable on whether he will live. A kettle
of scalding water was spilled by his wife on
their small child and it died Monday night.

BELL, JOHN HENRY - Quincy - Sep 20, 1895 - Will
of John Henry Bell was admitted to probate, he
leaves all his property to his widow to be
divided equally between his 2 children, George
and Lillie Bell at her death. Widow is exec.

BENGMAN, JOHN HENRY - Co. Seat - Jan 8, 1896
Will of John Henry Bengman has been admitted to
probate. He leaves all his estate to his widow
during her lifetime, at her death $50.00 to
each of his 3 children and rest equally divided
among his stepchildren.

BENNESON, ROBERT S. - Death - May 18, 1893
Robert S. Benneson died at his home in Quincy
Monday, age 85 years. Came to Quincy from
Deleware in 1837 and has always been a
prominent man in Quincy.

BENNETT, ORIN E. - Local - Mar 2, 1894 - Died,
Orin E. Bennett age 24 died at the home of his
parents, Mr and Mrs Robert Bennett, Clayton
twp, Tuesday eve. He was a brother of Otho H.
Bennett of Camp Point.

BENNETT, ORRIN E. - Obituary - Mar 9, 1894
Died, Orrin E. Bennett son of Robert S. and
Sianna Bennett at his fathers near Clayton,
Ill. Feb 28, 1894 age 24 years 5 months 8 days.
Attended Clayton High School and Gem City
Business College and took work in a bank.
Father, stepmother, 2 brothers survive him.
Services by Rev Chas. F. McKown at Clayton
Methodist Church. Buried in South Cemetery.

BENTON, ABRAM - Death of Abram Benton - Jan 8,

1896 - Died, Abram Benton at his home at 11
P.M. Sunday. He was the last of 7 children of
Lot and Hannah (Chittenden) Benton. His father
died 1822, his mother died 1861, both at
Guilford, Conn. where their forefathers had
lived back as far as 1639. He and his brother
Daniel arrived in Mendon 1834. Daniel died
1836. Mr. B. married at Guilford, Conn. 1837
to Miss Sarah Dudley Chittenden who was a old
schoolmate. Had 2 children, Sarah J. born Jul
17, 1838 wife of S.S. Arnold, of Whitehall,
Greene Co. Ill. and Ruth Francis, widow of A.J.
Leggett of St Louis, Mr Leggett died several
years ago. She still lives St Louis. Mrs
Arnold has 2 children and Mrs Leggett, 4.

BENZ, MRS MAGDALENE - Died in Quincy - Jun 16,
1897 - Mrs Magdalene Benz, mother of Mrs Mat
Huber, of this village died in Quincy Sat.
night in her 68th year. Husband had been dead
7 years. Leaves 6 children-2 sons, 4
daughters. Funeral this A.M. from St Mary's
Catholic Church.

BERRY, MRS M.P. - Death - Nov 12, 1902 - Mrs
M.P. Berry of Carthage died at her home Thurs.
eve. She was operated on last Sat. for
appendicitis and was the result of the shock
and complications. Husband survives her.

BERRY, MINNIE F. - Death - May 18, 1893 Minnie
F. Berry was born Aug 27, 1875. She was
married to J.F. Bogart, Coatsburg, Ill. Sep 16,
1891. Joined church Feb 1891. Leaves parents,
a brother, a sister and husband. Funeral
service by W.S. Lowe in Christian Church Sun.
afternoon, 17 years old.

BERRY, COL. W.W. - Death - May 7, 1895 - Col.
W.W. Berry died suddenly at his home in Quincy
2 P.M. Monday. Born Maryland 1837. Enlisted
in Louisville Legion and served during the war
as Colonel. Settled Winchester, Ill. after the
war. Came to Quincy 1873. Leaves wife and 7
children, one son lives in Chicago.

BERTSCHINGER, MR ERNST F. - Quincy - Feb 26,

1895 3 A.M. Sun. Mr Ernst F. Bertschinger died
at his home , 811 Kentucky St., from a
hemorrhage of the lungs, 47 years old. Leaves
4 children-2 sons and 2 daughters. His wife
died about 2 weeks ago.

BEUTEL, CASPER ADAM - Full of Years - May 6,
1903 Casper Adam Beutel was born in Germany
Jan 8, 1824 and came to U.S. 1858, married
Annie D. Bidle in 1876 and they had 3 children,
2 died in infancy, the other, Mrs Henry Hartung
was living with him and caring for him until
his death Apr 24, 1903. Services at Coatsburg
Methodist Church Sun. Apr 26th by Rev Hehner of
the German Methodist Church of which Mr B. was
a member since 1877 having been converted at
Columbus. Besides his daughter he leaves 7
grandchildren.   Card of thanks followed this
article signed by Mr and Mrs Henry Hartung.

BEVANS, CHARLES I. - Co. Seat - Apr 22, 1896
Charles I. Bevans of Canton, MO. committed
suicide at Tremont Hotel Monday A.M. by taking
morphine, under influence of liquor at the
time.

BIDDLE, MRS - Coatsburg - Jun 8, 1893 - Died,
last Wed. at the poor farm, Mrs Biddle at age
70 years from advanced age. Remains taken by
her children and buried I think (sic) at
Burton.

BILLINGS, JONATHON - Ancient History - May 15,
1894 May 15, 1874-Jonathon Billings of Clayton
twp died.

BIMSON, ROBERT - Quincy - Sep 7, 1895 Robert
Bimson, who had been a resident of the city
since 1848 died of Brights disease Mon. night.

BISSELL, MR - Ancient History - Sep 11, 1894
Sep 7, 1877 a deaf old man named Bissell was
run down by a Wabash engine east of town and
killed.

BLACKABY, MISS LILLIE - Our Unfortunate
Neighbors- Nov 20, 1894 Temporary insanity

caused by ill health suffered since childhood
caused Miss Lillie Blackaby, daughter of Hon.
Inman Blackaby, a wealthy farmer and ex member
of legislature residing 5 miles from Canton to
commit suicide Friday.

BLACKFORD, MRS IDA MAY - Quincy - Jan 29, 1895
Mrs Ida May Blackford, formerly of this city
died at Clatskaine, OR. age 38 years.

BLAISDELL, DR W.O. - Local - Mar 25, 1903 - Dr
W.O. Blaisdell, of Macomb who is widely known
over the military tract as a politician and a
fair manager, died, Friday of heart failure, 72
years old.

BLAISDELL, DR W.O. - Blaisdell's Monument - Jun
17, 1903 A unique monument will be erected
over the grave of the late Dr W.O. Blaisdell,
of Macomb. It will be a hugh boulder from his
boyhood home in Maine, he having expressed a
wish some years ago when on a visit to the old
home that he wanted it shipped to Macomb and
placed over his grave.

BLANCHARD, J.C. - Quincy - Sep 24, 1895 - J.C.
Blanchard age 72 years, a former resident of
Quincy died in Kansas City. Buried here Wed.

BLANCHARD, MRS WILLIAM - Murdered his Wife -
Aug 23, 1895 Murdered his wife at Prairie
City, McDonough Co. last spring. William
Blanchard's young wife left him after 4 years
of married life taking their 3 year old child
with her. Monday morn he shot her and then
himself. (He still lives when article was
written).

BLANK, JONATHON - St. of Ill. Co. Court - Feb
6, 1894 Adams Co. Ill. Feb. term George
Thrush, adm of the estate of Jonathon Blank,
deceased petitioner vs., to sell real estate to
pay debts, Henry Franklin Blank, Mary D. Blank,
Willoughby Blank, Laura Blank, Rosa Simmons,
Harry Simmons, Kate Ayers, Clyde Blank, Lewis
Blank, Susan Blank, Anna Louisa Snyder, Henry
Snyder, Frank S. Heil, Simon S. Heil, Esther

Jane Harvey and John T. Harvey, defendants
Harry Simmons, Kate Ayres, Clyde Blank, Anna
Louisa Snyder, Henry Snyder, Frank S. Heil,
Simon S. Heil, Esther Jane Harvey and John T.
Harvey all reside out of state of Ill.   Dated
Quincy Jan 16, 1894

BLATTER, G.W. - Accident - Aug 2, 1895 - On
Sat. eve the 13 year old son of G.W. Blatter of
Liberty twp came home from a trip to the
village of Liberty with horse and wagon. Lifted
gun out of wagon and set it butt down on the
ground, it discharged hitting him in back of
head.   Died Sunday eve.

BLENTLINGER, MRS - Death Record - Mar 3, 1897
Died, Mrs Blentlinger, mother of Mrs George
Akers died at her daughters home in Camp Point
Sun.   Funeral at Methodist Church Tues. A.M.

BLIVEN, MRS MARIA - Local - Jan 8, 1895 Mrs
Maria Bliven died Jan 1st at the home of her
daughter, Mrs McVay in Clayton twp.   She was
widow of the late Samuel G. Bliven of Burton
twp.   Funeral at Burton Thursday.

BLIVINS, CLARENCE - Quincy - Feb 25, 1903
Clarence Blivins mother died.

BLOOD, MRS HANNAH C. - Death - Sep 10, 1902
Mrs Hannah C. Blood died Wed. Eve Sep 3, 1902
at the home of her son, F.W. Blood.   Hannah
Cummings born in Temple, N.H. Mar 21, 1811.
Married at Canaan, VT. to Stillman Blood Jun 1,
1831.   Mr B. died 1874 when Mrs B. came to Ill.
to live with her son Frank W. Blood.   She had 4
children, 2 survive her-Frank W. and Mrs J.M.
Brooks of Winchester, Mass.   She united
Christian Church at Cameron, Ill. 1874.   Lived
Camp Point nearly 20 years.   Services at family
home Thurs. eve. by Rev R.A. Omer and at 9:40
Mr and Mrs F.W. Blood departed with remains for
old home at Coldbrook, N.H. to lay them beside
those of her husband who had gone before.

BLOOD, MRS HANNAH C. - Local - Sep 10, 1902   Mr
and Mrs F. W. Blood left Thursday night for

Coldbrook, N.H. with the remains of Mrs Hannah
C. Blood which were buried at her old home.

BOBBITT, CARRIE - Ancient History - Feb 18,
1903 Feb 15, 1883 Carrie Bobbitt, died on the
8th age 16 years. Was daughter of George C.
Bobbitt.

BOCKENPOOF, MRS - Quincy - Apr 28, 1897 Mrs
Bockenpoof of Maine St. stepped on a rusty nail
and died on Apr 14th of lockjaw.

BOESING, JOSEPH - Quincy - Sep 16, 1903 Body
of Joseph Boesing, who was drowned in the
Mississippi, was found a few miles south of the
city on Thursday night.

BOGER, FRED - Local - Jul 16, 1902 Fred Boger
returned Friday from Detroit, Mich. where he
was called by the illness of his father, who
died a few minutes before Fred arrived.

BOGER, MARY HELEN - The Babe is Dead - Nov 24,
1897 Little Mary Helen, infant daughter of Mr
and Mrs J.F. Boger died in Golden Friday age 6
mon. 9 days. Buried Camp Point Cemetery Fri.
PM.

BOHENREITH, EDWARD - Quincy - Mar 3, 1897
Letters received here from White Sulphur
Springs, Mont. inquiring for the relatives of
Edward Bohenreith, who had considerable
property and died interstate in the place
mentioned.

BOLDING, WILLIAM A. - Suicide in Quincy - Jan
18, 1895 Wed. eve about 9 the lifeless body of
William A. Bolding was found hanging by the
neck in his blacksmith shop. Located in the
deep ravine on the north side of Cedar St.
between Front and 2nd by his wife and another
woman named Mrs Ball. "Whig"

BOLING, HENRY - Double Assassination - Sep 3,
1895 Henry Boling, a Quincy barber who lived
Camp Point in early youth with his affianced
wife, Mrs Rose Swearingen were shot by Dora

Hellwagen Friday in the country north of
Quincy. Dora and Henry had been lovers before
Mrs S. who Mr H. was going to marry soon as she
divorced husband, Chet Swearingen.

BOLTON, SAMUEL - Quincy - Feb 22, 1895 Samuel
Bolton, who was formerly in business here died
last week in New York City, age 50 years.

BONNEY, MATTHEW C. - Quincy - Apr 8, 1896 Died
Matthew C. Bonney, age 40 years died Thursday
in Salvador, Central America. Was formerly
associated with his cousin, Judge O.P. Bonney,
in the law business here, but later chose the
vocation of an artist.

BOOTH, MRS - Columbus - Jan 22, 1902 George
Powell and wife of Bowen attended the funeral
of his grandmother, Mrs Booth.
Isaac Gray of Chebanse, Ill. a former resident
of Gilmer came to attend the funeral of his
aunt, Mrs Booth.

BOOTH, LAVINA - Quincy - Jan 22, 1902 Will of
Lavina Booth leaves 300 each to Charlotte
Colburn, George S. Powell and Charles S.
Coleman, 1/4 of her estate is set aside with a
direction that its annual income shall be given
to Mary Ann Wilson and then divided between
George S. Powell, Charlotte Colburn and Eleanor
S. Dickhut.

BOOTH, MRS LAVINA - Death - Jan 15, 1902 Mrs
Lavina Booth about 85 years old and a resident
of Adams Co. 66 years died at the home of her
daughter, Mrs John A. Dickhut, 4 miles W. of
Columbus, Sat. eve. Was widow of Stephen Booth
who died 1884. Services at Paloma ME Church at
11 AM Tues. Buried in Stahl cemetery near
Fowler. Leaves 3 daughters, Mrs Dickhut, Mrs
Mary Wilson and Mrs Charlotte Colburn of
Chicago.

BOOTH, MRS SARAH - Obituary - Jul 31, 1894
Died-Mrs Sarah Booth born in Shelby Co. KY Sept
14, 1816 in same Co. and state she married
James G. Welsh Aug 14, 1834 and at once came to

Adams Co. Ill. to Columbus about 1-1/2 years
then Camp Point twp. They had 8 children-4
boys, 4 girls-all living. Leaves husband and
children. Married 60 years. Died Jul 26,
1894. She was 78 years old. Services from
family home in Camp Point Jul 27th all present
but 1 son-George W. of Kingston, Mo. Buried
village cemetery. Services by Elder O. Dilley.

BOOTH, STEPHEN - Ancient History - May 8, 1894
May 8, 1884 Stephen Booth died at Paloma May
3rd.

BORDENKIRCHER, GEORGE W. - Jun 3, 1896 Geo. W.
Bordenkircher dead Mt Sterling, Ill. May 27th,
George W. Bordenkircher, pres. of the Brown Co.
fair assoc. and Co.'s best known farmer died
very suddenly this AM. Lived on his own farm
about 3 miles SE of Mt Sterling. Found dead in
field by son Albert, hogs had gotten at him,
idelity thru clothes. Was about 55 years old.
Leaves a wife and 6 children.

BORDNER, CHRISTINA - Local - May 10, 1895 The
oldest woman in Central Ill. if not in the
state, died recently near Lewiston, name
Christina Bordner. Born Penn. 1789. Married
1810. Leaves 13 children, 102 grandchildren,
228 gr. grandchildren and 26 gr gr
grandchildren.

BORNMAN, MRS KATHERINE - Quincy - May 11, 1894
Died, Mrs Katherine Bornman age 72 years, a
resident of Quincy 50 years. Died from lung
fever. Leaves 2 children, Henry Bornman,
editor of the "Germania" and Miss Wilhelmina
Bornman.

BOTTORFF, ANDERSON - Local - Feb 13, 1894
Mesdames Val and Frank Strickler of NW Missouri
arrived at Golden Sunday A.M. to attend the
funeral of their brother, Anderson Bottorff.

BOTTORFF, ANDERSON - Local - Feb 13, 1894 Died
Anderson Bottorff at his home in Houston twp
Thurs. night from pneumonia. Was son of Isaac
A. Bottorff of Camp Point twp and was married a

little more that a year ago to Miss Cora Omer
who is left with a little babe. Funeral at
Hebron Church at 11 A.M. Sunday.

BOTTORFF, ANDERSON - Obituary - Feb 16, 1894
Died, Anderson Bottorff born Jun 16, 1866 died
Feb 8, 1894 in his 28th year of lung fever.
Married Dec 1892 to Cora Omer who with 1 child
survive him. Services at Hebron Church on the
11th by Elder O. Dilley and Rev W.D. Atkinson
of Golden.

BOURNE, MRS MAGGIE - Coatsburg - Jul 20, 1894
Fri. the 13th inst, Mrs Maggie Bourne died at
the poor house of paralysis of the insane,
about 63 year old and came from Quincy.
Daughter lives at Hannibal, MO. Burial in Ursa
vicinity.

BOWER, WM - Suicide at Barry - Apr 2, 1902 Wm
Bower, living near Barry blew out his brains
Tues. eve of last week because his wife refused
to accompany him to Barry to attend a lodge
supper. Was about 35 years old. Leaves wife
and 6 little children, oldest 12 years old.

BOWERSMITH, MARY - Obituary - Sep 11, 1894
Died, Mary, infant daughter of Prof. H.W. and
Clara M. Bowersmith born Aug 20, 1893 died Sep
9, 1894. Services at the home Sunday at 5 P.M.
by Rev A.N. Simmons and Rev J. Miller. Arrived
in Camp Point recently so parents are among
strangers.

BOWLES, MRS ETTA - Death - Jun 23, 1897 The
death of Mrs Etta Bowles wife of L.W. Bowles at
Quincy Wed. Jun 16th at 9 A.M. She was
daughter of Mr and Mrs Jas. A. Wallace of this
place, was about 36 years old. Born and raised
on the old home place near town. Leaves
husband and 3 small children. Family had been
in Quincy but a short time. Remains brought to
this city Thurs. and services by Rev. Lorimer
at the U.P. church at 3. Buried Hebron
Cemetery. "Golden New Era"

BOWLES, JAMES STAFFORD - Co. Seat - Nov 18,

1896 Will of James Stafford Bowles gives
$5,000 cash to his sister Ella Bowles and a
$5,000 life insurance policy to his sister, Mrs
Oscar Heinze, residue of the estate to be
equally divided between the 2 sisters.

BOWLES, WILLIAM - Ancient History - Nov 2, 1894
Nov 3, 1881 William Bowles of Ellington twp
committed suicide in Brooklyn, N.Y.

BOWLING, OTTO - Local - Jan 30, 1894 Otto
Bowling, a barber at Elvaston, at one time
located in Camp Point, went to Keokuk and
Hamilton last Tues. and at night started to
walk home. His dead body was found 3 miles
from Elvaston frozen to death. Leaves a widow
and child.

BOWLING, OTTO - Quincy - Feb 2, 1894 Remains
of Otto Bowling who was found frozen to death
in Hancock Co. near Elvaston was brought to his
home in this city for burial Tuesday.

BOWLING, WILLIAM - Ancient History - May 24,
1895 - May 1875 William Bowling an aged German
attempted suicide while under mental
aberration. Died a week later.

BOWMAN, C.J. - Local - Feb 19, 1895 C.J.
Bowman, Wabash agent at Riverton committed
suicide Friday by shooting himself. Parents
reside in Meredosia.

BOWMAN, MR AND MRS JOHN - Local - Nov 2, 1893
Last Friday A.M. Mr and Mrs John Bowman, living
near Frederick, on awakening found their only
child, age about 6 months, cold in death. The
babe slept with parents. "Rushville Citizen"

BOYD, EDWARD - Obituary - Mar 23, 1894 Died,
at his home in Houston twp Wed. eve Mar 21,
1894 Edward Boyd of consumption. Funeral at
Ebenezer Church today (Fri.) at 11 A.M. Born
Penn. and about 30 years old. Leaves a wife,
the daughter of Charles F. Cate and 2 little
children.

BOYD, EDWARD - Obituary - Apr 3, 1894 Died,
Edward Boyd, born in Carbon Co. Penn. 1862.
Came to Adams Co. Ill 1878. 1890 he married
Miss Nancy Cate who with 2 children survive
him. He died Mar 21st 1894 of consumption.
Funeral at Ebenezer Mar 23rd by Elder O. Dilley
and buried church cemetery.

BOYD, MRS ROBERT - Fairview - Aug 26, 1903 Mrs
Robert Boyd died last Wed., age 71 years.
Leaves aged husband, 5 daughters and 1 son
living, having 2 children dead. Living are Mrs
Sallie Shroder, Mrs Jennie Stansbury, Mrs Orvel
Harris, Mrs George Pearce, Miss Mary Boyd and
Robert Boyd last 2 named lived with parents at
the home place. Buried Friday at Ebenezer.
Services by Rev Baughman of Loraine and Rev
Cubbage.

BOYER, FARMER - Drowned Himself - Apr 12, 1895
Farmer Boyer, who lived NE of Abingdon, Ill
drowned himself in the well on his farm Sunday
A.M. Had a large family and couldn't find work
to feed them or pay his rent.

BOYLE, MRS DANIEL - Local - May 27, 1896 Died
Mrs Daniel Boyle, of Benbow, MO. died at her
home in that city Sat. eve. She was a former
resident of Gilmer twp and daughter of Mr and
Mrs Joseph Pierce, of Quincy.

BOYLE, MRS SUSAN - Ancient History - Dec 10,
1895 Dec. 1879 Mrs Susan Boyle died Nov 29th.

BOYLE, MRS SUSAN - Ancient History - May 26,
1897 Nov. 1879 Mrs Susan Boyle died.

BRADBURY, AMELIA - Obituary - Apr 13, 1893
Amelia Bradbury born England Mar 12, 1810 died
Apr 7, 1893. Was 83 years 26 days old.
Married John Chandler in state of New York Nov
6, 1833 and came to Columbus, Ill. in 1846.
Mother of 11 children-2 sons survive, only 1
present. In 1871 while visiting one of his sons
in Cherokee Co. KS. she became a member of
Christian Church. Funeral at Christian Church
in Coatsburg Sun. at 2:30 by Elder O. Dilley.

Buried in Coatsburg cemetery.

BRADLEY, BENJ. - Local - Sep 16, 1903 Mrs
Jennie Watson and little son returned last week
to her home in Kansas, having been called here
by the death of her father, Benj, Bradley.

BRADLEY, BENJAMIN J. - Probate Notice - Oct 14,
1903 Benjamin J. Bradley, deceased 1st Mon.
of Dec 1903 (7th) Sarah E. Bradley, Exec.

BRADLEY, BENJAMIN J. - Death - Sep 9, 1903
Benjamin J. Bradley died Sun. A.M. the 5th inst
from cancer in the mouth. Services Sun.
afternoon by Rev E.A. Hedges at the family
home. Buried village cemetery. Was born in
Virginia Jan 15, 1830, came to Ill. 1843 and
lived since in Clayton and Camp Point. Married
Sarah E. Curry Nov 30, 1853. They had 5
children-2 sons, 3 daughters. For past 13
years Mr and Mrs B. have lived in Camp Point.

BRADLEY, DR CHARLES F. - Dr Bradley's Body
Cremated - May 13, 1896 Remains of Dr Charles
F. Bradley were taken to St Louis, Sun. for
cremation. Per "St Louis Republic" Body of Rev
Dr Charles F. Bradley of Quincy, Ill was
cremated at the Missouri Crematory yesterday
afternoon. 1st time where the body of a
minister was reduced to ashes in this manner
and was entirely devoid of any ceremony other
than a few words.

BRADLEY, REV DR CHARLES F. - Co. Seat - May 13,
1896 Died-Rev Dr Charles F. Bradley an eminent
minister in the Unitarian Church and for 10
years a pastor in this city died Thursday, age
56 years.

BRADLEY, CHARLOTTE - Quincy - Mar 10, 1897 The
will of Charlotte Bradley leaves all of her
property, real and personal to her niece, Julia
Arnold.

BRADLEY, MISS CHARLOTTE - Local - Feb 17, 1897
Died- Miss Charlotte Bradley of Mendon died
last week at age 83 years. She came to Ill.

from Connecticut in 1831.

BRADLEY, JOHN T. - Death - Jul 30, 1902 Mrs
N.J. Booth received telegram Mon. of the death
of her brother, John T. Bradley of Oakland,
Calif. age 67 years. Born in Kentucky. Came
to Ill. 1851 and in 1852 in company with
several others traveled by wagon from Quincy to
Calif. driving the team the entire distance,
began work as a miner. Mrs Mary Seaton of
Brookings, S.D. is also a sister and James M.
Bradley of Fort Madison, IA is a brother of the
deceased.

BRADLEY, MRS JOSEPHINE - Recent Deaths - Apr
15, 1896 Mrs Josephine Bradley died in Mendon
April 10th in her 91st year. Lived county for
65 years. Leaves 2 sons and 2 daughters, S.H.
Bradley and Miss Ellen Bradley of Mendon D.A.
Bradley of Peabody, KS and Mrs Solon W. Kimball
of Galesburg.

BRADLEY, ROBERT - Local - Jul 19, 1895 Robert
Bradley who lived 5 miles E. of Macomb was
killed by lightning Wed. afternoon.

BRADSHAW, SIMON P. - Ancient History - Aug 12,
1903 Aug 1893 Kingston White Caps were
arrested and lodged in jail for the murder of
Simon P. Bradshaw, who was visiting Mrs Kittie
Breckenridge, a notorious character.

BRADSHAW, SOLOMON P. - Kingston - Jul 27, 1893
Solomon P. Bradshaw a young sewing machine
agent of Quincy was shot and killed at the home
of Mrs A.C. Breckenridge with whom he had been
infatuated. She claims a hooded mob of about
20 came there and shot him.

BRADY, JOHN - Quincy - Aug 5, 1903 John
Seybold, a brother of D. Gates Seybold who is
held in jail on a charge of killing John Brady
is here looking after interests of his brother
and has offered $10,000 bonds for his
appearance when wanted. Bond not yet accepted.

BREEDEN, MAYOR RICHARD G. - Local - May 12,

1897 Died- Mayor Richard G. Breeden of Macomb died Friday of typhoid fever in his 37th year, was elected mayor last month.

BREESE, L.S. - Local - Oct 15, 1902 William I. Bates received telegram Mon. eve of the death of his brother in law, L.S. Breese. Death in Wilmette, near Chicago. He was in the employ of the Lake Shore Railroad and had several acquaintances in this vicinity.

BRENTS, THOMAS H. - Local - Jan 19, 1893 Thomas H. Brents was found dead in bed at the Park House, Clayton, on the A.M. of the 17th inst. Was over 84 years old and been in feeble health for some time.

BREWER, DOW - Ancient History - Sep 4, 1894 Sep 4, 1874 Dow Brewer committed suicide by hanging himself in the barn of Samuel B. Witt, Big Neck.

BRICK, MARTIN - May 26, 1897 Listed in Soldiers buried in Pleasant View Cemetery. Was in Co. D 10th Ill. Cav.

BRIGGS, HARVEY - Local - Jan 22, 1896 Shot and killed, Harvey Briggs, 7 years old was accidently shot and killed by a boy named Joe Dunn 13 years old. Both parents live at Mt Sterling.

BRINK, CHARLES B. - Coatsburg - Jul 14, 1897 Died- Thurs. eve at the old home farm of the Louis Nicolai family in Camp Point twp Charles B. Brink suffered a heat prostration and died. He had lived at Coatsburg since he was a child. Was 40-42 years old and unmarried. Leaves his aged mother and 3 brothers.

BRINK, CHARLES - Kill by the Sun - Jul 14, 1897 Charles Brink of Coatsburg was employed by Louis Nicolai on his farm 2 miles W. of town and became overheated by the sun. They took him to the house where he died 1 hour later. Was about 42 years old and brother of Joseph P. Brink.

BRINKMAN, WILLIAM - Quincy - Aug 26, 1896
William Brinkman age 24 years has disappeared
and friends fear he has committed suicide.

BROCKENFIELD, MRS ANNA M. - Co. Seat - Jan 22,
1896 The will of Mrs Anna M. Brockenfield
after making provision for masses in the
Catholic Church distributes her property
equally among her children. J.A. Siepker is
appointed exec.

BROCKMAN, JAMES R. - Local - Aug 13, 1895
James R. Brockman dropped dead suddenly at the
home of his sister, Mrs Medearis in this city
Thurs. 8 P.M. from asthma. Born near this city
Aug 9, 1839. 3 children, 4 brothers and 5
sisters survive him. Spent most of his life in
this city. Services by Rev F.P. Douglas at the
house. Buried city cemetery. Mt Sterling
Democrat-Message.

BROCKSCHMIDT, HENRY J. - Co. Seat - Dec 23,
1896 J.H. Brockschmidt has been appointed adm.
of the estate of his brother, Henry J.
Brockschmidt.

BROCKSCHMIDT, HENRY JOSEPH - Co. Seat - Nov 18,
1896 Died-Henry Joseph Brockschmidt, who was
engaged in the hat and cap business here for
nearly 40 years died Wed. afternoon, age 63
years.

BROME, MRS S.D. - Quincy - Nov 1, 1895 Mrs
S.D. Brome age 60 years formerly of this city
died in Chicago Sun. eve. Buried here
yesterday.

BRONAUGH, MRS L.F. - Quincy - Jun 7, 1895 Mrs
L.F. Bronaugh, a former resident of the city
died in Chicago and was buried here Sunday.

BROOKER, SIDNEY - Dead - Jul 8, 1903 Sidney
Brooker, editor of the Quincy Optic was found
dead in bed at his boarding house in Quincy
about noon Sat. died some hours before of heart
disease. His wife, who was daughter of Rev
A.M. Danely has been visiting her parents in

Champaign and was on her way home. Became
editor of the Optic about 18 months ago.

BROOKS, JARED - Jared Brooks Dead - Nov 26,
1902 Jared Brooks, a colored man who lived
many years in Camp Point twp and moved to
Quincy died Wed. in the insane hospital at
Jacksonville where he was taken for treatment a
few weeks ago. Brooks was a respected citizen
of Camp Point.

BROOKS, MARTIN - Local - Feb 26, 1895 The
little daughter of Mr Martin Brooks editor of
the Mt Sterling Examiner died last Friday.

BROOMFIELD, VERNON - Kicked by a Horse - Oct
14, 1903 Vernon Broomfield, age 13, living
with his widowed mother in Big Neck, near
Loraine was kicked by a horse last Wed. and
died the next A.M.

BROUGHAM, MRS THOMAS - Co. Seat - Apr 8, 1896
Mrs Thomas Brougham, a former resident of
Quincy died in Chicago on Thurs. and buried
here Sunday.

BROWN, MRS ANNA - Brown Estate - Dec 6, 1895
T.C. Poling, executor of the last will of Mrs
Anna Brown was in the county court Tues. to
arrange the distribution of the estate
according to the will. ($350,000)

BROWN, MRS ANNA E. - Will of Mrs Anna E. Brown -
Nov 2, 1893 Will of the late Anna E. Brown of
Quincy was admitted Tues. to probate, its value
$300,000, had no children. Most of left to
charitable and benevolent institutions. Some
to her nearest relatives. (Article carries a
list of all amounts and to whom.)

BROWN, MRS ANNA E. - Death - Oct 19, 1893 Mrs
Anna E. Brown died at her home in Quincy Sun.
A.M. She was regarded as one of the richest
women in the city, her wealth estimated at
anywhere from $300,000 to $500,000. She gave
to the city the beautiful fountain at the N.W.
corner of the court house square.

BROWN, CHARLES - Local - Feb 23, 1893 Charles
Brown, one of the old citizens and merchants of
Quincy died Sunday eve, age 73 years. Was very
wealthy and made his start in the shoe trade.

BROWN, FRANK - Co. Seat - Feb 12, 1896 The
body of Frank Brown, a stranger will be held
for identificaton. Was killed by a train.

BROWN, GEORGE M. - Died in Quincy - Oct 27,
1897 George M. Brown died at the home of his
parents in Quincy Sat. Oct 23rd age 44 years.
Born Camp Point Mar 27, 1853. Was a telegraph
operator for several years and then owned a
drug store at Galt, MO. Died from consumption.
Leaves his parents, Mrs and Mrs Richard Brown,
2 sisters, 4 brothers.

BROWN, MRS HANNAH C.S. - Quincy - May 22, 1894
Died-Mrs Hannah C.S. Brown, widow of Homer
Brown, age 79 years died. Taken to Hamilton for
burial. Settled Quincy 1834. Her 2 children
left are Capt. Horace S. Brown of this city and
Homer D. Brown of Hamilton.

BROWN, JAMES - Murder at Barry - Jan 19, 1894
On Monday John Parker inflicted a wound in the
arm of his father in law, James Brown and he
bled to death in about 10 minutes. They lived
together. Mrs P. had died and left several
children to their father. Mr P. was correcting
one of the children and Mr B. interfered.

BROWN, JOHN - Quincy - Mar 19, 1895 John Brown
who had been living with Mr and Mrs C.E. Baker
on Spring Street committed suicide Mon., was
brother of Mrs Baker, about 40 years old.
Suffered from mental trouble.

BROWN, JOHN A. - Quincy - Mar 26, 1895 John A.
Brown who committed suicide here Monday leaves
an estate valued at $30,000, gave his reason as
fearing insanity approaching.

BROWN, LETITIA - Death of Mrs L. McNeall - Sep
3, 1902 Letitia Brown was born near Baltimore,
MD Dec 22, 1816 died in Camp Point, Ill of

pneumonia, Sat. A.M. Aug 30, 1902 age 85 years
8 mon. 8 days. She was of Quaker parentage,
but early in life united with Christian Church.
Married Matthias McNeall, May 10, 1854 and soon
joined Methodist Episcopal Church until after
his death Dec 7, 1900 when she returned to
church of her choice. She reigned supreme in
hearts of her stepchildren. Leaves 1 sister
Mrs Martha Butler, now visiting in Kansas, 1
son and 4 daughters. Services at Bowen Sun.
A.M. by Rev L.A. Powell.

BROWN, M.H. - Local - Mar 10, 1897 Died- M.H.
Brown a well known farmer living 2-1/2 miles
S.W. of Bushnell died suddenly Thurs. A.M. of
last week. He was found dead in his chair
sitting before the stove. Cause-heart disease,
77 years old.

BROWN, MRS SARAH A. - Death - May 14, 1902 Mrs
Sarah A. Brown died near Dundee, NE Apr 24th,
age 71 years. Was daughter of Peter Thomas and
reared in Camp Point twp. Married John H.
Brown 1853. Lived a number of years between
Bowen and Augusta and later moved to NE. Her
husband, 2 sons and 2 daughters survive her.
Also a number of relatives in this vicinity and
at Augusta.

BRUNS, MISS BELLE KOBEL - Ancient History - Oct
26, 1894 - Oct 23, 1874 Miss Belle Kobel Bruns
died on the 19th.

BRUNS, BRUNE T. - Death of Brune T. Bruns Dec
1, 1897 Brune T. Bruns was thrown from his
wagon Fri. P.M. Nov 19th while driving from
town to his home near Home, KS and died the
next day. He was son of the late Wilkey T.
Bruns of Columbus twp and lived here 16 years
ago. Was 50 years old. Leaves a wife, a
married daughter and a daughter at home.
Wilkey Bruns, his brother was telegraphed but
did not reach him until after his death.

BRYANT, JOHN H. - 20 Years Ago - May 25, 1893
John H. Bryant died in Chicago.

BRYANT, REV THOMAS J. - Death - Mar 16, 1893
Rev Thomas J. Bryant, of Ill. Methodist
Conference died at his home in Versailles on
Mon. A.M. on the 7th inst. Born in Tenn. Sept
29, 1829, 64 years old. Came with parents as a
youth in Ill. and spent his youth near
Jacksonville. 1846 enlisted in Mexican War for
1 year. 1854 was ordaned as a member of Ill.
conference was active till last Sept. Married
Margaret A. Brady in Hannibal in 1836. Wife
and 5 children survive him. Funeral on the 9th
by Rev W.J. Rutledge and buried in Versailles
cemetery. (He was in Camp Point 3 years).

BRYSON, LEVI - Quincy - Nov 24, 1897 Levi
Bryson died some days ago in our city, age 90
years. He was reckoned a great fiddler many
years ago and was with General Thomas at
Chickamauga, serving among the colored troops.

BUB, VALENTINE - Probate Notice - Dec 29, 1897
Valentine Bub, deceased 1st Mon. of Feb 1898
(7th) Gustave Bub, Ex.

BUCKINHAM, MRS LINA - Death - Mar 5, 1902 Mrs
Lina Duckinham, known as Miss Lina Campbell,
died at St Mary's hospital, Quincy, Sat. A.M.
where she had an operation the week before.
Was daughter of the late John Campbell, of Big
Neck and a sister of Mrs Jacob Groves, of Camp
Point, 38 years old. Buried Big Neck Monday in
Curless cemetery.

BUD, ADAM - Jumped Into a Well - Dec 21, 1893
Adam Bud, a well known Griggsville farmer
jumped into his well Thur. where his body was
found. Cause probably temporary insanity,
caused by despondeny over family trouble.

BUERKIN, CHARLES F. - Quincy - Mar 17, 1897
Charles F. Buerkin age 50 years and his
stepson, Emil Barth age 28 years both living in
the same house died within a few hours of each
other Thursday eve.

BULL, MRS MARGARET H. - Death - Dec 2, 1903
Mrs Margaret H. Bull died in Quincy Nov 24th

age 83 years. Born in Mass. Came to Quincy in 1843. Married Lorenzo Bull 1844. Husband and 5 children survive her.

BULLION, PHILLIP - Co. Seat - Apr 1, 1896 Will of Phillip Bullion conveys all of the estate to his widow and she is named executrix.

BUNTE, WILLIAM - Quincy - Jul 23, 1902 William Bunte died Tues. eve from effects of a paralytic stroke, age 71 years. Native of Germany and lived Quincy 45 years.

BURCHUM, PHOEBE - Sudden Death - Dec 28, 1893 On Sat. night when James Skirviv reached his home in Gilmer twp he found his housekeeper, Phoebe Burchum, dead. Miss B. had been at home alone. Was 46 years old and her father lived in Hancock Co.--not married had lived with the Skirvin family about 20 years. Verdict death caused from heart failure.

BURGDORFF, MRS CARL - Quincy - Mar 12, 1902 Mrs Carl Burgdorff, who had lived here for nearly half century died Wed., age 58 years.

BURKE, MRS - Elm Grove - May 11, 1894 Mr and Mrs Jesse Leeper of Columbus attended Mrs Burke's funeral last Sat. Mrs B. was a sister of Mrs Leeper.

BURKE, MRS C.H. - Elm Grove - May 11, 1894 Frank and Willie Butler attended the funeral of their mother Mrs C.H. Burke last Sunday. Frank came from Kansas and accompanied the remains and Willie came from Henderson Co. where he is employed at farm labor.

BURKE, CYRUS H. - Golden - May 8, 1894 Cyrus H. Burke arrived Sat. eve from Partridge, KS with the remains of his deceased wife and she was buried in Horeb cemetery Sun. May 6th.

BURKE, CYRUS H. - Elm Grove - May 25, 1894 Cyrus H. Burke and little family have returned to Partridge, KS after the last rites of a wife and mother. They will probably return in the fall and live on the old homestead.

BURKE, MRS LILLIAN - Elm Grove - May 11, 1894
Died-The remains of Mrs Lillian Burke, wife of
Mr C.H. Burke were brought from Partridge, KS
last Sat. to Golden and buried Horeb Church
cemetery on Sun. Services by Rev R.A. Hartrick
at 11 A.M. Mr B. moved to Kansas during last
fall with the hope her health might be restored
but exposure to a storm and an attack of the
grippe ended with death on May 3, 1894.

BURKE, PATRICK - Killed by Fast Mail - Oct 7,
1898 Patrick Burke, section man between
Eubanks and the Soldiers home was killed Fri.
A.M. by the fast mail. Taken to Quincy where
he died at 12:30.

BURNHAM, WILLIAM A. - 10 Years Ago - Mar 16,
1894 Dead- William A. Burnham was found dead
in the woods in the vicinity of Newtown.

BURNS, CHARLES - Columbus - Jan 12, 1894 Mrs
Ed Stenbeck attended the funeral services of Mr
Charles Burns at Payson Sunday.

BURNS, MRS MARY F. - Quincy - Jul 1, 1896 Died
Mrs Mary F. Burns died Sat. at Los Angeles,
Calif. age 72 years. Born New York. Came with
parents to Payson 1839 and spent many years in
Quincy. Maiden name was Brown.

BURNS, PATRICK - Dropped Dead - May 19, 1897
Patrick Burns, one of the wealthiest farmers of
Mt Sterling twp died suddenly of apoplexy in a
field near his home Sat. A.M. the 8th inst.

BURR, WEBSTER - Local - Jan 2, 1896 Webster
Burr, an inmate of the Soldiers home committed
suicide by drowning in the lake on the grounds
Sun. A.M. Family lived Batavia, Kane Co.

BURTON, "GRANDMA" - Local - Jul 22, 1896
Grandma Burton of Mt Sterling, Brown Co. Ill.
the oldest resident of that co. and central
Ill. died, 98 years old on Wed. the 24 of last
June. Died Sun. at her home in Mt Sterling

where she lived with 2 daughters, Mrs Phoebe
Allen and Miss Pattie Burton who are 2 of her 5
surviving children.

BUSBAUM, MR AND MRS - Golden - Sep 14, 1893 Mr
and Mrs Busbaum, 2 miles E. of this place both
died Sun. A.M. within an hour of each other.
She had been an invalid for more than 20 years
but Mr B. seemed to be a stout hearty old
gentleman. He was sitting by his wife's
bedside when she died. Then he went out and
ate a lunch, come back and lay down on the bed
and in less than an hour was a corpse.

BUSCH, MISS EMMA - Quincy - Mar 2, 1894 Miss
Emma Busch age 20 died from typhoid fever.
Buried from Salem Church Sunday.

BUSCH, HENRY - Broke his Neck - Mar 26, 1902
Henry Busch, a Quincy carpenter kicked at a cat
on his porch, Thurs. afternoon, missed it and
the force of the kick caused him to fall off
the porch 4 ft. to the ground below, breaking
his neck. Died within a few minutes.

BUSHNELL, NEHEMIAH - Ancient History - Feb 11,
1903 - Feb 6, 1873 Nehemiah Bushnell, one of
the foremost lawyers of Quincy died Jan 31st.

BUSHONG, DR E.W. - Golden - May 20, 1896
Funeral for Dr E.W. Bushong at Augusta last
Thursday.

BUSS, G.J. - Golden - Jul 22, 1896 Mr and Mrs
Miller of Hulls, Ill and Mr Buss of Beatrice,
NE attended the funeral of G.J. Buss.

BUSS, G.J. - Golden - Jul 22, 1896 Died, at
his home here, G.J. Buss of typhoid fever last
Fri. at 7 P.M. Funeral Monday at Prairie
Lutheran Church.

BUTLER, MRS - Local - Mar 6, 1894 Died- Mrs
J.W. Corkins of Sedalia, Mo. arrived here Mon.
A.M. to see her sick sister, Mrs Butler who
died very shortly after her arrival.

BUTLER, DANIEL - Local - Sep 7, 1893 A fire at
Beardstown on Thurs. A.M. destroyed almost an
entire business block. Fire broke out in C.M.
Spring's livery stable and spread. Daniel
Butler who was sleeping in the Spring barn was
burned to death as were 6 horses.

BUTLER, MRS NEVA GRIMES - Death of Mrs Neva
Butler - Mar 6, 1894 Died, Mrs Neva Grimes
Butler died Mon. at 8 A.M. Services at Presby.
Church Wed. at 2 P.M. burial will be in village
cemetery.

BUTLER, MRS NEVA - Obituary - Mar 9, 1894 Died-
Mrs Neva (Grimes) Butler born Beverly Adams Co.
Dec 12, 1862, died at home of her parents in
this city Mar 5, 1894 age 31 years 2 mon. 23
days. Married Apr 19, 1892 to R.G. Butler and
moved to Butte, Mont. Stricken sick in a few
months. Came to folks and when well she
returned to husband again. In Sep. she
returned to folks for last time. Funeral in
Presby. Church by Rev Miner and Elder O.
Dilley. Her sister Mrs Corkin's of Sedalia, MO
came the night before she died. Left her young
son for her mother to care for.

BUTTS, AARON W. - Probate Notice - Aug 6, 1902
Aaron W. Butts, deceased 1st Mon. of Oct. 1902
(6th) Cyrus L. Butts, adm.

BUTTS, AARON WESTCOTT - Death - Jun 25, 1902
Aaron Westcott Butts was born in Coharie Co. NY
Oct 10, 1813, died in Columbus twp Jun 21,
1902, age 88 years 8 mon. 11 days. He came to
OH where he stayed a few years and on to Ill.
about 60 years ago and located in Columbus twp.
Leaves 3 sons, 2 daughters and a number of
grandchildren. Funeral Sunday.

BUTTS, MRS AMANDA - Death - Apr 22, 1903 Mrs
Amanda Butts, age 36 years died Wed. A.M. at
her home, 24th and Maple Sts., Quincy from
kidney trouble. Husband Walter Butts, 3 young
children, her parents, Mr and Mrs Dan Simmons
and 6 brothers survive.

BUTTS, AMY ZELINDA - Obituary - Apr 7, 1897
Died-Amy Zelinda Butts, infant daughter of Mr
and Mrs Walter Butts of Columbus twp of lung
fever Mar. 31st. Born Apr 14, 1896, age 11
mon. 17 days. Buried from Pleasant View Church
by Rev Parrick and Rev Knight, buried Pleasant
View cemetery.

BUTTZ, A.H.D. - Ancient History - Sep 25, 1894
Sep 20, 1883 A.H.D. Buttz, a wealthy citizen of
Liberty died on the 7th.

BUTTZ, A.H.D. - 10 Years Ago - Sep 28, 1893
A.H.D. Buttz, one of the prominent citizens of
Liberty died, age 74 years.

BUTTZ, ABRAHAM H.D. - Ancient History - Sep 16,
1903 - Sept 1883 Abraham H.D. Buttz, a pioneer
resident of Liberty, died on the 7th.

BUTTZ, MRS ANNA - 10 Years Ago - Mar 16, 1893
Mrs Anna Buttz died at the home of R.A.
Wallace.

BUTTZ, MRS ANNA - Ancient History - Mar 4, 1903
Mar 1, 1883 Mrs Anna Buttz died on the 22nd.

BYBEE, CLARENCE L. - Death - Nov 18, 1903
Clarence L. Bybee, a switchman, who lived in
Quincy was accidently killed at work in the Q
yards Friday A.M. Worked for the Co. about 30
years.

BYLER, MRS HARRIET - Obituary - Jun 1, 1894
Died Mrs Harriet Byler, nee Harriet Lakins,
born in Belpre, Washington Co. OH. Jul 11, 1820
Came to Ill. summer of 1840, Mother of 5
children-2 living, William H. Hezlep and Chas.
B. Johnson. She died May 24th age 73 years 10
mon 13 days. Services from Christian Church
Coatsburg by Elder O. Dilley. Buried Coatsburg
cemetery.

BYLER, MRS HARRIET - Local - May 29, 1894 Died
Mrs Harriet Byler at her home in Honey Creek
twp last Thur. Lived here many years.

CABBELL, JOHN - Quincy - Jan 19, 1894 Died
John Cabbell age 65 years. Died from heart
disease. He was an engineer in the U.S.
Service. Was one of the oldest and best known
engineers on the Mississippi River.

CABELL, CAPT. SAMUEL G. - Quincy - Apr 14, 1897
Capt Samuel G. Cabell, who died in Washington
D.C. the 1st of the week, was buried here
Friday afternoon.

CAHILL, COL. J.B. - 20 Year Old Items - Jan 16,
1894 Died in Chicago, Col. J.B. Cahill from an
overdose of morphine.

CAIN, ABEL - Golden - Jul 21, 1897 Died at his
home in this village Sat. July 17th 2:05 P.M.
Abel Cain age 70 years, been poor health
several years. Buried Horeb cemetery.

CAIN, LABAN - Local - Oct 22, 1902 Laban Cain,
a druggist of Carthage died Sun. Remains
brought to Golden, his former home and buried
Tuesday.

CAIN, LABAN - Sketch of Laban Cain - Oct 29,
1902 Laban Cain was born near Clayton Jun 27,
1841 died at his home in Carthage Oct 19, 1902.
Enlisted Co. I 84th Ill Inf. Vol. Served 3
years during war. Upon his return married
Letitia Grainger who died within 5 years after
their marriage leaving 1 child, Jesse Cain, who
died in 1890. He married May 1877 to Camilla
R. Selby who survives him. 1877 they moved to
Golden where he was in drug business for 16
years. Spring of 1893 he went to Carthage and
again went into drug business until his death.

CALDWELL, J.W. - Local - Apr 23, 1902 Harry
Caldwell of S. Omaha arrived Mon. night, he
came to attend the funeral of his father,
J.W.Caldwell.

CALDWELL, JAMES W. - Obituary - Apr 23, 1902
James W. Caldwell born in Butler Co. OH Sep 14,
1824 spent early life there and married Eliza
Ann Brooks Oct 6, 1850 and they had 3

daughters, 1 living, Alice B. Everson. Moved
to Columbus, Adams Co. fall of 1854 where his
wife died. March 1869 he married Mrs Catharine
McAnulty, by whom he had 1 son Harry S. who now
lives S. Omaha, NE also 1 brother and 3 sisters
survive him-Wm N. of Calif., Mrs Amos J. Linn
of Liberty Adams Co. and Mrs Maggie Kennedy.
Became an Odd Fellow at Columbus Apr 11, 1863.
Services from Methodist Church by Rev W.M.
Reed, Rev's C.N. Cain and F.A. McGaw. Died
probably of apoplexy.

CALKINS, JOHN W. - Quincy - Feb 12, 1902 John
W. Calkins, an old resident of the city,
formerly in the railway mail service, died on
Wed. A.M. age 69 years.

CALLAHAN, JOHN -Probate Notice - Nov 23, 1894
John Callahan, deceased   1st Mon of Jan 1895
M.W. Callahan, adm.

CALLAHAN, JOHN -Columbus - Oct 12, 1894
Funeral services of John Callahan at Mt
Pleasant on Mon. Oct 8th by Rev A.A. White and
A.N. Simmons of Camp Point after which he was
buried in the adjoining cemetery by the side of
his son who died 20 years ago.

CALLAHAN, ROY GILBERT - Obituary - Jan 28, 1903
Roy Gilbert Callahan, 2nd son of L.L. and Anna
Callahan, born near Columbus, Ill. Jul 23, 1894
died Wed. A.M. Jan 14, 1903, was 8 years 5 mon.
21 days old.

CALLAHAN, ROY - Dead - Jan 21, 1903 Roy
Callahan, young son of Lawrence Callahan and
grandson of Alex Callahan living about 1-1/2
miles S. of Columbus died at noon Wed. from
injuries after being thrown from his pony which
he was riding. Was about 8 years old and on an
errand to his uncle's farm, Albert Callahan,
about 1-1/2 miles away. He was dragged over
the frozen ground with foot in stirrup. Number
of relatives live in Camp Point. Services at
Mt Pleasant Church Friday.

CALLAHAN, ROY - Local - Jan 21, 1903 Dr J.H.

Callahan of Carthage came down last week and
attended the funeral of Roy Callahan Fri. and
visited his brother Alex in Camp Point.

CAMPBELL, MISS ALICE - York Neck - May 28, 1902
Ed Beatty and sister, Miss Helen and mother,
Mrs Beatty from Quincy attended the funeral of
their cousin, Miss Alice Campbell, Wed. of last
week.

CAMPBELL, MISS ALICE - Death - May 21, 1902
Miss Alice Campbell, a sister of Mrs Jacob
Groves, died Mon. at her home in Big Neck,
Keene twp, age about 30 years. Miss C. spent a
few years in Camp Point with Mrs R.H. Pearce
and was well known here. Funeral today at
Union Church, Big Neck. Burial in Curless
cemetery.

CAMPBELL, ALICE MATILDA - Obituary - May 28,
1902 Alice Matilda Campbell died at her home
in Big Neck May 19th after illness of a year.
Born in Gilmer twp, Adams Co. Sep 22, 1864,
died May 19, 1902 age 37 years 7 mon 27 days.
Leaves 5 sisters and 1 brother, they are--Mrs
Hannah Kelley, Fairmont Clark Co. MO., Mrs
Maria Powell, Bentley, Hancock Co. Ill., Mrs
Margaret Groves, Camp Point, Ill., Mrs Ellen
Dougherty, Mendon Ill. and Miss Sarah Campbell
and brother Samuel who lives on the home place.
Family have lost 2 sisters in less than 3
months. Services by Rev L.A. Powell at Union
Church Wed May 21st. Buried Curless cemetery.

CAMPBELL, CHARLES - Local - Dec 30, 1896 Died
in New York City, Charles Campbell who was born
and reared here. He was elder son of Mrs M.T.
Campbell now of Bloomington. Disease-
consumption

CAMPBELL, CHARLES CYRUS - Death of Charles C.
Campbell - Jan 6, 1897 Died-Charles Cyrus
Campbell in New York City, Christmas Day of
consumption. Born Camp Point Oct 27, 1869, his
brother Frank was with him at the time of
death. Frank lives N.Y. Burial Greenwood
cemetery.

CAMPBELL, CLYDE - Local - Mar 22, 1895   A
Wabash train killed Clyde Campbell age 13 years
at Versailles Wed. eve. He was on top of a car
and fell between.

CANTRELL, DAVID J. - Death - Mar 8, 1895 David
J. Cantrell died Feb 20th at Rowena, MO, 76
years old. Born Warren Co. TN. May 28, 1819.
Married Miss Sarah Derrick Feb 11, 1841, had 11
children-9 still living. Lived Camp Point twp
several years before moving to Rowena.

CANTRELL DAVID J. - Death of David J. Cantrell -
Sep 7, 1894 Died, David J. Cantrell at
Corning, Ark. last Mon. the 3rd inst. Remains
sent to Coatsburg. Funeral by Rev Elder Dilley
Thurs. Born Camp Point Aug 26, 1868 lived with
grandfather in Audrain, Co. MO then went to
railroading, was a brakeman on the Iron
Mountain road where he was killed. Was
grandson of Mr and Mrs John Frost of Camp
Point.

CANTRELL, JACKSON - Local - Sep 11, 1894 J.D.
Cantrell, a former resident of Camp Point twp
came last week with the body of his son,
Jackson Cantrell from Ark. to bury him at
Coatsburg, returned home Fri. to Redfield, Ark.

CAREY, HENRY - Quincy - Oct 4, 1895 Henry
Carey who had lived Quincy 24 years died at St
Mary's hospital age 47.

CARLIN, MRS WM F. - Obituary - Dec 16, 1903
Perlia Fredonia, eldest daughter of Mr and Mrs
Charles Garner, born Clayton twp Aug 31, 1881.
Married Wm F. Carlin Mar 2, 1902, died Dec 9,
1903 at her late home in Houston twp. Leaves
husband and parents. Services at Hebron Church
Dec 10 at 11 A.M. by Rev D.H. Hartley of
Golden. Buried in cemetery nearby.

CARNEY, C.J. - Local - Jul 15, 1903 C.J.
Carney, a well known citizen of Liberty died
Sat. of heart disease. He had been in the
undertaking business for years.

CARNEY, JOHN - Ancient History - Jan 15, 1895
Jan 1875 John Carney was killed near Golden by
being thrown from a hand car.

CARPENTER, WILL - Crushed by a Mule - Jul 23,
1902 Will Carpenter, a young man who has been
working for Fred Farlow was found in a small
stall with a mule with his skull crushed.
Small hopes for his recovery. His father lives
near Chester and 2 sister live in Quincy.

CARPENTER, WILL - Local - Jul 30, 1902 Will
Carpenter, the young man found in a stall at
Fred Farlow's on the eve of the 19th with his
skull fractured died Friday night without
regaining consciousness. Remains taken to
Clayton Sat. to the home of a sister for
burial.

CARPENTER, WILLIAM - Death - Jul 30, 1902
William Carpenter died at home of Fred Farlow
near Camp Point Friday eve from skull fracture
received Sat. evening before. Was 22 years
old. Parents lived near Chester. Mother and
brother came and assisted in caring for him.
Remains taken to Clayton Sat. to the home of
his sister and services held Sunday.

CARROLL, GEORGE - Plymouth Man Lost - Aug 27,
1902 George Carroll of Plymouth has
disappeared and nothing is known of his
whereabouts. He hired a boat in Quincy Mon. the
18th and gave his own name. Tues. a man found
the skiff, floating in the river, one of the
oars missing. In the bottom was the vest
belonging to George Carroll. Police notified
his family at Plymouth. They were told he had
been in the livery business there until
recently. He has a wife and 6 living children
there.

CARROLL, GEORGE N. - Quincy - Aug 27, 1902
John W. Carroll, of Plymouth has offered a
reward of $25.00 for the discovery of the
whereabouts of his father, George N. Carroll,
who mysteriously disappeared in this city on
Mon. and is thought to have drowned.

CARROLL, MARY ELIZABETH - Local - Aug 23, 1895
Mary Elizabeth Carroll died at the home of Ed
P. Smith Tues. age 21 years of typhoid fever.
She was a niece of Mrs S., her home being in
Ellington twp near Eubanks. Funeral at
Bloomfield Thursday.

CARROTT, JAMES FINLAY - Death - Dec 30, 1903
After a long illness James Finlay Carrott died
last Wed. afternoon. Born in Quincy 57 years
ago. Educated at DePauw Univ. and Harvard Law
school. He was in partnership the past year
with his son Matthew F. Carrott. Survived by
his wife, who was Miss Susan Culbertson, of
Bedford, Ind. and 3 children-Matthew Finlay,
Browning and Miss Helen Carrott--sisters, Mrs
Helen F. Bristol of Chicago and Mrs Minnie
Appler of Hannibal and a brother, M.W. Carrott
of Minneapolis.

CARSON, WILLIAM - Local - Oct 21, 1896 Mrs
J.F. Joseph left on the Eli this A.M. for
Moberly, MO to attend the funeral of her
nephew, William Carson.

CARTER, MARTIN - Ancient History - Jul 17, 1894
Jul 18, 1879 Martin Carter, a former resident
of this county was killed when a well caved in
that he was digging in Reno Co. Kansas.

CASE, WARREN - Death - Mar 12, 1902 Warren
Case, age 53 years died in Jacksonville Fri.

CASEY, JOHN - Death - Sep 24, 1895 John Casey
died suddenly at his home in Hamilton last Wed.
Lived Camp Point a number of years ago before
moving to Hamilton.

CASLEY, MRS SUSAN - Local - Aug 20, 1902 Mrs
Susan Casley, wife of Jacob Casley, a well
known Mendon farmer died suddenly at her home
west of the village Wed. and buried Mendon
cemetery Fri. afternoon. She had long been a
resident of this county.

CASTLE, RIAL - 20 Years Ago - May 4, 1893 Rial
Castle died at his home in Camp Point.

CASTLE, RIAL - Ancient History - Apr 29, 1903
May 1, 1873 Rial Castle died April 28th.

CASTLE, TIMOTHY H. - Ancient History - Jun 25,
1895 June 1880 Timothy H. Castle died in
Quincy.

CATHER, JUDGE WILLIAM H. - Judge Cather Dead -
Dec 18, 1894 Died - Judge William H. Cather in
Quincy Sun. night, age 82 years. Native of
Penn. Came to Quincy over 50 years ago. Wife
died several years ago in Blessing Hospital.
No children.

CHANDLER, MRS - Columbus - Apr 13, 1893 Mrs
Chandler of Coatsburg was buried last Sunday.
83 years old.

CHANDLER, FRANK - West Point - Jul 17, 1894
Died-July 8th at his home 1-1/2 miles west of
town Master Frank Chandler, age 13 years 1 mon
2 days. Funeral by Rev McDonald in the ME
Church Tues. Buried in West Point Cemetery.

CHANDLER, FRANK - West Point - Jul 17, 1894
Mrs Emma Boyles and daughter Leli of Quincy and
Chas. Kinney of Bowling Green, MO were present
at the funeral of their nephew, Frank Chandler.

CHAPMAN, MRS LAURA E. - Shocking Accident - May
20, 1896 Mrs Charles Chapman drowned in a well
on last Tues. at the farm home of Mr C. one
mile NE of Mounds. Less than a month ago Mrs
C. was Miss Laura McPhail, the pet of her
fathers family. 3 weeks ago she married
Charles Chapman. "Mt Sterling Examiner"

CHARPENTIER, MR JULES - West Point - Jun 28,
1895 Died, Sun. A.M. June 25th at 7, Mr Jules
Charpentier, age 55 years. Several years was
troubled with heart trouble and asthma.
Funeral at the house by Rev J. Miller. Buried
near his old home west of Basco. Leaves a
wife, 2 sons and 1 daughter.

CHASE, JUDGE SALMON P. - Ancient History - May
13, 1903 May 8-15, 1873 Judge Salmon P. Chase

died on the 6th.

CHASE, THOMAS S. - Death of Thomas S. Chase -
Mar 23, 1894 Died- Thomas S. Chase formerly of
Fowler this co. died at Buena Vista, CO Mar.
13th, 1894 age 70 years. He was the last one
of Abram Chase sons. Was once a wealthy farmer
in Gilmer twp, but at death had nothing.
Married twice, both wives dead. Had 12
children, 5 still living.

CHATHAM, MRS FRANK - Local - Jun 8, 1893 Mrs
Frank Chatham died at the home of her daughter,
Mrs Max Pollock, in Columbus Tues. of
hemorrhage of the lungs. Funeral Wed at 2.

CHILDS, THOS. D. - May 4, 1893 Soldiers buried
in Camp Point Cemetery. Listed in Co. L, 2nd
Ill. Cavalry.

CHILDS, WILLIAM O. - Ancient History - Sep 4,
1894 -- Sep 1, 1881 William O. Childs was
suffocated by gases in a well on the farm of
Jas. T. DeHaven and was dead when removed from
the well.

CHINN, FRANK - Memoriam - Jan 15, 1895
Preamble and resolutions of LaPrairie lodge
#267 A.F. & A.M. relative to the death of
brother Frank Chinn Dec 29, 1894 at his late
home in Galesburg. Leaves widow and children.

CHINN, FRANK - Primrose - Jan 1, 1895 Died at
Galesburg Sun Dec 30, 1894, Frank Chinn.
Worked for C B & Q. Died from typhoid fever.
Sick 40 days. Leaves wife, 2 children, a
mother, Mrs C.M. Kern and 1 brother at Golden,
a sister, Mrs W.L. Omer of Camp Point. Funeral
from Hebron Church today.

CHITTENDEN, MRS CAROLINE - Death - Jun 17, 1903
Mrs Caroline Chittenden, widow of Samuel R.
Chittenden, died Fri. A.M. at her home in
Mendon of old age, was 82 years old, had lived
Mendon over a half a century.

CHRISTIE, JOSEPH B. - 10 Years Ago - Jul 27,

1893 Joseph B. Christie fell from his horse and died in a few minutes about a block from home.

CHRISTIE, JOSEPH B. - Ancient History - Jul 15, 1903 July 1883 Joseph B. Christie died.

CHRISTIE, JOSEPH B. - Ancient History - Jul 24, 1894 July 19, 1883 Joseph B. Christie died on the 13th.

CHRISTIE, MRS M.B. - Local - Nov 26, 1895 Funeral of Mrs M.B. Christie took place from the Methodist Church Sat. afternoon. Remains brought from Quincy on the 2:20 train and taken to the church. Services by Rev A.N. Simmons. Buried village cemetery.

CHRISTIE, MRS DR R.J. - Local - Jan 15, 1902 Mrs R.J. Christie died in Quincy Fri. age 68 years of paralytic stroke. Was wife of Dr R.J. Christie and mother of Dr R.J. Christie Jr.

CHURCH, SAMUEL P. - Local - Sep 21, 1893 Samuel P. Church, one of the early settlers of Quincy died at his home in that city Fri. eve. Age 88 years, born in Rhode Island, came to Quincy 1835 and engaged in merchandising and amassed a modest fortune.

CLARK, MRS E.A. - Elm Grove - May 26, 1897 Mrs E.A. Clark, near Elm Grove Post Office died Sat. A.M. May 15th after several years of lingering illness. She was buried in the Night cemetery in Brown Co.

CLARK, FRANK - Clark will Hang - Oct 21, 1903 Jury in the case of the negro, Frank Clark on trial last week at Kohaka, MO on a charge of assaulting a white girl, returned a verdict of guilty and assessed the death penalty.

CLARK, GEORGE - Local - Jun 10, 1896 George Clark of Jacksonville came over Wed night to attend the funeral of Henry S. Whitford, his brother in law.

CLARK, GEORGE W. - Local - Oct 29, 1902 Harry
Folckemer went to Jacksonville Sun. to attend
the funeral of the late George W. Clark.

CLARK, GEORGE W. - Died - Oct 29, 1902 George
W. Clark one of oldest citizens of Jacksonville
died there Thurs. night age 80 years. Came west
in 1841 and settled Brown Co. and 1847 married
Margaret J. Taylor. Moved 1862 to Morgan Co.
where he lived since. Leaves wife and 7
children, 1 daughter being Mrs Mary E.
Folckemer of Camp Point. Services Sunday.

CLARK, NAT - Killed by Wabash Train - Nov 12,
1902 Wabash train #19 was cause of death of
Nat Clark of Schuyler Co. Fri. about 11:50.
Clark was driving from Mounds to Clayton and
had just reached the co. line when the train
came along and hit the buggy. Was about 65
years old. Leaves a wife and 8 children. Was
an uncle of Mrs Mary Folckemer.

CLARKE, C.D. & FRED J. - Card of Thanks - Jun
16, 1897 For sympathy toward us and our
beloved sister...etc. C.D. & Fred J. Clarke

CLARKE, S.L. - Local - Jan 8, 1895 Mr and Mrs
R.M. Kimber of Galesburg attended the funeral
of their uncle, S.L. Clarke last week.

CLARKE, SAMUEL LAYTON "LAY" - Death Record -
Jan 4, 1895 Died-Samuel Layton Clarke Thurs.
A.M. after a long illness from pneumonia.
Lived Camp Point nearly 36 years. Married Miss
Susan Kirkpatrick who with 2 sons and 1
daughter survive him. Almost 63 years old.
Funeral from ME Church 2 P.M. today.

CLARKSON, DAN - Accident at Pittsfield - Mar 1,
1895 Dan Clarkson was killed by the accidental
discharge of a revolver in the hands of Frank
Frazier Tues. night on Adams St. at a lunch
counter owned by Clarkson Bros. He was 19
years old.

CLARY, EDWARD - Co. Cullings - Dec 7, 1893
Liberty Dec 4th Edward Clary, aged 82 years

died Sunday afternoon. Native of Ireland but
had lived in this country about 50 years.

CLARY, WILLIAM - Killed by a Pole - Mar 22,
1895 A little son of William Clary of Liberty
was killed when the horses knocked over a pole
striking him in the head. Died Thursday eve of
last week.

CLEVELAND, EDWIN - Dead - Oct 21, 1903 Edwin
Cleveland, widely known over Adams Co. died
Thurs. night at his home in Quincy age 67
years. Lived most of his life in Adams Co.
Served as Co. Treas. from 1873 to 1877 and was
supervisor for a number of years. 3 daughters
survive him. Funeral Sunday afternoon and
burial by Bodley Lodge of Masons.

CLEVELAND, MISS NELLE - Local - Mar 19, 1902
Miss Ida Derrick was called to Bushnell last
week to attend funeral of Miss Nelle Cleveland.

CLIFFORD, MRS WILLIAM - Quincy - Jul 12, 1895
Mrs William Clifford age 43 years died at St
Mary's hospital Monday from the result of a
fall received last week.

CLOTHIER, OLD MRS - Columbus - Mar 2, 1893 Old
Mrs Clothier died at her home on Fri. the 24th
ult from a stroke of paralysis Mon. Leaves an
aged husband, 1 son Fred, 1 daughter Mrs Philip
Roseberry. Funeral by Rev C.F. Stecker Mon. at
10 A.M.

CLOTHIER, FRED - Columbus - Mar 9, 1893 Fred
Clothier was called back to attend his mothers
funeral, but expects to start for his home in
Kentucky next week.

COATS, MRS ELLEN - Local - May 12, 1897 Died
Mrs Ellen Coats, widow of the late William A.
Coats died last week at the home of her son
William in Liberty twp, age about 81 years.
Funeral last Wed.

COATS, MRS MARY - Local - Apr 27, 1894 Died
Mrs Mary Coats wife of William A. Coats of

Liberty twp died Wed. eve., daughter of Thos. McCreery of Macomb.

COCHRAN, WILLIS P. - Dropped Dead - Jan 21, 1903 Willis P. Cochran, of New Canton, a railroad contractor fell dead Sat. noon in a Quincy restaurant after eating his dinner. Was a widower and is survived by 3 sons, Elmer, Emmett and Eugene, of New Canton. Born at New Canton, 50 years old.

COE, H.P. - Local - Jan 20, 1897 All masons are invited to attend the funeral of H.P. Coe at Clayton Thursday.

COE, H.P. - Recent Death - Jan 20, 1897 Died H.P. Coe, an old resident of Clayton Sunday night of complications of diseases. Had been a hardware merchant there many years. Leaves a wife and 4 sons-James B. and Edward of Clayton, Porter of Chicago and Charles of Montana, besides a number of other relatives. Services Thurs. by masonic fraternity.

COE, PORTER - Local - Jan 20, 1897 Porter Coe of Chicago was in town Tues. A.M. on his way to Clayton, having been called there by the death of his father.

COFFIELD, MRS SARAH J. - Death of Mrs Coffield-Apr 8, 1896 Died-Mrs Sarah J. Coffield at the home of her son, Dr James Coffield in Mendon, Tues. Mar 31st in her 85th year. Born Washington Co. Penn. Came to this county 60 years ago and in 1837 married John Coffield had 2 sons Thomas, of Lincoln, NE and Dr J. of Mendon. Husband died a few years ago and she since has lived with her son. She was an aunt of Mrs G.W. Smith and Mrs J.M. Kern of Camp Point. Lived more than 40 years on Sect. 6 Camp Point twp, then she and her late husband moved to Mendon.

COLLIER, MRS - Funeral - Apr 12, 1895 Funeral of Mrs Collier was held at Christian Church Tues. 2:30 P.M. by Elder R.A. Omer. Buried village cemetery.

COLLIER, MRS G.S. - Local - Apr 12, 1895 Mrs
George Riedenger of Quincy came up to attend
funeral of Mrs G.S. Collier, Tuesday.

COLLIER, MRS GABRIEL S. - Death - Apr 9, 1895
Mrs Gabriel S. Collier died in Camp Point Mon.
Apr 8th in her 45th year after a brief illness.
Betty A. Haley was born in Lincoln Co. KY Jul
9, 1850, married Gabriel S. Collier Apr 18,
1866. They came to Camp Point Dec 1869 and
lived there since. Had 4 children-3 of whom
with husband survive her. Buried village
cemetery after services this P.M. at 2 at
Christian Church.

COLLINS, MISS CORNELIA A. - Death - Jul 2, 1902
Miss Cornelia A. Collins of Quincy died Fri.
night in Minneapolis at the home of her sister,
Mrs C.W. Keyes age 55 years. Was daughter of
the late Frederick Collins and was born in
Columbus 1846. She was the founder and chief
inspiration of the Cheerful Home in Quincy.

COLLINS, FREDRICK - 15 Years Ago - Feb 23, 1893
Fredrick Collins, an old citizen of Quincy
died.

COLLINS, HARRY - Quincy - Apr 8, 1903 Remains
of Harry Collins, age 23 years, who died in St
Louis were buried Thurs. at his old home in the
village of Liberty.

COLLINS, JAMES - Local - Oct 12, 1893 James
Collins, of Quincy, lay down on a folding bed
in his office Wed A.M. to take a nap. His
clerk went in to wake him and found him
smothering in the folding bed and unable to
help himself or give an alarm. He came to
Quincy from Canton, MO about 2 years ago.

COLLINS, WESLEY - Death - Jul 19, 1895 Wesley
Collins and wife left Camp Point for Missouri
last Sat. not Mon. as in Tues. paper. Collins
took sick on train after leaving Quincy to go
to his brothers place, but was forced to lay
down along the roadside where he died.

COLLINS, WESLEY - Local - Jul 16, 1895 Wesley
Collins who attempted suicide has moved to
Missouri. A telegram received this A.M. by
E.K. Dice stating that Wesley Collins died at
Durham, MO from the effect of a dose of poison
which is supposed to have been obtained
yesterday in Quincy as he passed thru.

COLMAN, RICHARD M. - Recent Death - Mar 19,
1902 Richard M. Colman died in Quincy on the
11th inst. Sick 5 days, 74 years old. Born
Indiana. Lived Camp Point in early 60's moved
Quincy about 35 years ago. Was a carpenter.
Leaves aged wife, 2 sons and 6 daughters.

COLVIN, DAVIS P. - Local - Aug 24, 1894 Died,
Davis P. Colvin died at Ursa Tues. He was one
of the early settlers of the county, coming in
1838.

COMSTOCK, MR WARD - West Point - Dec 22, 1897
Mrs James Major returned home from Keosauqua,
IO. where she attended the funeral of her
brother in law, Mr Ward Comstock.

CONNER, DANIEL L. - Dead - Aug 13, 1893 Word
Friday A.M. that Conner had been in feeble
health for a couple of months. Disease of the
stomach had wrecked his vitality and he passed
away suddenly. Daniel L. Conner was born in
Columbus twp Nov 20, 1836 and spent his whole
life in this county living in Camp Point about
30 years. Maried Jane Peyton of Marcelline who
with 2 sons and 3 daughters survive him.
Services at the family home by Elder O. Dilley
at 2, Aug 20th. Buried Pleasant View Cemetery.

CONNER, DANIEL L. - Ancient History - Aug 12,
1903   Aug 1893 Daniel L. Conner died on the
17th.

CONNERS, JOHN - Quincy - Feb 13, 1894 John
Conners age 65 years died from heart disease
Wed. Been a special policeman for merchants of
the city for nearly 30 years.

COOK, DR A.F. - Dead - Oct 14, 1903 Word

received of the death of Dr A.F. Cook in Butler
Co. KS. Dr Cook lived many years in Houston
twp. Moved to Kansas about 10 years ago.
Leaves a wife and several grown children. Wife
was daughter of the late Philip S. Judy of
Gilmer twp.

COOK, MRS SUSAN - Quincy - Oct 25, 1895 Mrs
Susan Cook, colored, died Mon. at the home of
her daughter, Mrs Caroline McMurray on 7th St.
between Jersey and York. 105 years old. Mrs
C. came here from Ellsberry, MO. 7 months ago.

COOKSON, ANDREW J. - Local - Jan 7, 1903
Andrew J. Cookson, about 80 years old died
Sunday at the home of his daughter, Mrs P.H.
Kerley, had been an invalid several years.
Buried Burton Tuesday.

COOPER, MRS MARY - Resulted in Murder - Mar 6,
1894 Mrs Mary Cooper age 24 a colored woman
from Louisiana, MO has been living in Quincy
for some time and a colored man named Richard
Taylor, better known as "Springfield Dick" has
been living with her. Neighbor claims he
knocked her down and kicked her. Died of
internal injuries.

COOPER, WM H. - Quincy - Jan 26, 1894 Died, Wm
H. Cooper the stranded actor who gained
celebrity with the Ben DeBar and Lawrence
Barrett Co.'s died at Blessing hospital.
Funeral Sunday. His widow is a member of the
Ida Lewis Co. and the where abouts of the
company is unknown.

CORBIN, MISS ANNA M. - Quincy - Feb 5, 1895
Miss Anna M. Corbin, age 30 years, died from
consumption Thurs. A.M. remains taken to West
Point for burial.

CORKINS, DR P.G. - Fell Dead in Harwood - Jul
22, 1896 Dr J.M. Grimes received telegram
Thurs. from Sedalia, MO that Dr Corkins had
fallen dead on his way from depot to his home
in Harwood, MO. He had spent 3 or 4 weeks
visiting in Adams Co. visiting old friends

starting home Wed.   Philip G. Corkins born
Chatauqua Co. N.Y. Nov 7, 1825.   Was nearly 71
years old.   Went with parents to Ind. in 1838
to Tippecanoe Co. began to study medicine in
1845 and graduated at Rush Medical College,
Chicago 1853, but in meantime came to Ill. and
located in Kingston.   1869 he moved to Liberty
till a few years ago when he went to Schell
City, MO.   Married Miss Amelia M. Babcock Jan
1, 1852 who died about 2 years ago, had 2 sons
and 1 unmarried daughter surviving.

CORN, CHARLES - Elm Grove - Jan 4, 1895 A son
of Charles Corn, near LaPrairie was buried in
Horeb cemetery Wed. of last week.   Died of
typhoid fever.

CORN, MARIA - Local - Nov 23, 1893 Maria Corn,
a colored woman died at the poor farm Tues. on
her 100th birthday.

CORNELIUS, REV JACOB - Death Record - Aug 11,
1897 Telegram received here Sun. the 1st inst
of the death of Rev Jacob Cornelius at Galena,
KS. He was widely known in Ind., Ill., and
Iowa.   Was father of our townsman G. B.
Cornelius who had been at his bedside since
July 26th.   Funeral at Pella, IA where the
family lives.   "Bowen Chronicle"

CORNWELL, EZRAEL - Quincy - Jan 1, 1902 Ezrael
Cornwell, formerly of Oberlin, KS died here in
Blessing hospital.

CORRIGAN, JAMES - Death Record - Jun 9, 1897
James Corrigan died at his home in Liberty twp
on Sat night age 84 years.   Born Ireland, but
came to America while still young, settling
upon the farm that has since been his home.

CORRIGAN, JAMES LEO - Death - Feb 19, 1902
James Leo, son of Daniel and Eva Corrigan died
near Liberty, Feb 17th age 7 months 3 days.

CORRIGAN, JOHN H. - Local - Aug 31, 1894 Died--
John H, Corrigan died at his fathers home in
Liberty twp Thurs.   Had been crippled with

rheumatism several years. Leaves a wife, the daughter of Benj. Acklam and 3 children.

CORRIGAN, JONATHAN H. - Death of Jonathan H. Corrigan - Sep 4, 1894 Died--Jonathan H. Corrigan died Aug 30, 1894 at the home of his father, James Corrigan in Liberty twp, age 35 years 2 mon. 17 days. Born Adams Co. in Liberty twp May 13, 1859 married Eva Acklam who with 3 children survive him. Buried in Catholic cemetery at Liberty in presence of parents, brothers and friends.

CORRIGAN, PATRICK - Quincy - Dec 3, 1895 Will of Patrick Corrigan admitted to probate leaves 30,000 to his widow and 1/6 to his children, Mrs Louis Hogan, Mrs R.A. Varner, Mrs W.J. Waters, Daniel Corrigan, Mrs D.P. Rinecker and grand daughter, Clara Waters. Daniel Corrigan appointed Executor.

CORRIGAN, MRS SARAH - Death of Mrs Corrigan - Sep 15, 1897 Mrs Sarah Corrigan, widow of Jas. Corrigan died at her home in Liberty twp Fri. age 80 years. Husband died last June age 84 years. She leaves 8 children, living--Bernard of Kansas, Catherine Gorman of Liberty, Ellen Dwyer of S. Dakota, Daniel of Liberty, James B. of Quincy, Frank of Louisiana, Felix of Louisiana, Sylvester of Oklahoma territory. Deceased was born Ireland and came to America when 18 years old and married James Corrigan at Buffalo. She came to Liberty twp and settled on the farm where she continued to live ever since her marriage and where she died.

CORSE, MR AND MRS EDWIN - Coatsburg - Dec 3, 1895 The infant child of Mr and Mrs Edwin Corse died Friday of membranous croup. Services at Lutheran Church at Coatsburg Sunday afternoon.

CORSE, WILLIE - Necks - Dec 6, 1895 Died-- little Willie, only child of Mr and Mrs Ed Corse died of membranous croup Friday eve Nov 29th, was 2 years 1 month 23 days old. Buried Coatsburg cemetery.

COSGROVE, MR AND MRS - West Point - Jun 30, 1897 Died--infant son of Mr and Mrs Cosgrove.

COSGROVE, SYLVESTER - Killed - Apr 7, 1897 Sylvester Cosgrove, the 12 year old son of James Cosgrove of Marblehead died Mon. A.M. after injuries on Sat. eve when he was struck by a horse rode by Jesse Lanham 18 year old son of Elijah Lanham. Lanham lives on farm about a mile NE of Marblehead and Cosgrove lives in the village and works at the lime kilns.

COSTELLO, MICHAEL - Quincy - Jan 5, 1894 Michael Costello, an old resident died Monday night.

COURTNEY, WALLACE - Local - Aug 13, 1895 Wallace Courtney, in Fulton Co. jail charged with making murderous assault on Samuel McLaughlin of Banner twp committed suicide by hanging himself with 2 towels from his cell.

COWARD, GEORGE - Quincy - Jul 2, 1895 George Coward, the murderer of Edward J. Prewitt, both colored was captured at his home on Zimmerman Hill Saturday A.M.

COX, MRS A.S. - Our Unfortunate Neighbors Burnt to Death - Nov 20, 1894 Mrs A.S. Cox of Canton, Thurs. dropped a lamp and caught her clothes on fire, death resulted.

COX, MRS ANNA ROWLAND - Quincy - Jan 29, 1895 Mrs Anna Rowland Cox an old resident of this city, widow of Capt John C. Cox died the past week in Plainsfield, N.J.

COX, JOHN - Soldiers buried in Camp Point Cemetery - May 4, 1893 - Listed in Co. L 2nd Ill Cavalry.

COX, MART - Local - May 15, 1894 Mart Cox of Mt Sterling committed suicide Thurs. night. Leaves a wife and 2 children.

COX, SHEP - Local - Jun 4, 1895 Shep Cox died at the home of his daughter, Mrs Heaton in Ursa

Saturday night.

COX, SHEP - Quincy - Jun 21, 1895 Will of the
late Shep Cox was admitted to probate in county
court Wed. James M. Sprigg was named executor.
3 wills were filed and last one was probated,
estate inventories $25,000 and was estimated a
few years ago at $100,000.

COX, SHEPHERD - Quincy - Mar 19, 1895 John W.
Miller of Ursa has been appointed conservator
for the estate of Shepherd Cox. His bond
$50,000.

COXE, RICHARD - Quincy - Dec 15, 1897 Richard
Coxe, formerly a leading hardware merchant in
this city, died at White Bear Lake, MN on Wed.
age 80 years.

CRAIG, C.H. - Ancient History - Sep 25, 1894
Sep 20, 1878 C.H. Craig, banker at Clayton died
on the 17th.

CRAIG, MRS HENRY C. - Local - Dec 8, 1897 Mrs
Henry C. Craig died at Clayton Tues. age 78
years.

CRAIG, MRS JOHANNA - Death of Mrs Craig - Sep
2, 1896 Died--Mrs Johanna Craig of Liberty
died Thurs. eve at her home from an ulceration
in her head which resulted in blood poisoning,
49 years old. Leaves 4 children, Wesley Craig
and Mrs George Ham of St Louis and Mrs Henry
Leifhelm and Jas. Craig of Quincy.

CRAIG, THOMAS D. - Killed by Cars - Mar 26,
1902 Word received Monday by Mrs E.B.O. Dean,
that her brother, Thomas D. Craig was killed by
the cars Sun at Fresno, CA. He was reared in
Camp Point and ran as brakeman between Quincy
and Galesburg several years before he drifted
west. Mrs D. ordered the body shipped here.
The mother, Mrs Belle Barnes lives at VEO,
Iowa.

CRAIG, THOMAS D. - Obituary - Apr 2, 1902
Thomas D. Craig died at Fresno, Calif. March

24th from injuries when run over by a train
while switching. Born Camp Point Aug 10, 1869
and reared here. Past 10 years he has been
railroading, 1st on C.B. & Q and later in the
west. His mother, Mrs Belle Barnes of VEO, IA
and 1 sister, Mrs E.B.O. Dean survive him.
Body arrived in Camp Point Sun. A.M. Services
at Methodist Church 2 PM Sun. by Elder O.
Dilley and Rev's C.N. Cain and W.M. Reed.
Buried village cemetery.

CRAIG, THOMAS D. - Local - Apr 2, 1902 Mr and
Mrs Bert Craig, Mrs E.J. Craig and Dudley Craig
of Kewanee, attended the funeral of Thomas D.
Craig here Sunday.

CRAIN, CHARLES - Soldiers buried in Camp Point
cemetery - May 4, 1893 - Listed in Co. L, 2nd
Ill. Cavalry.

CRAIN, MISS SERVILLE - Elm Grove - Jul 19, 1895
Burial of Miss Serville Crain who died in
LaPrairie Sunday A.M. took place at Horeb
cemetery Tuesday afternoon.

CRAM, WILLIAM - Primrose - Oct 18, 1895
William Cram died Tues. Oct 15th at his home in
Camp Point twp, age 22 years. Was only son of
Mr and Mrs Henry Cram. Death caused from
malarial fever. Funeral from Methodist Church
Coatsburg Wed. 10 A.M. Buried Coatsburg
cemetery.

CRAMBERG, MRS CALLIE - Obituary - Oct 19, 1893
Mrs Callie Cramberg, nee Davis, was born in
Camp Point Jul 28, 1876. She lived here many
years and attended Maplewood school. Went to
Wichita, KS last March for her health being a
victim of consumption and she died Oct 13,
1893.

CRAMER, FRED C. - Soldiers buried in Camp Point
cemetery - May 4, 1893 Listed in Co. L , 2nd
Ill Cavalry.

CRAMSEY, FRANCES - Local - Oct 8, 1902
Frances, 6 year old daughter of John Cramsey

living in Gilmer twp died Friday night from
congestion of the brain.

CRANE, REV E.C. - Local - Jul 6, 1893 Rev E.C.
Crane, at one time a Cong'l minister at Mendon
and later editor of the Ludlow Vermont Tribune
was killed by a fall from his bicycle a couple
of weeks ago. He was a talented young man.

CRAVER, M.D.L. - Local - Nov 11, 1903 Rev E.J.
Lampton, of Bowling Green, MO and a former
pastor at the Christian Church here, came over
Tues. to assist at the funeral of his old
friend, M.D.L. Craver.

CRAVER, MARCUS D.L. - Dead - Nov 11, 1903
Marcus D.L. Craver died Sun. night Nov 8th from
a stroke of paralysis, age 77 years 10 months.
Born Johnstown, PA Jan 9, 1826, father died
while he was a child and he made his own living
afterwards. Learned the tailor trade which he
followed until 4 years ago. Served a short
time in Penn. regiment in the Union army 1863.
Married, Jane L. Ensminger about 1844 and they
lived in Penn. until 1866 when they came to
Camp Point and lived since. Living in one
house 36 years. Was father of 9 children of
whom 5 and his aged wife survive him. Children
are--Mrs H. Folckemer and John Craver, Camp
Point; Mrs Mary F. Miller and James E. Craver
of Minneapolis and Harry E. Craver of
Galesburg. Also leaves an aged sister in York,
PA. Services Tues. at the family home by Rev
E.J. Lampton of Bowling Green, MO buried
village cemetery.

CRAWFORD, JESSIE G. - Local - May 10, 1895
Jessie G. Crawford, one of the earliest
settlers of Griggsville died Tues. night age 85
years.

CRAWFORD, MRS WM - Ancient History - May 8,
1894 --May 10, 1878 Mrs Wm Crawford died,

CREE, MRS J.M. (LIDA) - Death of Mrs J.M. Cree -
Jul 24, 1894 Died-- Mrs Lida Cree, only child
of Dr and Mrs G.O. Pond died at Griggsville

Mon. July 23rd survived by husband and parents.

CREE, MRS LIDA A. - In Memoriam - Aug 7, 1894
Mrs Lida A. Cree July 23rd. Born Oct 7, 1840
only child of Mr and Mrs G.O. Pond. Married
Mar 31, 1864 to Mr Jas. M. Cree who with her
aged parents survive her. Was an invalid many
years.

CREEKMUR, J.W. - Local - Dec 25, 1894 J.W.
Creekmur arrived Sun A.M. and will spend the
holidays in Camp Point. He was called to Tower
Hill by the death of his father and has been
spending a few weeks there.

CRENSHAW, GUY - Quincy - Jun 14, 1895 Guy
Crenshaw, a brakeman on the Quincy and
Louisiana line was killed Tues. afternoon in a
collision between 2 freight trains, 27 years
old. Married and lived at Louisiana.

CRIPPEN, THOMAS S. - Death - Dec 24, 1902
Thomas S. Crippen died at his home in Concord
twp Thurs. leaves wife, but no children. Lived
several years in vicinity of Camp Point. Was
member of Camp Point Lodge of Odd Fellows.
Buried Sat. in Hebron cemetery.

CRIPPIN, THOMAS S. - Probate Notice - Feb 25,
1903 Thomas S. Crippin, deceased 1st Mon of
April 1903 (6th) Julia A. Crippen, Exec.

CROCKER, ELLEN - Quincy - Jul 16, 1895 Remains
of Ellen Crocker who died in St Louis of heart
disease last week and was buried there as an
unknown, were brought to her home in this city
and reinterred Thursday.

CROMWELL, JOSEPH - Death - Jan 8, 1902 Joseph
Cromwell died at his home in LaPrairie Jan 1,
age 66 years after a long illness. Reared
Clayton twp 4 miles NE of Camp Point. Spent
most of his life in Adams Co. Married
Elizabeth J. Robbins Feb 14, 1856 - she and 4
children survive him. Buried Camp Point
cemetery by the masons of LaPrairie Lodge and
Camp Point masons.

CROOK, WILLIAM - Quincy - Apr 17, 1894 Died
William Crook age 40 years, of Burton twp died
in Comstock, Texas. Brought here for burial.

CULP, MRS - Columbus - Jan 12, 1894 Mrs Dudley
Chatham was called to New London, MO to attend
the funeral of her mother, Mrs Culp Saturday
January 6th.

CULP, MRS - Columbus - Jan 12, 1894 Died-Mrs
Culp, mother of Mrs Dudley Chatham, buried at
Stones Prairie Sat. 6th, 1894.

CUNNINGHAM, MR - Golden - Nov 17, 1897 J. and
Fred Cunningham of Chicago came down to attend
the funeral of their father week before last.

CUNNINGHAM, ANDREW J. - Local - Dec 30, 1903
Andrew J. Cunningham, a former resident of Camp
Point, who moved to Cherokee, KS about 30 years
ago, died a couple weeks ago at age 64 years.

CUPP, LEWIS C. - Local - Nov 17, 1897 Lewis C.
Cupp died at New London, Mo last week. He was
a brother of Henry C. Cupp of Fall Creek.

CURL, DAVID B. - Local - Nov 3, 1897 The will
of the late David B. Curl of Camp Point was
filed for probate Tuesday leaves household
furniture and 1 lot in Camp Point to Mrs Ann C.
Clarke, the rest to his 3 sisters-Mrs Francis
Bellew, Mrs Isabelle Clark and Mrs Rebecca
Pickler. Rev O. Dilley named executor.

CURL, DAVID - Death Record - Nov 3, 1897 Died
David Curl born Jeffeson Co KY Feb 10, 1813.
Died Camp Point Oct 27, 1897. Was son of John
B. and Charity Curl. Came with parents to Ill.
Oct 1831. Married Ann Curry Apr 5, 1838. Had
1 son, 1 daughter both dead. Son died in
services of his country. Mrs C. died Apr 18,
1890. 3 sisters are all that survive Mr C.'s
family-Mrs Francis Bellew of Camp Point, Mrs
Isabel Clark of Chandlerville, MO and Mrs
Rebecca Pickler of Chico, Calif. Lived in Camp
Point nearly 20 years. Services Friday P.M. at
Pleasant View by Elder O. Dilley buried Church

yard near the home of his early manhood.

CURL, DAVID B. - Probate Notice - Dec 15, 1897
David B. Curl, deceased   1st Mon. of Feb 1898
(7th)   Orrin Dilley, Ex.

CURL, JOHN B. - Soldiers buried Pleasant View
cemetery - May 26, 1897 - Listed in Co. G, 78th
Ill. Infantry.

CURL, MILDRED - Death of Mrs Anders - Jul 13,
1894 Died--Mildred Curl, born in Jefferson Co.
KY Apr 11, 1816. Came with parents to Adams Co
1831 settled on farm near Camp Point now owned
by Mr Frame. Married Richard Kelley Aug 13,
1840 they had 1 son, Samuel Kelley now of
Schell City, MO. After Mr Kelley died she
married John Anders Jan 7, 1855, they had 1
daughter, wife of Wesley Sammons at whose home
she died July 5th in her 79th year. Known as
Aunt Milly. Buried Pleasant View cemetery.

CURREY, LEWIS F. - Dead - Sep 24, 1902 Lewis
F. Currey born near Louisville, KY Apr 24, 1832
died at the home of his daughter, Mrs Henry
Vollmer in Roseville, Ill Fri Sept 12, 1902.
Sick one week, age 70 years 4 months 18 days.
He came to Ill 1852 and located in Columbus twp
for about 2 years and moved to Roseville to
live with his children there. Married Mar 30,
1856, Mary Jane Roseberry who died Oct 10, 1897
they had 9 children, 2 died in infancy-those
surviving are Mrs Cynthia Vollmer, Mrs Belle
Lake, George and Nelson Currey of Roseville,
William of Coatsburg, Frank of Kellerville, Mrs
Minnie Turner of Clayton. Funeral at the home
in Roseville Sat. A.M. Buried Pleasant View
Cemetery, Camp Point, Ill.

CURRY, MRS C.S. - Local - Oct 7, 1896 Died Mrs
C.S. Curry of Clayton Sat. eve, sick over 2
years of paralysis. Funeral from the home Mon.
at 2 P.M. by Elder G.H. Hendrickson, pastor of
the Christian Church of which she was a member.

CURRY, FRANK C. - Quincy - Oct 27, 1897 Died
Frank C. Curry, a prominent business man of Mt

Sterling died at Colorado Springs last week.

CURRY, GUY - Was it Suicide? - May 31, 1895
Richard S. Curry received letter from his
daughter at Kirksville, MO telling of the death
of Guy Curry, son of H.H. (Tip) Curry last
Sunday. Body was found between R.R. and his
boardinghouse. Note makes them think suicide.
Leaves a young wife.

CURRY, HARRY WARDELL - Death - Apr 16, 1902
Harry Wardell Curry was born at Mt Sterling
Brown Co. Ill. Oct 16, 1838 and died at the
home of his grandparents, Mr and Mrs Chas.
Baird in Camp Point Apr 10, 1902 at tender age
of 13 years 5 months 25 days. Came to Camp
Point at age 1 year. Leaves father and mother
and 2 half brothers. Services at Christian
Church by Elder J. Thos. Webb and Rev W. M.
Reed. Buried Village Cemetry.
Mrs Curry and her sons Dick and Charley
McGaughey wish to express their thanks.

CURRY, JAMES L. - Soldiers buried in Pleasant
View cemetery - May 26, 1897 - Listed in Co E,
50th Ill. Infantry.

CURRY, JOSEPH A. - Quincy - Jul 16, 1902
Joseph A. Curry, a prominent resident of Mt
Sterling died Friday age 65 years.

CURRY, MRS LEWIS F. (MARY JANE) - Obituary -
Oct 20, 1897 - Mary Jane Roseberry, wife of
Lewis F. Curry, died at her home in Columbus
twp Sun. Oct 10th 1897. Married Lewis F. Curry
in 1856 leaves 7 children-4 boys, 3 girls with
her husband. Samuel Roseberry a brother and Mrs
Volmer, a daughter of Roseville were at the
funeral which was at Pleasant View on 11th at 3
P.M. Services by Elder O. Dilley. Buried
Pleasant View Cemetery.

CURRY, MRS LEWIS F. - Local - Oct 13, 1897 Mrs
Lewis F. Curry, of Columbus twp died Sun. A.M.
after a lingering illness. Funeral Monday
afternoon.

CURRY, MRS LUCY - Ancient History - Oct 16, 1894 - Oct 13, 1881 Mrs Lucy Curry, wife of B.A. Curry of Clayton died on the 11th.

CURRY, SAMPSON - Soldiers buried in Pleasant View cemetery - May 26, 1897 - Listed in Co B, 50th Ill. Infantry.

CURRY, THOMAS S. - Sale of Real Estate - Mar 23, 1893 As Adm. of the late Thomas S. Curry, deceased by consent of the heirs the residence of the late Thomas S. Curry consisting of 3 acres more or less located 2 blocks S. of the P.O. in town of Clayton will be sold March 28th. C.S. Curry

CURTIS, MRS ANNA M. - Ancient History - Apr 26, 1895 - Apr 1879 Mrs Anna M. Curtis died age 61 years.

CURTIS, MRS ANNA M. - Ancient History - Mar 24, 1897 - April 1879 Died- Mrs Anna M. Curtis, widow of E_am B. Curtis, died.

CURTIS, ELAIN B. - Ancient History - Dec 18, 1894 - Dec 1880 Elain B. Curtis, the 1st merchant in Camp Point died Dec 7th.

CURTIS, ELAM B. - Ancient History - Jul 14, 1897 - Dec 1880 Elam B. Curtis died on the 7th.

DADE, LOUIS - Shot by Policeman - Sep 17, 1895 Policeman Sidney (colored) shot and killed Louis Dade in Quincy Sunday night.

DALY, JOHN F. - Local - Jul 13, 1893 - John F. Daly, a member of the police force of Quincy, was drowned Friday A.M. while bathing in the river. He and Frank Duker and a couple of women of the town had rowed up the river above the bridge early in the morning and cooked breakfast. After breakfast they waded across the sandbar, but Daly never was seen afterwards. His body was recovered a few hours later.

DALY, JOHN - Quincy - Oct 7, 1903 - John Daly, of this city, was killed on the railroad tracks at Memphis, Tenn. on Wednesday.

DANLEY, CHARLES - Local - Jan 19, 1893 Charles Danley, a coal hauler was killed last Tues. by the caving of a bank near Macomb. He was caught under the clay and crushed to death.

DARRAH, MRS A.T. - Local - Jul 6, 1893 Mrs A.T. Darrah, of Bloomington, daughter of Mrs Fugate of Camp Point died at her home last week. Miss Mattie Fugate was with her at the time of her death.

DARRAH, DR JOEL - Ancient History - Sep 20, 1895 - Sept. 1878 Dr Joel Darrah a pioneer physician living north of Coatsburg died on the 22nd, age 72.

DARRAH, DR JOEL - Ancient History - Jan 27, 1897 - Sept 1878 Dr Joel Darrah, an old time physician died near Coatsburg.

DAUGHERTY, MISS ESSIE - Local - Oct 28, 1896 Miss Essie Daugherty, daughter of Charles Daugherty died at her home in Quincy Thurs. the 22nd. Brought to Camp Point for burial, 19 years old.

DAUGHERTY, MICHAEL - Quincy - Jun 4, 1902 the heirs of Michael Daugherty have appointed the State Savings Loan and Trust Co. as trustees of the estate.

DAVIDSON, J.M. - Death of Editor Davidson - Oct 2, 1894 Lewiston, Ill Sept 30th died, J.M. Davidson, editor of the Carthage, Ill Republican died here Sat. A.M. age 65.

DAVIS, MRS CATHERINE - Obituary - Dec 31, 1902 Died, at the family home on York St in this city at 5 A.M. Dec 19th, Mrs Catherine Davis, age 79 years 8 months 2 days. Catherine Clingingsmith was born in Missouri Apr 17, 1824. Married the late Cornelius Davis Jul 10, 1842, lived together over 60 years. Reared 6

children. Mr Davis died 2 months ago (Oct
31st). Services from the family home by Dr
Owens of Hersman and Rev F.A. McGaw at 2 P.M.
Sunday Dec 21st. Buried beside her husband in
Camp Point cemetery. Amanda, the youngest
daughter and only unmarried one cared for her
mother.

DAVIS, MRS CATHERINE - Death - Dec 24, 1902
Mrs Catherine Davis, widow of the late
Cornelius Davis died at her home in Camp Point
Fri. Dec 19th age 78 years 8 months 2 days.
Had been an invalid for a long time. Mr Davis
died Oct 31st and since then she has failed
rapidly. Services Sun. 2:30 P.M. by Elder Owen
of Hersman. Leaves 3 sons and 3 daughters.

DAVIS, CATHERINE - Probate Notice - Jan 7, 1903
Catherine Davis, deceased 1st Mon. of Mar 1903
John W. Sherrick, conservater and Exofficio
adm.

DAVIS, CORNELIUS - Will - Nov 12, 1902 - The
will of the late Cornelius Davis, of Camp Point
was filed for probate at the courthouse Thurs.
leaves all real estate to wife and at her death
to be divided among 6 children-except that John
Davis received $250 less than the others.
Daughter Catherine also receives 2 lots in Camp
Point in addition to her share.

DAVIS, CORNELIUS - Death - Nov 5, 1902
Cornelius Davis, pioneer of Adams Co died at
his home in Camp Point Fri eve Oct 31, 1902 age
83 years. Born in Missouri, but in infancy his
family moved to Tenn. Came to Adams Co. while
he was in his youth where he lived nearly 70
years. Married in this county 60 years ago and
his wife who is an invalid survives him.
Celebrated their golden wedding nearly 10 years
ago. Leaves also 6 children-3 sons, 3
daughters. Sons are Henry of Camp Point - John
of Honey Creek and Charles of Idaho who arrived
to late to see his father alive. Services Sun
P.M. at family home by Elder D.W. Owens of
Hersman. Buried village cemetery.

DAVIS, CORNELIUS - Probate Notice - Dec 10,
1902 Cornelius Davis, deceased 1st Mon of Feb
1903 John W. Sherrick, executor.

DAVIS, ERNEST - Ancient History - Jul 24, 1894
July 21, 1876-Ernest Davis was killed in Barry
by William Mallory.

DAVIS, GEO. - Columbus - Nov 25, 1903 - Geo.
Davis and family of Hebron, Ill attended the
funeral of her sister.

DAVIS, JANE A. - Probate Notice - Jan 19, 1893
Jane A. Davis, deceased 1st Mon. of March 1893
(6th) Geo. W. Cyrus, Ex.

DAVIS, JAMES R. - Additional Locals - Sep 30,
1903 James R. Davis of Mt Sterling was killed
by a Wabash train Thurs night, 1/2 mile west of
Versailles. Mr Davis was 41 years old and
leaves a wife and 2 sons.

DAVIS, LEVI - Local - Jun 1, 1894 Died-Levi
Davis, of Lima twp died in Quincy Thurs. A.M.
age 66 years. Born in Penn. Came to Ill. 1851.

DAVIS, MISS MAGGIE - West Point - Jan 18, 1895
Died-Miss Maggie Davis, age 20 years 7 months
at the home of Mrs G.T. Tatman. Funeral by Rev
Lowe. Buried Payne Cemetery.

DAVIS, PHILIP - 78th Ill. Reunion at Plymouth -
Oct 15, 1895 Died during the year: Philip A.
Davis of Co. A - Wm A. Jenkins of Co. B -
Clayton McGill of Co. G - Ira Arnold and John
McClellam of Co. I.

DAVIS, V.D. - Ancient History - Jun 12, 1894
June 9, 1881-V.D. Davis died in Concord twp.

DAVIS, W.B. (WILLIAM) AND WIFE - Killed by
Wabash Train - Oct 19, 1894 Mr and Mrs William
Davis were both killed by the Wabash passenger
train here at 10 Tues. forenoon. Lives 2-/2
miles W. of Mt Sterling. Both were very old
and partially blind and very deaf. Mr D. was
89 years old and known as "Uncle Billy". Mrs

D. was about 70 years old. Both had lived in
Brown Co. all their lives.

DAVIS, WILBUR - Columbus - Nov 25, 1903 Wilbur
Davis and family of Camp Point attended his
aunt's funeral here last Saturday.

DAVISON, CHAS. T. - Murder at Bushnell - Nov
17, 1897 Midnight Sat. night, Chas. T. Davison
a traveling man was shot and killed by Charles
Clement over a quarrel due to the unwelcome
attentions to Clement's sister.

DAZEY, MITCHELL - Death Record - Sep 16, 1896
Died-Hon. Mitchell Dazey died at his home in
Lima Thurs. eve Sept 10th. Born Bourbon Co. KY
Oct 2, 1820, he and parents moved to Adams Co.
1830. Arrived here after a long and tedious
journey by water and wagon. Settled in Lima
twp. Married Sept 11, 1853 to Abina Conover,
daughter of Robert and Hannah Conover pioneers
of the same twp. She died 1857 leaving 1 son,
Charles T. Dazey the successful playwright who
was born 1855. Mr D. married 2nd in KY some
years later but his second wife has been dead a
dozen years. Services at Lima Sun. at 10 A.M.

DEAN, MARTHA - Local - Sep 7, 1893 Martha
Dean, an insane colored woman died at the poor
farm last Thurs. She was adjudged insane in
Quincy the week before and taken to the poor
farm. She neither ate nor drank during the
week she was there. Evidently died of brain
fever.

DEATHS - County Seat - Jun 17, 1896 Number of
deaths reported during the year ending May 1,
1896 were 541.

DECKER, CHARLES - Quincy - Jun 8, 1894 Charles
Decker, a cabinet maker who came here from St
Louis last Jan. has disappeared. His wife
fears he was one of the 2 men who were killed
in a collision of freight trains near Hannibal.

DEEGE, MR AND MRS DAN - West Union - Aug 11,
1897 The 8 month old child of Mr and Mrs Dan

Deege died August 2nd.

DEGITZ, GEORGE - Co. Seat - Jun 24, 1896
George Degitz, an old resident of the city died
from a complication of diseases, age 66 years.

DEGROOT, MRS JOHN - Ancient History - May 8,
1894 May 8, 1884-Mrs John DeGroot died in
North East twp on the 1st.

DEHAVEN, JACOB - Hunting for Heirs - Feb 20,
1894 A fortune of $4,000,000 awaits
descendants of Jacob DeHaven who in 1777 loaned
the U.S. government a large sum of money.
Heirs scattered in 1859 to Ohio, Ind. and Ill.
William DeHaven of Logansport, Ind. has been in
the city looking up heirs here and found
MrsOgan and Mrs Collier both are direct
descendants of DeHaven. James T. Dehaven of
Camp Point twp is one of the heirs and has
hopes of being able to realize on his share of
this claim.

DEHAVEN, JAMES T. - DeHaven's Delightful
Deposit - Mar 16, 1894 James T. DeHaven Camp
Point twp--New York Mar 15th another heir to
Jacob DeHaven money is Mrs Eliza Fackler, wife
of John Fackler an organ maker who lives at
#430 W. 44th St. New York. Mrs F. is daughter
of Jehu DeHaven who is one of the grandchildren
of Jacob DeHaven and lives at Harrisburg, PA.
Jehu was formerly Supt. of the Northern Central
Railroad of Penn. The original DeHaven came
from France just prior to the outbreak of the
Revolution and settled at Norristown, PA where
he is buried. Most of heirs live at
Harrisburg. R.E. Doan of Washington has the
case in charge.

DEHAVEN, MISS MARIA - Ancient History - Mar 24,
1897 - Feb 1879 Miss Maria DeHaven died.

DEKRIEGER, CHRISTIAN - Quincy - Nov 17, 1897
Christian DeKrieger, a resident of Quincy since
1844 died Wed. A.M. age 75 years. He was
gardener at the poor farm for several years.

DELAMETER, MRS MARY J. - Quincy - Oct 25, 1895
Mrs Mary J. Delameter of this city for the past
40 years died Sunday 76 years old.

DELL, RACHEL - Obituary - Mar 30, 1894 Died-
Rachel Dell, born Frederick Co. Maryland Dec
25, 1804. Married James Durbin in 1825 had
14children. Moved with children in 1835 to
Belmont Co. OH where the rest of children were
born except youngest born in Monroe Co. where
they lived 7 years. 1853 they came to Adams
Co. Died at her home near Kellerville March
2nd A.M. Husband died 2 years ago in coming
Apr. Buried Washington Grove Cemetery beside
her husband Sat. at 3 P.M.

DEMAREE, MRS ALBERT - Local - Dec 21, 1893 Mrs
Albert Demaree died in Quincy Sun. Leaves
husband and 5 children.

DEMAREE, ELIZABETH - Quincy - Jan 22, 1902
Elizabeth Demaree, a resident of this city
since 1842, died while sitting in her chair on
Thurs. eve.

DEMOSS, CALVIN JR. - Obituary - Feb 27, 1894
Died-Calvin Demoss Jr at the home of his
parents in Coatsburg Feb 23rd 1894 at the age
of 30 years 4 mon. 26 days. Had been sick the
last year or more. Leaves parents, brothers,
sisters. Funeral at Christian Church Coatsburg
Sun. Feb 25th at 2 PM by Elder O. Dilley.
Buried Coatsburg Cemetery.

DEMOSS, CALVIN JR. - Coatsburg - Mar 6, 1894
The death of Calvin Demoss Jr who had been a
sufferer of laryngeal consumption for about a
year has been noticed in the "Journal"

DEMPSEY, THOMAS - Ancient History - Nov 2, 1894
Oct 30, 1874-A runaway team caused the death of
Thomas Dempsey on the road east of Quincy.

DENIG, MRS H.E. - Quincy - May 21, 1895
Funeral of Mrs H.E. Denig was Friday afternoon
by Rev Mayo and Corbyn with impressive
Episcopal services.

DENNING, THOMAS - Quincy - Aug 20, 1902 Thomas Denning, one of the best known hackmen of the city, died on Wed. age 60 years.

DENNING, WILLIAM - Quincy - Feb 24, 1897 William Denning, one of the oldest clerks in the railway mail service died here Tues. night age 62 years.

DENNIS, LAWRENCE - Local - May 18, 1893 Lawrence Dennis, a Hannibal boy, age 17, stole a ride to Quincy on the steps of the Eli coming from Palmyra and was knocked off the step in the Quincy yards Sun. A.M. and run over. He died a short time later.

DENNY, JOHN - Local - Feb 26, 1896 James Baird received word last week of death of John Denny at Whitehall, Ill. He lived many years in Camp Point moving to KS and then to Whitehall.

DENNY, MRS WESLEY - Local - May 3, 1895 Mrs Wesley Denny died at the home of her daughter, Mrs J.F. Lowry in Clayton Tues. afternoon. She lived many years in Camp Point and is the mother of Mrs Jas. Baird.

DENSON, WM - Deaths - Feb 18, 1903 William Denson died at his home in Quincy Sat. afternoon of heart failure and disease of the kidneys which he had suffered many years. Born in Ursa twp 61 years ago and lived this co. all his life. Several years he was in merchandising in Mendon and 22 years ago moved to Quincy and opened an insurance loan and real estate office until this fall when he became sick. Leaves wife and 2 sons, Homer and Harry.

DESPANE, SOLOMON - Soldiers buried in Camp Point cemetery - May 4, 1893 Listed in U.S. infantry 1812

DETMER, HENRY - Local - Feb 4, 1903 Henry Detmers an old resident and native of Germany died in Golden Thurs. night, age 67 years. Leaves a wife and children.

DEVORE, WILLIAM - Local - Feb 17, 1897 William Devore, a deaf mute, at one time engineer of Casco Mills died Mon. night in Quincy from paralysis.

DICK, CRESCUTIA - Co. Seat - Oct 14, 1896 Crescutia Dick, the only child and daughter of the late Adrian Dick has received notice of an inheritance of 67,397 marks having fallen to her from her grandfathers estate in Germany. Geo. Ricker has been appointed her guardian.

DICKERMAN, IRA R. - Local - Apr 9, 1902 Ira A. Dickerman, a pioneer settler of Mendon, died Friday night 88 years old. Settled on Mendon Prairie, then known as Fairfield in 1839. Leaves wife and 3 sons.

DICKERMAN, REV DR LYSANDER - Quincy - Dec 31, 1902 Rev Dr Lysander Dickerman, one of the early pastors of the Cong'l church in this city died in Boston recently.

DICKHUT, ALICE M. - Death - Oct 7, 1903 Alice M. Dickhut was born at Fowler Feb 9, 1871. Married Samuel L. Petrie Sep 14, 1892, they grew up together from childhood. They had 4 children, Myra age 10 years, Helen 7 years, Mildred 4 years and Harland 11 months who with her husband survive her. Also leaves 5 sisters and 6 brothers, one of whom is Arthur Dickhut of Camp Point. Was member of Grace Methodist Church at Bloomington near where she lived. Died from typhoid fever Sep 28th. Brought to Camp Point and buried from Liggett Undertaking rooms Thurs A.M. and buried village cemetery.

DICKHUT, AUGUST - Local - Feb 12, 1896 Died-August Dickhut, one of the oldest citizens of Ellington twp died Sat. night at the home of his daughter, Mrs Geo. Harvey.

DICKHUT, C.C. - Quincy - Jul 1, 1896 Died-C.C. Dickhut, one of the pioneer druggists of the city died Friday age 67 years.

DICKINSON, B.W. - Suicide - Feb 26, 1902 B.W.

Dickinson of Quincy, the Peoria agent of the
Interstate Dispatch Fast Freight line was found
dead in bed at the National Hotel, Peoria, Sat.
A.M. bottle of morphine and laudanum was found
near by.

DICKINSON, MISS LIZZIE - Local - Jul 6, 1893
Miss Lizzie Dickinson, who has made her home
for many years with Madison Willard in Houston
twp died Mon. night, age 62 years. Funeral
yesterday.

DICKISON, SARAH ELIZABETH - Obituary - Jul 13,
1893 Died, at the home of Madison Willard, 9
miles S. of Camp Point on Mon. night Jul 3rd
Lizzie Dickison age 60 years 6 months 22 days.
Sarah Elizabeth Dickison was born Dec 11, 1832
in Jacksonville, Ill, without parents she lived
among relatives until maturity. Since her 9th
year she has been almost a helpless cripple.
51 years she got around with crutches. 18
years she lived with her cousin, Madison
Willard. United with Methodist Church over 20
years ago. She leaves 3 sisters, Mrs L.C.
Hamilton of LaHarpe, Ill, Mrs Mary Cunningham
of Bentonville, Ark. and Mrs Jane Comstock of
NE. with a host of other relatives. Services
by Rev Rose of Bowen, Ill on Wed. Jul 5th
buried in cemetery near the Ebenezer Church of
which she was a member.

DILLEY, J.W. - Ancient History - Oct 12, 1894
Oct 7, 1880 Died J.W. Dilley of Macomb died at
the Francis hotel.

DILLON, REV T.M. - Dead - Oct 28, 1903 Rev
T.M. Dillon, editor of the Rochester Item died
in the railroad station at Rochester Sat. from
heart trouble. Was a native of New York but
came to Ill about 30 years ago. Was stationed
at Methodist Church in Camp Point about 6 years
ago and remaining 2 years. Leaves wife and 2
adopted daughters. Remains buried at
Springfield.

DIMMITT, REV JAS. P. - Local - Nov 1, 1895 Rev
Jas. P. Dimmitt died in Jacksonville Tues.

night. Well known in Adams Co. Funeral today at Jacksonville.

DINES, J.B. - Quincy - Jan 4, 1895 J.B. Dines, age 21 a student in Chaddock College died Mon. A.M. from typhoid fever.

DISMORE, JOHN - Obituary - Mar 8, 1895 John Dismore died at his home in Houston twp Tues. March 5th, 2 days less than 38 years old. Leaves wife and 2 children and his aged mother who lived with him. 3 sisters, Mrs A.H. McFarland of Camp Point, Mrs T.S. Crippen of Concord, Mrs E. Bennett of Houston. Was a member of Union lodge ICMA at Golden. Buried Thurs. at Hebron cemetery with ceremonies of the order. Services by Rev McDonald of LaPrairie.

DITMER, HENRY - Coatsburg - Feb 2, 1893 Henry Ditmer who has lived in this neighborhood 1/4 of a century died Friday afternoon at his home in this village from acute pneumonia, 57 years old. Leaves a wife and 5 children-2 daughters and 3 sons. Funeral Monday.

DITTMER, HENRY - Probate Notice - Feb 9, 1893 Henry Dittmer, deceased 1st Mon. of Apr 1893 (3rd) Paulina Dittmer, adm. Alfred J. Brockschmidt, attorney

DIX, J.H. - Quincy - Apr 3, 1894 Died, J.H. Dix, age 80 years died at a late hour Wed. night from paralysis of the heart. Came to Quincy 1856. Leaves a 75 year old wife and following children-Mrs John C. Bell, Elmwood, Ind., Herman H. and Ernest F. Dix of Sedalia, MO, John C. Dix of Memphis, Tenn., Capt H.A. Dix, Mrs Henry Bauer and Mrs Charles H. Lehbrink, Quincy.

DODD, L.L. - Clayton - Feb 26, 1896 L.L. Dodd, having purchased his father's residence property from the other heirs, has moved to it and will make it his home.

DODD, MRS WILLIAM R. - Quincy - Oct 29, 1902

Mrs William R. Dodd, of Quincy for more than a
half century died on Saturday, age 70 years.

DODSON, MR - Paloma - Apr 29, 1903 Funeral of
Mr Dodson was held in ME Church last Friday.

DONALDSON, JAMES - Death of James Donaldson -
Jan 26, 1894 Died-James Donaldson Mon. at his
home in Quincy. Born Ireland. Been in USA 27
years and in Adams 19 years of that time.
Buried Burton twp Thursday.

DONLEN, TERRENCE P. - Quincy - Sep 4, 1894
Terrence P. Donlen who died last Wed. was
supposed to be a bachelor, but he was privately
married to Miss Mary Schafer of this city in
Vincennes, Ind. Aug 12, 1892. They had lived
apart as the wedding was never sanctioned by Mr
Donlen's mother. Wife took her proper place at
funeral.

DONLEY, HENRY - Local - Jul 27, 1893 Henry
Donley, an old citizen of Big Neck died Thurs.
eve and was buried Sunday.

DONLEY, HENRY - Probate Notice - Aug 31, 1893
Henry Donley, deceased 1st Mon. of Nov 1895
(6th) Jacob Groves, adm.

DONLEY, HENRY - Local - Sep 21, 1893 Jacob
Groves, adm, will sell the personal effects of
Henry Donley, deceased, at public sale next
Thurs., the 28th near Big Neck Post Office.

DOOMIS, HENDERSON - Quincy - Jul 5, 1895
Henderson Doomis assaulted Mary Smith (both
colored) with a knife Wed. and cut her
severely. Police officer shot him in side and
he died about an hour later. Girl in critical
condition.

DORSEY, MR A. - Local - Sep 28, 1894 Died-Mr
A. Dorsey, a well known stock breeder living
near Perry died last week and buried Sun. about
61 years old. Funeral from Christian Church
and at the grave by the Odd Fellows.

DORSEY, MOLLIE - Death - Feb 26, 1902 Received word of sudden death at her home in Los Angeles, Calif. on the 12th inst of Mrs Mary Emerton. Born York Neck as Mollie Dorsey. Married John Simpson of Houston twp who died several years ago. Later married again and lived Los Angeles.

DOUGHTY, WILLIAM J. - Eaten by Hogs - Jan 1, 1895 William J. Doughty of Lynn twp a few days ago was found in the feed lot by neighbors being eaten by hogs. His mother became anxious when he didn't come in for supper. Body was rescued, but mother not allowed to see it. Mr D. had been told by doctors he could be taken any time. "Galesburg Mail"

DOWNING, GRANDMOTHER - Ancient History - Jul 14, 1897 - Nov 1880 Grandmother Downing died on the 26th age 97 years.

DOWNING, EBON C. - Ancient History - Feb 5, 1902 - May 1884 Ebon C. Downing died on the 27th.

DOWNING, MRS ELIZABETH - Obituary - Dec 30, 1896 Died- Mrs Elizabeth (Robertson) Downing widow of the late Ebon C. Downing at her home in Camp Point twp Fri Dec 25th age 74 years. Born near Greencastle, Ind. May 10, 1822. Came with parents 1832 to Ill. settled Morgan Co. for short time then Camp Point. Lived on farm where she died for over 60 years. Married Ebon C. Downing Jan 18, 1842. He died 1884. They had 11 children-5 sons, 6 daughters-4 survive her Amos R. of Deerfield, KS, George Y. of Camp Point, E. Lincoln of Pomona, Cala. and Mrs Clara H. Stabler of Camp Point. Funeral held at the old Hebron Church of which she was a member. Buried beside her husband in the old cemetery nearby.

DOWNING, MRS NANCY - Ancient History - Dec 10, 1895 - Dec 1880 Among deaths reported 1st week was Mrs Nancy Downing age 97 years.

DOWNING, R.H. - Local - Feb 3, 1897 Funeral of

the late R.H. Downing at Hebron Thursday.

DOWNING, R.H. - Co. Seat - Feb 3, 1897 Will of
the late R.H. Downing leaves all his real
estate to his wife for life the rest to his
children. His daughter, Florence E. Downing
was appointed adm.

DOWNING, MRS REZIN - Ancient History - Dec 18,
1894 - Dec 1880 Mrs Rezin Downing died age 97
years.

DOWNING, REZIN A. - 10 Years Ago - Feb 13, 1894
Rezin A. Downing died Feb 11th.

DOWNING, REZIN HAMPTON - R.H. Downing - Jan 27,
1897 Died-Rezin Hampton Downing at his home in
Houston Jan 26th in his 70th year. Born Clark
Co. Ind. Apr 3, 1827 came with parents to Ill
1835. Came to Houston twp in the early 50's.
Married Rebekah Bennett Mar 14, 1850, had 11
children, 9 survive him-4 sons, 5 daughters.
Services at Hebron Thurs. at 11 A.M.

DOYAN, MRS ABBIE BROWN - Quincy - Aug 18, 1897
Mrs Abbie Brown Doyan formerly of this city was
killed in a runaway accident near Pantota,
Calif. the past week.

DRALLEY, MRS - Coatsburg - Oct 5, 1893 Sept
29th occurred the death of Mrs Dralley, mother
of Henry Dralley of this place. Remains taken
to Quincy for burial.

DRAPER, FRED - C.F. Draper Killed - Jun 25,
1895 Friday A.M. a man found lying near Brooks
crossing 3 miles W of town - dead- identified
as Fred Draper of Carthage. He has a brother
in business in Augusta and a mother and sister
in Carthage. Was the son of the late Henry
Draper a wealthy lawyer of Carthage who died a
number of years ago. Whig says--About 3 years
ago a girl came from Missouri with a claim
against him and he married her at the Franklin
House. They did not live together long, if at
all. No one knows where she is.

DRUDE, DR FRANCIS - Quincy - Apr 23, 1895 Dr
Francis Drude died Monday, age 75 years. Spent
50 years in Quincy.

DUDLEY, E.D. - Conductor Dudley Dead - Mar 30,
1894 Died-E.D. Dudley, the well known C.B. & Q
conductor dropped dead of heart disease in
Galesburg Thursday at 8 A.M., was 70 years old.
Leaves 1 son who is asst. trainmaster at
Galesburg and 1 daughter who lives in
Brookfield.

DUKER, JOHN HERMAN - Quincy - Dec 9, 1903
Simon Duker had filed an appoved bond of
$150,000 as adm of the estate of John Herman
Duker. Deceased left no will.

DUKER, J. HERMAN - Death - Nov 18, 1903 J.
Herman Duker, a wholesale liquor dealer in
Quincy died suddenly Sat. from hemorrhage
caused by the rupture of a blood vessel. Born
in Germany and came to Quincy 1847. Was Pres.
of Quincy National Bank and was 70 years old.

DUNCAN, CYNTHIA - Quincy - Nov 15, 1895 The
will of Cynthia Duncan gives $50 to each of her
children, James W. and Pendleton C. Duncan, Mrs
Josephine McMurray and Laura Stritch, rest goes
to her daughter Nancy as long as she stays
single if and when she marries it is to be
divided equally among all.

DUNCAN, GEORGE - Local - Oct 9, 1894 Died-
George Duncan, a professional baseball catcher
was killed by a train in LaHarpe Thursday
night, had been drinking.

DUNLAP, TONY - Local - Jan 7, 1903 Tony Dunlap
who has been on trial at Aledo for the murder
of Mary Alena Dool with poisoned chocolate was
acquitted by jury Sat.

DUNLAP, DR WARREN B. - Ancient History - Apr
22, 1903 Apr 19, 1883 Dr Warren B. Dunlap died
at Lincoln, NE of consumption.

DURANT, ELIZABETH (JOHNSON) - Death - Oct 11,

1895 Elizabeth (Johnson) Durant died at the
home of her sister, Mrs P.J. Rhea in Camp Point
Tues. Oct 8th after illness of several months.
Was widow of the late Thomas E. Durant of
Quincy and daughter of the late George Johnson
of Columbus. Buried Quincy in Woodland
Cemetery beside her husband Thursday A.M.

DURANT, ELIZABETH D. - Mrs Durant's Will - Oct
15, 1895 Will of Elizabeth D. Durant of Camp
Point was admitted to probate Mon. Leaves her
sister Mrs Parmelia Rhea of Camp Point $500, to
Miss Effie Rhea of Camp Point $200, to her
grandaughters Lucy G. and Lizzie D. Hardy of
Indianapolis, the rest of her estate after $100
is paid to her son in law, James B. Hardy. Wm
Hanna of Golden is named executor.

DURANT, FRANK - Co. Seat - Nov 11, 1896 Frank
Durant, a prominent farmer died in Melrose twp
age 67 years and James Stafford Bowles formerly
of Missouri died in Blessing Hospital.

DURBIN, MRS - Local - Mar 6, 1894 Died- Mrs
H.W. Childs was called to Kellerville Friday by
the death of her mother, Mrs Durbin Friday Mar
2nd. Funeral at 3 Sat. afternoon.

DURHOLT, MISS IDA (ADDIE) - Quincy - Nov 30,
1894 Died-Miss Ida Durholt age 24 died Sunday
eve from typhoid fever. Funeral of the late
Miss Addie Durholt took place Wed. A.M. at the
St Boniface Church.

DURLEIN, ADAM - Quincy - Jun 30, 1897 The body
of Adam Durlein was found in the lake at
Baldwin Park Monday night.

DUTTON, MR AND MR D.H. - Golden - Aug 26, 1896
Mr and Mrs D.H. Dutton lost their 5 month old
baby last week. It was too frail a mortal for
this world and God called it home. Services by
Rev P. Slagel at Horeb.

DUVALL, EDITH - Quincy - Feb 26, 1895 It is
now more than 100 days since the young woman,
Edith Duvall mysteriously disappeared from the

city, and time has failed to reveal the slightest trace of her whereabouts.

DUVALL, MISS EDITH - Quincy - Nov 16, 1894 Miss Edith Duvall, daughter of John Duvall of Maiden Lane disappeared from her home Tuesday.

DUVALL, EDITH - Quincy - Apr 2, 1895 Edith Duvall disappeared Nov 13th and her parents made many efforts to get a trace of her. Monday her body was found floating in the river and identified by her clothing and jewelry.

DWIGHT, HELEN RICHARDSON - Quincy - May 7, 1902 Remains of Helen Richardson Dwight, who died in Chicago, on Wed., were buried here on Fri. A.M.

DYER, DR I.T. - Quincy - Jan 29, 1902 Dr I.T. Dyer, well known resident of this city died on Tues. night, age 67 years. Buried LaBelle, MO on Thursday.

DYER, LEROY - Quincy - Oct 22, 1902 Leroy Dyer has started suit against the estate of Bertha Weber for $5,000 damages for alleged injuries received on the Tremont House elevator.

DYER, WALTER - Killed in a Runaway - May 1, 1894 Killed- Walter Dyer Thurs. afternoon near Cooperstown, Brown Co. about 6 years. "Mt Sterling Democrat Message"

EARL, MR AND MRS J.J. - Ancient History - Aug 7, 1894 - Aug 6, 1875 Mr and Mrs J.J. Earl lost a babe with colera infantum.

EASUM, CHARLES AUGUSTUS - Local - May 4, 1893 News received Tues. A.M. of the death of Charles Augustus Easum at his home near Shelbina, MO of dropsy. Lived the greater part of his life in vicinity of Camp Point. Buried at Shelbina.

EASUM, MRS JOHN - Local - Apr 2, 1902 Mr and Mrs E.B. Cramore and children went to Clayton Fri. to attend the funeral of Mrs John Easum, Mrs C.'s sister.

EATON, L.D. - Elm Grove - Aug 5, 1896 E.A.
Eaton of Union, Ore. was a recent visitor in
the neighborhood looking after the business
interests of his brother, L.D. Eaton, who died
in NE about 2 years ago.

EATON, MARY E. - Quincy - Jul 14, 1897 The
will of Mary E. Eaton leaves a piano to a niece
and $100 to a nephew both living in Linn, MO
and the rest of her estate to her husband John
Eaton.

EBER, MRS HENRY - Elm Grove - Oct 19, 1894
Died-Mrs Eber, wife of Henry Eber died last
Sunday A.M. of typhoid fever.

EBER, JOHN ROBERT - Quincy - Sep 10, 1895 The
will of John Robert Eber, who died in
California was admitted to probate, his
property goes to relatives in this city, to the
children of Rudolph Eber $500 and children of
William Eber $200 residue of the estate is
given to William Eber.

ECKERT, MRS ABLINE - Cremated in Her House -
Oct 19, 1894 Friday eve the house of Mrs
Abline Eckert burned with the old lady in it.
Mrs E. was a widow, 71 years old who lived in
the house with her 2 grandsons Louis and Jake
German. "Beardstown Star"

ECKERT, AUGUST - Ancient History - Mar 25, 1903
Mar 27, 1873 The adm. of the estate of August
Eckert sued the Camp Point Mfg Co. for damages
sustained by the death of Eckert from a bursted
emery wheel.

ECKERT, CHRISTIAN - Quincy - Jan 14, 1903
Christian Eckert, a resident of this city since
1862, died suddenly from a stroke of apoplexy
on Thursday.

ECKHOFF, HEYE - Found Frozen - Dec 30, 1903
Heye Eckhoff age 83, was found in his yard
Christmas Day frozen to death. Family had gone
to Golden to attend services at Lutheran Church
leaving the old man at home alone.

ECKLES, JAMES H. - Recent Deaths - Feb 10, 1897
Died- James H. Eckles Jan 31st at his home in
Nodaway Co. MO sick 2 weeks, age 78 years 7
months 8 days. Born Washington Co. Penn. 1818.
Came to Adams Co 1842. Married Nancy Coulter
1843 lived on a farm in Houston where they
stayed till 1883 when he went to Nodaway.
Leaves a wife and 8 children, all present at
the end. Services at the Presby. Church at
Graham, MO. Jan 15th buried in Prairie Home
Cemetery.

ECKOFF, MR - Primrose - Dec 30, 1903 Mr
Eckoff, who moved his family here about 10
months ago from east of Golden was found dead
in the yard about 10 P.M. Friday. Was about 83
years old.

EDIE, REV JOSEPH A. - Clayton - May 31, 1895
We learn of the death of Rev Joseph A. Edie at
his home in Beaver, PA. Wed. May 22nd. Was
pastor of the United Presby. Church of this
place several years in the 70's.

EDMONDS, CHARLES W. - Death of C.W. Edmonds -
Mar 24, 1897 Died-Charles W. Edmonds at Payson
on the 13th inst, age 50 years. Married at
Clayton where he lived a number of years.
Leaves a mother, sister and several brothers
and a son, Roe, who lives in Clayton.

EDMONDS, ROBERT F. - Late Deaths - Dec 21, 1893
Robert F. Edmonds, a wealthy citizen of Payson,
died last week. Was a native of Tenn. and came
to Payson in 1831. Leaves 3 sons, 2 daughters
of whom Charles and Robert F. are known in this
part of the county.

EDSON, MRS JENNIE - West Point - Dec 11, 1894
Funeral of Mrs Jennie Edson, of Denver was
preached by W.S. Lowe in the Christian Church
at this place Tuesday A.M. and buried in West
Point Cemetery. Born and raised in this
vicinity died from consumption. Leaves husband
and 4 children.

EDWARDS, GEORGE - Fell Dead - Dec 10, 1895

George Edwards, a farmer of Columbus twp fell
dead on his farm 10 A.M. Sat. from heart
disease. Buried Quincy. Born England, but
lived Ill. many years. Engaged in coal mining
at Augusta about 40 years ago and later went to
Quincy and kept a grocery store. About 2 years
ago came to Camp Point and last spring moved to
a farm in Columbus twp, about 5 miles from Camp
Point. Leaves a wife and several grown
children.

EDWARDS, JOHN - Co. Seat - Apr 8, 1896 Will of
John Edwards veteran soldier conveys all of his
belongings to the State Soldiers Home.

EELS, MRS FRED - Primrose - Oct 6, 1897 We
were sorry to learn of the death of Mrs Fred
Eels who was formerly one of our schoolmates at
Primrose.

EELS, MRS LENA - Local - Sep 29, 1897 Mrs Lena
Eels, daughter of Frank Thomas died at
Shelbina, MO Monday the 27th inst. Born Camp
Point township.

EGAN, MRS - Paloma - Jan 26, 1894 Died- Mrs
Egan last Wed. Services held at Catholic
Church near Bloomfield Friday.

EHMAN, JOHN - May 26, 1897 Soldiers buried in
Hebron Cemetery. Was listed as being in 65th
Illinois Infantry.

EICHEN, ANNA MARIE KATE - Death - Sep 16, 1903
Anna Marie Kate, infant daughter, of Dick
Eichen, died the home of her aunt, Mrs Hannah
Gilbert, York Neck, Sept 7th age 26 days.
Mother died at the time of the babe's birth.
Remains were buried at Fowler by the side of
the mother.

EISENBERG, WILLIAM - Quincy - Jun 30, 1897 The
will of William Eisenberg gives all of his
estate to the St John's German Evangelical
Lutheran Church.

ELBUS, HERMAN - Quincy - Nov 26, 1902 Herman

Elbus, age 25 years, while cutting wood near Mt
Sterling was killed by a falling tree.

ELLERMAN, MRS GOTTLIEB D. - Quincy - Feb 15,
1895 Mrs Gottlieb D. Ellerman, an old resident
of the city died at the age of 73 years.

ELLIOTT, "GRANDMA" - Local - Dec 14, 1893 An
old woman familiarly known as "Grandma"
Elliott, died at the poor farm on the 5th inst,
age 73 years.

ELLIOTT, MRS EMELINE M. - Quincy - Jan 4, 1895
Mrs Emeline M. Elliott of Nashua, N.H. died at
the home of her daughter, Mrs Charles E. Cook
in this city Monday A.M. Age 83 years.

ELLIOTT, WARNER D. - May 26, 1897 - Soldiers
buried in Pleasant View Cemetery. Listed in
Co. L, 2nd Ill. Infantry.

ELLIOTT, WILLIAM B. - Ancient History - Aug 21,
1894 - Aug 21, 1884 William B. Elliott died in
Coatsburg on the 15th.

ELLIS, CAPT - Deaths - Dec 27, 1895 Capt
Ellis, father of John B. Ellis and Al S. died
at his home in Liberty twp Tues., 74 years old.
Was a gallant soldier during the war at that
time he lived Schuyler Co. Moved Adams about
10 years ago. Leaves a wife and 2 sons in
Quincy and 2 daughters in Rushville-Mrs Davis
and Miss Jennie Ellis and a younger son James.

ELLIS, DR DAVID - Killed by Train - Jul 8, 1903
Dr David Ellis was killed at Augusta Sun. by
train #6 when he was walking down the tracks.
He had lived Augusta many years and practiced
medicine there for over a half century.
Retired from active work some time ago and his
son, Dr J.P. Ellis succeeded to the practice
and lived with him. He was 76 years old and
quite deaf.

ELLIS, MARY MYRTLE - A Carthage Tragedy - Mar
11, 1903 Mrs Alice Ellington, a nurse living
in Carthage was charged with performing an

abortion on Mary Myrtle Ellis, a country girl,
who lived nine miles S.E. of Carthage and as a
result the Ellis girl died, but before she died
said Mrs E. had performed the operation and she
paid her $5.

ELLIS, JOHN BRISTOW - Whig Publisher Dies - Mar
25, 1903 John Bristow Ellis, publisher of the
Quincy Whig died on the 17th inst of pneumonia
age 45 years. Born in Kentucky Nov 11, 1857.
Came to Ill. with parents in childhood and
settled in Schuyler Co. near Plymouth. At 11
years of age he went to Plymouth and learned
telegraphy in the Q station and was employed
for about 25 years by the C.B. & Q. Married
Miss Maggie Dick several years ago who survives
him. His brother is Alfred S. Ellis, city
ticket agent at Quincy. About 4 years ago Mr
E. bought the Quincy Whig and has been
publisher and manager since.

EMERY, MRS MARY - Death - Mar 12, 1902 Mrs
Mary Emery, wife of Samuel H. Emery of Quincy
died Tues. of last week from paralysis, age 64
yrs. Daughter of the late Rev Dr Alexander
McClure and had lived there since 1855.

ENGLE, ELLA - Quincy - Aug 23, 1895 Ella
Engle, a formerly well known resident of this
city died Monday in Ravenna, OH. Remains were
taken to Fort Smith, ARK for burial.

ENLOW, I.N. - 10 Years Ago - Jul 13, 1893 I.N.
Enlow died at his home in Burton of heart
disease.

ENLOW, WASHINGTON - Death - Jul 9, 1902
Washington Enlow, a prominent citizen of
Liberty twp died Monday, age 74 years. Born
Crayville, PA Jul 24, 1828. Came to Ill 1835.
Married 1864 to Miss Alice Southerland and
moved to a farm on Sect 26 where they lived
since. Had 11 children, only 3 and widow
survive him. Funeral at Liberty Tuesday.

ENLOW, WASHINGTON - Quincy - Aug 13, 1902 Will
of Washington Enlow leaves his entire estate to

his widow, Alice Ann Enlow and names her as
executrix.

ENSMINGER, JAMES - Death - Feb 25, 1903 James
Ensminger died at his home in Kansas City
Thurs. A.M. the 19th inst age 76 years. Leaves
wife, 1 son and 4 daughters. He was twin
brother of Mrs Jane Craver of Camp Point and
had visited here frequently. Services Sat.

ENSMINGER, JONATHAN - May 4, 1893 - Soldiers
buried in Camp Point Cemetery. Listed in Co.
B, 1st PA Infantry - 1845.

ENSMINGER, SAMUEL S. - Death of Samuel
Ensminger - Feb 2, 1894 Died-Samuel S.
Ensminger, a brother of Mrs Jane L. Craver and
Henry Ensminger died at his home in Harrisburg,
PA. Jan 24th 1894. Born May 1, 1829 spent his
whole life in PA. Enlisted in 137th PA
infantry during the rebellion and was a Sergant
of the company. Leaves a wife and 2 sons.

EPPSTEIN, MRS E. - Quincy - Dec 3, 1895 Mrs E.
Eppstein, wife of Rabb's Eppstein died Wed.
eve. Services last Fri. by Rev Dr's E.A. Ince,
S.H. Dana, C.F. Bradley pastors of the 2nd
Baptist Cong'l and Unitarian Churches.

ERB, MAJOR - Quincy - Dec 13, 1895 - Major Erb,
formerly landlord of the Sherman House in this
city and for about 18 years the proprietor of
the Walker House, Salt Lake City died recently
while sitting in his chair. His wife was a
Miss Chapman of this city.

ERDMAN, ANDREW - Death - Feb 26, 1902 Andrew
Erdman, 3rd son of Mr and Mrs Henry Erdman of
Camp Point twp died in Denver, Colo. Feb 6,
1902 of pulmonary hemorrhage. Born Nov 28,
1860 near Fowler, Ill and early life spent in
Camp Point. Was conductor for Atchison, Topeka
and Santa Fe Railroad. Leaves wife, 3
children, father, mother, 3 brothers and 3
sisters.

ERDSICK, MRS EMELIE - Local - Sep 17, 1902

Fred Mensendike received telegram that Mrs Emelie Erdsick died at Hudson, KS Monday. Was wife of Fred Erdsick and daughter of Fred Langenhagen of Coatsburg.

ERKE, MISS - Fowler - Sep 24, 1894 Funeral of an elderly maiden lady, Miss Erke 66 years old was at the Lutheran Church last Thurs. Buried Chase Cemetery.

ERNST, GEORGE - Quincy - Sep 10, 1895 George Ernst, the well known Maine St. saloon keeper died Sunday A.M., 64 years old. Born Baden. Lived Quincy since 1859.

ERTEL, FREDDIE - Local - Apr 14, 1897 Died-Freddie, the 15 year old son of Geo. Ertel died Tues. A.M. at his fathers home in Columbus twp.

ERTEL, JOHN - Local - Apr 21, 1897 John Ertel of Shelbina, MO came last week to attend the funeral of his nephew and spend a few days with his parents and brother.

ERTEL, VALENTINE - Quincy - Jan 4, 1895 Valentine Ertel died at his home in Quincy Tues. afternoon. Born on Christmas Day 1802 at Weisenburg, Germany. Came to Quincy 1835. Only 1 brother survives, Daniel Ertel near Coatsburg. The mother of Alderman Grimm was a sister and assistant postmaster Frederick Ertel is a nephew. Funeral Thursday P.M.

ERTZ, FREDERICK - Ancient History - Jun 23, 1897 - July 1880 Frederick Ertz of Columbus twp was killed when thrown from his wagon by his team running away from Casco Mills.

ERTZ, FREDERICK - Ancient History - Jul 16, 1895 - 1880 Frederick Ertz, of Liberty twp was killed in Camp Point by being thrown from his wagon by his team running away.

EVANS, BETSY - Local - May 20, 1896 Died-Aunt Betsy Evans, wife of Baylis Evans and only sister of Squire J.J. Pevehouse at Nauvoo on Tues. of last week. Lived in vicinity of Bear

Creek many years.   "Clayton Enterprise"

EVANS, JOHN J. - Ancient History - May 15, 1894
May 15, 1874-John J. Evans committed suicide at
Bowen.

EVATT, WILLIAM - Local - Oct 12, 1893 William
Evatt, a former well known citizen of Quincy
died at Lawrence, KS Sept 28th from an injury
received by a team running away. He was a
native of Ohio, 74 years old.

EVERETT, FRANK MILTON - Quincy - Aug 11, 1897
Frank Milton Everett an electrical engineer
died Thurs. eve.

EVERSON, WILLIAM - Ancient History - Oct 7,
1896 - June 1877 A daughter of William Everson
near Coatsburg committed suicide.

EWAN, HENRY - Local - Jul 19, 1895 - Strange
death near Golden last Sat. little 2 year
daughter of Henry Ewan had a grain of corn in
her mouth when it slipped down and lodged in
the windpipe, suffocating her.

EWENS, RENKIN W. - Obituary - Jan 28, 1903
Renkin W. Ewens was born in Bakanover, Germany
Apr 25, 1845. Died Thurs. eve Jan 22nd, 1903.
Came to America 1865 and located in vicinity of
Columbus, where Sep 25, 1874 he married Anka
Lena Wertz. Lived Columbus twp about 23 years.
Four years ago he moved to his present home 4
miles N. of Coatsburg where he died. Leaves
widow, 5 sons and 3 daughters. All children
were at his bedside. Funeral at Coatsburg Sun.
at 3 P.M. by Rev Drexel, of the Luthern Church.
Buried village cemetery.

FAIRFAX, MRS W.A. - Death of Mrs Fairfax - Apr
28, 1897 - Died on Apr 15th at her home on
Paonia, Delta Co. Colo. of consumption, Mrs
W.A. Fairfax nee Miss Carrie Bell. Born
Columbus this county and married in Quincy 1876
where she lived 12 years. Leaves husband, 3
sons and 2 daughters.

FARMER, GEORGE - Dead - Nov 11, 1903 George
Farmer, a prominent stockmen of Clayton, died
last Wed. night of cancer. He leaves a wife
and 1 child.

FARRELL, MRS ANNA - Quincy - Jul 1, 1896 Mrs
Anna Farrell died at the age 84 years Wed. eve
at the home of her daughter, Mrs J.W. Butler.
Lived the city for 55 years.

FARRELL, MICHAEL - Local - Nov 2, 1893 Michael
Farrell, police magistrate of Quincy died Wed.
night.

FARRELL, PATRICK - Quincy - Jan 28, 1903
Patrick Farrell, age 65 years, an inmate of the
Soldiers home, died on Thurs. eve from injuries
received in a fall.

FASTHOFF, ARTHUR - A Boy Missing - Apr 17, 1894
Arthur Fasthoff left home Fri. A.M. Apr 6th and
his not since been heard from. He is 14 years
old, large for his age, has light brown hair,
light complexion, blue eyes. When last seen he
was crossing the river in a skiff. Anyone
knowing his whereabouts write: Jas. Fasthoff
Warsaw, Ill.

FELD, MRS HANNAH - Quincy - Mar 8, 1895 Mrs
Hannah Feld died Sunday eve, age 55 years.

FELDMAN, F.W. - Co. Seat - Nov 4, 1896 F.W.
Feldman, age 75 years, a former resident of
Camp Point and many years a resident of this
city dropped dead in an alley near his home
Sat. A.M. of heart disease.

FELDMAN, F.W. - Co. Seat - Nov 18, 1896 Will
of F.W. Feldman mentions his wife, daughter
Emma, son Edward and 2 grandchildren (no names
given) daughter, Mrs H. Thesen and daughter,
Mrs William Gruetter.

FELDMAN, FREDERICK W. - Found Him Dead - Nov 4,
1896 Frederick W. Feldman, age 75 years, an
old resident of Quincy and a tailor by trade
died very suddenly of apoplexy Sat. A.M.

Leaves widow, 4 children, all grown and
residents of this city. "Herald"

FELGER, SIMON - Quincy - Dec 24, 1902
Inventory of estate of Simon Felger was filed
in county court Fri. real estate value $9,500
personal property at $1,000.

FELSMAN, LOUIS - Local - Sep 29, 1897 Louis
Felsman age 84 years died at his home on the
West side of Camp Point Sunday. Born Germany.

FERGUSON, REV H.T. - Killed by Lightning - Jun
26, 1894 Monmouth, Ill June 23, The Rev H.T.
Ferguson, pastor of the United Presby. church
at Sunbeam, NW of here was struck by lightning
and killed. His son was also struck, but will
live. Mrs Ferguson found him.

FERGUSON, J.H. - Suicide at Kinderbrook - Oct
28, 1896 J.H. Ferguson, a young man well known
in Kinderbrook, Ill and vicinity committed
suicide Sunday A.M. at 1. Was 24 years old and
unmarried.

FERGUSON, WILLIAM WEBB - Quincy - Dec 24, 1902
William Webb Ferguson, colored, who was
sentenced to 20 years for the murder of Dr Jos.
Barnes in Nov. 1901 died in the Chester
penitentiary on Tues.

FERRELL, JOHN - North Houston - Mar 3, 1897
Died-the infant child of John Ferrell at Ferris
Tues. 23rd at 1 A.M. Buried Ebenezer cemetery
next day. Services by C.F. Cate.

FERRIS, ANNA - Ancient History - Mar 26, 1895
March 1876 George Adams killed Anna Ferris in
Quincy, beating her to death with a hammer.

FERRIS, HIRAM G. - Local - Aug 13, 1893 Hiram
G. Ferris, Pres. of the Hancock National Bank,
of Carthage, died Sunday age 73 years.

FERRIS, NANCY - Ancient History - Sep 20, 1895
Sept 1876 George Adams was sentenced to
penitentiary for life for the murder of Nancy

Ferris.

FIELD, MRS - Paloma - Sep 13, 1895 Died-Mrs Field Monday A.M. Services at Methodist Church Thurs. A.M. Buried Chase Cemetery, south of Fowler.

FIELD, MRS ANNA - Death - Nov 23, 1893 Mrs Anna Field, wife of Daniel Field and sister of Thomas Bailey, died at West Phillips, Maine Nov 13th. Lived most of her life in that locality. Made a visit with her husband to Camp Point in 1881 to her brothers. She leaves 2 brothers, 4 sisters, Mr Thomas Bailey, Mr Silas Bailey, Mrs Benjamin Haines, Mrs Abigail Wing, Miss Lois Bailey and Mrs Lyman Bushnell.

FIELD, JOHN - Ancient History - Aug 12, 1903 Aug 1883 John Field, a prominent citizen of Quincy died on the 4th.

FINKHAUS, WILLIAM - Quincy - Jan 16, 1894 Died-William Finkhaus age 76 years Thursday eve.

FINLEY, HARRY - Co. Seat - Sep 30, 1896 Harry Finley age 23 years suffered from mental trouble caused by long illness and measles became violently insane. He died suddenly while in a spasm Thurs. A.M.

FINLEY, HARRY - Death of Harry Finley - Sep 30, 1896 Died-Harry Finley at the home of his grandmother, Mrs Nancy Judy in Quincy, Friday. Was 22 years old had been an invalid several years, subject to epilepsy. His father was killed by a train in Chicago about 2 months age. Funeral at Fowler Sat. afternoon. Mother is left childless and a widow.

FINLEY, LYCURGUS E. - L.E. Finley Killed- Aug 5, 1896 - Lycurgus E. Finley was seriously hurt Tues. the 28th at Union stock yards in Chicago. Crushed between the cattle shute and the side of the car. Remains brought to Fowler Tues. for burial. Lived Adams Co. about 30 years. Moved Chicago a few years ago. Leaves a wife and 1 son.

FINLEY, MISS SALLIE - Coatsburg - Sep 30, 1903
Died-Sat. about noon, Miss Sallie Finley, about
74 years old, had lived Coatsburg and vicinity
about 30 years. Came from Tenn. with her
family, never married. Leaves a brother, sister
and a niece. Buried beside her parents in
Coatsburg cemetery. Services Mon. A.M. 10:30
by Rev Rose of Paloma.

FISHER, ROBERT - Ancient History - May 13, 1903
Robert Fisher died on the 7th.

FISHER, ROBERT - 10 Years Ago - May 25, 1893
Robert Fisher died at his home in Camp Point.

FISHER, STANLEY O. - Obituary - Sep 7, 1893
Stanley O. Fisher was born near Paloma, Ill Nov
14th, 1870 and died at Monte Vista, Colo. Aug
31, 1893. In Jan. 1890 he went to Janesville,
Wisc. to study telegraphy which he completed in
9 months and received a position as night
operator at Truesdell, Wisc. which he held
until Jan 1892 when his health failed and he
went west. Spent 6 months in Denver, Colo. and
went to Monte Vista where he stayed only a
short time until his death. Funeral at the
Methodist Church in Paloma on Mon. Sept 4th by
Rev White. Buried Columbus Cemetery.

FISHER, STANLEY O. - Probate Notice - Sep 21,
1893 Stanley O. Fisher, deceased 1st Mon. of
November 1893 (6th) Royal I. Fisher, adm.

FITCH, SIMEON - Barry Adage - Mar 13, 1894
Died-Mr Simeon Fitch Tuesday night. Had been
identified with the twp for nearly half a
century. Was founder of the Unicorn Greenbach,
a paper published in Barry 10 years. Funeral
at ME Church this P.M.

FLAGG, DR - Local - Mar 30, 1894 Killed, Dr
Flagg who was here a couple of years ago with
the Kickapoo Indian Medicine Co. was killed a
few weeks ago by Plenty Horse, one of the
indians.

FLEER, HENRY - Quincy - Aug 7, 1894 Relatives

of the late Henry Fleer, a teamster who lost
his life by going over an embankment on 12th
St. Sat. night have started suit against the
city for damages.

FLEER, HERMAN - Quincy - Jun 1, 1894 Died
Herman Fleer age 54 died Sunday afternoon of
consumption.

FLEER, MRS MARY - Quincy - Sep 11, 1894 Mrs
Mary Fleer is suing the city for damages for
loss of her husband who was killed by an
accident on a defective road on a dark night.

FLEMING, MRS ELIZABETH - West Point - Jan 30,
1894 Rev McDonald was in Basco Wed. to preach
funeral of Mrs Elizabeth Fleming.

FLEMING, MATT - Local - Jan 19, 1893 Matt
Fleming a well known Quincy politician and
stove molder was killed Tues. in a railroad
accident at Villisca, IA.

FLESHNER, MR AND MRS HENRY - Elm Grove - Feb
15, 1895 An infant of Mr and Mrs Henry
Fleshner died last Sunday A.M. of lung trouble.

FLESNER, WILLIAM E. - Local - Jul 9, 1895
William E. Flesner of Golden died June 30th,
age 71 years. Lived that locality 15 years.

FLETCHER, JOHN - Ancient History - Jun 1, 1894
May 28, 1875- John Fletcher, colored, in Quincy
murdered an adopted son, 3 years old by
beating.

FLETCHER, MRS MARY JANE - Pickups from the
Necks- Mar 30, 1894 Mrs Sallie Maynard and
Miss Ada McGinley arrived home from Kansas
where they were at the last sickness and death
of their sister, Mrs Mary Jane Fletcher.

FOLCKEMER, ELLA ROBERTa - Sudden Death - May
13, 1903 Little baby daughter of Mr and Mrs
P.M. Folckemer died Sunday A.M. about 9 of
whooping cough. Ella Roberta Folckemer born
Dec 3, 1902 was 5 months 10 days old. Funeral

Monday.

FOLCKEMER, OLIVER E. - Death of O.E. Folckemer -
Apr 6, 1894 Died Oliver E. Folckemer after
suffering nearly 5 years died Wed. A.M. Apr
4th, 1894 in his 50th year. Born in Penn.
Came to Camp Point 1867 and was in tinning and
hardware business with his brother Harry.
Married Feb 17, 1873 to Mary Clark of
Jacksonville who with 1 daughter survives him.
Funeral at 2 P.M. Friday from his home by Odd
Fellows.

FOLCKEMER, OLIVER E. - Probate Notice - May 11,
1894 Oliver E. Folckemer, deceased 1st Mon of
Jul 1894 Mary E. Folckemer, Ex.

FOLCKEMER, OLIVER E. - Funeral of O.E.
Folckemer- Apr 10, 1894 Last rites of Oliver
E. Folckemer in the village cemetery Friday
afternoon by Camp Point lodge of Odd Fellows.
Services by Elder O. Dilley.

FOLTZ, MRS - Primrose - May 1, 1894 Died the
youngest son of Mrs Foltz of Big Neck died and
was buried at Fowler beside his father. Was 7
or 8 years old.

FOLTZ, FRANK RUSSELL - Obituary - May 22, 1894
Died-Frank Russell Foltz Apr 23rd, 1894 of
pneumonia at the home of his mother, Mrs A.M.
Foltz in Big Neck. Services at Centennial
Chapel Apr 25th by Rev King. Buried Fowler
cemetery between his father and brother.
Leaves mother, 2 sisters and 1 brother. Born
Dec 2, 1887. Father died Nov 12, 1887 and
brother January 1888.

FORDYCE, CURTIS - Local - Aug 11, 1897 A
number of Camp Point people drove to Bowen
Thursday for the funeral of Curtis Fordyce.

FORREST, CHAS. - Primrose - Mar 12, 1896 The
youngest child of Chas. Forrest age 4 months
was buried at Coatsburg cemetery one day last
week. Cause the croup.

FORSYTHE, MARY FAY - Local - Feb 4, 1903 Mary
Fay, 11 month old baby of Mr and Mrs Will
Forsythe died at their home on Knox St.
Galesburg, Friday night of pneumonia.

FOSTER, MRS A.M. - Northeast Burton - Apr 13,
1893 Died, on Thurs. night Apr 6th Mrs A.M.
Foster in her 77th year. Funeral next day at
family home by Rev White of the Paloma circuit.
Buried in Burton cemetery.
(Same paper Mrs A.L. Pottle of Chillicothe, MO
is at the bedside of her sick mother, Mrs A.M.
Foster.)

FOSTER, A.M. - Northeast Burton - May 4, 1893
A.M. Foster is residing with his daughter, Mrs
E.N. Wheeler since the death of his wife.

FOSTER, ALBERT M. - NE Burton - Feb 8, 1895
Died Jan 29th, 1895 Albert M. Foster at the
home of his daughter, Mrs E.M. Wheeler at age
80 years 11 months 9 days. Funeral at
Presbyterian Church in Burton Jan 31st at 11
A.M. by Rev A.A. White of Paloma citcuit.
Buried Burton Cemetery.

FOSTER, ALBERT M. - Local - Feb 1, 1895 Albert
M. Foster of Burton twp died at the home of
E.N. Wheeler Jan 29th, 90 years old. Came to
Ill. at an early day and settled this county
where he lived since.

FOSTER, HENRY - Local - May 24, 1895 Henry
Foster died Wed A.M. from consumption. Buried
village cemetery that evening. Leaves wife, no
children.

FOSTER, MARIA - Henry Foster's Mother - Dec 10,
1895 Aunt Maria Foster, an old colored woman
well known here died in Macomb, Ill last week.
There were 5 in the family when they left here.
But in last year 4 of them have died. Uncle
Charley died of old age, Aunt Maria had
paralysis, bad whiskey was cause of Henry's
death and Glover was killed for insulting a
white woman. With exception of Aunt Maria they
were a hard lot. "Palmyra Spectator"

FOWLER, JOHN - Killed by a Bull - Jul 21, 1897
John Fowler, of ElDara, Pike County went into
his pasture Wed. eve to get cows, not returning
they found him between 9 & 10 trampled to death
by a dehorned bull. He was about 50 years old.
Leaves a wife and 3 children.

FOY, JOHN - Co. Seat - Dec 2, 1896 A sick
stranger giving his name as John Foy and
apparently in the last stages of consumption
was taken in Blessing Hospital Saturday.

FRANCIS, MRS JOHN T. - Ancient History - Jul
24, 1894 - July 21, 1881 Mrs John T. Francis
died on the 15th.

FRANCIS, MR AND MRS V. - Local - Mar 2, 1893
Mr and Mrs V. Francis were called to Virginia,
Ill. Monday by the death of a relative.

FRANCIS, VINCENT - Fell at his Post - Jul 7,
1897 Died-Vincent Francis died Sat. 2:30 A.M.
Funeral Sun. A.M. at the Methodist Church by
Rev A.N. Simmons buried Mendon Cemetery. Born
in Bedfordshire England Aug 16, 1828. Died
July 3, 1897. Came to U.S. 1850 and located in
Mendon twp until 1885 when he came to Camp
Point and was a dealer and shipper of grain.
He married twice, 1st to Miss Sarah Hatchett
who left him with a daughter, Mrs Nellie
Townsend of St Louis. On Sept 11, 1883 he
married Miss Maggie Bean who survives him. His
2 nephews Charles and Fred Clarke were reared
in his family and treated as one. Leaves a
brother Samuel Francis and a sister, Mrs Martha
Longton of Lewiston, MO who are the only
survivors of a family of 6.

FRANCIS, VINCENT - Local - Jul 14, 1897 George
W. Francis has been appointed adm of the estate
of Vincent Francis.

FRANCIS, VINCENT - Local - Jul 7, 1897 Mr and
Mrs B. Townsend of St Louis attended the
funeral of her father, Vincent Francis.

FRANK, ED S. - Ed S. Frank Stricken - Aug 20,

1902   Ed Frank who lives 1 mile 1/2 SE of
Clayton was overcome by heat Fri. and his
recovery doubtful. "Whig"
Later in same article--Mr Frank died Tues. A.M.
from the effects of strangulated hernia.

FRANK, EDWARD SMITH - Edward S. Frank - Aug 27,
1902 Mention was made last week of the death
of Ed S. Frank of Clayton after illness of
about a week. Edward Smith Frank was born in
Davidson Co. N. Carolina near Lexington May 23,
1848. Came with parents to Ill. in fall of
1852 and located at Buckhorn, Brown Co. In May
1856 he located at Fargo until Sep 1891.
Married Feb 14, 1878 to Miss Martha Jane
Morehead of Buckhorn. They had 2 children-
Nonae Ruth and James Edward. First a farmer,
then blacksmith and later in undertaking
business at Fargo. During last few years lived
on farm SE of Clayton.

FRAZER, MELINDA J. - Notice - Sep 3, 1902 Oct
term 1902 in chancery: J. Henry Frazer, Mary E.
Frazer, James Frazer, Irene A. Chase and James
F. Kincaid, complaintants #1450 VS John H.
Kincaid, John H. Kincaid as adm of the estate
of Melinda J. Frazer deceased, Lucy Kincaid
Jansen, Enoch E. Wood, Isaac N. Wood, Sameul E.
Kincaid, Abraham L. Wood, Charles W. Kincaid,
Rollie E. Kincaid, Susie Kincaid, John T.
Kincaid, Henry Debert and Frank P. Grubb,
defendants   Lucy Kincaid Jansen, Charles W.
Kincaid, Rollie F. Kincaid, Susie Kincaid and
John T. Kincaid each reside out of state.
Hiram R. Wheat, clerk (Dated Aug 27, 1902
Quincy)

FREDERICK, MRS HELENA - Death Record - Nov 3,
1897 Died-Mrs Helena Frederick at her home
near Golden Oct 29th age 22 years. Was
daughter of Mr and Mrs John Flesner. Leaves a
husband and babe 1 month old. Services at
German Lutheran Church in Clayton twp Sun. P.M.

FREDRICKE, MRS ANNIE - Golden - Mar 10, 1897
Died last week, Mrs Annie Fredricke.

FREEMAN, ALFRED - Local - Jan 26, 1894 Alfred
Freeman an old soldier laid out Tues. night on
the streets of Quincy and froze to death. Had
been drinking.

FRIENDLICH, JACOB - Mt Sterling Postmaster Dead
Feb 4, 1903 Jacob Friendlich, postmaster at Mt
Sterling died there at 11 A.M. Sat. from an
attack of nervous prostration and other
ailments. Had lived Mt Sterling about 30 years
and was active in Republican politics in Brown
Co. Was about 80 years old. Leaves only his
wife. No living children.

FRIENDLICH, MARIA & JACOB - Mt Sterling
Postmistress Dead - Mar 25, 1903 Mrs Maria
Friendlich who was appointed to succeed her
husband, Jacob Friendlich as postmaster at Mt
Sterling after his death Jan 31st, died Friday
of consumption, age 62.

FROST, MRS W.W. - Local - Jan 25, 1895 Mrs
W.W. Frost of Columbus twp died Tues. Remains
taken to Fowler Thursday for burial.

FROST, MRS WILBUR - Columbus - Jan 25, 1895
Mrs Wilbur Frost died Tuesday the 22nd inst.
Her remains were taken to Fowler for burial.

FRY, JOHN W. - Our Unfortunate Neighbors - Nov
20, 1894 Died-John W. Fry an aged citizen of
Mt Sterling died last Friday from a dose of
strychnine.

FUGATE, MRS - Local - Dec 13, 1895 Remains of
Mrs Fugate arrived Tues. night from Urbana
accompanied by her son, Dr John Fugate and his
daughter. Funeral Wed. from Christian Church.
She was born N. Carolina 1811. Came to Ill.
with her husband 1835 settling in Pike Co.
Husband died several years ago.

FUGATE, MISS MATTIE - Death of Mattie Fugate -
Nov 20, 1894 Died- Miss Mattie Fugate from
tuberculosis Fri. Nov 16th. She came to Camp
Point about 11 years ago with her parents and
had taught school in Camp Point for a time.

Father died about 9 years. She lived with her
mother in Camp Point. Her mother and 3
brothers survive her. Buried village cemetery.
Services by Elder O. Dilley Sunday P.M.

FUGATE, MISS MATTIE - Local - Nov 20, 1894
Funeral -- Delmar D. Darrah, editor of the Ill.
Freemason, Bloomington arrived Sat. night and
attended the funeral of his aunt, Miss Mattie
Fugate. His sister accompanied him.

FUGATE, MRS W. - Death - Dec 10, 1895 Dispatch
received Monday by Postmaster Robertson
announcing the death at Urbana of Mrs W.
Fugate. Remains to arrive tonight via the
Wabash. Funeral tomorrow at 10:30 at Christian
Church.

FULLER, REV E. HALE - Additional Locals - Sep
23, 1903 Rev E. Hale Fuller, the new Methodist
minister, who was stationed last year at Golden
was called Monday to Benton Harbor, Mich. by
the death of his mother.

FULLERMAN, MRS CHRISTIAN - Local - Mar 1, 1895
The remains of Mrs Christian Fullerman, wife of
Jacob Fullerman were taken Sunday from Camp
Point twp to the German Lutheran Church in
Burton twp for services. Leaves a husband, a
son 7 years old and twin girls about 2 months
old.

FUNK, CHARLES - Ancient History - Apr 26, 1895
April 1877 Charles Funk committed suicide in
Beverly by shooting himself with a shot gun.

FUNK, JAMES E. - Local - Jan 26, 1893 James E.
Funk and Mrs L.G. Hoke went to Kentucky Friday
night to attend the funeral of a sister.

FUNK, JESSE - Local - Nov 30, 1894 Jesse Funk
was found guilty of murder in the 2nd degree.
Received 21 years in penitentiary for the Funk
murder.

FUNK, WM - Local - Nov 20, 1894 Two murder
cases are now in this term of circuit court-the

tragic death of Wm Funk of nearly a year ago is
recalled. Jesse Funk, the son did the shooting
has been in jail since the shooting.
John Parker who caused the death of James Brown
is also this term. He is out on bail. "Barry
Adage".

FUNKE, MRS J.H. - Quincy - Oct 19, 1894 Died
Mrs J.H. Funke, age 59 a native of this city
died Sunday A.M.

FUSSELMAN, MR - Coatsburg - Jan 15, 1895 On
Sun. 6th an old man named Fusselman was brought
to the poor farm. On Tues. A.M. while on his
way to breakfast he fell and was dead. Remains
taken to Richfield for burial by friends.

FUSSELMAN, GEORGE H. - Killed by Lightning -
Jun 3, 1903 George H. Fusselman, 19 years old
and living with his parents at Richfield was
struck by lightning Sun. May 24th on the porch
of his fathers home. Killed him instantly.

GABRIEL, WILLIAM O. - Local - Oct 14, 1896
William O. Gabriel, formerly of Payson was
kicked by a horse at Helena, Mont. and his leg
broken. It became necessary to amputate the
injured leg and patient died of shock. He was
a printer by trade and had worked at many
places in the west.

GADDIS, MRS STEWART - Golden - Aug 28, 1894
Died - Mr Stewart Gaddis, NE of LaPrairie lost
his wife and baby. Baby buried here, the wife
taken to Columbus, Ind. for burial a week ago
Sunday.

GAHAN, JOHN - Coatsburg - Jun 25, 1895 John
Gahan of the poor house fell out a window and
died. Lived Coatsburg vicinity last 25 years.
Greater part of last 1/2 in poor house. Was
about 75 years old. Far as we know was never
married and no known relatives.

GAINES, COL. THOMAS W. - Local - Jan 8, 1895
Died-Col. Thomas W. Gaines at Clarksville, TX
Dec 30th. Well known in Adams Co. as Lieut.-

Col. of the 50th Ill. Vol. and was County
Treas. from 1872 to 69. Went to Texas in 1872
and appointed P.M. by Pres. Harrison.

GALLAGHER, MRS JANE - Quincy - Mar 3, 1897 Mrs
Jane Gallagher, a resident of this city since
1860 died Tues. night age 86 years.

GALLAHER, JAMES - Local - Mar 16, 1894 Died
James Gallaher, city librarian of Quincy died
Thurs. A.M. Connected with newspaper work all
his life.

GALLAHER, JOHN H. - Local - Sep 2, 1896 John
H. Gallaher of Kansas City was here for the
funeral of his sister, Mrs Craig.

GALLIER, MRS MARGARET - Golden - May 8, 1894
Died Mrs Margaret Gallier of LaPrairie, wife of
the late Benjamin Gallier, died last Friday
night and buried at Pulaski Cemetery Sunday.
Services by Rev I.M. Johnson.

GANOE, ISAAC - Quincy - Dec 30, 1896 Died
Isaac Ganoe, one of the pioners of Adams Co.
age 82 years died while sacking wheat at his
home near Plainville.

GARARD, MRS MINNIE - West Point - May 11, 1893
Misses Margie Cavanaugh and Ethel Gordon were
in Basco Sat. to attend the funeral of Mrs
Minnie Garard.

GARDNER, HENRY J. - Jan 27, 1897 Died- Henry
J. Gardner at the home of his daughter in
Jacksonville Tues., age 73 years. Born
Scotland where he learned the book binding
trade and after worked at some of the famous
old shops of London. Came to America 1849 and
to Quincy 1855. Leaves 3 sons and a daughter,
James R. Gardner of the Whig, being one of the
sons.

GARNER, C.W. - Card of Thanks - Dec 16, 1903
To neighbors and friends in our late
bereavement.   C.W. Garner & family
W.F. Carlin

GARNER, SHIVEREL - Local - Aug 27, 1902
Shiverel Garner, well known farmer near Bowen,
Hancock Co. died while seated in his buggy at
his wife's side Thurs. eve. 70 years old.
Leaves wife, 2 sons and 4 daughters.

GARNER, SHIVEREL - Quincy - Aug 27, 1902
Shiverel Garner, age 70 years, a well known
farmer died while riding with his wife in a
buggy near Bowen.

GARNER, WM - West Point - Dec 28, 1893 Died,
Mr Wm Garner at the home of his son Fletcher,
in Quincy last Sat. Mr Garner lived at this
place. About once a week he was taken to
Quincy to be doctored. Dying at 1 P.M. Sat.
those present at death with him were his wife,
his son George, his son Fletcher and his wife.
Remains brought home on the train Sat. eve and
funeral was by Rev McDanold Mon. at 11 A.M.
Buried in the town cemetery. Leaves wife, 4
sons and 1 daughter. Relatives from a distance
to attend funeral were his daughter, Mrs Walker
and her son of Oklahoma, his son Geo. of Nebr.,
his son Henry and his family of Denver and his
son Fletcher and his wife of Quincy. Other
relatives were Mr Charles Overman and son of
Oquawka, Granville Garner and wife and Mr Shiv
Garner and family of near Denver.

GARNER, WILLIAM - Soldiers buried in Hebron
Cemetery - May 26, 1897 Listed as being in War
of 1812.

GARRETT, MRS ELIZABETH - A Good Woman Gone -
Nov 18, 1903 Mrs Elizabeth Garrett died early
Thurs. A.M. Nov 12th. Lived here 68 years.
Funeral Fri. 1:30 at the family home by Rev
F.A. McGaw and Elder James H. Smart of
Waukegon, a son in law of deceased and Elder
J.H. Garrison of St Louis, also a son in law.
Buried Pleasant View cemetery and buried beside
her husband who was buried there in 1865.
Elizabeth Welsh was born in Jefferson Co. KY
Apr 30, 1813. Married Peter B. Garrett Feb 16,
1832. They came to Camp Point 1835 and settled
on farm where they both died. Had 11 children,

9 survive her - Silas of Desota, IA, Mary W.
Miller of Graham, MO, Robert W., John H. and
Alvin A. of Camp Point, Sarah E. Smart of
Waukegan, IL, Judith E. Garrison of St Louis,
Geo. W. of Sheridan, WY and Christopher B. of
Arvada, CO. Mrs Susanah H. Boyle died Nov 29,
1879, Richard S. was killed Oct 17, 1862 near
Island #10 in a skirmish between the 2nd Ill.
Cav., of which he was a member and the rebels.
She left also 40 grandchildren and 27 gr.
grandchildren.

GARRETT, MRS ELIZABETH - Injured - Nov 11, 1903
Mrs Elizabeth Garrett, age 90 years received
fatal injuries in a runaway accident Friday
afternoon.

GARRETT, RICHARD S. - May 26, 1897 Soldiers
buried in Pleasant View Cemetery. Listed in
Co. L of the 2nd Ill. Cavalry.

GARTNER, DANIEL - Quincy - Nov 20, 1894 Died
Daniel Gartner age 60 died Fri. A.M. His
mother who is 89 years old is a resident of St
Louis.

GATES, CAROLINE - Obituary - May 20, 1903
Caroline Gates was born Nov 5, 1830 in Ind.
Married Linus Moores at Florence, Ind. Jan 1,
1850. Moved to Ohio for 2-1/2 years and on to
Adams Co. and a farm in Columbus twp where they
reared their family and where she died May 8th,
age 72 yrs 6 mon 3 days. Had 8 children-3 son,
5 daughters of whom the sons and 2 daughters
and the aged husband survive her. Belonged to
United Brethern Church. Funeral at Columbus
Christian Church. Buried Columbus cemetery.

GATES, MISS LAURA - Prairie - Aug 7, 1894 Miss
Laura Gates died from consumption.

GAULT, JOHN - "A Long Journey" - Dec 7, 1893
Died Mon. eve Nov 27th John Gault, age 93 years
6 months 27 days. Born Washington Co. N.Y. Apr
30, 1800. Married Eliza Armitage in 1827 and
1836 started west settling 8 miles N of Quincy
in Ursa twp for 6 years and moved to Hancock

Co. near Chili for 6 years when he returned to
Adams Co. til 1887. Was Postmaster at Columbus
during Pres. Pierce's adm. til <u>1856</u> when he
moved to Houston twp and was P.M. in Houston
until 1862. Was also 1st P.M. at York Neck
P.O., both of which have been discontinued. He
was remarried in 1854 to Mrs A.G. Cyrus of
Houston twp who died 1887 after her death he
went to his son, J. Wesley Gault, at Red
Bridge, Jackson Co. MO. Buried cemetery at New
Santa Fe, MO in presence of his children, W.J.
Gault of Oklahoma City, OK, Thomas L. of
Stockton, Calif., J. Wesley and Mrs Lydia M.
Sweaney of Red Bridge, MO. United with
Christian Church at Columbus 1853.

GAY, MRS - Local - Feb 12, 1896 Died Mrs Gay,
mother of W. Grant Gay at Zanesville, OH Sun.

GAY, VIXEN P. - Ancient History - Sep 20, 1895
Sept 1877 Vixen P. Gay died on the 19th.

GAY, VIXEN P. - Ancient History - Sep 25, 1894
Sept 21, 1877 Vixen P. Gay died on the 19th.

GAY, WILL E. - Local - Nov 13, 1894 Died Will
E. Gay died at Clayton Thurs. from consumption.
Married a daughter of Capt A.J. Griffith of
Concord twp and was engaged in merchandising in
Clayton.

GEM<u>BLER</u>, JACOB - Golden - Jan 16, 1893 H.H.
Emminga and J.L. Gem<u>ber</u> has been appointed
executors of the estate of Jacob Gem<u>bler</u>,
deceased.

GENTLE, JESSE - North Houston - Feb 3, 1897
Died-Jesse Gentle died in Chili Jan 10th.
Funeral Tues. at 11 A.M. Buried in cemetery
nearby, 18 years some months old. Parents both
died when he was 4 years old. Since then he
lived most of time with his Aunt Nancy Cray.

GEORKE, HENRY JR. - Columbus - Jan 20, 1897
Funeral of Henry Georke Jr. was held at the
German ME Church on Sun. Jan 17th at 10 A.M. by
Rev W.K. Herzog. Buried Coatsburg cemetery.

GERDES, JOHN - Local - Feb 4, 1903   John
Gerdes, a well known German resident of Golden
died Friday night age 78 years.   Leaves a wife
and children.

GIBSON, THOMAS - Death - May 18, 1893   News
received from Los Gatos, Calif. of the death of
Thomas Gibson, a pioneer of NE. and for a
number of years Secretary of the Omaha Board of
Trade.   He was a veteran newspaper publisher,
having established the Western Patriot in
Quincy in 1854 in connection with late Ansel
Warren.   He was also connected with a newspaper
in NE and Denver.   He taught school in this
county in the early 50's.

GILBERT, WILLIAM G. - Wm G. Gilbert Dead - Jul
28, 1897   William G. Gilbert, overseer of the
poor of the town of Quincy died early Wed. A.M.
at his home 410 Vine St.   Was 65 years old.
Born state of New York.   Came to county with
his parents when 4 years old to Payson and then
to Quincy.   Was a carpenter by trade.   Leaves a
wife and 2 sons and a daughter, George W.,
William and Mrs Lulu Tutt, all of Chicago.
Funeral Fri. afternoon from the family home in
charge of Knights of Pythias.

GILL, MRS ELIZABETH - Quincy - Jun 18, 1902
Mrs Elizabeth Gill, a resident of Quincy for
more than a half century died here Saturday.
Age 79 years.

GILLETT, ELI - Local - Mar 6, 1894   Died-Eli
Gillett a prominent citizen of Augusta died
Monday of last week.

GILLETTE, ELI - Elm Grove - Mar 2, 1894   Lem
Burke attended the funeral of Eli Gillette of
Augusta last Wed.

GILLILAND, WILLIAM P. - A Pioneer Gone - Jul
21, 1897   Mendon, Ill July 19th William P.
Gilliland, a pioneer of Adams Co. and the
oldest man in the twp died at his home 2 miles
S of town Sat. Eve in his 92nd year.   Born
Kentucky 1805.   Married Lettia Curry in 1827,

had 9 children, 5 still living. Came to Ill.
in early 30's and Adams Co. in 1843. Wife died
7 years ago. Funeral from his home Tues. 2
P.M. Buried family cemetery near his home.

GILLUM, DR JACKSON - Quincy - Jan 1, 1902 Dr
Jackson Gillum, colored, one of the best known
veterniary surgeons in Quincy died Tuesday
evening age 61 years.

GILMER, FRED A. - Local - Dec 1, 1897 Fred A.
Gilmer, of Mendon died Tues. A.M. of pneumonia.
46 years old. and never married.

GILMER, FREDERICK A. - Quincy - Dec 8, 1897
Frederick A. Gilmer of Mendon died on Tues.,
age 47 years.

GILMER, JOHN B. - Ancient History - Jul 16,
1895 1880 John B. Gilmer died near Coatsburg
age 42 years.

GILPIN, JOSEPH B. - Ancient History - Jan 27,
1897 July 1878 - Joseph B. Gilpin, a well
known real estate dealer in Quincy died.

GLASER, CHRISTOPHER - Fell Across a Manger -
Jun 9, 1897 Christopher Glaser, of Clayton
lost his footing while throwing hay down for
his horse and hit the manger. He was a large
fleshy man of 220 pounds and ruptured his
abdomen. Died at 5 P.M. Mon. Leaves a wife and
3 children. He told son Elmer he was going to
die. Funeral from family home at 2 P.M. today,
burial will be in South Side Cemetery by Odd
Fellows, M.W.A. adn A.O.U.W. of which he was a
member.

GLASER, JOHN C. - Quincy - Jul 13, 1894 Died
John C. Glaser, an old resident of Adams Co.,
died at Cliola, age 80 years.

GLAY, HENRY - Probate Notice - Aug 17, 1893
Henry Glay, deceased 1st Mon. of Sept 1893
(4th) W.E. Enlow, adm.

GODMAN, HATTIE - Local - Feb 11, 1902 Hattie

Godman, a colored girl age about 18 years died Mon. A.M. of consumption.

GODWIN, JOSEPH - Local - Jan 29, 1896 Died Joseph Godwin (colored) died at Mt Sterling and was buried at Camp Point Monday afternoon.

GODWIN, JOSEPH - Local - Feb 5, 1896 Joseph Godwin (colored) died at Clayton not Mt Sterling as reported.

GOERKE, MR - Columbus - Jul 23, 1902 Old Mr Goerke was buried here last Thurs. July 17th. Was an old resident of Columbus twp. Services at German ME Church by Rev C.F. Stecher of Camp Point and Rev E.D. Hahner of this place.

GOERKE, ADAM - Obituary - May 12, 1897 Died Adam Goerke May 8th at the home of his daughter, Mrs S.A. Erdman, Schell City, MO Had spent last 4 years at Schell City and had been feeble many years. Remains arrived here Sun. A.M. and buried beside his wife in village cemetery.

GOERKE, HENRY - Adm Sale - Aug 13, 1902 At the home of Henry Goerke, deceased, on sect 9 Columbus twp. Geo. W. Cyrus, adm.

GOERKE, HENRY - Death - Jul 23, 1902 Henry Goerke a farmer of Columbus twp, died on the 15th inst. Daughter, Mrs George Riutzel moved to his home to take care of him. Later another daughter came, Mrs Louisa Jabs of Wichita, KS. He was born in Hesse Cassel, Germany Aug 5, 1826. Age 16 came to U.S. and to Adams Co. Married in 1850 to _____ Oax, who died 2 years later. Leaving 1 daughter who became the wife of Louis Guenther, but died soon after her marriage. Married 2nd, 1857 to Katherine Hornecker who died 1873. They had 7 children, only 3 survive him, the 2 daugthers mentioned and Miss Lena Goerke of Jacksonville. Funeral at Columbus Thurs. by Rev C.F. Stecher. Burial in Coatsburg Cemetery.

GOERKE, HENRY - Probate Notice - Jul 30, 1902
Henry Goerke, deceased 1st Mon. of Oct 1902
(6th) Geo. W. Cyrus, adm.

GOERKE, HENRY - Oakwood - Jan 27, 1897 Henry
Goerke of Columbus twp died Tues. Buried
following Sun. in cemetery at Coatsburg.

GOERKE, HENRY JR - Probate Notice - Feb 3, 1897
Henry Goerke Jr., deceased 1st Mon of April
1897 Henry Goerke Sr., Adm.

GOERKE, HENRY JR. - Local - Jan 13, 1897 Died
Henry Goerke Jr a young farmer of Columbus twp
died about 1 o'clock from pneumonia. He lived
with his father and was 28-30 years old.

GOLDEN, MRS - Paloma - Apr 27, 1894 Funeral of
Mrs Golden who died in Quincy the 16th were
held at the Baptist Church last Wed. P.M.

GOLDEN, ROBERT R. - Local - Apr 16, 1895
Robert R. Golden died in Mt Sterling on the 8th
inst age 63 years. Kept a hotel in Golden a
few years ago. Has lived Mt Sterling since
1890. Leaves wife and 8 children. Buried by
G.A.R. and Masons.

GOLDEN, STEPHEN M. - Quincy - Dec 3, 1902
Stephen M. Golden, age 71 years, one of the
early settlers of Adams Co. died at
Jacksonville last Wednesday.

GOLDEN, STEPHEN M. - Quincy - Dec 10, 1902 The
will of Stephen M. Golden leaves all of his
estate to Francis H. St Clair, who is named as
executor.

GOLLIHER, MARGARET - Probate Notice - Jun 1,
1894 Margaret Golliher, deceased. 1st Mon of
July 1894 R.H. Bacon, Ex.

GOODING, MR - West Point - Mar 6, 1896 Mrs
James Rhoades and Mrs James Knott have returned
from Jasper, MO where they attended the funeral
of their father, Mr Gooding.

GOODNER, EMMA - Quincy - Jun 9, 1897 Edward
Shannon has been appointed adm of the estate of
Emma Goodner.

GORE, JOHN - Death - Dec 13, 1895 Died Monday
Dec 9th at Virginia, Ill, John Gore age 62
years 10 months 25 days. Funeral from Presby.
Church Wed. at Virginia. Buried Walnut Ridge
cemetery.

GRACE, PATRICK - Quincy - Feb 16, 1894 Died
Patrick Grace, formerly a prominent contractor
in this city died in Terre Haute, Ind.

GRAHAM, MRS - Burned to Death - May 11, 1894
Mrs Graham age 80 years living 2 miles N. of
Bowen was burned Tues. forenoon and died during
the night. Her pipe must have ignited her
dress. She lived with her daughter, her
husband died a great many years ago. Was
mother of Mrs W.F. Hughes of Golden.

GRAHAM, MRS J.M. - Local - Oct 1, 1902 Mrs
J.M. Graham was burned to death at Galesburg
Mon. by her clothes catching fire at a gasoline
stove. Mr Graham was a Q conductor and many
years ago was station agent at Golden.

GRAHAM, JAMES M. - Quincy - May 10, 1895 James
M. Graham died Tues. after a lingering illness
caused by a gun shot wound received in the
Civil War. He had charge of the baths at
Siloam Springs at the inception of that
enterprise and the father of Nellie Mae Vosburg
the elocitionist. Leaves widow and this
daughter.

GRAHAM, SIDNEY - Golden - Apr 6, 1893 Died,
suddenly last week at Galesburg, Sidney Graham
of lung fever. Brought to LaPrairie for burial
in Pulaski cemetery beside his father. Was
still in his teens.

GRAHAM, SIDNEY M. - Elm Grove - Apr 6, 1893
Sidney M. Graham, son of the late J.J. Graham
of LaPrairie died of pneumonia at Galesburg Mar
29th. Brought to LaPrairie and buried at

Pulaski cemetery after services by Rev R.A.
Hatrick in the ME Church. Born Mar 23, 1874
and lived at LaPrairie until a few months
before his death. He was with his sister, Mrs
Mat Rigdon at the time of his death.

GRAHAM, THOMAS - West Point - Jul 10, 1894
Died at his home 5 miles N.E. of here Thomas
Graham age 85 years. Leaves 2 sons-Thomas and
Charles. Funeral held in Baptist Church and
buried in the graveyard near his wife and
daughter.

GRANT, PROF. I. - 10 Years Ago - Feb 23, 1893
Prof. I. Grant an eccentric, scholarly man,
died at Coatsburg.

GRANT, PROF. I. - Ancient History - Feb 25,
1903 - Feb 22, 1883 Prof. I. Grant died at
Coatsburg he had been professor of Greek and
Latin in Knox college.

GRAY, FRANK - Killed by Falling Sand - Jul 1,
1903 Two boys, Frank Gray and Frank Weber of
Quincy were playing in a cave dug in a sand
bank on Locust St. Thurs. when the bank caved
in burying them. Another boy on the outside
gave the alarm. Gray was dead but Weber will
probably live.

GRAY, LAVINA - Obituary - Jan 22, 1902 Lavina
Gray was born in the Isle of Wright, England
Feb 22, 1817. Came with parents to U.S. in
winter of 1828-29. After remaining in New York
City a short period they moved to Ind. till
1836 when they came to Coatsburg, Ill. Married
Stephen Booth Jan 12, 1839 who died May 3,
1884. They had 4 daughters, Mary Wilson,
Charlotte Colburn, Louise Powell, who died
early womanhood and Eleanor Dickhut with whom
she lived. Had 11 grandchildrn and 3 gr.
grandchildren. She died 4 P.M. Jan 11, 1902
age 84 years 10 months 19 days. Services by
Rev W.E. Rose in the ME Church at Paloma 11
A.M. Tues. Jan 14th. Buried North cemetery at
Fowler by the side of her loved one.

GRAY, PROF. - Local - Aug 3, 1893 Mrs Rosa
Frost attended the funeral of Prof. Gray's
infant son Monday at Coatsburg.

GRAY, RUSSEL - Died - Aug 10, 1893 Died, Sun.
A.M. at age 1 year 9 months, Russel, beloved
babe of Mr and Mrs W.S. Gray. Sick one week.
Services by Rev White Mon. A.M. at the U.B.
Church. Buried village cemetery.

GRAY, RUSSEL - Coatsburg - Aug 10, 1893 Sun
July 30th about noon occurred the death of
little Russel Gray, youngest son of Prof. and
Annie Gray.

GRAY, SAMUEL W. - Local - Mar 27, 1894 Died-
Samuel W. Gray in Quincy Sunday, age 38 years.
Was a brother of Mrs J.H. Bottorff of
LaPrairie.

GRAY, WALTER - Paloma - Jul 22, 1903 Remains
of Walter Gray, an old resident of this place,
arrived here last week. Burial was at
Columbus.

GREEN, ELMER - Co. Seat - Nov 18, 1896 Elmer
Green age 35 arrived here on a midnight train
Sun. night from Ashburn, MO. He seemed in last
stages of consumption and said he was on his
way to St Mary's Hospital. As he showed no
permit to enter hospital he was taken to police
station. At 4 A.M. he was found dead on the
floor in a small room assigned to him.

GREEN, EVALINE - Obituary - Jun 24, 1896
Evaline Green born Aug 3, 1869 in Shelby Co.
Ill. moved with parents 1878 to Kansas and
lived there 14 years. 1892 moved to Camp
Point. Died 8 P.M. Sat. Jun 20th 1896.
Funeral ME Church 4 P.M. Monday.

GREENHALGH, MRS ELIZA C. - Death - Apr 2, 1902
Mrs Eliza C. Greenhalgh was born at Clinton, KY
July 31, 1832. Died at her home in Camp Point
March 25th age 69 years 7 months 24 days.
Maiden name was Eliza Catherine Cole. Parents
died when she was a child and when 12 years old

she was brought to Rushville, Ill. Married Apr 10, 1851 in Rushville to William Greenhalgh who died 12 years ago. They came to Camp Point in 1856 and lived here since. Leaves 3 children Mrs Hannah Garrett of Maryville, MO, Mrs Nevada Lizzett of Camp Point and Edgar W. of Jacksonville, Florida. Services Wed. afternoon at Methodist Church by Rev C.N. Cain. Buried village cemetery.

GREENHALGH, MRS ELIZA C. - Death - Mar 26, 1902 Mrs Eliza C. Greenhalgh died Tues. A.M. after a lingering illness of blood poisoning. Leaves 2 daughters, Mrs Hannah Garrett of Maryville, MO and Mrs Nevada Liggett of Camp Point and 1 son, Edgar W. of Jacksonville, Fla. Services at Methodist Church 2 P.M. today.

GREENHALGH, ELIZA C. - Probate Notice - May 14, 1902 Eliza C. Greenhalgh, deceased 1st Mon. of July 1902 (7th) Nevada Greenhalgh, adm.

GREENHALGH, JOHN - May 4, 1893 Soldiers buried in Camp Point cemetry. Listed in Co. B. 137th Illinois Infantry.

GREER, ALEXANDER - Local - Feb 20, 1894 Died Alexander Greer at the home of his brother in law, James McClintock, near Mt Sterling on the 1st inst, 58 years old. Lived with McC's 20 years and was a brother of Mrs M.T. Williams of Columbus twp. Buried at Mt Sterling.

GREER, JOHN - Local - Feb 19, 1896 Died, Sun., John Greer, father of Rev T.W. Greer of Chatham, Ill. "Rushville Republican"

GRIFFIN, WILLIAM - Local - Jun 22, 1893 A 2 year old child of William Griffin, of McDonough Co. was scalded to death last week by pulling off the table onto itself a bowl of hot rhubarb which had just been cooked by the mother. It died the next day.

GRIFFITH, MISS LIZZIE - Local - Dec 16, 1896 Died Miss Lizzie Griffith died at the home of her father, A.J. Griffith in Concord twp Fri.

She had been an invalid many years.

GRIFFITH, MISS SALLY A. - Died - Apr 14, 1897
Died, *Miss* Sally A. Griffith, *wife* of Capt J.
Griffith at her home in Concord Fri. the 9th
inst., 63 years old. Her husband, 3 sons and 4
daughters survive her.

GRIFFITH, WILLIAM H. - Local - Aug 31, 1894
Died William H. Griffith, cashier of the
Hancock Co. National Bank, Carthage died
suddenly from apolexy Tues. A.M. 45 years old.
Leaves a wife and 2 daughters.

GRIGSBY, MRS ANN - Death - Dec 3, 1902
Thanksgiving A.M. the family of John Grigsby
arrived with remains of the wife and mother,
Mrs Ann Grigsby who died at San Jose, Calif.
the 21st ult. Was daughter of Thomas White,
one of the very early settlers of Honey Creek
twp. Lived here all but 4 years of her life.
Married twice 1st to Alvan Murrah, they had 2
girls, the eldest died about 18 years ago. The
younger Miss Adella lived with her mother all
her life. About 33 years ago she married 2nd
to John Grigsby, who survives her. They had 2
daughters and 1 son, Grace, Viola and John Jr.
Viola died in infancy, other two lived with
parents. Also surviving her is 2 brothers,
James M. White of Honey Creek - Thos. C. White
of Wheeling, MO and 1 sister Mrs Eben Crouch of
Hamilton, Ill. Buried beside her children in
Coatsburg Cemetery at high noon on Nov 27th.
Services by Elder Orrin Dilley of Camp Point.

GRIGSBY, H.D.L. - Local - Apr 15, 1903 H.D.L.
Grigsby died in Pittsfield Mon. age 46 years.
Was a prominent Republican politician.

GRIGSBY, WEBB - Quincy - Mar 12, 1895 Webb
Grigsby, age 25 took morphine Sat. Died 4 hours
later. Formerly of Milan, MO but had worked in
this city last 2 years. Leaves wife and 1
child.

GRIMES, ALICE - Quincy - Aug 12, 1896 J.A.
Dunn, a merchant at Nebo, Pike Co. who is

charged with the murder of Alice Grimes has
been placed in jail in this city.

GRIMES, MRS CATHERINE A. - Obituary - Mar 25,
1896 Catherine A. Conrey born Genoa, N.Y. Oct
20, 1837 died Camp Point Mar 17th, 1896. Sick
2 months. Came to Beverly twp with her parents
Oct 1857 where hse married Oct 10, 1860 to Dr
James M. Grimes. They had 3 children a son and
a daughter died before her. Surviving is Mrs
Harriet Corkins of Sedalia, MO and a baby
grandson. Services at Presby. Church Fri.
afternoon by Rev L.H. Royce and Rev's A.N.
Simmons, W.M. Reed and O. Dilley. Buried
village cemetery. Relatives present was Mr and
Mrs J.W. Corkins, Sedalia, MO.; John M. Grimes,
Chicago; Miss Ida Grimes of Mt Sterling; Mrs
Lizzie Crocker of Springfield; Mr and Mrs
Cutforth of Newtown.

GRIMES, GEORGE W. - Local - Jan 29, 1896 Died
George W. Grimes, of Perry, Pike Co. a brother
of Dr J.M. Grimes of this city died in Chicago
on the 22nd inst. and taken to Perry for
burial.

GRIMES, MRS J.M. - Local - Mar 18, 1896 Died
Mrs J.M. Grimes died Tuesday night. Funeral
from Presby. Church Friday at 2 P.M.

GRIMMER, MR - Local - Jun 16, 1897 Mr and Mrs
E. Hornecker went to Quincy Saturday to attend
the funeral of Mr Grimmer.

GRIMMER, HENRY A. - Quincy - Jun 16, 1897
Henry Welsh, the lad who rode his pony over
Henry A. Grimmer causing the latters death has
been placed in jail in default of $200.00 bail.

GRIMSHAW, COL. JACKSON - Ancient History - Dec
10, 1895 -Dec 1875 Col Jackson Grimshaw died in
Quincy.

GRONEWALD, MR AND MRS - Local - Dec 23, 1903
Coroner Lummis was called to Chalten Friday to
hold an inquest on the babe of Mr and Mrs
Gronewald, which was found dead in bed with its

parents that A.M.

GROSH, MRS J.F. - Quincy - Jul 19, 1895   Mrs
J.F. Grosh died Wed. night from a stroke of
paralysis, 62 years old.   Leaves husband and
several children.   Sister of J.H. Clark and Mrs
Follansbee.

GROSS, MR AND MRS JOHN - Local - Nov 17, 1897
The babe of Mr and Mrs John Gross, LaBelle, MO.
died Friday.

GROVER, BENJAMIN FRANKLIN - Death - Feb 25,
1903 Benjamin Franklin Grover, for many years
of Adams Co. died last Wed. the 18th inst at
Dixon age 86 years.   Born at Sidney, Maine Feb
2, 1817 and came west 1837 and soon settled at
Liberty where he was in merchandising many
years.   Moved to Dixon 1890.   Married 1856 to
Annie E. Ferguson who with several children
survives him.   Ferguson A. Grover of Quincy, ex-
county surveyor, is a son.

GROVER, MRS PARDON B. - Quincy - Jul 19, 1895
Death of Mrs Pardon B. Grover at the family
home Mon. eve after a lingering illness.   85
years old, spent nearly all her life in Adams
Co.   Leaves husband and 3 children, 1 son-2
daughers, the son is John C. Grover of Ursa.

GROVES, STEPHEN - Primrose - Jan 29, 1895 A
little son of Stephen Groves was buried in York
Neck cemetery Wed. the 23rd, was 3 months old.

GROVES, MR AND MRS STEPHEN - Local - Jan 25,
1895 A babe of Mr and Mrs Stephen Groves of
Houston was buried at York Neck cemetery Wed.

GROVES, MRS STEPHEN - Ancient History - May 22,
1894 - May 23, 1884 Mrs Stephen Groves, of
Houston twp died on the 10th.

GRUNY, LEE - Passed Away - Oct 29, 1895 Lee,
the baby boy of Mr and Mrs George Gruny died
Friday eve Oct 25th after a brief illness with
flux, age 1 year 21 days.   Funeral Sunday
afternoon.

GUENTHER, FRED - "From the Necks" - Sep 22, 1897 Mr and Mrs John Geibert were present at the funeral of Mr Fred Guenther at Coatsburg Wednesday.

GUENTHER, FREDERICK - Recent Death - Sep 22, 1897 Frederick Guenther died at his home 2 miles N of Coatsburg Mon. the 13th inst. Funeral Wed. Sept 15th has lived here since 1855. Born Germany May 18, 1833. Came to America 1853 landing at New Orleans where he went to St Louis and then to the farm in Honey Creek twp where he died. 1859 he married Ernestine Rauschel who died in 1865. They had 4 children- 3 daughters and 1 son who survive.

GUTH, HENRY - Quincy - Feb 27, 1894 Killed, Henry Guth a brakeman of this city was killed in a railroad wreck at Rock Springs, Wyo. Thursday A.M.

GUTHRIE, JOHN C. - West Point - Feb 13, 1894 Will Guthrie and daughter of Hamilton, and Miss Lib Guthrie of Mendon attended the funeral of John C. Guthrie.

GUTHRIE, JOHN C. - West Point - Feb 13, 1894 Died, Feb 5th, of pneumonia, John C. Guthrie eldest son of Geo. and Mary Guthrie. Born Dec 9, 1868, age 15 years 1 month 26 days. Born and raised in this vicinity. Member of ME Church since 1893. Leaves a father, mother, 3 sisters and 4 brothers. Services by Rev McDonald at ME Church Wed. at 11 A.M. Remains were followed to their resting place by a large concourse of friends.

GUTHRIE, MOSES - Ancient History - Aug 7, 1894 Aug 7, 1874 Moses Guthrie, a wealthy and well known citizen of Columbus twp died on the 1st. He was the father of James R. of Camp Point.

GWINN, MRS DOW R. - Quincy - Jul 23, 1902 Mrs Dow R. Gwinn, (nee Bessie M. Duff) a native of this city and formerly a well known school teacher, died in Terre Haute, Ind. on Wed. burial will be here.

HACKNEY, W.D. - Quincy - Nov 19, 1902 W.D.
Hackney, an old resident of Adams Co. died in
Golden, age 74 years.

HAFNER, VITUS - Probate Notice - Mar 4, 1903
Vitus Hafner, deceased 1st Mon. of May, 1903
(4th) Barbara Hafner, ex.

HAGERTY, MRS CLARA - Ancient History - Aug 7,
1894 - Aug 7, 1874 Mrs Clara Hagerty died on
the 1st.

HAGERTY, J.T. - Ancient History - Aug 25, 1897
March 1881-J.T. Hagerty died at Stanberry, MO.
His remains were brought here for burial.

HAGERTY, JOHN T. - Ancient History - Mar 26,
1895 - March 1881 John T. Hagerty died at
Stanberry, MO.

HAGUE, WALTER E. - Quincy - Nov 12, 1902
Walter E. Hague, formerly employed in R.R.
offices in Kansas City, died at his home here
Wed. night age 22 years.

HAINES, MRS GEO. R. - Ancient History - May 15,
1894 - May 16, 1879 Mrs Geo. R. Haines died at
Baylis.

HAINES, MRS SALLY - Death - Jan 1, 1902 Mrs
Sally Haines died at Baylis Sat. Dec 21st in
her 81st year. Was sister of Thomas Bailey of
Camp Point and lived here with her husband, the
late Benjamin R. Haines from 1869 to 1876 when
they moved to Baylis. Leaves 3 sons and 1
daughter.

HAINES, SAMUEL - Suicide at Augusta - Sep 13,
1895 Samuel Haines killed himself at the home
of John Shepherd near Augusta Tues. Leaves a
wife and a large family in poor circumstances.
Was about 38 years old.

HAINLINE, JOHN D. - Local - Jan 1, 1902 John
D. Hainline age 86 years, father of publisher
of the Macomb Journal died last Fri. in
McDonough Co. where he lived 63 years.

HAIR, MRS ANNA - Death of Mrs Anna Hair - Jun 23, 1897 Died Aunt Anna Hair, wife of D.L. Hair, Esq. of Gilmer twp at her home in Gilmer Friday 9 P.M. Services at ME Church in Columbus Sun. June 20th 3 P.M. by Rev A.A. White of Paloma. Anna Elizabeth Elliott born near Westchester, Butler Co. Ohio Nov 19, 1828, died at her home, Columbus, Ill Jun 18, 1897 age 68 years 6 months 19 days. Married Mar 6, 1851 to Daniel L. Hair and in the next spring they came to Adams Co. First year to Quincy then to Gilmer twp. Had 7 children-1 daughter and 6 sons. The daughter and 2 sons died in infancy. Leaves husband and 4 sons-Clement W., William H., Delano C. and David L. all live in the neighborhood of their old home. Also a foster daughter, Miss Anna Bell. Also leaves 2 brothers, David Elliott of Idaho and John Elliot of Ohio and 1 sister, Mrs Sarah Williamson of Hartwell, Ohio.

HAIR, MRS D.L. - Columbus -Jun 30, 1897 Died Mrs D.L. Hair from cancer of the stomach.

HAISE, WILLIAM - Quincy - Mar 12, 1902 William Haise, for several years connected with Quincy telephone exchange died at Blessing hospital, age 63 years.

HALEY, ALFRED - Local -Feb 9, 1893 Alfred Haley died Sat. afternoon at the home of his brother William. He had been an invalid for a long time. Funeral Monday A.M.

HALEY, MR AND MRS JOE - Columbus - Dec 29, 1897 Infant daughter of Mr and Mrs Joe Haley was buried afternoon Christmas Day in village cemetery.

HALL, FRED - Local - May 31, 1895 Word received of death of Fred Hall at Macomb.

HALL, FRED - Death of Fred Hall - Jun 4, 1895 Fred Hall born Camp Point, Ill Oct 7, 1876 being 18 years 7 months 24 days. Lived there till about 2 years ago when he came to Macomb with parents. Was a graduate of Macomb High School 1894. Mrs H. and daughter had just left for Vliss, N.Y. and arriving there was told of death of her son. Returned to Macomb Sat. eve. Funeral to be Monday. Remains arrived on fast mail Monday A.M. from Macomb, taken to home of Louis A. Hall for services by Elder O. Dilley. Buried village cemetery.

HALL, FRED - Cause of Fred Hall's Death - Jun 7, 1895 Macomb Bystander says death of Fred Hall caused by -- He ran half a dozen foot races in rapid sucession which resulted in complete exhaustion and an acute affliction of the heart, causing death the following morn at 4 A.M.

HALL, CAPT. MOSES - Local - Mar 12, 1902 Capt Moses Hall, a well known steamboat man, died in Quincy Sun., 83 years old.

HALL, S.F. - Local - Apr 15, 1903 The will of S.F. Hall was filed Tues. leaves property to the widow and at her death to be divided among his 5 children. Widow appointed executrix.

HALL, SAMUEL F. - Death of Prof. Hall - Apr 15, 1903 Prof Samuel F. hall died Sat. eve, cancer of the stomach, about 5:30 P.M. Funeral Monday P.M. by Rev Corey of Mt Sterling at the family home, buried village cemetery. Born Oswego, N.Y. Nov 14, 1838. Died Camp Point, Ill. Apr 11th. Reared in New York and began teaching there where he met and married Artemisia Burroughs another New York school teacher. Came to Ill. 1862 settled Princeton for 5 years. Fall of 1867 he came to take charge of Camp Points Maplewood school. Leaves a widow, 4 daughters and 1 son, Louis A. who has a grocery store in Camp Point. Daughters are Mrs Nina B. Gabriel and Mrs Maggie M. Gabriel of Payson, Mrs Bessie A. Dunn of Quincy and Miss Edith E. Hall who is also a teacher.

HALL, SAMUEL F. - Probate Notice - May 13, 1903 Samuel F. Hall, deceased 1st Mon. of July, 1903 (6th) Ellen Artemisia Hall, executor.

HAMAN, ROMONA - Local - Oct 22, 1902 Romona

Haman, of Quincy age 15 years was engaged in
blacking the stove with a gasoline preparation
when the gasoline burned, burning her
dreadfully. She died a short time later.

HAMILTON, GEN. ELISHA B. - Dead - Mar 26, 1902
Death of Gen. Elisha B. Hamilton announced
Thurs. afternoon. He had gone to home of Capt
Barnes in Riverside twp near Soldiers Home and
was attacked by paralysis of the heart and died
before medical assistance could get there.
Born Carthage Oct 5, 1838, 64 years old.
Served 3 years in Ill. 118th and saw much hard
service. Married Miss Mary E. Fisk Sept 10,
1878, she with a son and daughter survive him.

HAMILTON, HENRY - Local - Jun 18, 1902 Henry
Hamilton of Quincy was working in a field in
Melrose twp Friday afternoon when he was struck
by lightning and killed. His body was found
Sunday.

HAMMER, MRS ANTONE - Coatsburg - Feb 23, 1893
Mrs Hammer, relict of the late Antone Hammer is
lying at the point of death from a cancerous
trouble.

HAMMER, MARY - Probate Notice - Apr 13, 1893
Mary Hammer, deceased 1st Monday of May 1893
(1st) Fred Hammer, executor.

HAMMOND, MRS ELVIRA - Quincy - May 22, 1894
Died-Mrs Elvira Hammond, the oldest colored
woman in the city died, age 93 years.

HAMPTON, MRS A.E. - Local - Jul 20, 1893 Mrs
A.E. Hampton, widow of the late Benjamin R.
Hampton died in Macomb on the 8th inst. Her
son D.H. Hampton, editor of the By-Stander is
the only member of the family.

HANBACK, LEWIS - Lewis Hanback Dead - Sep 8,
1897 Mrs W.T. Kay received a telegram Mon. of
the death of her brother, Lewis Hanback at
Armourdale, KS, age 58 years from typhoid
malarial fever. He was born Winchester, Ill
and lived as a boy in Camp Point. Went to

Kansas in the 60's.

HANCOCK, EDWIN E. - Suicide at Barry - Feb 23,
1894 Edwin Hancock a prominent farmer of Pike
Co. committed suicide at Barry at 3 Monday.
Had sold his farm and was preparing to move to
Kansas but rather than go he killed himself.
Note was signed E.E. Hancock.

HANCOCK, JAMES - Ancient History - Aug 12, 1903
Aug 1873-James Hancock, of Burton twp, hanged
himself after killing his wife with a hammer.

HANCOCK, JAMES - 20 Years Ago - Aug 31, 1893
James Hancock, of Newtown killed his wife and
committed suicide by hanging himself.

HANKS, ISAAC E. - Quincy - May 25, 1894 Died
Isaac E. Hanks age 36, died at the home of his
parents in Melrose twp Sunday A.M.

HANKS, JOSEPH - Death - Jan 8, 1902 Joseph
Hanks, 77 years old _____ since 1828 ___ east
of Melrose Chapel, ____. Born ___ Co., Ind.
May 14, 1825 moved with parents to Sangamon Co.
Ill same year. Fall of 1828 moved to Melrose
twp where the family lived since. May 14, 1851
he married Miss Martha Bartholomew a native of
Ind. had 10 children of which 6 are still
living. Mrs H. died some years ago. He was
director of the Adams Co. Fair for a number of
years and a breeder of cattle. (The print on
the first part of this article is very hard to
read.)

HANKS, JOSEPH - Quincy - Jan 8, 1902 Joseph
Hanks, a relative of the family of Abraham
Lincoln, died at his home in Melrose twp on
Wed. age 76 years. He had lived on the same
farm since 1839.

HANKSLER, MATTHEW - Local - Jun 10, 1896
Matthew Hanksler, a German laborer, 30 years
old was found dead on outskirts of Rushville
Monday eve. He had committed suicide because
he could not find work.

HARBIN, MRS ADALINE - Local - May 13, 1896
Died Mrs Adaline Harbin, colored, died at the
home of her son in Concord at 9 P.M. Sunday of
cancer of the breast. Family came from
Mississippi 4 years ago. Mother of 10
children, 9 still living-3 in native state and
other in Ill. Funeral Tuesday. Buried Camp
Point beside a son in law who died a few months
ago. "Clayton Enterprise"

HARDING, NELLIE - West Point - Nov 18, 1896
Died Nellie Harding, age 13 years, died last
Wednesday. Buried Friday. Services by Rev
Hedges.

HARRIS, DANIEL - Quincy - Dec 17, 1902 Daniel
Harris, formerly a prominent resident of Quincy
who died in St Louis was buried here Thursday.

HARRIS, JAMES M.R. - Ancient History - May 24,
1895 - May 1876 James M.R. Harris died on the
15th.

HARRIS, JAMES M.R. - Ancient History - May 15,
1894 - May 19, 1876 James M.R. Harris died in
Quincy May 15th.

HARRIS, JAMES MADISON - Death - Jan 14, 1903
James Madison Harris was born near Memphis,
Ind. Feb 28, 1838 died Dec 31, 1902 age 64
years 10 months 3 days. Came to Ill. March
1866 and married Anna M. Strickler Feb 18,
1868. Two brothers, 4 sisters, widow and 6
children survive him. He served 3 years during
Civil War in Co. D 4th Reg. Ind. Cavalry Vol.
Funeral at home in Houston twp Jan 2nd by C.F.
Stecher.

HARRIS, JOEL - A Fatal Accident - May 21, 1895
A fatal accident in Burton twp Sat. in which a
carpenter named Joel Harris of Plainville was
killed when a scaffold fell. He was about 55
years old. Born and raised in Adams Co. Had a
number of grown children.

HARRIS, NEWTON - Plead Quilty - Dec 16, 1903
Fred Mink, who was indicted in Pike Co. circuit

court for killing Newton Harris and his step
mother June 13th was arrainged at Pittsfield
Sat. where he plead guilty both indictments and
received 99 years on each.

HARRISON, MISS NELLIE - Quincy - Feb 20, 1894
Died, Miss Nellie Harrison, formerly of this
city died at the home of her brother, Rev R.M.
Harrison, New York.

HARRON, SAMUEL T. - Ancient History - Oct 12,
1894 - Oct 4, 1884 Sameul T. Harron, a widely
known stock dealer of LaPrairie died Sept 26th.
(Incorrect spelling on Harron, see Herron)

HARRY, JOHN - Local - Jan 22, 1895 John Harry,
an inmate of the poor farm died last week. He
was sent to the farm from Quincy.

HART, AMOS - 15 Years Ago - Feb 16, 1893 The
home of Amos Hart, in Big Neck was burned and
his remains were found in the ruins. Was about
70 years old and lived alone.

HART, AMOS - Ancient History - Feb 22, 1895
Feb 1878 The home of Amos Hart in Big Neck was
destroyed by fire and his charred remains were
found in the ruins. He lived alone.

HART, ISAAC - West Point - Apr 10, 1894 Died
Isaac Hart in Quincy Thurs. A.M. remains
brought here Friday to the home of his brother
William. Services by Rev McDonald on Sat. A.M.
Buried West Point Cemetery.

HARTMAN, RUDOLPH - Local - Feb 2, 1894 Died
Rudolph Hartman a well known postal clerk died
in Quincy Thurs. He was one of the oldest
clerks in the service.

HARTUNG, FREDERICK - Quincy - Aug 27, 1902
Frederick Hartung, formerly an old resident of
this city, died at his home in Fremont, NE,
during the past week.

HARTUNG, MRS LOUISE - Obituary - Jan 20, 1897
Mrs Louise Hartung died at the home of her son,

Louis Steiner in Columbus twp Jan 13th. Born
Germany 1816. Came to America 1847 lived Adams
Co. since. Married twice. Services by Elder
O. Dilley and Elder John Parrick on the 15th.
Buried Jefferson cemetery.

HARVEY, JAMES M. - Ex-Gov. Harvey Dead - Apr
24, 1894 Died James M. Harvey 5th governor of
Kansas at his home in Riley Co., Sunday P.M.
Born Sep 21, 1822 in Monroe Co. Virginia.
Father was Thomas Harvey. Mother was Margaret
Walker both native of Virg. He lived Beverly
twp Adams Co. several years. Moved to Kansas
1859. Married Oct 4, 1854 to Miss Charlotte
Cutter of Adams Co. Ill. They had 6 children.

HASELWOOD, MRS ELIZABETH - Died - Nov 8, 1895
Mrs Elizabeth Haselwood, the mother of Co.
clerk Haselwood and one of the oldest residents
of Adams Co died at her home in Payson Wed.
eve. Born Grant Co. KY Aug 8, 1814. Was 82
years old. Came to Adams Co. with husband
1836. Lived Payson twp nearly 60 years.
Leaves 5 sons and 1 daughter-William & Perry of
Knox City, MO- Willis of Quincy - James and
John of Payson - Mrs Mary E. Shields of
LaHarpe, Ill. Her husband died in 1867.

HASELWOOD, WILLIS - Dead - Jun 17, 1903 Willis
Haselwood at his home in Quincy Monday A.M.
Born in Payson twp Sept 8, 1838 and lived there
as a boy and man, school teacher and farmer
until elected county clerk in 1873 and moved to
Quincy. Married Oct 14, 1858 to Olive S. Bean,
a neighbor girl. She survives him with 1 son
and daughter. Invalid since 1900.

HASTING, MISS LIZZIE - Paloma - Jun 2, 1897
Word received Monday of the sudden death of
Miss Lizzie Hasting, near Mendon.

HASTING, WILLIAM - Paloma - May 5, 1897 On
April 20th occured the death of William
Hasting. Funeral and burial took place in
Mendon.

HATCHER, P.E. - Suicide - Aug 2, 1895 P.E.

Hatcher, an inmate of the Soldiers Home
committed suicide Tuesday A.M. by drowning
himself in a pond on the grounds. He came from
Pearl, Pike Co. about 4 months ago and was
considered mentally unbalanced. 56 years old.
Married twice.

HATFIELD, ANNA - Died - Jun 22, 1893 At the
residence of George Longcer, Camp Point Friday,
June 16th Anna Hatfield, age 20 years. Funeral
by Elder O. Dilley and buried in the village
cemetery.

HAUGHMAN, J.W. - A Brakeman Meets Death - Dec
29, 1897 J.W. Haughman, a C.B. & Q brakeman
was run over by #92 freight train at Plymouth
Tuesday about noon. Died almost at once.
Remains taken to Galesburg on night train. He
was 32 years old. Had a wife and 2 children in
Galesburg. "Macomb Bystander"

HAUSER, DAMON - Quincy - Jun 28, 1895 Damon
Hauser, who was a citizen of Quincy 20 years
ago died Tues. at Denver, Colo., 94 years old.
Back in the 40's he was receiver of the land
office at Quincy.

HAUSER, DAMION - Quincy - Jul 2, 1895 Damion
Hauser, one of the early merchants of this city
died this week in Denver, Colo. age 94 years.

HAWKER, REV WILLIAM - Local - Dec 23, 1903 Rev
William Hawks, an aged pioneer Baptist
minister, died at his home at Perry Tues. of
last week, age 87 years. He has preached in
Adams and Pike counties for 60 years. He has
often visited Camp Point.

HAXEL, PHILIP - Quincy - Jan 1, 1902 Philip
Haxel, an old resident of Adams Co. died in
Burton twp, age 68 years.

HAYNES, WAKEFIELD - Was Murder & Suicide - Apr
28, 1897 Wakefield Haynes and his 15 year old
niece, Lizzie Hudson. Haynes was 24 years old
and a brother of Lizzie's mother. The two were
found shot Sat. A.M. in the woods a mile from

Loraine. They chose to die because they knew
they could not marry. Father of girl was
Washington Wren Hudson.

HAZLETT, CHARLES - Local - Aug 6, 1902 Charles
Hazlett, son of James Hazlett of Clayton, and
well known in Camp Point died Sat. eve of
apoplexy. Was 31 years old and married.

HAZLETT, MRS JACOB - Recent Deaths - Feb 10,
1897 Died Mrs Jacob Hazlett at her home in
Clayton Sat. age 51 years. Leaves husband and
6 children. Services Monday 1:30 P.M. at
family home.

HEAD, WILLIAM T. - Death - Dec 21, 1893
William T. Head died Sat. A.M. at his home in
Quincy near Oak and 5th. Had been confined to
his home since spring of 1890 from a stroke of
paralysis. For 16 years he was a deputy county
clerk under Willis Haselwood and a servant of
the public for 60 years. Born Washington Co.
KY Feb 26, 1816 according to his wife. He
himself used to put his birthday on the last of
Feb and as 1816 was a leap year he celebrated
his birthday every 4 years. His folks moved to
Ill. when he was young. His brother, Daniel E.
Head was the first circuit clerk in the county
of Hancock. The deceased also became sheriff
of McDonough Co. and elected several times.
Was then chosen county treasurer. Moved to MO
and lived there about 4 years. 1870 he came to
Quincy.

HEADLEY, G.W. - Paloma - Feb 22, 1895 Died
last Friday A.M., G.W. Headley. Funeral next
day at Baptist Church by Rev Dodge of Prairie
City. Buried in the cemetery on his farm which
was laid out some time ago.

HEADLEY, GEORGE W. - Quincy - Mar 1, 1895
Naomi Headley has been appointed adm of the
estate of George W. Headley.

HEANY, MRS SAMUEL - Quincy - Apr 10, 1894 Died
Mrs Samuel Heany at her home Thursday A.M.

HEARNE, MISS GRACE GARLAND - Quincy - Dec 4,
1894 Died, Miss Grace Garland Hearne of St
Louis age 16 died here from consumption
Thursday at the home of her aunt, Mrs T.J.
Lemley.

HEARNE, DR JOSEPH C. - Dr Hearne Acquitted -
Dec 24, 1895 Bowling Green, MO Dec 21st Dr
Joseph C. Hearne this eve was acquitted of the
murder of Amos J. Stillwell. Wife, daughters
and an uncle were there with him. Wife's trail
set for Jan 2, 1896.

HEARNE, DR & MRS JOSEPH C. - The Hearne's
Indicted - Aug 20, 1895 Hannibal, MO Aug 17th
Dr and Mrs Joseph C. Hearne were indicted today
for the murder of Amos J. Stillwell the woman's
husband who was killed in bed Dec 1889.

HEATON, MRS BETSY - Obituary - Jan 12, 1894
Betsy Heaton born Danville, Vermont Aug 15,
1818. Married Samuel Heaton, deceased, in 1839
and they came to Liberty twp, Adams Co. same
year. Lived many years with her son in law
R.A. Wallace of Camp Point. Services at
Christian Church Dec 27th at 3 P.M. by Elder O.
Dilley and Rev E.B. Miner of Presby. Church.
Buried Pleasant View Cemetery.

HEATON, BETSY - Will of Betsy Heaton - Jan 19,
1894 Last will of the late Betsy Heaton was
admitted to probated Tues. dated Jun 21, 1890.
Witnessed by Thomas and Rebecca Bailey. To her
grandaughters Myrta Ross and Lillie Wallace
$500.00, rest to her daugther Hattie Wallace.
Richard A. Wallace named executor.

HEATON, MRS BETSY - Local - Dec 28, 1893 Mrs
Betsy Heaton died Tues. at the home of her
daughter, Mrs R.A. Wallace after a brief
illness with heart disease. Age 75 years.
Funeral Wed. P.M. at the Christian Church.
Remains were laid to rest beside her husband in
Pleasant View Cemetery.

HECKRODT, A.M. - Ancient History - Jul 24, 1894
Jul 20, 1882 A.M. Heckrodt a well known German

farmer of Columbus died on the 14th.

HEDGES, MRS C.N. - Quincy - Jun 30, 1897 Mrs
C.N. Hedges of Ursa age 52 years died suddenly
at Blessing hospital Tues. night. She was a
sister of Fred Taylor of the Journal of
Industry.

HEIDBREDER, MISS FREDERICKA - Quincy - Oct 27,
1897 Died Miss Fredericka Heidbreder, of
Quincy died Tuesday night, age 55 years.

HEILAND, MRS AND MRS JOHN - Columbus - Jul 23,
1902 Funeral of the infant child of Mr and Mrs
John Heiland were held in German ME Church by
Rev E.D. Hahner, the pastor on Sat. July 19th,
1902.

HEILAND, WILKIE JOHN - Death - Jul 23, 1902
Wilkie John, youngest son of John and Sophia
Heiland, died July 17th of inflamation of the
bowels, age 1 year 10 months 27 days. Services
Sat. afternoon in German Methodist Church,
Columbus by Rev E.D. Hahner. Buried Columbus
cemetery.

HEINE, MISS ANTOINETTE - Quincy - Dec 3, 1902
Miss Antoinette Heine died last Thursday night,
age 30 years.

HEINS, MRS FRED - Local - May 15, 1894 Died
Mrs Fred Heins died Saturday eve.

HEINS, HENRY - Ancient History - Mar 30, 1894
March 30, 1882 Henry Heins of Camp Point twp, a
brakeman on the Q was killed while switching at
Macomb.

HELHAKE, CARL A. - Quincy - Feb 26, 1902 Mrs
Adelaide M. Helhake has filed suit against
Quincy humane Society claiming $5000 damages
for the loss of her son, Carl A. Helhake, who
was drowned in the swimming pool constructed by
the humane society last July.

HELLER, MRS WILLIAM - Quincy - Jun 15, 1894
Dead Mrs William Heller age 62 was found dead

in bed Monday A.M. had suffered from heart
trouble long time.

HELLMER, WEIMKE MARGARITA KATHERINE - Death -
Mar 18, 1903 Died at her home in Camp Point
twp Mar 10th Weimke Margarita Katherine Hellmer
(nee Jurgens) beloved wife of Fred Hellmer.
She was born Ruttels, Germany May 3, 1861 died
Mar 10, 1903, 42 years 10 months 7 days old.
Married in her native country in 1885 to Fred
Hellmer and came to U.S. shortly afterwards.
Had 10 children-4 sons, 5 daughters are living,
1 son dead. Services by Rev Drexel at Lutheran
Church Coatsburg Thurs. Buried village
cemetery.

HENDERSON, ELDER D. PAT - Local - Feb 24, 1897
Elder D. Pat Henderson, a pioneer minister of
the Christian Church died at Canton, MO on the
11th last. 30 years ago he was well known in
this vicinity.

HENDERSON, JOHN - Quincy - Sep 10, 1895 Mrs
Ida Henderson, widow of the late John Henderson
has commenced suit against Dr E.B. Montgomery
for malpractice in attending her husband.

HENDRICKS, MRS THOS. - Clayton - Mar 8, 1895
Mrs Thos. Hendricks of Kellerville died Sat.
Buried Monday.

HENDRICKSON, GARRETT - Quincy - Aug 4, 1897
Elizabeth Hendrickson has been appointed adm of
the estate of Garrett Hendrickson.

HENGESBECK, THEODORE - Coatsburg - Nov 27, 1894
Died Fri the 22nd inst, Theodore Hengesbeck
died. He was a victim of the morphine habit.

HENNING, HENRY - Death - Dec 23, 1903 Henry
Henning, a well known German farmer living in
west side of Gilmer twp died Sun. night, age 73
years. Born Germany, lived this country many
years. His wife was Eliza Beutel, who with 6
children survive him- 2 daughters are Mrs W.H.
Michels of Camp Point and Mrs J.B. Rutledge of
Houston. Services in German Methodist Church

in Columbus Tuesday 10 A.M.

HENNING, HENRY & ELIZA - Death of Mr and Mrs
Henning - Dec 30, 1903 Henry Henning died at
his home in Gilmer twp December 20th and the
following Saturday, December 26th his wife,
Eliza followed him. Services of both were held
in Columbus German Methodist Church by Rev
Hehner. Mr Henning's on 22nd and Mrs Henning's
on the 27th. Buried side by side. Both were
born near Muehl Hasen, Germany. At age 13 Mr
H. came to U.S. At age 7 Mrs Henning came with
her parents, Mr and Mrs Conrad Beitel who
alsolived Quincy. Married Nov 1855 and had 8
children-1 son and 1 daughter are dead. 3
sons, 3 daughters survive, they are John A. of
Loraine; Gus A. of Chatten; Mrs J.B. Rutledge,
Mrs W.H. Michels and Geo. of Camp Point; Mrs
J.A. Smith of Quincy. 14 grandchildren. He
also leaves one half brother, Arthur Beitel of
Montana. Mr and Mrs H. lived on a farm in
Gilmer twp 1 mile N of St Joseph Church all
their married lives.

HENNING, JOHN A. - Local - Dec 15, 1897 John
A. Henning, age 70 years died at his home in
Gilmer Friday A.M. of a paralytic stroke. Born
Germany. Came to Adams Co. 1845. Leaves 8
children.

HENNING, MR AND MRS JOHN - Columbus - Apr 6,
1894 Funeral Mr and Mrs John Henning, family
of Big Neck came to attend the funeral of her
brother.

HENRY, ALEXANDER - Local - Aug 9, 1895 John
and Charles Henry executors of the will of the
late Alexander Henry of Quincy filed their
inventory of estate Wednesday. It is a big
one.

HENRY, ALEXANDER - Death - Jul 26, 1895
Alexander Henry born in Co. of Londonderry,
Ireland Aug 16, 1821 was 3rd child and 2nd son
of John and Rachel Henry both of Scotch
extraction. His Father had 6 sons and 6
daughters. At age 20 Alex came to U.S. Nov

1852 married Miss Julia Ann Morgan who with 7
children survive him. Moved to Quincy when
unable to farm. Died July 24th at 10 P.M. at
Camp Point surrounded by wife, children and
friends. Services at Methodist Church 10 A.M.
today. Buried village cemetery.

HENRY, GEO. - Quincy - Apr 7, 1897 Capt J.V.
Henry was called to Sandwich, Ill on Wed. by
the death of his brother, Mr Geo. Henry who was
well known in this city.

HENRY, MRS H.G. - Sudden Death of Mrs Henry -
Feb 19, 1896 Died Sat. A.M. Mrs H.G. Henry
taken to LaHarpe for funeral Tues. afternoon.
Lived Camp Point little over 3 years. Leaves
husband and 3 little children.

HENRY, MRS H.G. - Local - Feb 19, 1896 Dr and
Mrs Jas. Henry and daughters of LaHarpe were
called here Sat. by the death of Mrs H.G.
Henry.

HENRY, MAUD S. - In Memoriam - Feb 26, 1896 Of
Maud S. Henry by Corona Chapter #246.

HENRY, MAUD - Baby Henry is Dead - Aug 19, 1896
Baby Maud Henry died Tues. A.M. from an attack
of cholera infantum at the home of Mrs Ford who
had cahrge of her since her birth and her
mothers death, Feb 15th. The father H.G. Henry
is in northern Minn. and can not be reached.
Dr James Henry came Mon. eve and took remains
this A.M. to LaHarpe where they will be buried
beside the mother.

HERMAN, LUDWID - Local - Dec 28, 1893 Ludwid
Herman was trundling a wheelbarrow down the Q
track, south of Quincy Friday A.M. when he was
struck by a train and killed.

HERNDON, FREDDIE - Recent Deaths - Feb 10, 1897
Died Freddie, 8 year old son of James Herndon
on Feb 2nd. Born Camp Point Jan 23, 1889.
Mother died of consumption when he was a baby.
Services by Rev A.N. Simmons Thurs. 2 P.M.
Buried village cemetery.

HERNDON, JAMES R. - Local - Feb 3, 1897 Little
son of James R. Herndon died Tues. afternoon.

HERNDON, MRS MARY J. - Deaths Latest Doings -
Apr 1, 1896 Died Mrs Mary J. Herndon Mar 30,
1896 sick many months, age 73 years 7 months 8
days. Married Apr 10, 1838 to Mr H. they came
to Camp Point 1857. Also lived Jacksonville a
few years. Mother of 3 sons and 3 daughters.
Two sons and 1 daughter and her husband survive
her. Last few years she and husband lived with
their son, Dr P.M. Herndon Jr where she died.
Funeral this morn at 10, burial later in the
village cemetery.

HERRON, HARRY - Golden - Jul 13, 1893 Harry
Herron an old german living on the Wabash in
the N part of town committed suicide this A.M.
by shooting himself. He was a peculiar old
fellow and has been queer in actions for
several years.

HERRON, SAMUEL T. See incorrect spelling
Harron. This is the compilers great
grandfather.

HESS, MRS APPALLOS - Ancient History - Aug 21,
1894 - Aug 20, 1875 Mrs Appalos Hess died in
Chicago from the effects of poison taken by
mistake. She had been a resident of Camp
Point.

HESS, GRANDERSON M. - Ancient History - Nov 12,
1895 - Nov 1877 Granderson M. Hess an early
settler in this locality died in Brown Co. age
69 years.

HESS, GRANDERSON M. - Ancient History - Dec 16,
1896 - Nov 1877 Granderson M. Hess, a pioneer
of Camp Point died at Mt Sterling.

HESTER, DOCK - Local - Mar 24, 1897 Dock
Hester, who was severly cut on the wrist a
couple weeks ago died Monday as a result of the
injuries. Was about 30 years old. Leaves wife
and 2 children.

143

HESTER, JOEL - Death Record - Mar 24, 1897
Died Joel Hester died Mar 22nd as a result of a
cut received 2 weeks ago from an ax. Born
Adams Co. May 7, 1866. Married 1891. Leaves a
wife and 3 children. Funeral from Methodist
Church, Coatsburg Tues. by Rev W.K. Herzog of
Columbus. Buried Coatsburg cemetery.

HESTER, JOHN H. - Local - Mar 31, 1897 In
noting the death of John H. Hester last week we
erroneously printed Joel Hester. Mr H. was
known as Dock. Sorry for the wrong name used.

HESTER, JOHN HENRY - Primrose - Apr 7, 1897
Rebecca Hester, wife of the late John Henry
Hester, better known as "Dock" Hester had a
sale Sat. Mrs H. will go to the home of her
folks near Chili.

HETRICK, MRS JOHN - Golden - Jun 8, 1893 Mrs
S. Hendricks and son and Dr E. Hetrick attended
the funeral of Mrs John Hetrick at Carthage
last Saturday.

HEUBNER, ALBERT - Primrose - Nov 19, 1895
Philip Peters of near Coatsburg came to Church
at York Neck Sunday eve to inform L.C.
Schroeder and family of the death of Louis
Heubner's little boy, Albert.

HEUBNER, ALBERT R. - Local - Nov 26, 1895
Albert R. Heubner, age 2 years 1 month 15 days
died Nov 17th from disease of the throat.
Services by Rev Klein. Burial in Coatsburg
Cemetery.

HEUBNER, MRS FRANK - Primrose - May 19, 1897
Mr and Mrs L.C. Schroeder attended the funeral
of Mrs Frank Heubner at Horeb Church, North
East twp.

HEUPTNER, MRS FRANK - Golden - May 12, 1897
Died at her home, Mrs Frank Heuptner, of
consumption Mon. May 10th. Services by Rev
Bell of Mt Sterling Tues. at Horeb Church.
Buried Horeb cemetery.

HEWITT, FRANCIS - Quincy - Mar 2, 1894 The will of Francis Hewitt which was admitted to probate Monday, the Presby Church of this city received a bequest of $200.00.

HICKS, MRS SUSAN - West Point - Mar 17, 1897 Died March 9th at 12:25 A.M., Mrs Susan Hicks age 75 years 5 months 9 days. Born Sep 30, 1821. She and husband came to Ill. 1851. He died 1878. Leaves 3 children and his 3 dead, alive are William and John Hicks and Miss Minerva Slattery. Funeral at ME Church. Buried in Cooke cemetery 6 miles W. of West Point.

HICKS, WILLIAM - Local - Sep 3, 1902 William Hicks, an old resident of Carthage and an old soldier, committed suicide last Wed. with carbolic acid. His wife took her own life in the same way about 2 years ago. He was a hard drinker.

HIETT, MISS MYRTLE - Local - Nov 18, 1903 Friends of Miss Myrtle Hiett will be pleased to learn that she is doing nicely in her school work at Sidney, NE. She is inclined to believe that the story of her death was somewhat exaggerated.

HIGGINS, CHARLES - Ancient History - Aug 21, 1894 - Aug 25, 1881 A tramp printer was killed while trying to get on a freight train in the yard here. Identified as Charles Higgins of Carthage.

HIGGINS, CHARLEY - Local - Sep 8, 1881 Charley Higgins who was supposed to have been killed a couple of weeks ago arrived at his mothers in Carthage.

HIGGINS, CHARLES - Mendon - Sep 8, 1881 Mrs Higgins of Carthage received a telegram from Springfield yesterday and signed by Charles Higgins saying it was not him who was killed at Camp Point by the cars and would be home today.

HILDEBRAND, THEODORE - Quincy - Oct 4, 1895

Theodore Hildebrand, an old resident of Adams Co. died at Eubanks age 62 years.

HILLS, WILBUR Z. - Suicide in Macomb - Jun 3, 1903 Suicide in Macomb Monday A.M. May 25th Wilbur Z. Hills, about 25 years old who for several years worked for Whitman and Price Hardware shop shot himself.

HILLYER, CHARLES - Murder at Bushnell - Sep 9, 1898 Killed Monday night Charles Hillyer of Macomb was killed at Bushnell during a heated political discussion. Frank Black, a Bushnell hack driver has been arrested and in jail in Macomb. Ed Kelley also suspected of having been connected.

HILMER, MRS HENRY - Sensation near Camp Point Mar 18, 1903 Northeast part of Camp Point twp, Mrs Henry Hilmer died. It appears Mrs H. gave birth to a child and that she was left without medical attention until neighbors sent for Dr Brown of Golden and Dr Bates of Camp Point. They done all they could for her. Child is still living. "Quincy Herald"

HILTON, REV T.B. - Local - Mar 27, 1894 Died Rev T.B. Hilton, pastor of the Vermont St. Methodist Church in Quincy died Sunday afternoon. Funeral this afternoon and remains taken to Chicago by train for burial.

HOBBS, DR WILLIAM T. - Death of Dr Hobbs - Jul 28, 1897 Died-Dr William T. Hobbs of Mounds at his home at that place Sun. P.M. at 10 July 18th. Born 4 miles S. of Clayton Jan 27, 1839. Raised on a farm. Married Miss Alice Young Feb 6, 1861 they had 4 children.

HOBBS, C.S. (JAB) - Was Hobbs Murdered - Dec 25, 1894 Think C.S. Hobbs (Jab) has met foul play in Oklahoma territory while visiting his sister, Mrs Jordan Maiden in Southern Kan. He was son of Josephus Hobbs of Concord twp. Father has written to Alva for more information.

HOBBS, JAB. - Local - Jan 4, 1895 Jab. Hobb,
the Concord man who was supposed to be killed
in Oklahoma has written to his friends that he
is all right.

HOFFMAN, CHARLES H. - Death - Jan 15, 1902
Charles H. Hoffman age 78 died at his home in
Mendon early Sat. A.M. Served as its
postmaster 20 years. Member of Episcopal
Church. Leaves a wife.

HOFFMAN, CHARLES W. - Quincy - Apr 16, 1902
William W. Benton has been appointed adm of the
estate of Charles W. Hoffman.

HOFFMAN, HARVEY - Local - Oct 12, 1893 Harvey
Hoffman, ex supervisor of McKee died in
Kellerville Tues. eve age 46 years. Leaves
wife and several children.

HOGAN, THOMAS - Local - Apr 13, 1893 Thomas
Hogan was instantly killed by lightning at
Bardolph Monday night of last week.

HOGSETT, MISS ANNA - Golden - Aug 12, 1896
Quite a number attended the funeral of Miss
Anna Hogsett, at LaPrairie Saturday.

HOGSETT, MISS ANNA - Death of Miss Anna Hogsett
Aug 5, 1896 Died Miss Anna Hogsett died Friday
A.M. at the home of her parents, Mr and Mrs
William Hogsett, LaPrairie. Sick 2 years from
consumption. Age 23 years. Services by Rev
W.H. McDonald at noon Saturday. Burial was at
York Neck cemetery in the afternoon.

HOKE, CATHERINE - Death Record - Mar 10, 1897
Died Catherine Hoke, daughter of Leonard and
Barbara Hoke, born Jefferson Co. KY Mar 5, 1817
died at the home of her nephew, J. Edward Omer
near Camp Point, Feb 25th age 79 years 11
months 20 days. Funeral from Pleasant View
Church Friday Feb 26th at 2 P.M. by Elder O.
Dilley. Buried church cemetery.

HOKE, MISS CATHERINE - Death Record - Mar 3,
1897 Died Miss Catherine Hoke died Thurs. at

the home of J. Ed Omer, age 80 years. She was
a sister of the late John A. Hoke and Mrs
Daniel Omer and has lived many years in Quincy
with Mrs Omer. Funeral at Pleasant View
Friday.

HOKE, MRS EUNICE - Full of Years - May 6, 1903
Mrs Eunice Hoke died May 2, 1903, age 87 years
3 months 9 days. Eunice Welsh was born in Ky.
Jan 23, 1816 and married John A. Hoke Nov 22,
1840. Came to Adams Co. 1844 and settled on a
farm in Clayton twp where she lived since. Mr
H. died Apr 1889 and since Mrs H. has had her
grandaughter, Mrs W.O. Smith for her companion.
Had 2 sons, both living and 1 daughter Mrs Mary
C. Manholland, who died in 1869, leaving a
daughter Mrs W.O. Smith. Also leaves a sister,
Mrs Elizabeth Garrett and a brother Moses S.
Welsh. Services Monday P.M. in Pleasant View
Church where she worshipped many years.

HOKE, MRS L.G. - Local - Jan 26, 1893 James E.
Funk and Mrs L.G. Hoke went to Kentucky Friday
night to attend the funeral of a sister.

HOLLENSTEIN, MRS AUGUST - Local - Dec 3, 1902
Mrs August Hollenstein of Columbus twp died
Monday age about 70 years. Had been an invalid
many years.

HOLT, JAMES - Co. Seat - Oct 14, 1896 James
Holt an inmate of the Soldiers Home who
recently came here from Peoria dropped dead
from heart disease while mopping the floor of
one of the cottages.

HOLTMAN, HENRY - Quincy - Jun 21, 1895 Henry
Holtman age 7 years died Wed. A.M. with
lockjaw, result of stepping on a rusty nail
nearly 3 weeks ago.

HONNOLD, GEORGE R. - Ancient History - Nov 26,
1902 - August 1884 George R. Honnold, father of
Mrs G.S. Collier was killed in Decatur when
struck by a train on the Illinois Central
Railroad.

HOOD, JOSEPH - Local - Jun 22, 1893 Monday
Joseph Hood a citizen of Payson fell from a
cherry tree hitting his head and died. Was
about 65 years old.

HOOTEN, PROF. J.E. - Suicide of Prof Hooten
Jun 18, 1902 Joliet, Ill June 14th Prof J.E.
Hooten, one of the best known educators in Will
Co. and for several years at the head of
Lockport Public Schools was found dying
yesterday in the Duncan hotel of this city.
Had turned on the gas. Died about 9 P.M. was
married and about 36 years old. Had been in
Lockport 7 years. Prof Hooten was well known
in Adams Co. and was principal of Mendon School
for 3 years and was an applicant as Supt of
Maplewood School 1895.

HORN, ADAM E. - Death - Feb 18, 1903 - Adam E.
Horn died in Chicago Thurs., the 12th inst,
after a brief illness. Lived several years in
Mendon twp. Was a conductor on the C.B. & Q
between Quincy and Galesburg from 1857-62.
Married 1860 to Miss Mattie Naylor of Macomb
who died about 3 years ago. Moved to Chicago
several years ago and was in livestock
commission business. Leaves 3 sons and a
daughter.

HORNAKER, MRS ANDREAS - Quincy - Mar 24, 1897
Died Mrs Andreas Hornaker, an old resident of
Adams co. Died in Gilmer twp age 80 years.

HORNEY, MRS CORA - Elm Grove - Apr 6, 1893 Mrs
Cora Horney, wife of Rev B.F. Horney, died at
her home in Bellflower, Ill Mar 29, 1893.
Brought to her former home and buried in Horeb
Church Cemetery last Sat. Was daughter of
Thomas and Mary Hulen (nee Burke). Born in Elm
Grove neighborhood where she grew up. Married
Rev B.F. Horney of the ME Church who is a
member of the Ill. Conference. Leaves husband
and a young daughter.

HORNEY, MRS CORA (FRANK) - Golden - Apr 6, 1893
Mrs Cora Horney (nee Hulen), wife of Frank
Horney was brought back from the east part of

the state last Friday night to be buried beside her mother in family lot at Horeb Church.

HORNEY, REV J.F. - Elm Grove - Apr 13, 1893 Rev J.F. Horney returned to his home at Bell Flower, Ill Friday eve after the burial of his wife here. His little daughter is left without a mother.

HOSTETTER, CARRIE - Quincy - Dec 22, 1897 The case of Carrie Hostetter, of St Louis who has the care and custody of William Byrd Lee vs Dr J.B. Shawgo, adm of the estate of Dr Alexander Lee, father of the boy, came to trial last week. She sued the adm. for $1,500 for care of the boy. Case dismissed.

HOSTETTER, MRS MARGARET - Obituary - May 11, 1894 Died Margaret Grosh born Washington Co. Maryland Jan 16, 1829 where she lived till 12 years old at which time her mother died. Taken by relatives in Penn. where she married Christian Hostetter Dec 7, 1848. He died Dec 24, 1861. She came to Adams Co. in 1865. Joined Evangelical Lutheran Church in 1862 at Elizabethtown, Penn. Mother of 4 sons and 1 daughter - 3 sons & 1 daughter survive her. Services at Methodist Church Tues. May 8th by Elder O. Dilley. Buried village cemetery.

HOSTETTER, MRS MARGARET - Local - May 8, 1894 Died Mrs Margaret Hostetter Monday afternoon. Funeral from Methodist Church at 3 PM Tues.

HOUGH, MRS JULIA - Local - Feb 16, 1893 Mrs Julia Hough, wife of John Hough, of the Wabash road and daughter of Geo. W. Lester, of Clayton died at Keokuk Sat. of heart disease. Remains were buried at Clayton Mon. Leaves husband and a daughter 2 years old.

HOWELL, WILLIAM - Probate Notice - Jan 2, 1894 William Howell, deceased 1st Monday of March 1894 (5th) Nancy J. Howell, adm.

HOWES, MISS OLIVE - Clayton - Mar 8, 1895 Miss Olive Howes died Sunday eve age 72 years.

Funeral Tues. at Presby Church. Came to
Clayton from Virginia in 1830.

HOWSER, JOHN - Local - Jan 22, 1895 John
Howser, a laborer dropped dead in a saloon in
Quincy Monday just as he received his pay for
working in the ice.

HOYT, MRS ALBERT - Death Record - Mar 3, 1897
Died Mrs Albert Hoyt died suddenly in Hannibal
Monday night where she and her husband were
visiting. Body brought to Camp Point Tues. and
taken to Thomas Willard's in Houston where the
funeral will be today. She was a sister of Mr
Willard's.

HOYT, MRS ALBERT - Local - Mar 3, 1897 Mrs
L.W. Miller was called to Hannibal Tuesday by
the death of her aunt, Mrs Albert Hoyt.

HOYT, MRS ALBERT - Local - Mar 10, 1897 A.G.
Hoyt of Johnstown, MO was here for his mother's
funeral, Mrs Albert Hoyt last Thursday.

HOYT, MRS E.G. - Golden - May 1, 1894 Died Mrs
E.G. Hoyt, sick only a few days.

HOYT, MRS E.G. - Golden - May 1, 1894 William
and Hiram Bacon of Huntsville attended the
funeral of their sister, Mrs E.G. Hoyt last
Friday.

HOYT, MRS MARY ELLEN - Obituary - May 1, 1894
Died Mrs Mary Ellen Hoyt, wife of Edwin G.
Hoyt. Born Jun 3, 1841 at Pulaski, Ill. Died
at her home in Golden Apr 25th, 1894. Was
daughter of Benjamin Bacon. Married Edwin G.
Hoyt Nov 26, 1861 by Rev A. Semple at the home
of her parents in Pulaski and moved with
husband to Houston twp Dec 25 of that year.
Where they stayed till Oct 10, 1893 when they
retired from farm and moved to Golden. They
had 5 children, 2 are dead. Leaves a husband
and Mrs Maggie C. Thomas, Benjamin F. and
Charles C. Hoyt. Services at ME Church in
Golden by Rev W.D. Atkinson and Rev R.A.
Hartrick of LaPrairie. Buried in the Pulaski

cemetery near those who proceded her.

HOYT, MRS SAMANTHA - North Houston - Mar 10, 1897 Died Mrs Samantha Hoyt, wife of Albert Hoyt died at Hannibal, MO Mon. A.M. Mar 1st age about 70 years. Buried Ebenezer cemetery. Services at Ebenezer Church Thurs. A.M. Leaves an aged husband and 4 children. Daughter of old Mr Willard who died in this neighborhood a number of years ago. Born Tenn. Came to Adams Co. Ill in early day and lived many years in North part of Houston twp. Was member of ME Church.

HUBER, MRS - Local - Mar 10, 1897 Mr and Mrs W.H. Scott and sons, Arny and Charlie of Quincy came Friday to attend funeral of Mrs Huber.

HUBER, MRS ANNA - Death Records - Mar 10, 1897 Died Mrs Anna Huber March 3rd at her home in Camp Point from pneumonia. Born in Niederlenz, Canton Argan, Switzerland Jun 3, 1823. Was 73 years 9 months old. Married in her native country in 1848 to Solomon Huber and same year they came to U.S. Stopped at New Orleans about 6 months and a short time in St Louis on to Quincy about 11 years. Camp Point remaining (Over 30 years) husband died Feb 10, 1885. Had 10 children, 4 still living-Mrs W.H. Scott, Quincy; Mrs J.E. Landon, Chicago; Miss Emma and Chas S. Huber of Camp Point. Services at family home Friday 2 P.M. March 5th. Buried village cemetery.

HUBER, CHARLEY - Local - Apr 9, 1895 Charley Huber was called to Chicago last week by the death of his little nephew. Returned home Saturday.

HUBER, FRANK - Local - Nov 26, 1902 Mr and Mrs C.K. Conner of New Philadelphia came down Sat. to attend the funeral of Frank Huber, who was Mrs C.'s nephew.

HUBER, HELEN - Local - Nov 4, 1896 Died Helen, little daughter of Mr and Mrs Lambert Huber died Mon. from croup. About 3 years old. Was the only daughter.

HUBER, MRS AND MRS MATT - Local - Nov 26, 1895
An infant son of Mr and Mrs Matt Huber was
buried Monday.

HUBER, ROY - Local - Aug 11, 1897 Mrs Nick
Schleicher and Mrs Fred Bash of Hannibal and
George Schleicher and Mrs E. Reeder of Quincy
attended the funeral of little Roy Huber
Thursday.

HUBER, ROY - Death Record - Aug 11, 1897
Little baby Roy Huber died last Wed. Buried
Thursday afternoon in village cemetry. Parents
are Mr and Mrs Mat Huber.

HUBER, WILLIAM FRANKLIN - Death of Frank Huber
Nov 26, 1902 William Franklin Huber, son of Mr
and Mrs Lambert Huber, died Friday eve, Nov
21st from typhoid fever. He was born Nov 4,
1885. Was 17 years 17 days old. Leaves
father, mother, 3 brothers and 1 sister.

HUDSON, MRS - "Necks" - Sep 20, 1895 Died on
Monday 3 P.M. at her home, Mrs Hudson age 78
years. Suffered cancer 3 years and it was the
cause of her death. Funeral by Rev Rose at
Union. Buried Coatsburg cemetery. Leaves 4
daughters and 3 sons.

HUDSON, CYRUS H. - 20 Years Ago - Jul 13, 1893
Cyrus H. Hudson while intoxicated, laid down on
the railroad tracks near Loraine and was killed
by a train.

HUDSON, MARY ELIZABETH - Death of a Babe - Oct
8, 1902 Mary Elizabeth, 6 month old daughter
of Mr and Mrs Elmer Hudson died Oct 4th been
ill several weeks. Funeral at family home in
Camp Point Sunday Oct 5th by O. Dilley.

HUFFMAN, NICHOLAS - Quincy - May 22, 1894 Died
Nicholas Huffman age 71 years for 41 years a
resident of this city. Died Wednesday A.M.

HUGHES, MRS DANIEL - Obituary - Oct 5, 1893

Mrs Daniel Hughes, daughter of William and Martha Poteet died at the home of her daughter, Mrs J.F. Bird in Mechanicsburg, Ill Sep 29th, 1893. Since death of her husband she had lived with her children and had gone the last week of July to Sangamon Co. where she took sick. Elizabeth Poteet was born near Winters Run, Hartford Co. Maryland Oct 4, 1814 and married Daniel Hughes in fall of 1837 and started across the Allegheny mountains reaching Hughes Station, Ohio and 18 years of her wedded life was spent here. They crossed the prairie of Ill. in wagons in Oct 1855 locating in Burton, Adams Co. on the Joseph Leverett farm. Mar 1, 1870 they moved to Payson, Ill to stay till Jan 30 1892 the date of Mr H.'s death. Was a member of Methodist Church over 50 years. Leaves 4 children--Mary Susan, wife of Senator Dean; James F. living in Adams Co.; Elijah B. of Hancock Co. and Annie E., wife of J.F. Bird of Sangamon Co.

HUGHES, JAMES - Killed by his Engine - Nov 11, 1896 James Hughes, fireman was killed by his engine Sat. at Perry, IA. Remains brought to Augusta Monday for burial. Was son of J.M. Hughes who lived Camp Point many years. Buried Augusta Cemetery. Worked for C.B. & Q.

HUGHES, JAMES A. - Death - May 21, 1902 James A. Hughes died at the home of his daughter, Mrs J.R. Downing, Greshane, NE on the 16th inst. age 77 years. Remains brought to LaPrairie where funeral services were held Tues. A.M. Buried Hebron cemetery near Camp Point. Came to Ill from Ind. when a lad and spent nearly his whole life in Adams Co. first near Camp Point, later at LaPrairie. Wife died 2 years ago, since then he has lived with his children.

HUGHES, NATHAN - Ancient History - Jul 14, 1897 Nov 1880 Nathan Hughes died on the 25th.

HUGHES, NATHAN - Ancient History - Dec 10, 1895 Dec 1880 Among the deaths reported first week was Nathan Hughes.

HUGHES, MRS W.M. - Ancient History - Jun 12,
1894 - Jun 8, 1877 Mrs W.M. Hughes died on the
2nd.

HULL, JOHN T. - Sale of Land - Dec 9, 1896
Sale of Land to pay estate bills of John T.
Hull, deceased by William J. Franks, adm. vs
Ellen Hull, Martin L. Hull, Eliza Hull, William
T. Hull, Frances Hull, Levi R. Hull, Rebecca
Hull. Sanford Hull, Lucy Hull, Curtis C. Hull,
Della Hull, Grant Hull, Belle Hull, Cora
Fusselman, Charles Fusselman, Effie Baker, John
Baker, Elizabeth J. Franks, Otis Sprague,
Stella Sprague, Claude Sprague, Bert Sprague,
Fred Sprague, Phebe A. Hartshorn, Emma Elliott
and William Grewe, defendants. Living out of
state is Wm T. Hull, Frances Hull, Levi R.
Hull, Rebecca Hull, Sanford Hull, Lucy Hull,
Otis Sprague, Stella Sprague, Bert Sprague,
Claude Sprague and Fred Sprague. Dated Quincy
Nov 11, 1896.

HUMKE, MRS CONRAD - Death Latest Doings - Apr
1, 1896 Mrs Conrad Humke died Mar 19th after
about a years illness. Was sister of John P.
and Herman Hokamp. Born Prussia Apr 14, 1833.
Came to U.S. Nov. 1852 and married Conrad Humke
Aug 1, 1855 in St Louis. During the war they
settled McKee twp where they lived since. Had
10 children, 6 of whom and her husband survive
her. Buried Sunday in the Lutheran cemetery in
Concord twp. Services by Rev Neumeister.

HUMMER, JOSEPH - Suicide of Macomb Man - Jul
23, 1902 Joseph Hummer, a former resident of
Macomb committed suicide Fri. eve last week at
his late home in Trenton, MO where he had a
photography gallery. Cause was poor health, 33
years old. Leaves wife and 6 children. Taken
to Macomb and buried Tuesday.

HUNSAKER, MRS ANNA E. - Co. Seat - Dec 9, 1896
Mrs Anna E. Hunsaker, widow of Perry Hunsaker,
the fireman who was killed by falling from a
burning building, died Thursday age 34 years.

HUNSAKER, CLIFFORD - Sad Bereavement - Aug 6,

1895 Clifford, the baby boy of Mr and Mrs W.L.
Hunsaker died Sat. with cholera infantum buried
village cemetery Monday.

HUNSAKER, MRS DAN - Local - Mar 16, 1894   Mrs
Dan Hunsaker went to Maryville, MO Tuesday
night to attend the funeral of her niece, Miss
Eva Kimmons.

HUNSAKER, ELMER - Recent Deaths - Jan 20, 1897
Died at the home of his parents, Jan 14th Elmer
Hunsaker of consumption. Born Nov 30, 1873 at
Liberty. Moved with parents to Camp Point 1875
where he lived since. Services by Rev Edwards
and Rev Simmons at the family home Sat. Jan
16th. Buried village cemetery. Parents Mr and
Mrs D. Hunsaker.

HUNSAKER, ELMER - West Point - Jan 20, 1897   Mr
Linn started last Sat. to Camp Point to attend
the funeral of his oldest grandson, Elmer
Hunsaker, but had to come back after getting
out of town 2 miles on account of the rain.

HUNSAKER, ELMER - Local - Jan 20, 1897   A.J.
Linn and Rolla Linn of Quincy attended the
funeral of Elmer Hunsaker Saturday.

HUNSAKER, MRS FERNANDO - Co. Seat - Nov 18,
1896   Died Mrs Fernando Hunsaker, a resident of
the city since 1850 died Thursday eve, age 70
years.

HUNSAKER, PERRY - Fire in Quincy - Jul 23, 1895
Perry Hunsaker, a fireman at Quincy was killed
when a wall fell in while fighting a fire last
night about 10 P.M. at Wright and Adam's
machine shop.

HUNSAKER, RACHEL - Obituary - Feb 27, 1894
Died Miss Rachel Hunsaker Sunday A.M. Feb 25th,
1894 at the home of her brother, Wiley Hunsaker
in Camp Point. Deceased was born Liberty twp
Adam Co. Jan 3rd, 1845. Had been an invalid a
long time. Services Mon. by Rev Dilley.
Buried at Kimmons burial ground near Liberty
where her brothers and parents are buried. She

leaves 2 sisters and 3 brothers.

HUNT, MRS LEM - Suicide - Mar 20, 1894   Mrs Lem
Hunt cut her own throat Fri.   Funeral Sunday.
About 50 years old.   Leaves husband and 3 grown
daughters, one married.   "Macomb Journal"
Lived and farmed 2 miles E. of Bushnell.

HUNT, MR T.G.M.   - Quincy - Nov 29, 1895   Mr
T.G.M. Hunt, who died Tues. night was one of
the pioneers of Quincy.   Came here between 1840
and 50 and ran a grocery store under the old
Quincy Pouse.   H.F.J. Ricker worked for him at
one time.   79 years old.   Leaves a wife who is
a daughter of the late Thaddeus Munroe.

HUNTER, A.J. & LAURA - North Houston - Mar 18,
1896   Died an infant child of A.J. and Laura
Hunter of Stillwell was buried in Ebenezer
cemetery Wed. of last week.   Mother is said to
be in critical condition.

HUNTER, MRS HUGH SR. - Death - Dec 6, 1895   Mrs
Hugh Hunter Sr who has been ailing for about a
year died at her home in Honey Creek twp Wed.
Dec 4th age about 75 years.   Funeral at Mendon
today.

HUNTER, MRS HUGH SR. - Necks - Dec 6, 1895   Mrs
Hugh Hunter Sr is very low.   The end expected
at any time.   She died Wednesday.

HUNTER, JAMES - Ancient History - Dec 9, 1903
Dec 1883 James Hunter, a well known Irish
citizen died after an illness of many years.

HUNTER, MRS JANE EDMONDS - Died - Dec 10, 1895
Mrs Jane Edmonds Hunter born Timby,
Pembrokeshire, Wales, Mar 21, 1821 died Dec 4th
at her home in Honey Creek twp, near Mendon.
At age 9 with her parents she moved to Ireland
and in her 20th year came to U.S. landing at St
Johns, Lower Canada and moving to Adams Co.
1844.   1845 she married Hugh Hunter by
RevAshbel G. Harned at Summer Mill, Carbon Co.
Penn.   Leaves 5 sons and 3 daughters who were
with her when she died.   Also leaves 2 sisters

of her father one of them is Mrs Mary Daugherty
of this vicinity. Joined Presby. Church 1841.
Funeral at Mendon ME Church by Rev R.A.
Hartrick. Buried Mendon Cemetery.

HUNTER, JOHN - Ancient History - Feb 1895 - Feb
1877 A lad named John Hunter was killed in
McKee twp by the falling of a dead tree.

HUNTER, JOHN - West Point - Nov 11, 1896 The 4
year old baby boy of John Hunter died on Wed.
Nov 4th at the home of his father near the
Webster school house. Funeral at Christian
Church Thursday. Buried West Point cemetery.

HURLEY, MIKE - Local - Jun 5, 1894 Died Mike
Hurley a switchman on the Q at Galesburg was
run over by the engine. Taken home and died at
8 Saturday eve.

HURST, S. - Quincy - Apr 8, 1896 The German's
Old Peoples Home received 60 acres of land
valued at $2,500 from the estate of S. Hurst in
Burlington twp Iowa.

INGLES, THOS. J. - Local - May 1, 1894 Killed
News from Rushville says Fri P.M. the 2 year
old daughter of Thos. J. Ingles of that city
was killed when her older brother dropped a
pitchfork on her head.

IRVIN, EDITH ALMA - Paloma - Jul 29, 1903
Edith Alma, daughter of J.F. and C.L. Irvin was
born in Houston twp Sept 20, 1886. Died July
23, 1903 age 16 years 10 months 3 days. Joined
Methodist Episcopal Church Sep 16, 1900.
Leaves father, mother, 3 sisters, 2 brothers.
Funeral at York Neck Church Friday July 24th by
Paloma ME Church pastor.

IRVIN, MISS EDITH A. - Local - Jul 29, 1903
Miss Edith A. Irvin died at the home of her
parents in Houston twp Thursday night, age 16.
She was daughter of Mr and Mrs John F. Irvin.
Cause of death was consumption. Funeral Sat.

IRWIN, DR C.N. - Local - May 7, 1902 Dr C.N.

Irwin, a widely known physician of Mt Sterling, died Apr 26th. His wife was a daughter of the late Rev L.W. Dulnap, a one time pastor of the Presbyterian Church here.

IVINS, MRS J.R. - "Mrs Ivins Laid to Rest" - May 22, 1894 Funeral of Mrs J.R. Ivins was at the Methodist Church Sun. P.M. Rev S.H. Whitlock was present. He had officiated at the baptism and marriage of Mrs Ivins. Mrs Ivins parents are Mr and Mrs Glascow of Mt Sterling.

IVINS, MRS JAS. R. - Death of Mrs J.R. Ivins - May 18, 1894 Died Mrs Jas. R. Ivins this A.M. from puerperal fever. Mr Ivins has been in Florida several months trying to recruit his broken health and is expected home tomorrow. Leaves 2 babes.

IVINS, REV J.R. - Rev J.R. Ivins at Rest - Feb 1, 1895 Funeral of Rev Jas. R. Ivins who died Sunday A.M. Jan 27th were held at Methodist church Tues. P.M. the 29th inst. Buried village cemetery beside Mrs Ivins who died last May. Leaves 2 little boys.

IVINS, REV J.R. - Local - Jan 29, 1895 It is expected that nearly all of the Methodist preachers in the Quincy district will attend the funeral of Rev J.R. Ivins today.

IVINS, REV JAMES R. - Death - Jan 29, 1895 Rev James R. Ivins died Sunday A.M. Jan 27th at 7. 29 years old. Suffered Brights disease 2 years forced to abandon ministry 1894. Went to Florida for his health and while gone his wife died. Leaving a little boy and baby girl. Was sent to Camp Point 1890. Leaves parents, 2 brothers and a sister. Funeral at Methodist Church this P.M.

IVINS, REV JAMES R. AND WIFE - Ivins in a Suit - Nov 5, 1895 Rev James R. Ivins and wife of the Ill. conference both died last year, leaving one small child, which at present is at James Glasgow's, the father of Mrs Ivins who was appointed guardian. Now Joseph Ivins of Camp

Point, father of Mr Ivins enters suit in county court to void Glasgow's guardianship and secure the same and the custody of the chid. Case comes up next Mon. "Mt Sterling Old Flag"

IVINS, MARY E. - Obituary - May 25, 1894 Died Mary E. Glascow born Jul 17, 1868 in Brown Co. Ill. Married Rev J.R. Ivins Dec 24, 1890. Went to Camden to live. In fall of 1891 they came to Camp Point for 2 years. Died May 18, 1894 at 6 A.M. Leaves 2 little ones, little Morris 2 -1/2 years old and a beautiful babe. Services at ME Church Sun. at 2:30 P.M. by pastor Rev S.H. Whitlock and Rev D.W. English.

IVINS, MORRIS - Local - Nov 15, 1895 Trial before Judge Vandeventer in county clerks office Mon. for custody of a child, one Morris Ivins, a son of the late Rev James R. Ivins who died in Camp Point several months ago. There were 2 children and Mrs and Mrs James Glasgow of this county was appointed guardian and given custody of the children. The grandparents on the fathers side, Mr and Mrs Joseph Ivins of Camp Point wished to raise 1 boy and therefore brought suit to get custody of the boy, Morris. Court sustained its previous action and left Mr Glasgow in possession of the children. "Mt Sterling Republican"

IVINS, PROF W.C. - Local - May 22, 1894 Prof W.C. Ivins, principal of Stronghurst public school came down to attend the funeral of his brothers wife.

JACKSON, JOSEPH - Drowned at Warsaw - Jul 1, 1896 - Joseph Jackson of Keokuk was drowned in the Mississippi just above Warsaw Friday while seining for minnows. Jackson was married in a balloon at Quincy on July 4, 1893 and his wife survives him.

JACOBS, BENJAMIN FRANKLIN - Aeronaut Killed - Aug 19, 1896 Quincy, Ill. Aug 16th before a large crowd of people in Baldwin Park at 6 this eve Benjamin Franklin Jacobs balloon collapsed and parachute failed to open. Killed. Jacobs

was 32 years old and married. He formerly
lived here with parents but recently had
traveled.

JACOBS, CLARENCE & EVA - North Houston - Jul
15, 1896 - Died the infant daughter of Clarence
and Eva Jacobs died July 7th age 2 years 4
months 2 days of cholera infantum. Funeral by
Elder Peck of Bowen at Ebenezer Church Thurs.
Buried in the cemetery nearby.

JACOBS, MRS ELIZA A. - Death - Sep 10, 1902
Mrs Eliza A. Jacobs, wife of Henry F. Jacobs
died Fri Sept 5th age 61 years. Eliza Ann
Barnaby was born in Ind. Jun 19, 1841. Married
Henry F. Jacobs Oct 29, 1859. Came to Ill.
fall of 1864. They had 5 sons, 3 daughters of
whom 1 son and 2 daughters died before her.
Her father and 6 brothers also survive her.
Joined the Methodist Church at Ebenezer about
25 years ago. Family has lived in Camp Point a
few years. Funeral Sun A.M. at Ebenezer Church
Houston twp by Rev F.A. McGaw.

JACOBS, GEO. M. - Local - Apr 17, 1894 Died
the little daughter of Geo. M. Jacobs,
Plainville. Died Friday, buried Camp Point
cemetery Sat. P.M.

JACOBS, JOHN - Primrose - Jul 13, 1894 We are
sorry to learn of the death of John Jacobs, a
well known farmer of Houston twp. Near 60
years old. Leaves a wife and 6 children.

JACOBS, JOHN W. - Local - Jun 22, 1894 Died
John W. Jacobs, of Houston twp who has been an
invalid for several weeks. Died Thurs. A.M.
Leaves a widow and several children. Funeral
at Ebenezer tomorrow A.M.

JACOBS, JOHN WILLIAM - Adm's Sale - Aug 14,
1894 Sept 6, 1894 at the late home of John
William Jacobs, deceased in Houston twp,
personal property, livestock, implements, etc.
Henry F. Jacobs, adm. Aug 13, 1894

JACOBS, M. - Local - Dec 18, 1894 Died M.

Jacobs, a clothing merchant of Quincy died Mon.
Native of Germany but lived Quincy since 1860
and 25 years had a clothing store.

JACOBS, SAMUEL - Death - Apr 8, 1903 Samuel
Jacobs died at the Soldiers Home. Born
Louisville, KY Feb 28, 1837. Came to Columbus
as a child and lived most of his life there.
Served 3 years in 78th Ill. Inf. Married
Martha L. Sawin 1867 and she and 2 sons survive
him. Leaves also 2 brothers, James H. of Camp
Point and Peter S. of Chicago, 1 sister Mrs
M.K. Johnson of Chili. Buried at Columbus.

JACOBS, MR AND MRS W.P. - Local - Oct 22, 1902
Infant daughter of Mr and Mrs W.P. Jacobs died
at their home in Quincy Tuesday. To be buried
in Camp Point cemetery Thursday afternoon.

JACOBS, WILLIAM - Kicked by a Horse - Nov 3,
1897   William Jacobs a liveryman of LaGrange,
MO was kicked in the stomach by a horse at
Williamstown Thurs. Died Sat. 11 P.M. Was son
of Mr and Mrs Henry Jacobs of Camp Point.
Remains reached Camp Point Monday P.M.
Services Tues. at Ebenezer Church in Houston
twp near Mr Jacobs former home. Was about 30
years old. Lived LaGrange about 3 years.

JAHN, CHARLES - Quincy - Nov 5, 1902 Charles
Jahn, age 38 years died at Blessing hospital
Tuesday night from lockjaw.

JAMISON, WILLIAM - Is Jamison Insane? - Jul 6,
1893 The question of sanity of William Jamison
the comdemned murderer of Charles Aaron was
brought before Judge Bonny of circuit court
last week. Jury returned verdict, sane.

JANES, REV LESTER - Quincy - Jan 6, 1897 Three
members of the Methodist Church in this city
have died recently - Rev Lester Janes, H.H.
Markley and Mrs Lyford, who died in Calif.

JANES, REV LESTER - Death of Rev L. Janes - Dec
23, 1896 Rev Lester Janes died at his home in
Quincy Fri. A.M. 84 years old. Was a Methodist

minister. Pastor of Camp Point church 30 years ago. Leaves a widow and 5 sons of whom George M. Janes is well known in Camp Point.

JANSEN, ALF - Local - May 15, 1894 Alf Jansen of Canton a young tailor Friday forenoon started up town and was struck by a freight train and ground to pieces. He was under the influence of liquor.

JASPER, GEORGE E. - Quincy - Feb 12, 1902 George F. Jasper Jr. has been elected treasurer of the Quincy Building and Loan Assoc., vice George E. Jasper, deceased.

JASPER GEORGE F. - Local - Jan 29, 1902 George F. Jasper, cashier of Quincy National Bank was stricken with apoplexy last Tues. and died Thurs. night. Was son of the late Thomas Jasper. Leaves a wife and several children.

JASPER, HON. THOS. - Ancient History - Aug 25, 1897 Dec 1880 Hon. Thos. Jasper died in Quincy on the 25th.

JEANS, JOE - Quincy - Jul 30, 1895 Joe Jeans, a farmer living 1 mile E. of New Canton, Ill. committed suicide Friday at 2. Was a farmer 66 years old married on the 4th of this month to his 2nd wife. She being a widow living in St Louis, having 2 children. He owns 110 acres.

JEFFREY, JOHN - Columbus - Dec 23, 1903 John Jeffrey, one of the oldest residents of Gilmer twp died at the home of his son, George in Paloma, Ill Dec 16th. Services by Rev W.E. Rose in Baptist Church of Paloma of which he was one of the founders, Dec 13, 1903. Buried our cemetery.

JENNINGS, MRS MOLLIE - Prairie - Jun 8, 1893 Funeral sermon of Mrs Mollie Jennings was at Pleasant Grove last Sunday A.M. Death caused by consumption. Leaves husband and son and many relatives.

JESTER, FLORA - Local - Mar 23, 1894 Word

received of death at Liberal, KS of Mrs Bahr,
formerly Flora Jester who was well known here a
few years ago.

JIMISON, JOHN - Clayton - Jan 26, 1894   James
Jimison who has been here since the death of
his brother, John, departed for Oklahoma.

JIMISON, JOHN - Funeral - Jun 8, 1893   Funeral
of John Jimison was at Christian Church in
Clayton 10 A.M. Tuesday by Elder H.G.
VanDervoort.

JIMISON, JOHN - Death - Jun 8, 1893   John
Jimison, Co. Supt of Schools died at Liberty
Sat. eve, the 3rd inst from a complication of
the bowel and bladder and malaria.   Remains
taken to Clayton Mon. and buried Tues. by the
Odd Fellows.   Born in Liberty twp about 48
years ago. Began teaching at 18.   Never
married.   Parents are dead, but he has 3
sisters and a brother surviving him.   He was in
the drug business in Clayton with his brother
in law, David A. Davis.

JOHNSON, C.D. - Death - Sep 13, 1895   Mr C.D.
Johnson died at his home on Pea Ridge Monday
A.M. of heart disease after digging potatoes.
Age 3 score years and ten.   Two other members
of his family died of heart disease, brother,
Willis died at the show ground here a few years
ago and a sister, Mrs Ann Piles died of same in
MO.   Mr Johnson leaves wife and 11 children-9
sons and 2 daughters.   Funeral Wed. by Elder
Jacob Crawford.   "Clayton Enterprise"

JOHNSON, CHARLES - Ancient History - Sep 16,
1903 - Sept 1883   Charles Johnson and O.B. Ward
were poisoned by drinking "Prickly Ash Bitters"
and died in a short time.   Leander Miller was
with them and suffered severly but recovered.

JOHNSON, CHARLEY - 10 Years Ago - Sep 28, 1893
O.B. Ward and Charley Johnson were poisoned by
drinking bitters and both died.

JOHNSON, CHURCHILL J. - Our Neighbors - Aug 26,

1896 Sat. the 15th inst, Churchill J. Johnson
died at his home in Camden twp age 87 years.
Born Tenn. and settled Rushville 1829. Had
lived Schuyler Co. for more than 60 years.

JOHNSON, JOHN - Soldiers buried in Camp Point
Cemetery - May 4, 1893 - Listed in Co. D, 153rd
Illinois Infantry.

JOHNSON, HORACE G. - Inquest - Sep 23, 1903 At
Kellerville, the death of Horace G. Johnson, a
farmer living on the Brown Co. line, 70 years
old, fell from a hay mow and was found by a
grandson. Was a resident of McKee twp. Leaves
wife and family. "Whig"

JOHNSON, REV I.M. - Death Record - Aug 11, 1897
Rev I.M. Johnson a Methodist clergyman died at
LaPrairie Sunday A.M. He was at Lima and
Kinderbrook before going to LaPrairie. Forced
to quit 1892 for health. Was about 55 years
old. Leaves wife and 4 daughters. Funeral at
Methodist Church in LaPrairie Tuesday by Rev
English. Buried in Pulaski cemetery.

JOHNSON, IDA M. - Local - Jul 23, 1895 Judge
Glenn has granted a new trial to Ida M. Johnson
sentenced at Galesburg to 10 years last week
for the manslaughter of her husband.

JOHNSON, JAMES W. - Quincy - Jul 14, 1897
James W. Johnson, a newspaper solicitor died
suddenly from an attack of cholera morbus
Friday A.M. age 62 years.

JOHNSON, MRS JUDITH - Local - Mar 12, 1902 Mrs
Judith Johnson died Monday at Independence, MO
age about 80 years. Was sister of the late
William A. Booth and married in Ursa twp.
Lived number of years in Hancock Co. Remains
brought to Quincy Mon. night for burial.

JOHNSON, MRS JUDITH - Death - Mar 12, 1902 Mrs
Judith Johnson, widow of the late John S.
Johnson and sister of the late William A. Booth
died at Independence, MO March 10th, about 80
years old. Remains brought to Quincy Mon.

night. Funeral today. Leaves 4 children and 2
sisters, Mrs John L. Moore and Mrs E.B. Turner
in vicinity of Quincy.

JOHNSON, MISS LUCY - Quincy - Jul 24, 1894
Died Miss Lucy Johnson of Mendon age 49 years
died at Blessing hospital Thursday night.

JOHNSON, MRS RICHARD - Recent Death - Oct 14,
1896 Mrs Richard Johnson, of Columbus twp died
Mon. night during confinement.

JOHNSON, MRS SARAH A. - Ancient History - Jun
12, 1894 - Jun 7, 1878 Mrs Sarah A. Johnson
died in Coatsburg on the 4th.

JOHNSON, SIDNEY - Quincy - Dec 30, 1896
Chauncey H. Castle has been appointed
conservator of the estate of Sidney Johnson.

JONES, GEORGE - Local - Oct 14, 1903 George
Jones, a Colchester miner, was killed Tues.,
being crushed in a mine under timbers and rock,
owing to the breaking of the timbers. He
leaves a wife and 6 children.

JONES, JOHN - Elm Grove - May 20, 1897 Died,
John Jones age 75 at his home near Pine Grove
Wed. of last week from heart disease.

JONES, MYRA - Murder at Carthage - Dec 20, 1895
Myra Jones of Siloam a waitress at the Phoenix
Hotel, Carthage died Monday from effects of an
abortion about 2 weeks ago. Remains taken to
Siloam Springs Tuesday for burial. A
Burlington, IA dispatch says -- Dr W.H. Veath,
a doctor at Carthage, Ill was held in $10,000
bond and Charles Stepp and Wm Currier, young
men of the town in $5,000 each for causing the
death this afternoon of Miss Myra Jones a
domestic, from criminal operation.

JONES, THOMAS - Suicide in Ellington - Sep 24,
1902 Thomas Jones, living with his brother in
law, Henry Henhoff, near Locust Grove,
committed suicide last Wed. by hanging himself
in the barn. 35 years old had suffered from

the effects of a sun stroke from which he never
recovered.

JONES, WILLIAM - 10 Years Ago - Feb 23, 1893
William Jones, father of Mrs Benjamin Wigle,
died at her home.

JORDINE, MAUD - Late News - Jul 15, 1903 Maud
Jordine, 17 years old was arrested at
Bloomington Monday for the murder of her baby
sister, age 2 years.

JOSEPH, MAUD - Death - Jun 1, 1893 Maud
Joseph, daughter of Mr and Mrs J.F. Joseph died
Wed. eve after a surgical operation for a tumor
on Tues. A.M. Died about 9 P.M. Wed. Funeral
10 A.M. Friday from the family home.

JOSEPH, MAUD - Obituary - Jun 8, 1893 Maud
Joseph was born in Camp Point Apr 9, 1879 and
died at her home in Camp Point May 31st. Was
14 years 1 month 22 days. Converted and joined
ME Church during winter of 1889. Leaves mother
and father.

JOSEPH, SALO D. - Quincy - Feb 20, 1894
Remains of Salo D. Joseph who died in Cannes
France arrived here Thurs. funeral from the
home of his parents, Mr and Mrs Martin Joseph
Friday afternoon.

JOSEPH, SALO - Quincy - Feb 2, 1894 Cablegram
received from Mr and Mrs Martin Joseph saying
they have started for home with the remains of
their son, Salo, who died in Cannes, France.
Will arrive here in about 10 days.

JOSSLYN, MRS ELIZABETH - Quincy - Jul 30, 1902
Mrs Elizabeth Josslyn and Elijah Brobst, of
this city have been notified to attend the
meeting of the Brobst heirs, in Philadelphia
within a short time. Heirs claim property in
the Penn. coal regions valued at more than
$1,000,000,000.00.

JUDY, MRS E.V. - Local - Feb 12, 1902 Mrs E.V.
Judy died Mon. A.M. at the home of her

daughter, Mrs G.P. Stump near Columbus. She
was widow of Philip Judy and well advanced in
years.

JUDY, PARIS T. - Ancient History - Jun 26, 1897
Apr 1880 Paris T. Judy, of Gilmer twp died.

JUDY, PARIS T. - Ancient History - May 24, 1895
May 1880 Paris T. Judy of Gilmer twp died.

JUDY, PARIS - Local - Apr 9, 1902 Mrs W.A.
Berrian went to Decatur last week to attend the
funeral of Paris Judy's little girl, the little
girl had scarlet fever some months ago, from
which she never recovered.

JUDY, PHILIP S. - Probate Notice - Oct 20, 1897
Philip S. Judy, deceased 1st Monday of Dec.
1897 (6th) Elizabeth V. Judy, Ex.

JUDY, PHILIP S. - Will of Philip Judy - Oct 20,
1897 The will of the late Philip S. Judy was
admitted to probate Sat. wife was named exec.
bond set at $52,000. Will was dated Sep 21,
1892. Heirs were Elizabeth V. Judy, Sarah Ann
Cook, Catherine Aaron, Luella Grosh, Eli F.
Judy, Olive Stump, Philip S. Judy and Wm Roy
Judy the latter is a grandson. Estate valued
at about $60,000.

JUDY, PHILIP S. - Sale of Real Estate - Jun 18,
1902 Sale of real estate by Executors of
Philip S. Judy, estate. Eli F. Judy   Philip
S. Judy as executors of the last will and
testament of Philip S. Judy, deceased. F.M.
McCann, attorney.

JUDY, PHILIP S. - Philip S. Judy Dead - Sep 1,
1897 "Uncle Phil" Judy died Sat. A.M. at the
home of his daughter, Mrs G.P. Stump in Gilmer
twp, age 85 years. Born Kentucky came to Adams
Co. 1840 and engaged in farming and stock
raising. Became one of the wealthiest men in
the county. Leaves a wife and 6 children: Mrs
C. Aaron, Mrs E.L. Grosh of Big Neck, Mrs A.F.
Cook of Leon, KS, E.F. Judy of Houston twp, Mrs
G.P. Stump of Columbus and P.S. Judy Jr. of

Gilmer twp.   Funeral in Methodist Church
Columbus Monday afternoon.

KAELTZ, ADOLPH - Quincy - Oct 8, 1895 Will of
Adolph Kaeltz admitted to probate leaves son,
Andrew Kaeltz $100.00 rest of estate divided
between his daughters Mrs Joseph Vanden-Boom of
Quincy and Mrs Solon Harwood of Middleton, OH.

KANE, HENRY - Quincy - Nov 5, 1895 Will of
Henry Kane admitted to probate left property to
his daughter, Mrs Christian Reushold. Fredrick
Quest appointed executor.

KAUFFMAN, EDWARD - Brakeman Killed - Nov 30,
1894 Monday 6 P.M. Edward Kauffman, a brakeman
on the Pittsfield branch fell between the cars
and was killed instantly. He had lived
Pittsfield and was 26 years old, unmarried.
Was brother of William Kauffman, the present
engineer in the local freight. "Griggsville
Reflector"

KAUFFMAN, FRANK - Death - Jan 15, 1902 Frank
Kauffman of Clayton twp died Wed. eve. Was of
German birth. Leaves a wife and several
children.

KEATH, CLARENCE R. - Suicide of Clarence R.
Keath - Apr 17, 1894 Died-News received in
Quincy Friday of the death of Clarence R. Keath
at Dayton, Ohio. Was son of Capt U.H. Keath of
Quincy. Suicide. Traveled for E. Silverthorne
and Co. Lumber dealers of Chicago.

KECK, EVERETT E. - Local - Sep 22, 1897 Died
Everett E. Keck, a traveling grocery salesman,
formerly of Quincy died at Wichita Saturday.
He was well known in Camp Point. His wife was
Miss Fannie Butler, a niece of Geo. W. Butler.

KEENAN, MRS HIRAM T. - Local - Dec 16, 1903
Mrs Hiram T. Keenan died at Ft. Worth, Texas,
on the 8th, age 63 years. She was daughter of
the late J.W. Fawbush of Lima twp. The
Keenan's lived in Camp Point in the 60's.

KEENAN, JOSEPH - Ancient History - Aug 14, 1894
Aug 14, 1874 - Joseph Keenan died on the 9th.

KEENAN, MRS REBECCA A. - Ancient History - Feb
22, 1895 - Feb 1875 Mrs Rebecca A. Keenan widow
of Joseph Keenan died January 31st.

KEENER, MISS EMMA - Miss Keener's Suicide - Jul
15, 1896 Macomb, Ill July 14   Miss Emma
Keener living in Sciota twp committed suicide
Sunday afternoon by shooting herself. Family
was downstairs. Brother found her.

KEGLEY, MRS JACK - Local - Feb 4, 1903 Mrs
Jack Kegley was called to Lake Geneva, Wisc.
Saturday night by the death of a sister.

KEGLEY, JOHN L. - Local - Mar 4, 1903 John L.
Kegley, of the Pioneer Creamery received a
telegram Monday A.M. telling of the death of
his mother at West Salem, Edwards Co. He and
Mrs Kegley left Monday night for West Salem.

KELLER, C.H. - Killed at Zearing - Nov 4, 1903
C.H. Keller, of Golden, a brakeman for the
Burlington R.R. died Thurs. afternoon in the
hospital at Galesburg after being run over by
his train at Zearing, a little station on the
run from Streator to Galesburg. Sister is Rose
Keller who was called and reached Galesburg
before he died. Leaves parents, Mr and Mrs
Henry Keller, 3 sisters Misses Emma, Lena and
Rose and a brother Henry. He was 24 years old
and worked for C.B. & Q for nearly 3 years with
headquarters out of Galesburg. Burial at
Golden Friday.

KELLER, GEORGE - Quincy - Jan 28, 1903 Will of
George Keller provides for an annual income for
his widow during her life time and then directs
the estate to go to his children in equal
amounts 5 years after the death of the mother.

KELLER, GEORGE - Dead - Jan 21, 1903 George
Keller, a farmer of Liberty died Friday eve in
his 73rd year. Born in Germany and came to
U.S. when he was 20 years old and a few years

later settled at Liberty. Leaves widow, 7 sons and 1 daughter.

KELLER, HENRY - Local - Jul 23, 1895 Word has been received of the death of Henry Keller at Stillwater, Oklahoma on the 4th. He was charging a cannon when it exploded. Former resident of Liberty, 47 years old, son of George Keller.

KELLEY, A.B. - Local - Jun 3, 1896 - W.S. Tobie, Mr West and Free West of Augusta came down Sunday to attend the funeral of A.B. Kelley.

KELLEY, A.B. - Sudden Death of A.B. Kelley - June 3, 1896 Died Friday night Col. A.B. Kelley was found dead. Adolphus B. Kelley born Fairhaven, Mass. Dec 21, 1839. Came to Ill. 1860 stopped short time Springfield then to Camp Point where he had a jewelery store. Enlisted in Ill. Inf. during the war at Springfield. Married Oct 8, 1867 to Miss Eleanor Bailey, daughter of Thomas Bailey who lived only a few years after marriage. Second he married Miss Annie Leach Jun 18, 1884 who with 3 children survive him. Funeral at his home Sunday afternoon by Rev Wm Stewart of Quincy, an old time friend. Buried village cemetery.

KELLEY, MR AND MRS A.B. - Local - Aug 7, 1894 Mr and Mrs A.B. Kelley lost their babe Saturday. Funeral from their home Sunday P.M.

KELLEY, ADOLPHUS B. - Probate Notice - Jun 24, 1896 Adolphus B. Kelley, deceased 1st Monday of Sept., 1896 (7th) Anne F. Kelley, adm.

KELLEY, G.E. - Burned to Death - Sep 10, 1895 Saturday A.M. Orpha Johnson, a domestic in the family of G.E. Kelley, Macomb was burned to death when her clothes caught fire while preparing breakfast. Lived Bardolph, 24 years old, father dead, mother survives her.

KELLEY, THOMAS - County Seat - May 6, 1895

Died Thomas Kelley in the insane ward of the
county farm Sat. was formerly inmate of the
Milwaukee Soldiers Home. Was member of Co. D
16th Ill. Inf. George M. Janes was his
conservator. Was taken to county farm because
no room at Jacksonville. 70 years old.
Remains were brought to this city and Sunday
eve they were taken to the Home, where funeral
was held. No relatives.

KELLY, THOMAS - A Member of the 16th - May 27,
1896 Died at the poor farm Thomas Kelly
formerly of the Co. D 16th Ill Vol. Inf. He
drew $72.00 pension per month for many years.
65 to 70 years old had lost track of a brother
in America and his people in Ireland. Buried
at Soldiers Home cemetery. (The complete
obituary was to long to copy)

KEMP, MRS RHODA C. - Ancient History - Nov 12,
1895 Nov 1881 Mrs Rhoda C. Kemp died age 61
years.

KENDALL, MRS H.W. (Dr.) - Died from Fright -
May 29, 1894 Died Mrs H.W. Kendall (Dr.) was
out driving with another lady when the horse
runaway. Mrs Kendall died of a heart disease
in a few minutes after horse stopped by a
fence. Maiden name Collins, born Liberty Apr
8, 1840 leaves husband, son and a daughter.

KENDALL, DR HENRY W. - Death - Dec 2, 1903 Dr
Henry W. Kendall, of Quincy died last Wed., age
72 years. Was a surgeon of 50th Ill. during
the Civil War and since war practiced medicine
in Quincy.

KENDRICK, WILLIAM - Local - Mar 2, 1894
William Kendrick of Clayton died Sunday.

KENNEDY, GEORGE - Ancient History - Apr 1, 1903
Mar 29, 1883 George Kennedy, a one time
resident of Columbus was killed at Emerson, MO
by Henry C. Williams who shot Kennedy in a
quarrel about William's wife who had deserted
him.

KENNEDY, SARAH J. - Death - Jun 28, 1895 Sarah
J. oldest daughter of William and Rachel
Kennedy born Ligonier Valley, PA Nov 25, 1833.
Moved with parents to Adams Co. 1851. Married
J.H. Kirkpatrick Apr 1, 1853 lived Camp Point
till 1860 when they moved to Durham and on to
Carthage 1864. Died at her home in this city
2:30 A.M. Tuesday June 25th. Had 8 children, 5
and husband survive her; Mrs Crit Sympson,
William A., Fletcher, Stella A. and Arthur C.
"Carthage Republican"

KENNEY, MRS JERUSHA - Ancient History - Apr 21,
1897 - May 1879 Mrs Jerusha Kenney died.

KERLEY, PLEASANT H. - Death - Mar 5, 1902
Pleasant H. Kerley born at Hartsville, Tenn.
Jan 13, 1840 died at Camp Point, Friday Feb
28th, age 62 years 1 month 10 days. At age 11
went with parents and 2 sisters to Brown Co.
Ill. 1851. Enlisted in 3rd Ill. Cavalry during
Civil War and served 3 years and reenlisted
1more year. Married Mrs Lucy Hicks Jul 10,
1883. Leaves wife, an adopted daughter, his
aged father, King Kerley of Brown Co. and 4
half brothers. Services Saturday 3 P.M. in
Christian Church by Elder J. Thomas Webb.
Buried village cemetery.

KERN, C.M. - Golden - Apr 2, 1895 Abner Sears
and wife of Clayton attended the funeral
services of C.M. Kern at Golden last Sunday.

KERN, C.M. - Golden - Apr 2, 1895 Funeral of
C.M. Kern, one of the old landmarks was Sunday
at 2 P.M. at the ME Church. Buried York Neck
graveyard by LaPrairie Lodge #267 A.F. & A.M.
of which he was a member 35 years.

KERN, CHARLES M. - Death - Apr 2, 1895 Charles
M. Kern died at Jacksonville insane hospital
Sat. A.M. where he was taken 2 weeks ago.
Remains brought to Golden Sun. A.M. and funeral
at Methodist Church 2 P.M. Burial in York Neck
Cemetery. Leaves a wife, 4 sons, 1 daughter.
Lived this vicinity 54 years. Spent his youth
in Houston and about 40 years in La Prairie.

KERN, JOHN - Quincy - Feb 5, 1902 John Kern,
of McPherson, KS age 57 years died at the home
of his sister, Mrs Mary Lesem on Wednesday.

KERN, ROBERT - Golden, - Apr 2, 1895 Robert
Kern of Decatur, engineer on the Wabash R.R.
came home Sunday A.M. to attend his fathers
funeral.

KERROLINE, WILLIE - Columbus - Dec 2, 1903 On
Sunday A.M. Nov. 29th little Willie, son of
Stanley Kerroline died. His mother died just 3
years ago.

KESPOHL, MISS IDA - Quincy - Feb 15, 1895 Miss
Ida Kespohl died Sunday A.M. age 21 years.

KESSLER, WALTER - Local - Aug 6, 1902 Walter
Kessler was called to Cowden Sunday by the
death of his sister.

KESTINGSCHAFER, HENRY - Probate Notice - Nov
12, 1902 Henry Kestingschafer, deceased 1st
Monday in Jan. 1903 William P. Simon,
Executor.

KETCHUM, WILLIAM - Ancient History - May 26,
1897 - December 1879 William Ketchum was
murdered in Warren Co. He lived at a former
period in Camp Point.

KETCHUM, WM B. - Echo of Mormon War - Mar 26,
1902 Wm B. Ketchum whose obituary was
published last week was one of a detail of 12
of the Augusta Cavalry Co., Capt Jas. E. Dunn,
who during the Mormon troubles in 1844 were
sent by Gov. Ford to serve summon on Joseph
Smith and bring him to Carthage. They returned
without finding him and next day the Smith's
gave themselves up and next night were murdered
in the jail. Of the 12 only 2 are known to be
alive. S.S. Benson, Esq. of Huntsville and
R.H. Bacon of Golden. Capt Dunn at one time
ran a hotel on the Matilda Graham property now
owned by Henry King. Mr B. also of Augusta at
that time and after run a wagon shop near where
Dr Grigson now lives. "Augusta Eagle"

KEYES, EDWARD - Quincy - Aug 6, 1902 Edward
Keyes, formerly of this city was killed last
week in a runaway accident in Oklahoma.

KICKHOEFEL, HENRY - Death - May 7, 1895 Henry
Kickhoefel died at his home in Concord twp May
2nd, age 75 years 2 months 11 days. Born
Germany Feb 19, 1820. Came to U.S. 1850 and
settled in Concord twp where he married Mrs
Elizabeth Klempp in 1865. Leaves his wife and
4 grown children. Services at Union Church in
Columbus twp Sat. May 4th by Elder O. Dilly.
A large group followed them to the grave.

KICKHOEFEL, HENRY - Local - May 7, 1895 Death
of Henry Kickhoefel Thursday night. Funeral
at Union Church in Columbus Sat. P.M. Mr K.
was a German who settled in Concord twp nearly
30 years ago. Leaves a wife and several
children.

KICKHOFEL, HENRY - Probate Notice - May 17,
1895 Henry Kickhofel, deceased 1st Monday in
July 1895   Annie E. Kickhofel

KIEFER, MRS CLARA - Quincy - Jan 15, 1902 Mrs
Clara Kiefer, widow of Jacob Kiefer and a
resident of this city since 1853 died Thursday
night age 69 years.

KIMBER, R.M. - Dead - Nov 11, 1903 R.M.
Kimber, Supt of the Galesburg division of the
C.B. & Q died in Galesburg Thursday night of
cancer. Funeral Sunday. Dick Kimber lived a
few years of his youth in Camp Point. Was a
nephew of the late S.L. Clarke and married Miss
Emma Thompson, a niece of Mrs Clarke. The wife
and one son survive him.

KIMBER, R.M. - Local - Nov 11, 1903 Mr and Mrs
L.O. Sutton and Mrs P.C. Folckemer attended the
funeral of R.M. Kimber in Galesburg Sunday.

KIMMEL, MR HENRY - West Point - Dec 28, 1893
Mr Henry Kimmel was called to Creal Springs
last week on account of the death of his
mother.

KIMMONS, EVA - Took Strychnine - Mar 16, 1894
Died-Maryville (MO) Democrat reports Eva
Kimmons went to Maryville Monday afternoon and
purchased strychnine and took it while going
home and died on the highway.

KIMMONS, EVA - Kimmons Suicide - Mar 23, 1894
She left 2 letters, one to parents and one to
her lover to whom she was engaged, William
Hughes.

KIMMONS, EVA - Suicide of Eva Kimmons - Mar 13,
1894 Word received by Mrs Kenner Seaton from
R.H. Duncan of the suicide of Eva Kimmons, the
17 year old daughter of Mr and Mrs George
Kimmons formerly of this county. Mrs Kimmons
was here a few weeks ago at the time of the
death of her sister, Miss Rachel Hunsaker.

KIMMONS, SARAH JANE - Death - Jul 30, 1902
Sarah Jane Kimmons born Adams Co. Ill. Oct 16,
1842. Married Howard J. Vickers Dec 16, 1891
died at her home 7 miles south of Columbus, Ill
July 24th, 1902. Leaves husband, 2 sisters,
Mrs J.K. Ruth of Pueblo, Colo. and Mrs John
Schnur of Adams, Ill. also 2 brothers G.T. and
O.B. Kimmons of Maryville, MO. Funeral from
Pleasant Grove ME Church Saturday July 27th by
O. Dilley of Camp Point and Rev W.E. Rose of
Paloma and Elder W.T. Beadles of Quincy.
Buried in cemetery at Burton.

KING, MRS A.M. - Death - Mar 18, 1903 Mrs A.M.
King died at Hot Springs, Ark. Tuesday, age 28
years. Was daughter of the late Edward A.
Yeargain and reared in Gilmer twp. Learned
millinery business and conducted an
establishment in Texas where she met Dr A.M.
King and married him last June. Body brought
to Quincy Friday and taken to Mt Pleasant
cemetery in Gilmer twp Saturday and buried
beside her father. She was a niece of Mrs M.E.
Honnold of Camp Point.

KING, BERG - Local - Aug 6, 1902 - Berg King, a
young man of Augusta and a son of F.M. King,
the merchant died Saturday afternoon of typhoid

fever, 22 years old.   Funeral Monday.   He was a
nephew of Miss Addie King who went to Augusta
to attend the funeral.

KING, BERG - Local - Aug 6, 1902 - Mr and Mrs
Louis Olberg went to Augusta Monday to attend
the funeral of Berg King.

KING, MRS RUTH - An Old Pioneer Gone - Jan 15,
1895 Thursday afternoon, Mrs Ruth King died at
the home of her daughter, Mrs H.D. Morton near
Ursa of pneumonia, age 81 years.   Ruth Chase,
daughter of Abram Chase born in Penn.   Came to
Ill with parents 1832 settled Adams Co. and for
a great many years lived Gilmer twp where she
married Elijah M. King.   Only 1 is now left of
her fathers family Mrs Jane Miller of
Mansfield, Ohio.   Mrs King leaves 4 children,
Clinton E. King of Quincy; Mrs Lizzie Chase of
Melrose; Mrs A.R. Frazier and Mrs H.D. Morton
of Ursa.   Had lived several years with the
latter.   Services Saturday.   Buried Chase
burying ground near Fowler.

KING, SUSAN - Quincy - Dec 8, 1897 The will of
Susan King divides her estate equally between
her 2 daughters, Mrs Martha Yale and Mrs Thomas
J. Heirs.

KINNEY, MRS JERUSHA - Ancient History - May 24,
1895 - May 1879 Mrs Jerusha Kinney died on the
15th.

KINNEY, MRS JERUSHA - Ancient History - May 22,
1894 - May 23, 1879 Mrs Jerusha Kinney died on
the 15th.

KINNEY, MRS JOSEPH - West Point - Feb 16, 1893
Died Feb. 7th at her home 3 miles NW of town,
Mrs Joseph Kinney, age 65 years.   Sick only a
few days. Was member of Baptist Church and
Epworth League.   Funeral by Rev McDonald and
Finlay.   Buried in Chili Cemetery.   Leaves 2
sons and 4 daughters.

KIRKPATRICK, REV A.B. - 15 Years Ago - Feb 13,
1894 Rev A.B. Kirkpatrick died in his 79th year

KIRKPATRICK, REV A.B. - Ancient History - Mar
24, 1897 - March 1879 Died, Rev A.B.
Kirkpatrick a pioneer of this county died.

KIRKPATRICK, REV A.B. - Ancient History - Mar
30, 1894 - Mar 28, 1879 Died March 25th Rev
A.B. Kirkpatrick in his 79th year.

KIRKPATRICK, REV AUGUSTUS B. - Ancient History -
Apr 26, 1895 - April 1879 Rev Augustus B.
Kirkpatrick died, age 78 years.

KIRKPATRICK, J.H. - Death - Dec 20, 1895 - J.H.
Kirkpatrick, a long time resident of this place
died at his home in this city last Thursday 3
A.M., 64 years old. Services at M.E. Church
Friday 5 P.M. by Rev Robert Barton. "Carthage
Republican" Deceased was a brother of Mrs
S.L. Clarke of Camp Point.

KIRKPATRICK, MRS LYDIA A. - Obituary - Apr 27,
1894 Died-Mrs Lydia A. Kirkpatrick, nee
Brooks. Born in state of New York July 12,
1824. Died Apr 18, 1894 at her home in Camp
Point. Came to Ill. with fathers family in her
youth. Lived Will Co. where she married Caleb
Comer and had 4 children. After his death she
married in 1875 to A.B. Kirkpatrick who died in
1879. She leaves only 1 child, her daughter,
Mrs Sell. Funeral at M.E. Church last Friday
at 2 P.M.

KIRKPATRICK, MRS LYDIA A. - Local - Apr 17,
1894 Died Mrs Lydia A. Kirkpatrick died
Wednesday afternoon. Funeral will be at 2 P.M.
today.

KIRKPATRICK, MRS LYDIA A. - Local - Jun 8, 1893
Mrs Lydia A. Kirkpatrick received a certificate
last week allowing her a pension of $12.00 a
month on account of a son who died in service.

KIRKPATRICK, LYDIA ANN - Probate Notice - May
11, 1894 Lydia Ann Kirkpatrick, deceased 1st
Monday of July 1894 H.W. Childs, Ex.

KLING, MRS ADAM - Paloma - Jan 12, 1893 Mrs

Adam Kling died last Wednesday afternoon.
Funeral at Methodist Church at Fowler Saturday
A.M. by Rev Peck of Mendon. Buried in cemetery
south of Fowler. Mr Kling and his daughter,
Miss Kate has our sympathy.

KLING, HENRY - Had His Skull Crushed - May 20,
1896 Henry Kling, a german farmer who lived
about 4 miles SW of Barry, Ill. met with a
fatal accident about 3 P.M. Saturday. The
front wheel of his wagon went over his neck and
the rear wheel struck his head. Died within a
few minutes. Sons were helping him.

KNOWLES, CHAS. - Local - Aug 5, 1896 Monday
the 27th ult at Rushville, Chas. Knowles age 17
years was standing near an electric light pole
and leaned against it and was electrocuted.

KNOWLES, NORA MABEL - Drowned in a Tub - Oct
20, 1897 Nora Mabel, the youngest child of Mr
and Mrs George Knowles of Buenavista twp was
drowned in a tub of lime water Tuesday
afternoon. Was 2 years 5 months 11 days old.
A year ago August their oldest son was killed
by a shock from an electric light wire in
Rushville. "Rushville Times"

KNOX, JAMES - Death - Feb 26, 1902 James Knox,
age 51 years, a well known farmer of Cliola
died at his home early Friday A.M. of pleurisy
and other ailments. Died Friday 5:30 A.M.
Leaves wife, 6 children-Mary, Grace, Pearl,
Samuel, Everett and James and 1 brother Samuel
Knox survive him. Born Jan 16, 1851. Lived
locality where he died all his life.

KOBEL, MRS JACOB - 20 Years Ago - Sep 14, 1893
Mrs Jacob Kobel died.

KOCH, MRS ANNA - Recent Deaths - Feb 10, 1897
Died Mrs Anna Koch at her home near Mendon
Sunday night from consumption. She was
daughter of Valentine Reuschel of Honey Creek
and married about a year ago.

KOCHANOWSKI, CAPT V. - Ancient History - Mar

24, 1897 December 1878 Died Capt V.
Kochanowshki of the Polish Legion died at Adam
Goerke's in Columbus twp.

KOCHANOWSKI, CAPT VINCENT - Ancient History -
Jan 15, 1895 - January 1879 Capt Vincent
Kochanowski an officer of the Polish Legion
from New York City in the War of 1861 died at
the home of Adam Goerke.

KOELLER, MRS HERMAN - Ancient History - Jan 15,
1895 - January 1875 Mrs Herman Koeller died on
the 22nd.

KOETZLE, GOLDIE - Accident - Aug 2, 1895
Goldie Koetzle, daughter of Mr and Mrs John
Koetzle of Liberty was buried in Lutheran
cemetery there Sunday. Died Saturday from
lockjaw. Father is a butcher at Liberty.

KRAMER, MRS ROSENA - Co. Seat - Dec 9, 1896
Police received letter from George Kirkhoff Jr.
Consul. of the Netherlands, living in Chicago
asking him to find Mrs Rosena Kramer. Her son
was Captain in the Dutch Army and died in East
Indies last summer. The Netherlands wishes to
pension the mother of the deceased. She has
been located in this city.

KRAMER, MRS ROSENA - Co. Seat - Dec 9, 1896
Mrs Rosena Kramer whose whereabouts was sought
by the Consul. of the Netherlands has been
located in this city. She is the mother of Rev
J.C. Kramer and the family will receive a good
pension on account of her son, Capt Oscar
Kramer who was killed on the Island of Sumatra.

KROGMAN, ALF - Shot His Friend - Oct 28, 1896
Alf Krogman of Quincy shot and killed his
friend, Henry Riley at that place Tuesday
night. The two were fast friends and were
looking at an old fashioned revolver. Purely
accidental.

KRUISE, MRS ETTA - Quincy - May 22, 1894 Died
Mrs Etta Kruise, an old resident of Adams Co.
died near Ursa, age 63 years.

KUBLER, JOHN B. - Probate Notice - Mar 9, 1893
John B. Kubler, deceased 1st Monday of May
1893   Wilkie Bruns, adm.

LAACKE, HENRY WILLIAM - Quincy - Mar 22, 1895
Henry William Laacke, age 88 years, was found
dead in bed at his home in Ellington Sun. A.M.

LAAGE, MRS GEORGE J. - Quincy - Aug 23, 1895
Mrs George J. Laage died Thursday A.M. 66 years
old. Born Germany, came to Quincy 1847 when
she married Mr Laage. She was a sister of
Anton and John Heine.

LAIN, MR AND MRS A.H. - Local - Nov 20, 1894
Mr and Mrs A.H. Lain of Bloomington, who were
returning home from a wedding trip, came via
Camp Point and attended the funeral of Miss
Fugate, Mrs Lain's aunt.

LAKE, DOUGLAS - Dead - Dec 17, 1902 Douglas
Lake died at his home in this city Monday
afternoon of tumor on the brain. Had lived in
Bowen only about 6 weeks coming here from south
of Camp Point. Services at the house by Elder
Lee. Leaves his widow and 6 children, 2 little
girls still at home. He was born 1854 in
Columbus twp, Adams Co. Married 1875 to
Samantha Wear. Burial was at Union Church, 6
miles south of Camp Point. "Bowen Chronicle"

LAKE, MRS HERMAN - Local - Apr 17, 1894 Mrs F.
Boger received telegram from Quincy Monday of
the death there of Mrs Herman Lake. Mrs Boger
does not know Mrs Lake nor can anyone be found
here who knows her.

LAKE, JAMES - Killed - Jun 24, 1903 James
Lake, a young man reared in Columbus twp was
shot and killed Saturday night at Plymouth by
Isaac Miller, the village marshall. Miller was
taken to Carthage and placed in jail.

LAKE, JAMES - Local - Jul 1, 1903 Isaac W.
Miller the Plymouth town marshall, who killed
James Lake of near Bowen June 20th had his
preliminary hearing Saturday in Carthage and

committed to jail without bond until the
October term of court.

LAMMA, KATE - Local - Dec 15, 1897 "Boxer"
Jones charged with the murder of Kate Lamma's
new born child at Rushville who was sent to
Leiston for safe keeping escaped from the
Fulton Co. jail Sunday night. Was caught at
Plymouth 2 days later where his mother lives.

LAMMA, MISS KATE - Infant Murdered - May 19,
1897 Miss Kate Lamma, of Huntsville was
arrested last week on a charge of murdering her
new born infant. The Republican says--the girl
is 17 years old, superstitious and illiterate.
She says the child came to its death naturally.

LANCASTER, WARREN I. - Death - Feb 18, 1903
Warren I. Lancaster died at Carthage last
Thursday, age 43 years. Born near LaPrairie,
Ill where his father still lives. Went to
York, NE some years ago and was sheriff of York
Co. for 4 years. About a year ago he came to
Keokuk and bought a livery stable. Was brother
of Sherman Lancaster, formerly of this city and
has a wife and 5 children at York, NE. His
oldest son was here and took the body to York
for burial. "Carthage Republican"

LANDON, CHARLES A. - Death - Apr 9, 1895 Died,
April 3rd at the home of Mr and Mrs J.E.
Landon, Chicago, Charles A. Landon age 16
months 9 days. Funeral on the 4th to Oakwood
cemetery.

LANDON, DR M.W. - Local - Sep 16, 1903 Dr M.W.
Landon died in Quincy Thursday age 75 years.
Practiced medicine at Burton, Golden, Columbus,
Fowler, etc. Was brother of Jerome A. Landon
of Camp Point and father of Dr D.M. Landon of
Quincy.

LANGDON, DR CHARLES E. - Found Dead - Oct 23,
1894 Springfield, Ill. Oct 22nd This A.M. Dr
Charles E. Langdon a young doctor of New
Berlin, this county was found dead in his
office with a bullet hole in his head and a

revolver in his hand.

LANGDON, JAMES J. - Ancient History - Feb 22, 1895 - February 1875 James J. Langdon, at one time publisher of the Quincy Whig died in Quincy on the 11th.

LANNING, MRS JAMES - Coatsburg - Jul 23, 1895 This A.M. after a long and painful illness the remains of Mrs James Lanning were buried in Coatsburg Cemetery. Was mother of a large family, who with her aged husband survive her.

LANNING, MRS JAS. - Primrose - Jul 23, 1895 Mrs Jas. Lanning who has been an invalid for the past 10 months was buried in Coatsburg Cemetery Saturday at 10 A.M.

LANOIX, DR - Ancient History - Jun 1, 1894 May 31, 1878 Dr Lanoix of Quincy was on trial for the murder of Mrs Fannie Price of Pittsfield by criminal malpractice.

LANOIX, DR FREDERICK W. - Quincy - Dec 17, 1902 Dr Frederick W. Lanoix, formerly of this city, died in the Cook Co. hospital, Chicago, Thursday A.M. age 36 years.

LANTIS, MRS WILLIAM (MINNIE) - Death Record - Jun 9, 1897 Mrs Minnie Clarke Lantis died Tuesday June 8th of consumption, age 29 years. Leaves husband and 3 small children. Funeral from Christian Church this P.M. at 2. Minnie Clarke was born St Louis where both her parents died during her early childhood, afterwhich she and her brothers lived with their Uncle Vincent Francis, at Mendon and later at Camp Point. Married William Lantis in 1886.

LAPHAM, DR - Local - Nov 30, 1894 Died Dr Lapham of Victoria, Ill died Thursday eve of typhoid fever. He was known in Camp Point as the husband of Anna Ross.

LARIMORE, FRED - Assassination in Plainville - Oct 29, 1902 Fred Larimore was shot and killed within a few yards of his fathers door at

Plainville Thursday night. Body found by
brother, Clarence. He was son of I.M. Larimore
of Plainville, 25 years old. Had been to town
and visited his aunt. Sunday eve Quincy police
arrested Millard F. Lester a farmer of
Plainville and charged him with the murder.
Lester is a well to do farmer. It is said that
Larimore was intimate with Mr Lester's married
daughter, Mrs Lura McKee and that Lester had
threatened him.

LARIMORE, FREDERICK - Quincy - Nov 19, 1902
The spot where Frederick Larimore was murdered
in the village of Plainville has been marked by
the planting of an elm tree.

LASLEY, LEE DOWNING - In Memoriam - Apr 5, 1895
T.W. Green Chapter, Epworth League in memory of
Lee D. Lasley ------ our loved brother, Lee
Downing Lasley ------- . Copy sent to his
mother.

LASLEY, MARTIN - Death Record - Dec 8, 1897
Martin Lasley died at his home in Bowen
Saturday, aged about 83 years. Came to Ill.
with his parents in the 20's and lived in Camp
Point twp nearly all his life. Moving to Bowen
a few years ago. Married twice, 2nd wife
surviving. Leaves 2 sons, one Judge Lasley of
Kansas. Had been an invalid several years.

LAUBER, GEORGE - Runaway - Aug 16, 1895
Runaway out at Mill Creek some 7 miles from
Quincy Monday P.M. Mrs Margaret Bonnet, Mrs
Esther Doty and Mrs Elizabeth Byler, the 2
former of Quincy and the latter of Mill Creek
were coming home from the funeral of Mrs
Bonnet's brother, George Lauber. Mrs Bonnet's
other brother, Uriah had his buggy broken also.

LAUGHLIN, MRS T.B. - Death - Nov 1, 1895 News
received of the death of Mrs T.B. Laughlin in
Albuquerque, New Mexico on Tuesday. Remains
arrived in Quincy Wed. Was wife of U.S. Postal
Inspector Laughlin. Lived Quincy many years.
Leaves husband and 1 son, the latter being
Harry Laughlin, the actor.

LAUPHEIMER, MISS PAULINE - Motorman Held
Responsible - Aug 7, 1894 Miss Pauline
Laupheimer was knocked down and rolled by an
electric street car in Quincy last Sunday.
Died Saturday of blood poisoning. She lived
Sedalia, MO. Father was Henry Laupheimer of
Sedalia. Driver of car was Joseph Williams.

LAWLER, MRS ALICE - Quincy - Apr 6, 1894 Died
Mrs Alice Lawler, age 76 years and a resident
of Quincy 40 years. Died Sunday at the home of
her daughter, Mrs Kate Schlausler.

LAWLESS, MRS DAVE - Columbus - Mar 8, 1895 Mr
and Mrs Morton of Hamilton, Hancock Co. were
called to Gilmer to attend the funeral of Mrs
Dave Lawless Wednesday.

LAWLESS, MRS LULU - Columbus - Mar 8, 1895
Died at her home in Gilmer twp Mrs Lulu Lawless
(nee White) of consumption. Leaves husband and
1 son. Services by Rev A.A. White at Mt
Pleasant Wednedsay.

LAWLESS, MRS LULU - Prairie - Mar 26, 1895
Died Mrs Lulu Lawless. Leaves husband and a
little son. Died of consumption.

LAWLESS, THOMAS T. - Death Record - Mar 3, 1897
Died Thomas T. Lawless at his home in Gilmer
twp Sunday. Had been a physical wreck since
his incarceration in Andersonville prison where
he was confined about 14 months. Funeral
Tuesday at Mt Pleasant. Born in 1830. Came to
Adams Co as a boy with his parents. Crossed the
plains in 1849 looking for gold. Leaves a wife
and 3 sons.

LAWLESS, THOMAS T. - Probate Notice - Apr 28,
1897 Thomas T. Lawless, deceased 1st Monday
of July (5th) Ann M. Lawless, adm.

LEACH, A.H. - Coatsburg - Dec 14, 1893 On
Saturday the remains of A.H. Leach was buried
in Coatsburg cemetery. Died Thursday A.M. Was
3 years past 3 score. Leaves an aged wife and
8 children, 4 sons, 4 daughters. Was called

the old Sheriff. He came here with his family
from Easton, Buchanan Co. MO. during war times
so had lived here over 30 years.

LEACH, MRS A.H. - Coatsburg - Mar 6, 1894 Died
last evening (Wed.) Old Mrs Leach relict of the
late A.H. Leach. Mrs Leach had been in poor
health after the death of her husband. Born
Kentucky 77 years ago. Mother of 10 children,
2 dead. Oldest child lives in state of
Washington. Buried beside husband in Coatsburg
Cemetery Friday.

LEACH, ALBURN H. - Sale of Real Estate - Jun
26, 1894 Albert H. Gray, adm of the estate of
Alburn H. Leach, deceased petitioner vs. John
Leach, Mary Leach, Jeremiah Leach, Elizabeth
Leach, Epperson Leach, Mary Leach, Elizabeth
Gray, Harriet Asher, William Asher, Addie
Felsman, Christopher Felsman, Frederick Frike,
Emma Jones, Edward Jones, Daniel Carr, Alice
Carr, Ollie Obenlander, Fred Obenlander, Ida
Woods, Geroge Woods, Cora Sewall, R.H. Sewall,
William Leach, Charles Carr, Etta Carr, Alta
Carr defendants   Willis Haselwood   Clerk
Co. Court   June 18, 1894

LEACH, ALBURN H. - Probate Notice - Apr 6, 1894
Alburn H. Leach, deceased 1st Monday of June
1894 Albert H. Gray, adm.

LEACH, NANCY - Probate Notice - Jan 1, 1895
Nancy E. Leach, deceased   1st Monday of
February (4th) Albert H. Gray, adm.

LEBRASH, LOUIS - Dead - May 20, 1903 Louis
LeBrash, a blacksmith who lived in Camp Point
several years ago, died in Quincy Saturday age
67 years. Born Michigan but came to Ill. as a
young man and since live in this county.
Served in Civil War in Co. D., 13th Ill.
Cavalry. Leaves wife and several children, one
is Mrs E.P. Thompson of Camp Point.

LEE, GEO. H. - Dead - Jun 17, 1903 George H.
Lee, a former prominent attorney and supt. of
schools at Mt Sterling died at Colorado Springs

Monday of last week of consumption. Went to
Colorado about 5 years ago for his health.
Body brought to Mt Sterling for burial.

LEE, MISS LENA - Primrose - Apr 28, 1897 Miss
Lena Lee, who died in Quincy Friday was a
visitor last summer at L.C. Schroeder's for a
couple of weeks. She was forewoman in the
Noxall factory.

LEE, MARTHA A. - Probate Notice - Jan 13, 1897
Martha A. Lee, deceased 1st Monday of March
1897 Stewart Woods, adm.

LEE, MRS MARTHA - North Houston - Nov 4, 1896
Mrs Martha Lee died Sunday Oct 25th was a
daughter of Steward Strickler. Married Wm Wood
Sep 24, 1864 by whom she had 4 children, 3
still living, Annie Jackson in Rhode Island the
other 2 in this vicinity. After the death of
Mr W. she remained a widow for some years after
which she married Reed Lee. They had 3
daughters, leaving total of 6 children to
survive her. Services by Elder Carpenter of
Augusta on Tuesday at 11 A.M. at Ebenezer
Church. Buried in cemetery near by.

LEE, REV T.B. - Local - Dec 8, 1897 Rev T.M.
Dillon was called to Springfield Tuesday by the
death of his brother in law Rev T.B. Lee who
has lived in that city for more than 50 years
and a member of the First Methodist Church.

LEFERINGHAUS, MR - Primrose - Jan 15, 1895 Mr
and Mrs Chris Luckel attended funeral of Mr
Leferinghaus at Liberty, Thursday.

LEFERINGHAUS, JOHN - Terrible Accident at
Liberty - Jan 11, 1895 John Leferinghaus was a
german farmer living on the Buttz farm near
Liberty. He and wife were in field shucking
fodder. He loaded his wagon and started, but
horses became frightened and dragged him 40
rods. Crushing his head and breaking his neck.
Wife followed close behind but couldn't stop
it, age 52 years. Was a brother in law of
Jacob Luckel of Camp Point. Had 5 sons and

lived near Liberty 2 years.   Was unable to
speak English.

LEFERINGHAUS, WILLIAM - Primrose - Jan 15, 1895
William Leferinghaus, who was killed at Liberty
last week by falling from a load of fodder.
First settled in York Neck when he came from
old country, living with his brother in law,
Chris Luckel. He leaves 5 sons, the eldest
Louis lived at Big Neck the others ages are 18,
12 and 6.

LEFERINGHOUSE, MR AND MRS - Columbus - Aug 24,
1894 The infant child of Mr and Mrs
Leferinghouse was buried in the village
cemetery Wednesday, the 15th.

LEFERINGHOUSE, MRS MAMIE - Columbus - Oct 2,
1894 Died, Mrs Mamie Leferinghouse (nee
Henning) was buried on Thursday Sept 27th.
Funeral by Rev Herzog her pastor in the German
M.E. Church.

LESAGE, COL. J.B. - Col. J.B. LeSage - Sep 30,
1903 Died Col. J.B. LeSage in Clayton Sat.,
age 79 years. Native of Canada. Came to Ill.
1839. Served in regular army including the
Mexican War and during the rebellion was Capt
of the 101st Ill. Lived Clayton since the war.
Leaves 2 daughters. Funeral Sunday P.M. under
Masonic fraternity.

LESLIE, C.W. - Columbus - Oct 22, 1902 Charles
Hofmeister of Barry, Ill placed 2 monuments in
our cemetery Saturday Oct 17th, 1 for C.W.
Leslie and 1 for parents of Benjamin and Zelma
Morton.

LESLIE, OLIVER - Paloma - Nov 26, 1902 Babe of
Oliver Leslie was buried in Columbus Cemetery
last week.

LESLIE, ROSCOE WILLIAM - Columbus - Dec 3, 1902
Roscoe William, infant son of Oliver M. and
Dora B. Leslie died at Springfield, Ill Nov
17th, 1902 age 5 months 29 days. Remains
brought to his fathers home. Services by Rev

W.E. Rose.   Buried Columbus Cemetery.

LESTER, J.M. - Clayton - Feb 23, 1894 Among those who attended the funeral of J.M. Lester was Charles Locke of Versailes.

LESTER, JAMES - Local - Feb 13, 1894 Died James Lester at Clayton Thursday night. Formerly lived in Camp Point and had many relatives here.

LESTER, MILLARD FILLMORE - Lester Discharged - Nov 12, 1902 The trial of Millard Fillmore Lester, charged with the murder of Fred Larimore at Plainville a couple weeks ago was held in Quincy Wednesday and Thursday. Discharged because of no evidence.

LETTON, RAPHAEL E. - Local - May 27, 1903 Raphael E. Letton, the oldest musician of Quincy, died Monday, age 88 years. He had been in music business at Quincy about 60 years.

LEVY, L.D. - Death of Mr L.D. Levy - Aug 19, 1896 Died Mr J.D. Levy, one of Quincy's most prominent business men. Died very suddenly at the sanitarium at Hartford, Conn. at an early hour Wednesday A.M. of apoplexy. His wife and he sailed to Europe 1st of April and a week ago returned from Germany. Went to sanitarium accompanied by his son David. Mrs Levy went on to Chicago to visit a daughter, Mrs Silberman. He was founder of J.D. Levy Clothing Mfg Co.

LEWIS, MR AND MRS CHARLES E. - Local - Jan 18, 1895 The 3 month old babe of Mr and Mrs Charles E. Lewis living 3 miles E. of town was found Wednesday dead in bed.

LEWIS, MRS G.T. - Northeast Burton - mar 12, 1896 Funeral of Mrs G.T. Lewis was held at Burton Presbyterian Church Monday at 1 P.M. afterwhich she was buried in cemetery at that place.

LEWIS, MRS LUCY - Local - Mar 12, 1896 Mrs Lucy Lewis, daughter of H.J. Vickers of Burton,

died in San Antonio, Texas March 4th.   Remains
brought here to Burton for burial.   Mrs Lewis
went here to school at Maplewood many years
ago.   She leaves a husband and daughter.

LEWIS, MARY - Obituary - Feb 6, 1894 Died Mary
Lewis, born Maryland 1824 moved with parents as
a small girl to Green Co. Penn. where she
married Wm Sowers 1850. Soon they moved to
Iowa where 2 children were born. Then to Camp
Point in 1870 where Wm her husband died 1892.
She died Feb 3rd, 1894. Funeral Feb 4th at
Christian Church by Elder Orin Dilley. Buried
village cemetery. Leaves 1 son, Albert. Her
daughter died several years ago.

LEWIS, PERLANDER - Local - Jan 15, 1902
Perlander Lewis, a well known citizen of Bowen,
died Thurday age 72 years.

LEWIS, W.E. - An Editor Dead - Jun 2, 1897
W.E. Lewis, editor of the Prairie City Herald
died Monday. He was a lawyer as well as editor
and a man of ability. Leaves a wife and
family.

LIKES, MRS FINLEY - Local - Jan 29, 1895 Mrs
Finley Likes of Barry has received information
of the death of a brother in South Carolina
whose estate of $75,000 she inherits.

LIKES, WILLIAM - Death of William Likes - Dec
22, 1897 William Likes died at his home in
Richfield Dec 12th in his 70th year. Born
Indiana. Came to Adams Co. as a child with
parents. Funeral at Kinderhook on the 14th
services by the masonic fraternity.

LINDSAY, MRS JAMES - Local - Mar 2, 1894 Died
a telegram to S.L. Clarke Wednesday tells of
the death of his sister, Mrs James Lindsay at
Libertyville, Lake Co. Mrs Lindsay lived at
one time in Camp Point and was known by the
older citizens.

LING, JOHN - Ancient History - Nov 13, 1894
Nov 15, 1878 A chinese laundryman, named John

Ling was killed in Quincy by an unknown murderer.

LINN, PROF. ALBERT - Ancient History - Mar 26, 1895 - March 1875 Prof Albert Linn died at Abingdon.

LINN, PROF. ALBERT - Ancient History - Mar 23, 1894 - March 19, 1875 Prof Albert Linn died at Abingdon on the 11th. Born in Adams Co. and a son of Mrs Nancy Linn of Camp Point.

LINN, MRS EMILY - Local - Feb 24, 1897 A.J. Linn of Liberty came up to attend the funeral of Mrs Emily Linn Tuesday.

LINN, MRS EMILY - Local - Feb 24, 1897 Geo. W. Linn of West Point came down Monday to attend the funeral of his sister in law, Mrs Emily Linn.

LINN, MRS EMILY - Local - Feb 24, 1897 Mr and Mrs Rolla Linn of Quincy attended the funeral of his aunt, Mrs Emily Linn, Tuesday.

LINN, MRS EMILY - Recent Deaths - Feb 24, 1897 Died Mrs Emily Linn Feb 22nd after an illness of two weeks in her 59th year. Born Woodville, this county Apr 27, 1838 was eldest daughter of the late Theron B. Warren. Lived all her life in Adams Co. Married Feb 1868 to John F. Linn who died Oct. 1886. Her niece lived with her since Mr Linn's death, Miss Mary Bradley, now Mrs T.F. Leetch (niece). No children but her niece was like a daughter to her. Services Tuesday P.M. at the Methodist Church. Buried village cemetery.

LINN, MRS G.W. - Mrs G.W. Linn Dead - Aug 5, 1896 Mrs G.W. Linn died Thursday eve at her home in West Point. Born Ohio. Came to Adams Co. when a child with her parents who settled in Richfield twp. She and her husband lived West Point about 20 years.

LINN, MRS IRENE - Mrs Irene Linn - Aug 12, 1896 Died Thursday eve July 30 at 6 P.M., Mrs Irene

Linn age 49 years 10 months 10 days. Irene
Browning born Ohio Sep 20, 1846. Moved with
parents to Richfield, Ill. 1854. Married E.F.
Taylor, they had 2 children Otis and Edward.
Mr Taylor died soon and 1873 she married G.W.
Linn of Liberty, Ill. The year they married
they moved here. They had 4 children-George,
Cora, Nora and Mabel, all surviving her.
Funeral from M.E. Church Saturday 10 A.M. by
Rev Evans and Finlay. Buried West Point
cemetery.

LINN, JOHN - Ancient History - Nov 12, 1895
November 1881 John Linn an early settler died
in Columbus twp, age 77 years.

LINN, MRS MARY TRUITT - Local - Dec 27, 1895
Word received of the death Monday the 23rd inst
at Agricola, KS of Mrs Mary Truitt Linn, wife
of Charles Linn formerly of Adams Co.

LITCHERING, MRS - Livingston - Jan 5, 1893 Mrs
Litchering, of Burton twp died Dec 24th.
Funeral by the Lutheran minister and buried
Monday in the Independence graveyard.

LITTLE, MRS JOHN T. - Local - Jul 6, 1894
Died, Mrs John T. Little, a sufferer from
cancer the last few years died at the home of
her sister in Quincy about 1:30 P.M. Wednesday.
Brought out from Quincy to Camp Point and taken
from here to Clayton where she will be buried
today.

LITTLE, JOSEPH - Obituary - Dec 20, 1895
Joseph Little died at his home in this village
on the A.M. of the 14th of paralysis, 75 years
old. Born Washington Co. Penn. and came to
Adams Co. spring of 1841. Taught school in
Houston and Honey Creek twps. Fall of 1843 he
married Mary White and settled Houston twp on
farm now owned by Thomas Marshall. In 1850 was
J.P. of Houston twp. About 1852 he moved to
Warsaw vicinity wife died and in fall of 1853
he married Mary Long. 1855 he came to Camp
Point and built a hotel and ran a livery. Fall
of 1861 enlisted in Co. F 3rd Ill. Cavalry.

Served 3 years. 1865 was assessor of N. half
of Adams Co. for 2 years. Funeral Tuesday P.M.
under Camp Point Lodges of Odd Fellows and J.P.
Lasley Post, G.A.R. Buried village cemetery.
Member of I.O.O.F. for 39 years, Lodge #215.

LITTLE, JOSEPH - Death - Dec 17, 1895 Joseph
Little died at his home in Camp Point Sunday
A.M., age 75 years after a protracted illness
produced by paralysis. Came to Camp Point
1855, 40 years ago, and lived here since. Was
J.P. for a number of years and later was town
and village clerk. Leaves widow and 8
children. Funeral at 2:30 P.M. today and will
be attended by the Odd Fellows and G.A.R.

LITTLE, JOSEPH - In Memoriam - Jan 1, 1896 In
memoriam of Joseph Little by Post #543 G.A.R.

LITTLEFIELD, EATON - Quincy - Apr 19, 1895
Eaton Littlefield died Wednesday A.M., 80 years
old. Came to Quincy from Maine 1838 and was
prominently known as a builder for many years.

LITTLEFIELD, CAPTAIN N.R. - Death Record - Jun
9, 1897 Captain N.R. Littlefield died Saturday
at 3:20 P.M. at the home of his daughter, Mrs
H.N. Wheeler, Quincy. 82 years old, lived Mt
Sterling until recently. Buried there.

LITTLETON, GLENN - Local - Dec 30, 1903 Glenn
Littleton, age 4 years was burned to death
Thursday P.M. by her clothing catching fire
from the stove while her mother was out of the
house. The parents live 3 miles E. of Loraine.

LIVINGSTON, BENJAMIN - Death - Jun 17, 1930
Benjamin Livingston died Thursday, June 11th.
Suffered a stroke of paralysis several years
ago and practically helpless for past 2 or 3
years. Born in Fulton Co. Jan 8, 1833. Was 70
years 5 mon. 3 days old. Married Rebecca
Hankins 1858. They had 6 children, only 2
survive-Mrs B.T. Earl of Camp Point and Mrs
Chas. Hart of Avon and 2 grandchildren. Served
in Civil War in 10th Ill. Cavalry. Funeral
Friday at home of his daughter, Mrs B.T. Earl

by Elder R.A. Omer.   Buried village cemetery.

LIVINGSTON, BENJAMIN - Death - Jun 17, 1903
Benjamin Livingston died Thurs. June 11th
suffered a stroke of paralysis several years
ago and practically helpless for past 2 or 3
years.   Born in Fulton Co. Jan 8, 1833, was 70
years 5 months 3 days old.   Married Rebecca
Hankins 1858.   They had 6 children, only 2
survive, Mrs B.T. Earl of Camp Point and Mrs
Chas. Hart of Avon and 2 grandchildren.   Served
in Civil War in 10th Ill. Cavalry.   Funeral
Friday at the home of his daughter Mrs B.T.
Earl by Elder R.A. Omer.   Buried village
cemetery.

LIVINGSTON, JENNIE - Died - Nov 1, 1895   Jennie
Livingston died at her home in Chicago last
Monday.   Remains brought to Bushnell Wednesday
eve.   Funeral at Methodist Church Thursday 10
A.M. by Rev Wooley.   "Bushnell Democrat"

LIVINGSTON, MR AND MRS JOHN - Local - Nov 1,
1895 Mrs Jane Ensminger, Fillmore J.
Ensminger, Mrs Wm Livingston and Benj.
Livingston went to Bushnell Thursday to attend
the funeral of a daughter of Mr and Mrs John
Livingston.

LIVINGSTON, THOMAS - Ancient History - Apr 21,
1897 August 1879 Thomas Livingston, father of
Benjamin and William Livingston died at
Bardolph and was buried in Camp Point cemetery.

LIVINGSTON, THOMAS - Ancient History - Aug 7,
1894 Aug 8, 1879 Thomas Livingston, father of
Ben and William died on the 2nd.

LLOYD, ELI - Died - Jul 7, 1897 Eli Lloyd died
in Bradley, South Dakota June 16th age 78
years.   He was a resident of Camp Point about
20 years ago and spent several years in Clayton
where he was postmaster.

LOCKWOOD, ROBERT C. - Quincy - Jun 11, 1895
Remains of Robert C. Lockwood, who died in
Denver, Colo. in March were buried in this city

Thursday afternoon.

LOGAN, GEORGE - Boy Shot at Fowler - Jan 14,
1903 George Logan, a boy 15 years old was shot
and killed by Floyd Stahl near Fowler Saturday
while they were hunting, also with them was
Frank Logan 18 years old. Floyd also 18 years
old and a son of Hanby Stahl of Fowler.

LOHMILLER, J.C. - Quincy - Feb 8, 1895 Grand
jury failed to find an indictment against J.C.
Lohmiller for the murder of his wife and her
niece.

LOHMILLER, MRS KATHERINE - Quincy - Oct 23,
1894 The coroners jury in the case of Mrs
Katherine Lohmiller and niece, Orlinda Searls
has finally adjourned.

LOHR, DONALD - Crushed his Skull - Dec 2, 1896
Accident at Columbus, this co. on Saturday eve
in which Donald, 11 year old son of Mr and Mrs
Jas. Lohr lost his life. Chunk of frozen dirt
fell from hillside knocking him down a steep
hill side while he was rabbit hunting with
David Trout.

LOMILLER, MRS J.C. - Murdered - Oct 12, 1894
Mrs J.C. Lomiller and her 10 year old niece
were brutally murdered Tuesday night at their
home about 3 miles S.E. of Liberty.

LONG, MRS A.G. - Columbus - Apr 1, 1903 W.C.
Leslie and family attended the funeral of his
sister, Mrs A.G. Long of Mendon, Ill. which was
held at the Cong'l Church 2:30 Monday
afternoon, March 30, 1903.

LONG, DAVID - Death of Eccentric Man - Dec 3,
1895 Rushville, Ill Nov 29th David Long, who
died at the almshouse in Schuyler Co. was 94
years old. Had lived at the institution as an
inmate 40 years. Lost his mind in 1856.
Veteran of Mexican War.

LONG, MRS SOPHIA - Quincy - Nov 20, 1894 Died
Mrs Sophia Long age 44, wife of John M. Long

died Thursday of cancer.

LONGCOR, GEORGE - Death Record - Dec 29, 1897
George Longcor born Athens Co. Ohio 1826 died
Friday Dec 24, 1897. Was member of Co. G 78th
Ill. Infantry. Lived Camp Point many years.
Leaves a wife and 8 children.

LONGCOR, WILLIAM - Local - Dec 9, 1903 A
little daughter of William Longcor died Sunday
of meningitis. Funeral Monday.

LOOMILLER, MRS KATE - Quincy - Nov 16, 1894
Last will of Mrs Kate Loomiller who with her 10
year old niece Viola Searles was recently
murdered near Liberty has been filed for
probate.

LOTT, LEN B. - 10 Years Ago - Jul 13, 1893 Len
B. Lott was suffocated in a fire at
Jacksonville.

LOTT, LEN G. - Ancient History - Jun 10, 1903
June 1883 Len G. Lott lost his life in a fire
at Jacksonville.

LOUDERMAN, JOHN - Hung Himself - Aug 5, 1903
John Louderman, an old and well known resident
of Tenn., McDonough Co. committed suicide
Thursday while mentally unbalanced. Was 72
years old.

LOUIS, ZILANE - Quincy - Jun 19, 1894 Zilane
Louis age 38 a member of Kelly's Commonwealth
Army who was left here in St Mary's Hospital
died from pneumonia Friday A.M. Born Belgium
and joined army in San Francisco.

LOWARY, THOMAS - Death - Mar 19, 1895 Thomas
Lowary died at his home in Houston twp Friday
eve March 15th. Born Penn. Feb 24, 1817.
Married Martha Markley 1840. Fall of 1850 they
came to Ill. settling in Houston twp where he
died. 10 children born to them, 7 survive him.
Wife died about 2 years ago. Sons are Thomas
M. of Houston, William of Colorado, daughters
are: Mrs Al Bennett, Mrs M. Nelson, Mrs M.

Stone all of Houston and Miss Jane of Colo.
Buried Sunday in Ebenezer cemetery after
services by Rev McDonnald of LaPrairie in the
church.

LOWARY, THOMAS - Local - Jan 19, 1895 Died,
Thomas Lowary of Houston twp at his home
Saturday A.M. about 80 years old.

LOWE, CHARLES - Quincy - Jan 18, 1895 Charles
Lowe, a well known man about Quincy died
suddenly Tuesday eve from the rupture of a
blood vessel. 52 years old. Leaves a wife and
1 daughter.

LOWE, CHARLES - Local - Feb 16, 1894 Charles
Lowe of El Paso, New Mexico was called home by
the death of his brother at Mt Sterling.

LOWE, JAMES - Local - Aug 20, 1895 James Lowe,
living near Pittsfield accidently shot himself
while cleaning a revolver. Lived only a few
hours.

LOWE, MERTYN M. - Obituary - Feb 16, 1894 Died
Mertyn M. Lowe, son of John E. Lowe formerly of
Camp Point, died of pneumonia at his home in Mt
Sterling Feb 9th, 1894 in his 20th year.
Funeral in Christian Church in Mound Station on
the 13th by Elder Sharpless pastor of the
Chrisitan Chruch at Mt Sterling. Buried
Pleasant View Cemetery at Camp Point.

LOWERY, MRS THOMAS - Golden - Feb 23, 1893 Rev
Rose was called to Ebenezer last Sunday to
preach the funeral sermon of Mrs Thomas Lowery.

LOWRY, MRS SUSANNA - Death - Apr 26, 1895 Mrs
Susanna Lowry died Sunday night at the home of
her son Jacob F. in Clayton, 81 years old.
Susanna (Frost) Lowry was born in Ohio March 1,
1814. Married David Lowry in October 1833.
Came to Ill 1845 and settled on Sect. 36 in
Keene twp where they lived 20 years. Then came
to Camp Point and on to Clayton. Leaves 2 sons
and 1 daughter.

LUBBE, CLEM - Dead - Jul 22, 1903 Clem Lubbe, an advertising manager of Joseph Stern and Sons, Quincy died Saturday. Was 45 years old and was born and reared in Quincy. Married Nicholas Heintz, she died about a year later and he never remarried. Funeral Tuesday at St. Boniface Church.

LUBBE, MRS HENRY - Quincy - Nov 20, 1894 Died Mrs Henry Lubbe, formerly of Louisville, KY died from typhoid fever Friday evening.

LUBBE, JURDEN - Elm Grove - Jan 5, 1893 Jurden Lubben was thrown from his buggy. Died Monday A.M. at the home of a neighbor.

LUMMIS, MRS ANNA - Death - May 18, 1893 Mrs Anna Lummis died last week at the home of her daughter in Quincy, age 83 years. Born in Ohio. Came to Adams Co. with her husband in 1844. Funeral at Mt Pleasant Church, Gilmer twp Saturday.

LUNKIN, AMY - Local - Nov 18, 1896 Died Amy Lunkin, a colored woman who lived in Camp Point several years. Died in Quincy Wednesday, age 56 years.

LUPIN, JERRY - Local - Jan 5, 1893 A german named Jerry Lupin was out with a team Saturday afternoon when the horses ran away throwing Lupin out and against a fence fracturing his skull. Taken home where he died Monday eve. He lived about 5 miles east of Golden.

LUSK, SARAH M. - Doings of Our Neighbors - Mar 13, 1894 Died Sarah M. relict of Levi Lusk at the family home in this city Thursday A.M. Born Georgetown, KY Jul 13, 1800. Married 1823 and came to Rushville 1836 and on to this city 1866. 3 children survive her, Mrs Eliza J. Kendrick and Miss Ann Lusk of this city and Mr L.H. Lusk of Great Bend, KS. Funeral at family home 2 P.M. yesterday (Friday) by Elder M.D. Sharples. "Mt Sterling Examiner"

LYLE, HUGH - Death Records - Nov 3, 1897 Died

Hugh Lyle a former resident of Houston died at his home in Nodaway Co. MO last week. He was a brother of Mrs A.R. Wallace of Camp Point and Mrs Daniel Smith of Golden.

LYLE, MARY M. - Obituary - Oct 28, 1903 Mrs Mary M. Lyle died at the home of her son, John T. Lyle, Waco, Neb. Oct 9, 1903, 72 years old. Mrs Lyle was born Hagerty, native of Kentucky. Came to Rushville as a child where her father died of cholera in early 30's. Family later came to Adams Co. and settled Houston twp where she married James Lyle in 1849. They stayed Houston until about 30 years ago when they moved to Nodaway Co. MO. Mr Lyle died 1885 and she since has lived with children, having 3 sons and 1 daughter surviving her. Remains taken to Bernard, MO for burial. Mrs Lyle was the sister of the late J.T. Hagerty of Camp Point.

LYLE, WILLIAM J. - Local - Dec 29, 1897 William J. Lyle of Nodaway Co. MO was taken ill at Golden. Returned to his home in MO on the 19th, reached home much worse and died soon after. Born Houston twp about 40 years ago.

LYON, MRS ELIZA - Ancient History - Sep 11, 1894 - Sep 10, 1875 Mrs Eliza Lyon died on the 2nd.

LYON, DR T.A. - Death - Apr 8, 1903 Dr T.A. Lyon died from cancer on his lower lip Sunday A.M. Apr 5th, 1903 age 72 years. Services Tuesday P.M. in the Methodist Church by Rev E.A. Hedges. Buried village cemetery. Born in Franklin Co. Penn. Jan 29, 1831 and grew up there. Attended dental school at Philadelphia and graduated. 1859 came to Clayton to locate. In July 1860 he returned to Penn. and married Rebecca C. Leighty and came to Camp Point where he's lived since. Had 6 children, only 2 survive him, Miss Ida E. and Mrs Ella F. McClintock. Mrs Lyon died in 1871 and he married 2nd to Miss Clarrissa L. Christie Mar 8, 1873 who with 2 daughters survive him, 1 son dead.

MADISON, ZACH H. - Local - Aug 31, 1893 Zach
H. Madison of the firm of Madison Bros.
opticians of Chicago and St Joseph, MO
committed suicide at the Tremont House in
Quincy. He came there Saturday somewhat under
influence of liquor and at noon drained a 2 oz.
vial of laudanum in his room. Was discovered
dying at 4. At 1 A.M. Sunday left word to
notify his father, Harvey Madison of Milwood,
Ill. His wife and family arrived Sunday A.M.
from Girard, Ill and were horrified to find him
dead. He formerly lived Quincy but most of his
time was spent on the road.

MAGNUS, LOUIS - Co. Seat - Feb 5, 1896 Will of
Louis Magnus who froze to death last Sunday
night has been admitted to probate. He leaves
all his property to his widow, Franciska from
whom he was divorced several years ago. She
has since married and is a widow for the 2nd
time.

MAHONEY, CHARLES W. - Fell From a Window - Jun
11, 1895 Charles W., son of Mr and Mrs D.A.
Mahoney former resident of this city, but now
of Jacksonville fell from a 3rd story window to
the payment last Sunday night, instantly
killed. Charley had been living and working in
Chicago for 7 years and had sat down in the
window to fan himself. C.W. was born in this
city Feb 24, 1866 and with parents moved to
Jacksonville about 12 years ago. Funeral at
parents home Wed. "Mt Sterling Democrat
Message"

MAJORS, JAMES - West Point - Oct 12, 1893
James Majors is now sick at Wooster, OH where
he was called a short time ago on account of
the sickness of his brother. News reached here
a few days ago that the brother is dead.

MALLORY, JOHN - Suicide in Brown Co. - Sep 30,
1896 Last Saturday night John Mallory age about
40 years living with his father, Reuben Mallory
in Cooperstown committed suicide. Mother found
him. He was single and scarely up to average
mentally. "Mt Sterling Democrat Message"

MANARD, MR AND MRS BEN - Primrose - Nov 9, 1893
Mr and Mrs Ben Manard lost their infant child,
aged 3 months last Tuesday.

MANARD, WILLIAM - Ancient History - Feb 22,
1895 February 1879 William Manard was killed
by being thrown from his horse into a ditch
while going home from Coatsburg.

MANIER, WESLEY H. - Death Record - Mar 10, 1897
Died Hon. Wesley H. Manier one of the oldest
members of the bar of Hancock Co. and for 20
years supreme court reporter. Died at his home
in Carthage Feb 24th. Born Kentucky Oct 2,
1829. Came to Quincy 1851 where his uncle,
Archibald Williams was a lawyer. Studied law
under his uncle and admitted to bar 1852.

MANNING, ALBERT C. - Quincy - Nov 8, 1895
Albert C. Manning, age 22 years, of this city,
who recently lived in St Louis died suddenly
from dropsy while sitting in his chair.

MANSON, MRS REV JOSEPH R. - Quincy - Dec 18,
1894 Died Mrs Manson, wife of Rev Joseph R.
Manson, a former pastor of the Vermont St
Baptist Church, this city, died the past week
in Richfield, Minn.

MANUEL, PETER - Quincy - May 26, 1897 Peter
Manuel, a stranger stopped at the Sherman House
Sunday A.M. having arrived on a long line train
and soon retired to his room. His body was
found Monday eve dead on the floor, having
never been in the bed. Cause unknown.

MARCY, FREDERICK V. - Ancient History - Nov 26,
1902 July 1884 Frederick V. Marcy, a well
known lawyer, died on the 13th.

MARCY, FREDERICK V. - Ancient History - Jul 17,
1894 July 17, 1884 Frederick V. Marcy a
leading attorney of Quincy died.

MARKS, M. - Fatal Fire at Hannibal - Feb 24,
1897 Early Sunday A.M. M. Marks, prop. of the
"New York Store", his sons, Irwin and Harold

age 13 and 11 year and William C. Reed were the 4 victims. Police rescued Mr Marks wife, daughter and mother. Mr Marks lived on the 2nd floor of store and Mr Reed on 3rd floor.

MARKUS, ARNOLD - Quincy - Jul 21, 1897 Died, Arnold Markus, an old resident of the city died at St Marys hospital Friday A.M. age 74 years.

MARLOW, JENNIE - Local - Aug 31, 1893 Jennie Marlow, age 22 years, daughter of Levi Marlow of Camden twp was killed Saturday eve. Miss Marlow and George Lawson was riding in a road cart when their horse ran away and her foot was caught and she was drug a mile. When found she was dead. He escaped.

MARRETT, SAMUEL S. - 10 Years Ago - Oct 19, 1893 Samuel S. Marrett, a prominent farmer of Clayton, died suddenly.

MARRETT, LEWIS CASS - Additional Locals - Sep 23, 1903 Lewis Cass Marrett died in Clayton Tuesday, age 45 years. Was well known in Camp Point.

MARRETT, SAMUEL S. - Ancient History - October 21, 1903 - October 1883 Samuel S. Marrett, a well known farmer of Clayton died suddenly on the 6th.

MARSH, ARTHUR - Death - May 3, 1895 Arthur W. Marsh, son of Congressman Marsh died at his home in Warsaw Monday A.M. from rheumatism and a stroke of paralysis. Was about 30 years old. Parents and brother were in Washington but were telegraphed for.

MARSH, MISS ETTA - Killed at Bluffs - Oct 12, 1893 Accident at 3:30 P.M. Saturday, Miss Etta Marsh and Jennie Drescher, both deaf mutes who reside at Bluffs. While walking the Wabash track they were struck by a locomotive. Miss Marsh was killed and Miss Drescher was hurt but will recover it is thought.

MARSH, JUDGE JOHN W. - Death Record - Jul 14,

1897   Warsaw, Ill July 12 - Judge John W. Marsh
brother of Congressman B.F. Marsh died today 81
years old.   Judge Marsh was the oldest
practitioner at the Hancock Co. bar if not in
western Illinois.

MARSH, NATHANIEL - Local - Nov 20, 1894 Killed
Nathaniel Marsh, age 20, son of Ephriam Marsh
of Hickory twp Schuyler Co. had a horse fall on
him.   Died a few hours later.

MARSH, JUDGE WM - Quincy - May 1, 1894 Will of
Judge Wm Marsh was filed for probate names:
widow, Cornelia Marsh; daughter Mary M. Sweet;
daughter Cornelia W. Babcock; son Lawrence W.;
grandaughter Cornelia Sweet.

MARSH, JUDGE WILLIAM - Death of Judge Marsh -
Apr 17, 1894 Died Judge William Marsh in
Quincy Saturday night.   Born Moravia, Cayuga
Co. N.Y. May 11, 1822.   Was 4th born of 7
children.   Came to Quincy 1854.   Married Miss
Cornelia M. Woods, daughter of Hon. J.L. Woods
of Lockport, N.Y. Aug 29, 1845 who survives
him.   Leaves 2 daughters and 1 son, Mrs Don A.
Sweet of Groton, N.Y., Mrs Chester A. Babcock
and Mr Lawrence W. Marsh.   Also a brother Caleb
W. Marsh who is in Paris on his return from a
trip around the world.

MARSHALL, EV_ - Primrose - Dec 30, 1903 Little
Ev_, eldest daughter of Mr and Mrs Lilburn
Marshall died at her home in Big Neck last
thursday eve of bowel trouble, age 4 years.
Funeral at Coatsburg Saturday P.M. by Rev Rose
of Paloma.

MARSHALL, JAMES - Primrose - Nov 5, 1902 Oscar
Miller and wife and Will Donley and wife of
Bowen attended the funeral of little James
Marshall Sunday.

MARSHALL, JAMES - Primrose - Nov 5, 1902 James
Marshall, eldest son of Mr and Mrs Lilburn
Marshall of Big Neck died Saturday A.M. Nov.
1th.   Sick 9 days of congestion of the bowels.
4 years 7 months old.   Funeral here at

Coatsburg Sunday afternoon by Rev Rose. Buried
Coatsburg cemetery.

MARTIN, MRS ANNA - Elm Grove - Nov 23, 1893
The telegraphic announcement Sunday of the
death of Mrs Anna Martin, near Gothenberg, NE
on Saturday after illness of 2 weeks from
typhoid fever. Was wife of Charles Martin and
daughter of Mr and Mrs Cobus Franzen who were
at her bedside at the time of death.

MARTIN, MRS ANNA - Elm Grove - Nov 30, 1893 Mr
and Mrs Cobus Frazen arrived from Gothenberg,
Nebr. where they attended the funeral of their
daughter, Mrs Anna Martin, who died some time
ago.

MARTIN, DR L.A. - Golden - Mar 10, 1897 Died
last week, Dr L.A. Martin.

MARTIN, DR L.A. - Golden - Mar 10, 1897 Died
Dr L.A. Martin. Wife died 8 years ago.
Funeral from ME Church last Monday by Rev Mays
of the Episcopal Church of which the Dr. was a
communicant. Leaves 2 sons and 2 daughters.
Remains shipped to Rhode Island on Wabash train
Monday eve to be buried beside his wife. It
was accompanied by Miss Sadie Martin, youngest
daughter of the Dr.

MARTIN, DR L.A. - Death Record - Mar 10, 1897
Dr L.A. Martin for 37 years a citizen of Golden
died Saturday A.M. from grip. Came from Rhode
Island. Remains sent to native state for
burial. Leaves 2 sons and 2 daughters.

MARTIN, PHEBE - Quincy - Jun 16, 1897 The will
of Phebe Martin conveys all her property to her
sister, Jennie Bales, to go to her children
equally when they shall become of age.

MARTIN, MRS PHOEBE A. - Death Record - May 26,
1897 Mrs Phoebe A. Martin died at her home in
Camp Point twp May 21, 1897 the 44th
anniversary of her birth. Leaves her husband
and 5 children, the youngest only 8 week old.
Phoebe A. Manard was born in neighborhood where

she died May 21, 1853.   Married William W.
Martin Feb 20, 1877 and has spent her entire
life in that vicinity.   Services in the
Christian Church at Camp Point Sunday afternoon
by Elder Dilley buried village cemetery.   3 of
her sisters and her only brother attended the
funeral.

MARTIN, MR U. - Golden - Mar 10, 1897 Mr U.
Martin of Iowa attended the funeral of his
father at this place last Monday.

MARTLETT, ALFRED - West Point - Aug 17, 1893
Died, Sunday August 13th at 9:30 P.M., little
Alfred, son of Mr and Mrs Fred Martlett, aged 1
year 3 months.   Funeral at ME Church by Rev
McDonald buried West Point cemetery.   Pall
bearers were Misses Nettie and Maud Lines,
Belle Worth and Emma Martin.

MASON, MR - West Point - Apr 13, 1893 Mr and
Mrs Berger attended the funeral of Mr Mason, of
Basco yesterday.

MAYBACK, CAPT J.F. - Death - May 18, 1893 Capt
J.F. Mayback, a well known secret society man
in Quincy died Sunday, age 48 years.   He was
married a 2nd time a few weeks ago.

MEACHAM, W.H. - Quincy - Jan 14, 1903 W.H.
Meacham, age 70 years, a native of Liberty,
recently died in Great Bend, Kansas.

MEAD, CHARLES W. - Local - Jun 15, 1894 Died
Charles W. Mead, formerly division supt. of the
Q at Quincy died yesterday at Los Angeles.   He
was in the real estate business.

MEANS, MISS GEORGIA - Local - Mar 30, 1893
Miss Georgia Means, daughter of the late John
Means, died at the home of her mother in Mt
Sterling Sunday A.M.   Funeral Tuesday A.M. by
Rev E.B. Miner.

MECKES, MRS CATHERINE - Quincy - May 21, 1895
Mrs Catherine Meckes met her death in a cistern
at her home Sunday night.   3 sons were in the

house who made no effort to get her out, but
one ran a mile to police station for help.

MECKLE, JACOB - 20 Years Ago - Aug 17, 1893
Jacob Meckle of Augusta, Ill was killed by his
horse while trying to lead it across the
railroad. It reared and struck him in the
breast with its fore feet.

MEHAFFEY, ROBERT - Columbus - Feb 25, 1903 The
body of Robert Mehaffey who died in Idaho is on
the way here. Funeral services will be held in
Pleasant Grove Church.

MEIER, GOTTLIEB - Adm's Sale - Feb 5, 1896
Public sale at home of the late Gottlieb Meier
1/2 mile north and 1 mile east of Coatsburg and
3-1/2 miles west of Camp Point at 10 A.M.
Tuesday Feb 11th.   Jacob Reichert

MEIND, MRS CAROLINE - Quincy - Feb 10, 1897
Mrs Caroline Meind of Carroll, Iowa sister of
Rev Father Sturn died at St Mary's hospital
Thursday age 44 years.

MEIS, HENRY - Quincy - Oct 12, 1894 Died,
Henry Meis, an old resident of the city died at
the age of 60 years.

MELLEN, JAMES R. - Killed by a Kick - Sep 14,
1894 A young man, James R. Mellen living with
his uncle James Mellen, 4-1/2 miles NW of
Hamilton was kicked by a horse and killed. His
parents live in LaPorte, Texas. "Carthage
Republican"

MENIER, GEORGE - Local - Jan 26, 1894 George
Menier, formerly a baggageman between Galesburg
and Quincy died at his home in Oswego, Kansas,
Monday of consumption. Buried in Plymouth.

MERCER, ROBERT - Local - Mar 10, 1897 Died,
Robert Mercer one of the early settlers at
Rushville died Feb 28, age 87 years.

MERIAM, CAPT A.S. - Co. Seat - Dec 16, 1896
Will of Capt A.S. Meriam who killed himself in

Minneapolis, was sent here the past week to
have signature checked. Dated Nov 12, 1879
leaves all to his widow.

MERKEL, PHILIP J. - Quincy Carpenter Killed -
May 22, 1894 Killed Friday afternoon at
Quincy, Philip J. Merkel by falling about 20
feet. Died Blessings Hospital.

MERRETT, S.S. - Ancient History - Oct 16, 1894
Oct 11, 1883 S.S. Merrett, a prominent farmer
of Clayton died suddenly.

MERSSMAN, FENNA M. - Quincy - Feb 10, 1897
Rosalie Kreitz has qualified as adm of the
estate of Fenna M. Merssman.

MERZ, MRS RACHEL - Deaths - Dec 27, 1895 Mrs
Rachel Merz was born in East Tenn. Jan 1, 1840.
Married W.H. Merz in Ark. in fall of 1857.
Came to Adams Co. 1864 and settled Melrose twp.
Next year moved to Burton where they lived
since. Mrs Merz died Dec. 20th age 55 years 11
months 21 days. Leaves her husband, 2 children
and 2 grandchildren. Services by Rev W.K.
Herzog of Columbus.

MESSICK, JOHN M. - Death - Sep 17, 1902 John
M. Messick age 79 years, living in Houston twp
died Sunday of paralysis which he had had 15
years. Mr Messick had buried 2 wives and 3
children. Buried Monday at Ebenezer.

MESSICK, SAMUEL T. - Local - Apr 9, 1902
Samuel T. Messick, a well known undertaker of
Quincy died Sunday in his 61st year.

MEWTON, JUDSON - Local - Mar 16, 1894 Died
Judson Mewton of Nauvoo drank 1/2 gallon of
wine one day last week and in 3 hours was dead.

MEYER, CAROLINE - Quincy - Mar 4, 1903 Vedict
of the coroner's jury in case of Caroline
Meyer, who met her death by jumping from a
moving train, attaches no blame to any employes
of the railroad.

MEYER, MISS CARRIE - Fatal Accident - Mar 4,
1903 Miss Carrie Meyer, daughter of Mr and Mrs
August F. Meyer was killed Tuesday eve by
jumping from a moving train at the "Q" station,
Quincy. She had boarded train to say goodbye
to a friend and train started up and she
jumped. Died 10:40 P.M. at St Mary's Hospital.

MEYER, MRS GEORGE W. - Local - Feb 11, 1903
Mrs George W. Meyer died Thursday at her home
in Coatsburg, 66 years old. Leaves husband and
7 children, John Meyer and Mrs Emma Knuffman,
of Quincy, Mrs Mary Leach of Coatsburg, Mrs
Lizzie Brown of Kansas City, William Meyer of
Kansas City, Mrs Hattie Stacy of Coatsburg and
Miss Annie Meyer at home.

MEYERS, C.C. - Quincy - Aug 11, 1897 Sarah E.
Meyers has been appointed adm of the estate of
C.C. Meyers.

MEYERS, JOHN A. - Local - Dec 16, 1896 Died
John A. Meyers, an insane man, died at the
county farm the 3rd and was buried in the
Coatsburg cemetery Saturday. Was brother of
Mrs Henry Renken of this place. Services were
by Rev Herzog. "Coatsburg Review"

MEYERS, WILLIAM - Northeast Burton - Dec 14,
1893 A number from this place will attend the
funeral of William Meyers, eldest son of P.R.
Meyers this (Monday) morning. Services at Mt
Pleasant Church and buried in Mt Pleasant
Cemetery.

MEYERS, WILLIAM - Suicide at Barry - May 24,
1895 William Meyers, a well to do farmer who
lives near Barry, Ill committed suicide Tuesday
P.M. No reason given.

MICHEL, WALTER - Primrose - Aug 5, 1896 Little
Walter Michel died Friday A.M. of brain fever.
He was the only son of Mr and Mrs Wm Michel of
Houston twp and 3 years old. Buried Lost
Prairie cemetery Saturday afternoon.

MICHEL, MR AND MRS WILLIAM - Local - Aug 5,

1896   A 3 year old son of Mr and Mrs William
Michel of Houston twp died Friday.   Buried
Saturday at Lutheran cemetery in Columbus twp.

MIDDLEBURG, FREDERICK - Dropped Dead - Mar 24,
1897 Frederick Middleburg an old man died in
Fowler Friday P.M. of heart failure.   Had lived
Fowler a number of years.   Leaves a wife and
several children.

MILBURN, F.H. - Local - Jun 1, 1893   F.H.
Milburn, son of the blind chaplain of the
National House of Representatives committed
suicide in his room at the Saratoga Hotel in
Chicago.   He was found with his throat cut.

MILBY, GEO. D. - Soldiers Buried in Camp Point
cemetery - May 4, 1893   Listed in Co. B, 50th
Illinois Infantry.

MILEHAM, SAMUEL - Soldiers Buried in Camp Point
cemetery - May 4, 1893   Samuel was surgeon in
Tenn. infantry.

MILLER, DR - Columbus - Jul 13, 1894   Died Dr
Miller's father of Clayton was buried on
Tuesday Jul 3, 1894.   Death caused from eating
canned tomatoes.

MILLER, MRS BERNARD H. - Quincy - Jan 1, 1902
Mrs Bernard H. Miller died Friday A.M. age 26
years.

MILLER, EDWARD - Clayton - Nov 15, 1895   Mr
Edward Miller died at his mother's home in
Clayton little before noon Wednesday, after
illness of several years and confined to house
last several months.   About 30 years old.

MILLER, ELI S. - Elm Grove - Oct 11, 1895
Recent information received of the death of Eli
S. Miller, formerly a resident of this
neighborhood after a residence of about 25
years near Oxford, Kansas.

MILLER, FRANK - Co. Seat - Nov 4, 1896   Frank
Miller, a stranger in the city died at St

Mary's Hospital of Brights disease, age 50 years.

MILLER, FRED - Preferred Death to Arrest - May 14, 1895 LaHarpe, Ill May 11th Fred Miller who came in from the West last fall and worked for John A. Edmunds as a farm hand shot himself this P.M. in the timber 3 miles north of this place. He had been drinking several days and yesterday went to William Carroll's, a neighbor and attempted to assault his 13 year old daughter. Carroll swore out an arrest and rather than be caught he fled and shot himself. He is a cowboy and nothing is known of his antecedents.

MILLER, MRS H.T. - Death of Mrs H.T. Miller - May 27, 1896 Telegram from Pasadena, Calif of the death of Mrs Miller, wife of Rev Dr Henry T. Miller pastor of the Presbyterian Church in Quincy. Suffered consumption for some years. Went to Calif. with husband in February for her health. Husband returned to Quincy. She lived only a few months. "Whig"

MILLER, HENRY - Brush Prairie - Mar 23, 1893 Died Monday the 13th inst Henry Miller, leaves a wife and 5 children. Funeral by Farmers Alliance of which he was a member. Sermon by Rev C.F. Stecker of Columbus in German. Buried Union Church Cemetery.

MILLER, MRS REV DR HENRY T. - Co Seat - May 27, 1896 Died the wife of Rev Dr Henry T. Miller pastor of the Presbyterian Church in this city on Wednesday of consumption in Pasadena, Calif., age 40 years.

MILLER, J.H. - Co. Seat - Dec 23, 1896 J.H. Miller, a resident of Quincy since 1851 died Wednesday, age 79 years.

MILLER, REV JAS. - Murdered a Minister - Nov 25, 1896 Bloomington, Ill Nov 24th Rev Jas. Miller, pastor of the Grace Methodist Church at Bloomington was found murdered and robbed in an alley at Decatur, Ill this A.M.

MILLER, MRS JOE S. - Local - Dec 10, 1902 Mrs
Joe S. Miller died at her home in Clayton
Friday night. Services Sunday.

MILLER, JOHN - Local - Sep 28, 1893 We learn
from the Enterprise of the death of John Miller
at Clayton Tuesday A.M., age 58 years. His
wife and 3 sons survive him.

MILLER, JOHN EDWARD - Obituary - Jun 1, 1893
John Edward Miller, son of the late Nathan
Miller died at his mothers home in York Neck
May 5th, age 19 years. Born in Columbus twp
Adams Co. and came to York Neck with his
parents when quite young. Funeral by Rev J.R.
Ivins at York Neck Church.

MILLER, NATHAN - Ancient History - Dec 16, 1896
November 1877 Nathan Miller, a prominent old
citizen committed suicide by hanging himself in
a grove near his home.

MILLER, NATHANIEL OSCAR - Death - May 27, 1903
Nathaniel Oscar Miller, eldest son of Mrs Eliza
Miller of Camp Point twp died May 23rd at the
home of Mrs Mary Wartick of consumption. Was
27 year 9 months 13 days old. Born Gilmer twp
Aug 10, 1875 and came to Camp Point twp in
early childhood with parents. Married July 24,
1902 to Miss Rose Wartick who, with his mother,
4 brother and 1 sister survive him. Funeral
Monday 10 A.M. by Rev C.S. Baughman at York
Neck Church. Buried York Neck Cemetery.

MILLER, OSCAR - Primrose - May 27, 1903 Gene
Poling and wife of Loraine attended the funeral
of Oscar Miller at York Neck Monday.

MILLER, OSCAR - Primrose - May 27, 1903 Will
Miller and wife of Ursa were called here
Saturday by the death of his brother, Oscar.

MINER, ROBERT H. - Death Record - Dec 8, 1897
Robert H. Miner died at Vinita, Ind. terr. (per
paper) Dec. 3rd of typhoid fever. Was son of
Rev and Mrs E.B. Miner of Pawnee, Ill who
during their residence in Camp Point became

known to many of our people. He was asst
principal of Worcester Academy at Vinita. Age
25 years 1 month 13 days. Leaves parents, 1
brother and 3 sisters. Remains brought to Camp
Point and services from Presbyterian Church
Monday P.M. by Dr W.H. Penhallegon, pastor of
the Presbyterian Church at Decatur. Buried
village cemetery.

MINTLE, MISS HATTIE - Local - Jun 17, 1896
Miss Hattie Mintle of Liberty died in Blessing
Hospital Tuesday, age 24 years.

MITCHELL, CHARLES R. - Quincy - Nov 12, 1902
Charles R. Mitchell, formerly a clerk in the
Burlington freight office died on Friday, age
24 years.

MITCHELL, H.M. - H.M. Mitchell Dead - Jun 16,
1897 Hugh M. Mitchell, for over 60 years a
resident of Adams Co. died at his home in
Mendon twp Tuesday June 8th. Leaves a wife and
3 children. Born West Virginia Aug 16, 1831
and brought to Ill. when a child. Farmed Adams
Co. and was for many years one of the directors
of the Adam Co. Fair.

MITTLEBERG, JOHN HENRY - Quincy - Jul 7, 1897
C.M. Giener has been appointed adm of the
estate of John Henry Mittleberg.

MITTS, MINNIE - Local - Aug 19, 1896 Minnie
Mitts age 15 years formerly of Livingston Co.
Missouri committed suicide in Burton twp Sunday
by taking paris green.

MITTS, MRS NANCY - Quincy - Feb 26, 1895 Mrs
Nancy Mitts, who had lived in Adams Co. since
1829 died in Burton twp age 74 years.

MIXER, MR AND MRS JOE - Local - Jun 26, 1894
Died an infant child of Mr and Mrs Joe Mixer,
of Columbus twp died Tuesday.

MOECKER, FRED AND PEARL - Homicide and Suicide -
Mar 19, 1902 Fred Moecker of Quincy shot his
wife twice Sunday at 9:30 P.M. and then fired a

bullet into his worthless brain. She was shot
in right breast and arm. It is thought she
will recover. Mrs Robertson, mother of Mrs
Moecker tells the story. He asked Pearl to go
to gate with him and shot her in the yard.
(Article was to long to copy entirely)

MOECKER, HERMAN - Doings of our Neighbors - Mar
20, 1894 Heirs of the late Herman Moecker are
trying to break his will. Mr Moecker died Mar
18, 1893 leaving an estate of about $30,000.
Son, Herman of this city and William of Deer
Lodge, Montana, daughter, Amelia Frederick of
Quincy, Bertha Lomas of Chicago and Elizabeth
Peffenrath of Omaha. Most left to his widow by
his second marriage, Nancy Moecker. Daughter
Amelia died same day as her father, first wife
is still living.

MOFFETT, MRS SARAH M. - Quincy - May 21, 1895
The late Sarah M. Moffett left no will and her
daughter, Mrs W.R. Lockwood has been appointed
adm of the estate with approved bond of
$80,000.

MONTGOMERY, MRS G.W. - Recent Deaths - Nov 18,
1896 Died Mrs Montgomery, wife of Geo. W.
Montgomery of Clayton Monday A.M. after illness
of almost a year, about 46 years old. Leaves
husband and 1 son. Funeral Tuesday P.M.

MONTGOMERY, MRS MARY T. - Dead - Aug 26, 1903
Mrs Mary T. Montgomery died in Clayton Thursday
eve after a years illness of old age. Was
mother of Dr Frank Montgomery of Mt Sterling
and Mrs James Staker of the Clayton Enterprise.
Was 76 years old. Lived Clayton nearly all her
life. Funeral at Clayton Saturday P.M.

MONTGOMERY, MRS WM - Recent Deaths - Nov 18,
1896 Died Mrs Wm Montgomery at her home in
Kansas City, Saturday A.M. She formerly lived
in Clayton and was well known by our older
citizens. She leaves her husband and 2
daughters.

MOORE, AMANDA J. - Probate Notice - Dec 10,

1902 Amanda J. Moore, deceased   1st Monday of
Feb, 1903 (2nd) Jesse E. Moore, adm.

MOORE, EDWIN - Suicide - Jun 11, 1895 Body of
Edwin Moore a pension attorney of Canton, MO
who has been missing since May 20th was found
Friday A.M. hanging from a tree on Ill. side of
river 1/2 mile S.E. of Canton ferry landing.
Was about 59 years old and leaves a wife and 3
daughters. Lived Canton 15 years, before that
lived Quincy.

MOORE, JAMES - Local - Nov 5, 1895 James Moore
an old citizen and many years an invalid
confined to his bed died Sunday night. Born
Tenn. Came to Ill. in the early 50's. Leaves
aged wife, but no children.

MOORE, JOHN L. - John L. Moore Dead - Oct 14,
1903 John L. Moore, or as known John Moore III
died at his home at Quincy Tuesday from
paralysis, age 83 years. Was rather eccentric,
but an excellent citizen. His wife was Miss
Catherine F. Booth, a sister of the late
William A. Booth of Camp Point .

MOORE, JOSEPH - Local - Jan 12, 1893 Joseph
Dixon and Joseph Moore were driving across the
Santa Fe tracks in a buggy at Stronghurst last
week and hit by a train. Moore was instantly
killed and Dixon badly hurt.

MOORE, MR S.W. - Golden - Jun 9, 1897 Died Mr
S.W. Moore was taken sick May 25th and died
Tuesday June 1st from pneumonia. He had lived
here only about a year. Buried at Huntsville
on June 3rd. Leaves a wife and son.

MOORE, THOMAS - Kills the Wrong Man - Feb 12,
1896 Rushville, Ill Feb 9, 1896 Dead man is
Thomas Moore, shot by Fred Johnson in Rushville
Saturday night. Fatally wounded is Marcus
Spillars who was stabbed by Arthur Randall in
Frederick, a small village 8 miles east of
here.

MOORE, MR AND MRS TOM - Killed in a Runaway -

Oct 20, 1897 Mr and Mrs Tom Moore, Jeff
Griffith and Mrs J.A. Boren were driving in
Clayton Sunday in a carriage when the neckyoke
broke. The ladies jumped, Mrs Moore's head
struck the pavement fracturing her skull. Died
Tuesday A.M.

MOORES, MRS LINUS - Local - May 13, 1903 Mrs
Linus Moores, of Columbus twp died Friday night
after a lingering illness in which old age was
a factor.

MOREY, MRS JANE A. - 10 Years Ago - Dec 28,
1893 Mrs Jane A. Morey died in Clayton.

MORGAN, GEN J.D. - Quincy - Jun 9, 1897
Alderman Anton Binkert has been appointed
appraiser of the estate of Gen J.D. Morgan,
under the inheritance tax law.

MORGAN, GEN JAMES D. - Co. Seat - Sep 23, 1896
Will of Gen James D. Morgan was admitted to
probate dated Jan 5, 1891, names a widow, son
James, son William. William McFadon named Ex.
Estate valued at $200,000 to $300,000.

MORGAN, JAMES D. - Death Record - Sep 16, 1896
Died James D. Morgan of Quincy Saturday A.M.
Born Boston, Mass. 1810 located in Quincy 1834.
Leaves a widow, the 2nd wife and 2 sons.

MORLEY, JOHN - Local - Jul 22, 1896 William
Morley received news from England of the death
of his brother John Morley who visited here 2
years ago. Lived Bradford and served as mayor.
Died June 30th.

MORRIS, ISAAC N. - Ancient History - Nov 2,
1894 - Oct 31, 1879 Isaac N. Morris died in
Quincy on the 22nd.

MORRISON, THEODORE - A Curious Coincidence -
Aug 17, 1894 - At Adams Express Co. sale Mr
Theodore Morrison bought a valise. Turned out
it belonged to a son of his who had died in
Colorado 2 years ago from exposure in a ship
wreck in the Pacific Ocean. Mr Morrison's sons

George and Neal left here several years ago and
went to Australia. On their way home the ship
wrecked in Pacific and they were exposed for
days. Finally made it to land and reached San
Francisco. They started for home and shipped
the valise by express. After the son dying in
Colorado his remains were shipped to Quincy and
buried. "Whig"

MORROW, MCDONALD J. - Local - Mar 19, 1902
McDonald J. Morrow, a spanish war soldier and
an inmate of the Soldiers Home in Quincy
committed suicide in the back room of the White
House saloon, Quincy Monday afternnon by taking
carbolic acid. Was tried in county court Jan
15th on question of his sanity, but was
discharged.

MORTON, COL. C.H. - Ancient History - Jun 23,
1897 - June 1880 Col. C.H. Morton committed
suicide in Quincy.

MORTON, COL. C.H. - Ancient History - Jun 25,
1895 - June 1880 Col. C.H. Morton committed
suicide in Quincy.

MORTON, CO. C.H. - Ancient History - Jun 12,
1894 - June 3, 1880 Col. C.H. Morton committed
suicide in Quincy.

MORTON, HENRY - Quincy Whig - Jun 25, 1902
Quincy Whig Tuesday says: news received here
yesterday of the death of Henry Morton at the
home of his daughter in Colur d' Alene, Idaho
last Friday. Formerly lived Quincy. Was a
soldier in Civil War from "61" to "65" in the
50th Ill. Inf. Lived for awhile in Soldiers
Home until some time ago when he went to Idaho.
Was 63 years old. Leaves 1 brother, John E.
Morton of Perry, Ill and 1 sister, Mrs Anna
Ferrill, the late Mrs C.E. King of this city,
who died a little over a year ago was a sister.

MORTON, MISS MERINDA - Sorrow of the Sabbath
School - Sep 28, 1894 Memorial to memory of
Miss Merinda Morton. Miss Merinda Morton came
to her death Jul 23, 1894 by accidental

drowning in the San Joaquin River, Fresno Co.
Calif. near the home of Mr V.B. Cobb.

MORTON, MISS MERINDA - Local - Jul 27, 1894
Telegram received this week by Mr and Mrs B.
Morton of Gilmer telling of the death of their
daughter, Miss Merinda Morton at Fresno,
Calif., where she was keeping house for her
brothers.

MORTON, MISS MERINDA - Prairie - Aug 7, 1894
Died Miss Merinda Morton of Fresno, Calif who
drowned while trying to save the life of a lady
companion while in bathing. Both ladies died.

MORTON, WILLIAM ELLIS - Obituary - May 4, 1893
William Ellis, infant son of Wm C. and Mary A.
Morton, died very suddenly at their home west
of LaPrairie Friday April 28, 1893. Funeral at
Ebenezer M.E. Church on Saturday by 3 P.M. by
Rev R.A. Hartrick.

MOSS, MRS S.C. - Golden - Jul 21, 1897 Word
received here Monday of the death of Mrs S.C.
Moss of Burlington, Iowa, wife of Dr S.C. Moss,
ex-surgeon of the 78th Ill. Inf. was dead.

MOTTER, MRS H.R. - Local - Jan 29, 1902 Mrs
H. R. Motter died at Clayton last Wednesday of
cancer of the face. Funeral was Saturday
afternoon.

MOURNING, F.G. - West Point - Jul 19, 1895 Mr
and Mrs F.L. Fulmer of Hamilton attended
funeral of F.G. Mourning.   Charles Overman,
an old resident of this palce but now of
Oquawka, attended funeral of F.G. Mourning.

MOURNING, FELIX G. - Death - Jul 19, 1895 Died
Felix G. Mourning age 76 years 7 months 20
days. Born Nov 23, 1818. Married Nancy Watson
Feb 27, 1839. Had 6 children, 4 still living.
Wife died few years ago. Married second to Mrs
M.S. Carrier Aug 3, 1887. He died Saturday
A.M. July 13th at 4. Services at ME Church
Sunday A.M. at 10 by Rev Miller. Buried West
Point cemetery. Services at grave by G.A.R.

post and order of Free Masons.

MUEGGE, MRS LOUISA - Quincy - Jan 12, 1894
Died Mrs Louisa Muegge, age 71 years of Quincy.
Had lived Quincy 28 years. Died from cancer.

MUELLER, HENRY B. - Probate Notice - Apr 6,
1893 Henry B. Mueller, deceased 1st Monday of
June 1893 (5th) Dore Mueller, adm.

MULL, CLARENCE - Quincy - May 5, 1897 Clarence
Mull, formerly a telegraph operator in this
city died Friday night in Hot Springs, Ark.

MULLER, MRS AMELIA - Died in Asylum - Jul 26,
1895 Mrs Amelia Muller a inmate of the insane
ward of the Adams Co. alms house for many years
died Sunday, age 80 years, from cancer on her
face. Left an estate valued at $50,000 and not
a relative in U.S. The fortune goes to
relatives in Germany. Buried Quincy.

MULLER, NATHAN - Ancient History - Nov 13, 1894
Nov 9, 1877 Nathan Muller, a prominent citizen
committed suicide by hanging while laboring
under mental depression.

MUNDON, MISS - West Point - Jul 6 1893 Mr and
Mrs Capt Mourning attended the funeral of their
niece, Miss Mundon, of Basco, last Saturday.
Funeral by Rev McDonald of that place.

MUNSON, BRYON P. - Ancient History - Dec 18,
1894 - December 1877 Bryon P. Munson died in
Quincy.

MURPHY, MRS CATHERINE - Co. Seat - Jan 22, 1896
Mrs Catherine Murphy of Hannibal age 84 years
died at St Mary's hospital Wednesday.

MURPHY, MRS JACOB - Paloma - Jan 4, 1894 Died
last Tuesday Dec 25th Mrs Jacob Murphy.
Services at Columbus Thursday by Rev Wahlforth
of Urbana.

MURPHY, MRS JACOB - Columbus - Jan 4, 1895
Died Christmas Day 1894, Mrs Jacob Murphy age

76 years. Leaves aged husband, 1 son and 5 daughters. Funeral at Columbus Thursday Dec 27th by Rev J.L. Wahlforth.

MURPHY, JOHN - Suicide at Augusta - Feb 19, 1902 John Murphy, age about 65 years, an old bachelor living in Augusta committed suicide Saturday 9 A.M. by blowing off the top of his head with a shot gun. Lived with an uncle at one time and also lived with 2 aunts.

MURPHY, JOSEPH - Columbus - Nov 25, 1903 Joseph Murphy of Kohaka, MO came to attend the funeral of his sister which was held at this place last Saturday.

MURPHY, MISS MARGARET - Columbus - Nov 28, 1903 Miss Margaret Murphy died at her home in Gilmer twp, 3 miles west of Columbus on the A.M. of Nov 19th. Was 52 years old. Funeral at ME Church of this place Saturday, Nov 21st by Rev W.E. Rose, her pastor. Buried village cemetery by the side of her mother.

MURPHY, MARY - Quincy - Sep 13, 1895 Mary Murphy, an employee of the Newcomb Hotel was killed Thursday A.M. on the elevator when she was getting on a boy started it up. Her head being caught between the floor of the elevator and the floor above.

MURPHY, WILLIAM - Switchman Killed- Dec 16, 1903 William Murphy, a switchman in Quincy yards, age 25, was killed Friday by falling from the top of a car. Worked in the yards several years and was a sober, industrious young man.

MURPHY, WILLIE - Local - Jan 1, 1895 Willie Murphy, a Monmouth lad of 16 years was found dead in an alley there with a rifle beside him. His father had threatened to whip him shortly before he was found. Thought to be suicide.

MUTZ, MRS CAROLINE - Death Record - Jul 14, 1897 Died Mrs Caroline Mutz the night of the 7th inst in Quincy, age 76 years 6 months.

Leaves a son and 2 daughters. She and her
husband settled in Quincy 1844. Funeral from
St Boniface Church Friday A.M.

MYERS, C.C. - Paloma - Jun 2, 1897 Quite a
number from here attended the funeral of C.C.
Myers at Mendon last Saturday.

MYERS, CYRUS C. - Death of C.C.Myers - Jun 2,
1897 Cyrus C. Myers, supervisor of Honey Creek
died Thursday night at his home near Mendon age
56 years. Born Penn. Came as a boy to Ill.
with parents. Large family 4 brothers - Jacob,
John, Lee and Lutellus, and 7 sisters - Mrs Dr
Gilliland of Coatsburg, Mrs Moses Worman, Mrs
Frank Ogle of Paloma, Mrs F.F. Dudley, Mrs
Simon Young of Oklahoma and Mrs William Osborne
of Quincy and Mrs James Evans survive him.
Also his aged mother who lives in the old
homestead between Mendon and Fowler. He leaves
a wife, Sarah, daughter of James Dudley, also 2
daughters, Mrs Samuel Tallcott and Mrs J.B.
Frisbie Jr., 4 sons D.H., Irving and Walter of
Mendon and Fred C. of Conway Springs, Kansas.
Funeral from family home Saturday afternoon.

MYERS, MR AND MRS WILBUR - Local - Aug 5, 1896
An infant child of Mr and Mrs Wilbur Myers of
Gilmer was buried Tuesday.

MYERS, WILLIAM KING - Died - Dec 14, 1893
Died, William King Myers at the home of his
uncle C.E. King, Quincy, Ill on Saturday the
9th of Dec. 1893. Was eldest child of P.R. and
Mary K. Myers of Gilmer, 10 miles east of
Quincy. His mother died 4 years ago and Billy
was almost heart broken over her loss. Was
sick about 6 weeks. Leaves brothers and
sisters. Funeral at Mt Pleasant Church by
Elder White. Buried Mt Pleasant cemetery
beside his mother and little sister.

MYERS, WM - Local - Dec 14, 1893 Wm Myers, the
young man who drank muriatic acid by mistake,
about 2 months ago died after suffering untold
agony Saturday.

MCAFF, Mrs Emily - Quincy - Dec 21, 1894   Died
Mrs Emily McAff, age 79, one of the pioneers of
the city died Sunday A.M.

MCANULTY, MRS ANNA - Death - Apr 9, 1895   Mrs
Anna McAnulty died in Bangor, Calif. Mar 17,
1895. Was the relict of the late William
McAnulty of Camp twp who died nearly 50 years
ago. She lived many years in Columbus and
later Quincy. About 10 years ago went to
California.

MCBRATNEY, MRS THOMAS - Local - Mar 25, 1903
Mrs Thomas McBratney was called to Louisiana,
MO Monday by the death of a relative.

MCBRATNEY, WALTER - Clayton - Sep 18, 1894
Died Walter McBratney died Sept 15th, age 17.

MCBRIDE, ARTHUR - Northeast Burton - Jan 14,
1903 Mrs Phil Spangler received sad news of
death of her nephew, Arthur McBride, of Loraine
last Saturday. Funeral on Sunday Jan 4th at
Loraine. Buried in cemetery of that place.

MCCAFFREY, EDWARD - Death - Aug 27, 1902
Edward McCaffrey died last Wednesday afternoon
after a long illness, about 83 years old. Born
in Ohio. Came to Ill. in early 50's when he
drove the stage between Mt Sterling and Quincy.
Lived Camp Point for a number of years.
Funeral at the house Friday afternoon. Buried
Coatsburg Cemetery. Leaves wife and 7
children.

MCCALISTER, MARIA - Death Record - Jan 4, 1895
Maria McCalister born near Circleville, Ohio
Sep 3, 1818 died Dec 25, 1894 age 76 years 3
months 22 days. Married Jul 21, 1842 to Jacob
C. Murphy. Mother of 10 children, 6 and her
husband survive her. Services by Rev Wahlforth
of Urbana, Ill.

MCCANN, LILLIE HAZEL - Columbus - Mar 13, 1894
Died Lillie Hazel McCann infant child of Mr and
Mrs John McCann Sunday eve Mar 4th of brain
fever. Services by Rev Herzog at the home.

Buried village cemetery.

MCCANN, MARJORIE FAAET - Quincy - Nov 1, 1895
Died Wednesday A.M. Marjorie Faaet, only child
of Mr and Mrs F.M. McCann, 8 months old. Taken
ill with cholera infantum dying Wednesdy A.M.

MCCLAIN, ROBERT - Ancient History - Jul 16,
1895 July 1879 Robert McClain of Clayton twp
committed suicide by hanging.

MCCLAIN, ROBERT - Ancient History - Jul 24,
1894 July 1879 Robert McClain of Clayton twp
committed suicide by hanging himself.

MCCLANE, JOHN - Elm Grove - Apr 29, 1896 John
McClane died last Wednesday A.M. of typhoid
fever. Lived near Pine Grove and about 70
years old and leaves a family of grown children
all 8 themselves but one, a daughter and his
aged wife.

MCCLELLAND, DR COCHRAN - Death - Feb 25, 1903
Dr Cochran McClelland, a noted physician of
Philadelphia, died recently and remains were
brought to Mendon, his early home for burial.
Dr Thomas McClelland president of Knox College
is a brother.

MCCLINTOCK, MR AND MRS DAVID - Primrose - Dec
9, 1903 A little girl was born at Mr and Mrs
David McClintock on Thursday, but died the same
day.

MCCLINTOCK, JAMES A. - Obituary - Mar 6, 1896
Died James A. McClintock at his home in Clayton
twp March 1st age 54 years 8 months 11 days.
Native of Ohio. Came to this vicinity in
childhood. Lived with his mother until she
died 15 years ago. Since then he lived with
brother, Samuel W. Services at Hebron Church
Tuesday, buried in cemetery there. Services by
Rev Peter Slagel.

MCCLINTOCK, JAMES - Death - Jun 9, 1897 Died
James McClintock in this city on Friday May
28th. Born Ireland in county Formaugh in 1816.

Came to U.S. 1834 and settled Adams Co. where
he lived till 1872 when he moved to Missouri
twp where he lived till last Dec. when he moved
to this city. In 1852 he married Miss Lucy
Greer of Rushville had 5 children-1 son and 4
daughters, Mrs McClintock and son Samuel
survive him. Services at ME Church in this
city of which he was a member since 1854 by Rev
F.B. Madden on last Sunday afternoon. "Mt
Sterling Republican"

MCCLINTOCK, JAMES - Local - Jun 2, 1897 Moses
Vance received telegram Saturday of the death
of his brother in law James McClintock who
lived near Mt Sterling. Lived on Dean farm
until about 15 years ago when he moved to Brown
Co.

MCCLINTOCK, MRS LUCY - Death - Mar 18, 1903
Mrs Lucy McClintock died at her home near Mt
Sterling Sunday, Mar 15th age 70 years. Her
maiden name was Greer. She was reared near
Rushville. After her marriage to James
McClintock she lived several years in Camp
Point twp moving to Mt Sterling 30 years ago.
Leaves a son, Samuel W. McClintock of Camp
Point. Funeral Monday.

MCCLINTOCK, MRS S.W. - Local - Nov 12, 1902 Mr
and Mrs J.G. McClintock went to Sterling Friday
to attend the funeral of Mrs S.W. McClintock.

MCCLINTOCK, MRS SUSANNA - Ancient History - Nov
26, 1902 - July 1884 Mrs Susanna McClintock
widow of Thomas McClintock died on the 17th.

MCCLINTOCK, MRS SUSANNAH - Ancient History -
Jul 24, 1894 - July 24, 1884 Mrs Susannah
McClintock died on the 14th.

MCCLINTOCK, THOMAS - 10 Years ago - Mar 16,
1894 Thomas McClintock died.

MCCLINTOCK, THOMAS - Ancient History - Feb 5,
1902 - March 1884 Thomas McClintock, a pioneer
died on the 5th age 87 years.

MCCLINTOCK, WILLIAM - Ancient History - Nov 12,
1895 - Nov 1881 William McClintock died age 84.

MCCLUNG, WILLIAM L. - Co Seat - Feb 5, 1896
Will of William L. McClung leaves all his
property to his widow, Rachel, during her
lifetime to be devided at her death among the
children-Samuel McClung, Charity Smith and
Clara Zern.

MCCORMACK, THOMAS - Co Seat - Dec 2, 1896
Thomas McCormack, a former prominent and well
to do citizen of Brown Co., but who has been
blind several weeks died at St Mary's hospital,
age 88 years.

MCCOY, BEN W. - Local - Feb 19, 1896 Mrs H.C.
Sawyer of Cornell who was called to Kirksville,
MO by the death of her brother, Ben W. McCoy is
guest of Mrs E.E.B. Sawyer.

MCCOY, BENJ W. - Death of Ben W. McCoy - Feb 5,
1896 Death of Benj. W. McCoy at Kirksville, MO
Monday of heart disease. Born Clayton and
spent most of his life there being in jewelry
business part of that time. 10 or 12 years ago
he moved to Kirksville and was a traveling
salesman for a society regallia house.

MCCOY, MRS ELIZA - Clayton - May 31, 1895 Died
Mrs Eliza McCoy relict of John C. McCoy Esq.
and sister of Mrs M.T. Montgomery of this
place. Word received from relatives from
Georgetown, Colorado.

MCCOY, F.A. - Died - Oct 8, 1902 F.A. McCoy,
age 48 years of Clayton died at 1 A.M. Monday
of cancer. Sick several months. Was a well
known stock buyer in this city. Leaves widow,
1 son and 1 daughter. Funeral at Clayton
tomorrow 2 P.M. by Rev Rice at Presbyterian
Church. Burial to be in South Side cemetery.
Quincy Journal, Monday

MCCOY, JOHN D. - Additional Locals - Oct 21,
1903 John D. McCoy, a former resident of
Clayton and a brother of Blatchford A. McCoy,

supervisor of that twp died at Lordsburg,
Calif. on the 8th inst. from cancer. He was
reared in Clayton twp and moved to Calif. 8 or
10 years ago.

MCCOY, MRS MARTHA - Local - Jan 12, 1894 Died
Mrs Martha McCoy widow of the late John McCoy
died at her home at Clayton Tuesday age 73
years. Funeral yesterday at Presbyterian
Church. Was mother of B.A. McCoy who is well
known in Camp Point.

MCCREARY, THOMAS - Death Records - May 20, 1896
Died Thomas McCreary at his home in Macomb May
13th of apolexy. Born Ireland Aug 13, 1831.
Came to U.S. when 16 years old settled in
Virginia. About 1850 he moved to Schuyler Co.
Ill. Short time later to Camp Point. Married
Miss Rebecca A. Carden in Dec 1858. Lived Camp
Point 17 years then moved to Macomb. Had 4
children - Mrs Emma Covert of Chicago; Mrs Mary
Coats, deceased; Mrs Nettie Taylor, Columbus,
Ill; Mrs Laura Pollock, Victor, Colo. Buried
Columbus Saturday.

MCCREERY, DAVID - Golden - May 12, 1897 Quite
a number of Golden people attended the funeral
of David McCreery at Huntsville last Sunday
A.M.

MCCRONE, GEO. C. - Co Seat - Dec 2, 1896 Lyman
McCarl was appointed adm of the estate of Geo.
C. McCrone.

MCCRONE - George C. - Recent Deaths - Nov 25,
1896 Died George C. McCrone Friday night after
illness of several weeks at his home in Quincy.
Born Vermont 39 years ago. Came to Quincy
about 20 years ago and taught school and
studied law. Had necrosis of the bones of his
foot. Was in Blessing Hospital 2 years.
Leaves a wife, no children.

MCCRORY, MRS JOHN - Death Record - Aug 11, 1897
Mrs John McCrory, daughter of Mrs and Mrs Chas.
Kay, former residents of this vicinity died at
Hull on the 29th ult. She leaves a husband and

4 children.

MCCUTCHEON, WILLIAM - Death record - Dec 22,
1897 William McCutcheon born Deerhurst, Canada
Jun 22, 1855. Died in Camp Point, Ill Dec 15,
1897 age 42 years 5 months 23 days. Came to
U.S. 1867 settled near Trenton, Ill. Married
Aug 19, 1886 to Miss Lu E. Johnston of
Pocahontas where he taught school. Leaves 2
sisters, a widow and 6 small children. Moved
to Camp Point about 18 months ago. Worked for
Railway Mail Service since April 1889. Buried
Pocahontas.

MCDANNOLD, MRS T.I. - Local - Sep 29, 1897 Mrs
T.I. McDannold of Mt Sterling died on the 23rd
in her 70th year. She was mother of
excongressman John J. McDannold.

MCDAVITT, DR J.E. - Local - Apr 23, 1902 Jack
R. Pearce, county clerk was in town Tuesday
making arrangements for the funeral of Dr J.E.
McDavitt Thursday.

MCDAVITT, DR JAMES E. - Death - Apr 30, 1902
Died Dr James E. McDavitt at his home in Quincy
on the 22nd inst. Brought to Camp Point on the
24th and buried in Ebenezer in Houston. Born
near Bowling Green, KY Sep 8, 1826. Came to
Adams Co. after graduating in St Louis Medical
College and located on Sect 5 in Camp Point.
Married Miss Mary McGinnis Apr 29, 1852 and
settled near Chatten until 1879 when they moved
to Quincy to be with their daughter, Mrs Sam
Woods. Surviving are the widow and daughter
and 1 brother, Dr Virgil McDavitt.

MCDAVITT, DR JAS. E. - Local - Apr 23, 1902 Dr
Jas. E. McDavitt died at his home in Quincy
Tuesday. Funeral at Ebenezer Church in Houston
twp Thursday afternoon.

MCDAVITT, DR VIRGIL - Death - Oct 7, 1903 Died
Dr Virgil McDavitt, Friday A.M. age 74 years
from blood poisoning from a scratch on his hand
from an instrument he had been using. Native
of Kentucky. Came to Ill after graduating from

medicine. Locating in Houston twp where he
married Miss Caroline McGinnis in 1854.
Started housekeeping in Camp Point twp on the
farm now occupied by L.C. Schroeder, in Sect 5.
Dr McDavitt served in army during the rebellion
and settled after in McDonough Co. until 1880
when he moved to Quincy. His wife, 2 daughters
and 5 sons survives him.

MCDONALD, THOMAS - Ancient History - Aug 9,
1895 - August 1876 Thomas McDonald was killed
by Zach Wilson at Plymouth.

MCDONALD, THOS. - Ancient History - Aug 21,
1894 - Aug 18, 1876 Thos McDonald was killed at
Plymouth by Zach Wilson.

MCDOWELL, ABNER - Death - Dec 7, 1893 Clayton-
Dec. 1st - Abner McDowell, an old citizen of
this place was found dead in his yard
yesterday. Had evidently been there all night.
He lived alone, his wife being in the insane
asylum for a number of years. Cause of death
not determined.

MCDOWELL, SAMUEL K. - Death - Dec 10, 1902
Samuel K. McDowell, oldest son of Capt A.S.
McDowell, Clayton, died at Oklahoma City
December 1st. Was employed by a big
construction co. and 44 years old. Remains
brought to Clayton. Funeral Thursday.

MCELROY, ELLA - Quincy - Jun 12, 1894 Died
Ella McElroy age 16 died after a short sickness
Wednesday A.M.

MCELROY, JAMES A. - Obituary - May 13, 1896
James A. McElroy born near Lancaster, Fairfield
Co. Ohio Dec 29, 1833. Came to Ill. 1853
settled McDonough Co. In 1861 he married
Elizabeth Kions and about 1875 moved to
Chicago. Then to Kansas City where his wife
died 1887. Returned to Chicago till last fall
when he came back to Camp Point and married Mrs
Mary Lasley Nov 27, 1895. He died May 7th at 1
A.M. Leaves wife, a son and daughter both
married and living in Chicago. The son and

little grandaughter came down and remained till
the end. Services at the house Thursday at
6:30 P.M. by Rev A.N. Simmons. Buried
McDonough Co.

MCELWEE, HARRY - Death - Apr 8, 1903 Harry
McElwee, an widely known hotel clerk died in
Quincy, Thursday. He came to Quincy from
Washington, D.C. about 1867 and spent most of
his time in the Occidental hotel. Had no
family, but left 1 brother and 2 sisters.

MCFADDON, ANNA C. - Quincy - Feb 12, 1902 W.A.
Richardson, executor of the will of Anna C.
McFaddon petitioned to sell real estate valued
at $33,000.

MCFARLAND, BEN - Events of 1878 - Jan 12, 1893
Ben McFarland died at the home of his brother,
Daniel.

MCFARLAND, CLIFTON HUGHES - Died - Jan 26, 1893
Clifton Hughes, infant son of Thomas and Ada
McFarland, died January 20th. He was 1 month
and 2 days.

MCFARLAND, D.B. - Ancient History - Dec 16,
1896 January 1878 D.B. McFarland died at the
home of his brother D.G. McFarland.

MCFARLAND, EPHRAIM - West Point - Sep 2, 1896
Died Uncle Ephraim McFarland died Tuesday at 10
A.M. of a complication of diseases. Born Ohio,
came to Quincy in early manhood and learned
cooper trade. Lived West Point last 20 years.
Services Wednesday A.M. 10 o'clock by the
Masons. Buried West Point cemetery.

MCFARLAND, GUY - Overcome with Gas - Jul 1,
1903 Guy McFarland, a nephew of Mrs Arthur
Baird, age 13 years lost his life last week
when overcome with gas in an abandoned shaft.
He was son of Mr and Mrs D.B. McFarland.

MCFARLAND, JAMES - Primrose - Aug 28, 1894
Died a child of James McFarland died Tuesday.

MCFARLAND, LEWIS - Probate Notice - Apr 8, 1896
Lewis McFarland, deceased   1st Monday of May
(4th)   Samuel Woods, adm.

MCFARLAND, MARTHA - Obituary - Dec 10, 1895
Martha McFarland was born in Greene Co. Ohio
Aug 25, 1834.   Left an orphan at age 8 years.
Reared by her brother.   In fall of 1853 she
went to live with a sister in Vermillion Co.
Ill and the next year to another sister in
Houston twp, Adams Co. Ill.   July 19, 1855 she
married D.G. McFarland, had 4 sons and 4
daughters, 2 sons and 1 daughter died before
her.   Joined ME Church at Hebron 1865 under Rev
B. Newman.   Last 10 years sufferd heart
trouble.   Died Saturday at 10:30 P.M. Dec. 7th.
Services 11 A.M. Monday at Hebron Church by Rev
A.N. Simmons and Rev W.M. Reed and Rev P.
Slagel of Golden.

MCFARLAND, MR AND MRS OL - Local - Apr 28, 1897
A little child of Mr and Mrs Ol McFarland died
Tuesday A.M.

MCFARLAND, William W. - Death of W.W. McFarland
Jun 22, 1894 Died William W. McFarland, one of
the pioneer settlers of Houston twp died June
13th age 75 years.   Buried Hebron Cemetery on
the 15th.   Born Greene Co. Ohio May 29, 1819
and with his parents located near Hebron Church
when about 20 years old.   43 years ago he
settled in Houston 1 mile west of Golden.
Married Miss Maria Bishop of Xenia, Ohio in
1840.   She died 5 years ago.   1 daughter and 3
sons survive him: Mrs Will Finley and Isaac
McFarland of Golden, Thomas McFarland of
Plymouth and H.M. McFarland of Kentland, Ind.

MCFARLAND, WILLIAM M. - Probate Notice - Sep
30, 1896 William M. McFarland, deceased   1st
Monday of December 1896 (7th)   Martha L.
Forsythe, adm.

MCFARLAND, WILLIAM M. - Death Record - Sep 16,
1896 Died William M. McFarland died Friday
A.M. Sept 11th age 82 years.   Born Ohio Aug 12,
1814.   Came to Adams Co. 1832 to Houston twp.

Son of Capt John and Rebecca McFarland.
Married Eliza McFarland Nov 30, 1837 had 1 son
and 3 daughters, 2 daughters survive, 1 brother
D.G. McFarland and 1 sister Mrs Priscilla
Powers also survive him. Joined Methodist
Church at Hebron 1841 and was baptized in Bear
Creek north of the church. Funeral at Hebron
Church Saturday by Rev W.M. Reed.

MCGAUGHEY, MRS CAROLINE - Ancient History - Oct
7, 1896 - May 1877 Mrs Caroline McGaughey died.

MCGAUGHEY, MRS CAROLINE - Ancient History - Jul
15, 1896 - May 1877 Mrs Caroline McGaughey
died.

MCGAUGHEY, WOODIE - Local - Oct 15, 1895
Woodie McGaughey, little son of Mrs Georgie
Snider, formerly of Camp Point died recently in
Anselmo, NE where his mother lives.

MCGILL, CLAYTON - Accidently Killed - Jun 11,
1895 Clayton McGill was killed Monday at 7
A.M. on his farm while taking down a hay press.
Son, Sidney was helping him. Born Ohio. Came
to Camp Point about 1856. Entered army and
served 3 years in Co. G 78th Ill. On return
from army he married Miss Sophronia Gay who
with 8 children survive him. For about 25
years he had lived on the county line 2-1/2
miles south of Bowen. Funeral from the family
home Wednesday 10 A.M. by G.A.R. Post at Bowen
held services at grave.

MCGILL, CLAYTON - Local - Jun 11, 1895 Charles
V. Gay received word Monday A.M. of the death
of Clayton McGill who lived on county line
south of Bowen.

MCGILL, CLAYTON - Funeral of C. McGill - Jun
14, 1895 Funeral of Clayton McGill was from
the family home in Chili twp Wednesday 10 A.M.
Buried Bowen cemetery.

MCGINLEY, JOHN - Primrose - Oct 9, 1894 A
child of John McGinley was buried at Coatsburg
Saturday.

MCGINLEY, MR AND MRS JOHN - Pick ups from the
Necks - Oct 12, 1894 Died the youngest child
of Mr and Mrs John McGinley died on Thursday
night and buried Coatsburg cemetery Saturday.

MCGINNIS, MARTHA - Quincy - Sep 10, 1902 Heirs
of Martha McGinnis have instituted suit to
break her will, which gave all of her estate to
one brother, John McGinnis.

MCGINNIS, SMITH - Ancient History - May 22,
1894 - May 26, 1881 Smith McGinnis, an old
settler of Houston twp died at the home of Dr
V. McDavitt in Quincy.

MCINTYRE, MRS ROBERT - Death of Mrs McIntyre -
Jan 6, 1897 Mrs Robert McIntyre died at the
home of her son in Ellington Friday, age 75
years.

MCINTYRE, W.H. - Local - Feb 16, 1893 The
sister of W.H. McIntyre, editor of the Mendon
Dispatch died last week. She was her brothers
housekeeper and was nearly 60 years old. Born
England. W.H. is the last survivor of the
family.

MCKEE, MISS ELIZABETH - Local - Oct 14, 1903
Miss Elizabeth McKee of Augusta was found dead
in bed Tuesday A.M., 70 years old.

MCKENNEY, JOHN - Quincy - Jul 1, 1896 John
McKenney was killed at Burlington Wednesday
night by a train. He was on his way home to
Quincy from Des Moines.

MCKINNEY, JOHN - Two Boys Drowned - Jun 24,
1896 John McKinney of Mt Sterling, age 10
years fell into the public reservoir Saturday.
His companion, Frederick Guthery made a heroic
effort to save him, but both boys were drowned.

MCLAUGHLIN, ALEXANDER - Quincy - Mar 18, 1903
Word received here that Alexander McLaughlin, a
former resident of Adams Co., was shot and
killed in Paris, Texas.

MCLAUGHLIN, MRS NANCY A. - Quincy - Feb 24,
1897 Died Mrs Nancy A. McLaughlin, one of the
pioneers of Adams Co. Died in Ursa, age 77
years.

MCLEAN, E.H. - Quincy - Jan 7, 1903 E.H.
McLean, a traveling man who was born in this
city, died on Friday A.M., age 54 years.

MCLEAN, JAMES - Killed by a Fall - Jul 29, 1896
Tuesday afternoon James McLean was instantly
killed and Charles Purvis was hurt. The 2 were
employed by H.F.J. Ricker and were painting the
outside of the bank and were on the ladder when
one of the hooks gave way. Mr Purvis was taken
to his home 525 N. 10th St.

MCMAHAN, DR ROBERT W. - Dr McMahan Dead - Mar
18, 1896 Died Dr Robert W. McMahan a widely
known physician of Quincy died in Chicago
Sunday, age 64 years. Native of Kentucky.
Buried Quincy today.

MCMECHAN, JAMES - Local - Jun 22, 1893 Tuesday
night at his home in Lima occurred the death of
James McMechan, age 78 years 4 months 15 days
from kidney disease. He was an old settler of
Adams county. Lived Burton twp and will be
buried there. Leaves wife and 5 children they
are-T.F. McMechan, a lawyer in Oklahoma City,
Okl., James of Lima and 3 single daughters
living in Lima.

MCMEIN, HUGH - Local - Aug 31, 1894 Died Hugh
McMein, father of Harry McMein, of the Whig
died at his son's home in Quincy Thursday age
69 years. Born Scotland. Lived Quincy 30
years.

MCMILLAN, JOSEPH - Quincy - Mar 1, 1895 Joseph
McMillan, one of the pioneers of this city died
at West Point, age 73 years.

MCMILLAN, JOSEPH - West Point - Feb 22, 1895
Died Feb 11th at 10:30 A.M. Joseph McMillan age
73 years after a short illness. Born Ireland,
but his home has been here for many years.

Leaves a wife, 2 sons, 2 daughters all with him at death. Funeral by Rev Miller at ME Church Wednesday. Buried West Point cemetery.

MCMURRAY, MRS G.M. - Choked to Death - Nov 20, 1894 Mrs G.M. McMurray of Quincy had a piece of meat lodged in her throat Monday. Causing death Friday. She was Miss Eliza A. Reed of Boone Co. MO. Married G.M. McMurray in 1869. Was treasurer of WCTU. Buried Clayton.

MCNAY, JOHN - Death of John McNay - Aug 26, 1896 Died Mr John McNay at his home about 4 miles NE of Mendon Saturday A.M. Born Burbon Co. Kentucky Oct 15, 1819. Came to Adams co. in early manhood and lived here since. Leaves a wife and 3 sons- Mitchell of Loraine, Charles of Lima and Frank of Quincy.

MCNEALL, DR A.B. - Ancient History - Jun 25, 1895 - June 1880 Dr A.B. McNeall died in Columbus, age 70.

MCNEALL, DR A.B. - Ancient History - Jun 23, 1897 - June 1880 Dr A.B. McNeall died in Columbus.

MCNEALL, LETITIA B. - Probate Notice - Dec 17, 1902 Letitia B. McNeall, deceased 1st Monday of Feb. 1903 (2nd) Permelia H. Butler, exec.

MCNEALL, DR N.H. - Events of 1888 - Feb 2, 1893 Dr N.H. McNeall died at Paloma.

MCNEIL, COLONEL - Local - Dec 10, 1895 Colonel McNeil a member of the Soldiers Home died Sunday night. Found dead in bed. Came to the home from Rock Island where he was once deputy circuit clerk and was colonel of a reg. of Union soldiers during the war.

MCVAY, ALVIN - Obituary - Jan 5, 1894 Alvin McVay was born in Knox Co. Ohio Oct 15, 1830 and came to Adams Co. 1845 where he has lived most of the time since. He died in Camp Point at the home of his daughter, Mrs Milton McVay Dec 29, 1893. Married Phebe Sparks 1857 who survives him and 6 children. Funeral Saturday 2 P.M. at ME Church.

MCVAY, ALVIN - Obituary - Jan 5, 1894 Died Alvin McVay. Born Knox Co. Ohio Oct 15, 1830 came to Adams Co. 1845 and lived here most of time since. Died Camp Point at the home of his daughter, Mrs Milton McVay Dec 29, 1893. Married Phebe Sparks 1857. She and 6 children survive him. Recently when west he became a member of the Peoples Church at Denver, Colo. where his membership remained till death. Services Saturday at 2 P.M. at M.E. Church.

MCVAY, EDITH POWERS - Quincy - Dec 4, 1894 Died Edith Powers McVay died from consumption Thursday A.M.

MCVAY, GEORGE - Co Seat - May 6, 1896 Died George McVay, the baseball player died in St Mary's hospital Sunday.

MCVAY, MR AND MRS M.A. - Local - May 21, 1895 A 9 month old baby boy of Mr and Mrs M.A. McVay died Sunday.

NADERHOFF, ALBERT D. - Pick ups from the Necks Oct 12, 1894 Died Albert D. Naderhoff. Born Mar 27, 1872. Died Oct 2, 1894 of typhoid fever. Buried beside his mother in Coatsburg cemetery Thursday.

NADERHOFF, ALBERT D. - Obituary - Oct 5, 1894 Died Albert D. Naderhoff at the home of his father L.N. Naderhoff Oct 3, 1890. Born near Coatsburg Mar 27th, 1872. Attended school at Bushnell, Ill. Funeral from Christian Church Coatsburg Oct 4th by Elder O. Dilley.

NADERHOFF, BERT - Primrose - Oct 12, 1894 Died Bert Naderhoff died Tuesday night at his fathers with typhoid fever, about 23 years old. Had just finished school at Bushnell and about to teach at Coffield school. Brother Otis Naderhoff returned from Kansas for funeral.

NANCE, MRS PERMELIA - Death - Apr 8, 1903 Mrs

Permelia Nance, widow of the late Clement Nance
died at her home in Quincy Saturday A.M. 83
years old. Back in the 40's and early 50's she
lived in Columbus. Went to Quincy about 1854
and lived there since. Survived by 4 children,
R.W. Nance, Mrs B.F. Berrian, Mrs T.M. Rogers
and Miss May Nance, all of Quincy.

NATIONS, DAVID - Dead - Jun 30, 1897 David
Nations, an old citizen of Liberty twp died
this A.M., age 76 years. Was an elder brother
of Stephen and Joseph Nations and father of
Morris Nations of Camp Point. Funeral
tomorrow.

NATIONS, MRS SUSAN - Death - Jan 8, 1902 Mrs
Susan Nations, widow of the late David Nations
died at the home of her son, Maurice Nations in
Camp Point Jan 2nd. Maiden name was Gardner,
being the 6th and last surviving child of a
family of 7 children born to her parents, Mr
and Mrs James Gardner. Born Canaan, Vermont
May 8, 1821. With parents moved to Cincinnati,
Ohio when 12 years old. Married David Nations
April 1854 they had 2 children, Maurice and
Jessie. Jessie having died at age 20 years.
Mr Nations died Jun 3, 1897. Services at home
of the son at 3:30 P.M. Jan 3rd by Elder O.
Dilley. Buried Nation cemetery, near Liberty.

NAYLOR, CHARLES - Local - Aug 18, 1897 Charles
Naylor, postmaster at Liberty died Tuesday
night of last week. Buried Friday. He took
charge of the P.O. on July 1st.

NAYLOR, RICHARD - 10 Years Ago - Nov 16, 1893
Richard Naylor died in Columbus twp.

NEAL, MRS REBECCA - Quincy - Jul 30, 1902 Mrs
Rebecca Neal, who came to Quincy in 1841 died
in Memphis, MO Friday, age 90 years.

NEASTA, H.W. - Local - Dec 28, 1893 H.W.
Neasta died at his home in Columbus Wednesday,
age 71 years.

NEASTE, MRS MARY - Death Record - Mar 24, 1897

Died Mrs Mary Neaste, one of the old residents of this county at her home in Columbus twp Monday A.M. Came to U.S. in 1849 and lived here the past 48 years. Leaves 3 sons, Frank and John of Quincy and Henry of Columbus. Also 5 daughters, Mrs B. Enck, Mrs M. Geigel and Mrs Henry Schuerfield of Quincy and Mrs F. Bauman and Mrs Ida Bauman of Columbus.

NELKE, FERDINAND - Co. Seat - Dec 16, 1896 Will of Ferdinand Nelke leaves all to his widow and at her death it is to be devided equally among the 4 children, Harry, Emil, David and Johanna Nelke.

NELKE, FERDINAND - Local - Dec 2, 1896 Died Ferdinand Nelke, the dry goods merchant of Quincy died suddenly Sunday A.M. from heart disease. He was born Germany. 66 years old.

NELSON, BERTHA PAULINE - Local - Sep 29, 1897 Bertha Pauline, daughter of Mr and Mrs T.L. Nelson, died near Barry on the 23rd, age 5 months. Remains brought to Camp Point for burial Friday.

NELSON, MRS CLARA - Local - Apr 22, 1896 Mrs Clara Nelson, widow of the Q section hand who was recently killed near Colmar by a tie that fell from a passing train will sue the Railroad Co. for $5,000 damages.

NELSON, PETER N. - Local - Jun 1, 1893 Peter N. Nelson, a farmer was driving across the Chicago, Burlington and Quincy Railroad track at Galesburg, Ill when he was struck by the fast train, the "Eli" and instantly killed.

NELSON, WILLIAM - Local - Jan 5, 1893 William Nelson, one of the pioneer settlers of Houston twp died Dec 12th in Saline Co. MO of paralysis. He improved the farm now occupied by Elias Stahl.

NESTLERODE, S.P. - Dropped Dead at Bowen - Oct 4, 1895 About 8:15 A.M. Tuesday S.P. Nestlerode an old merchant and eccentric

character age 78 dropped dead from heart
disease. He had been a grocery merchant in
Bowen many years. Owned what is known as the
Nestlerode block of frame houses including the
Wells Hotel building. Wife survives him.

NEUMAN, CHARLIE - Death Record - Mar 24, 1897
Little Charlie Neuman, only child of Mr and Mrs
W.H. Neuman died Monday the 22nd inst. For
many years Charlie had been an invalid and has
never known the joys of happy healthy
childhood. Funeral today at 3 P.m. at
Christian Church.

NEUMAN, WILLIAM - Quincy - Mar 30, 1894
William Neuman who had lived St Louis past 8
years died at the home of his mother, Mrs X.
Neuman Monday A.M., age 33 years.

NEUSTADT, LOUIS G. - Quincy - Jul 22, 1896
R.W. Gardner has qualified as adm of the estate
of Louis G. Neustadt.

NEWHOUSE, FRED - Local - Mar 15, 1895 Fred
Newhouse died at his home in Griggsville
Thursday A.M. of dropsy. Leaves a wife, the
former Miss Hattie Conner of Camp Point and 1
child. Funeral at Griggsville.

NEWHOUSE, FRED MORRIS - Obituary - Mar 22, 1895
Fred Morris Newhouse born Griggsville Jun 20,
1866, youngest son of Mr and Mrs William
Newhouse. Married Miss Hattie Conner of Camp
Point Jun 25, 1890. They had 1 daughter,
Hattie. He was an invalid about 11 months. He
died March 14th. Funeral at family home by Rev
A.C. Armentrout. He worked for Wabash
Railroad. Leaves wife and the little daughter,
parents and brother. "Griggsville, Ind Press"

NICHOLS, HENRY CLAY - Additional Locals - Aug
5, 1903 Henry Clay Nichols, a former resident
of Camp Point died in Kansas City Saturday.
Served in the rebellion in the 50th Ill. and at
close of war settled in Camp Point. Went to
Quincy and later to Kansas City.

NICHOLS, JAMES - Died in the Berry Patch - Aug 25, 1897 James Nichols, an old citizen of Texas settlement, Keene twp was found dead Thursday night in the woods near his home. Wife couldn't find him, but one of his sons and the neighbor found him about 8 P.M. He was about 70 years old and lived with his wife and 3 children about 2 miles north of Big Neck Post Office. His children are grown.

NICHOLS, MRS MARY C. - Death - Aug 6, 1902 Mary C. (Arnold) Nichols wife of Nicholas Nichols died at her home in Big Neck Sunday Aug 3rd about noon from lung trouble, 38 years old. Leaves husband, 4 brothers and 1 sister, Mrs J.R. Frazier of Camp Point. Funeral by Rev L.A. Powell at Union Church Monday 4 P.M. Buried Curless Cemetery.

NICOLAI, OTTO - Local - Nov 5, 1895 Otto Nicolai, a young man living 3 miles west of town died Sunday A.M.

NIEBUHR, MR - Primrose - Jan 1, 1895 Mr Niebuhr, a well known citizen of Golden, died Sunday afternoon. He leaves a large family. Funeral from the East German Lutheran Church Tuesday.

NIEKAMP, MRS ERNEST - Quincy - Feb 15, 1895 Mrs Ernest Niekamp a resident of Adams Co. for 40 years died in Ellington twp, age 60 years.

NIEMAN, ANTON - Local - Jan 5, 1893 A 3 year old daughter of Anton Nieman, living in Quincy was burned to death last week while playing with a fire of dead leaves.

NIESTE, MR AND MRS - Prairie Pickings - Jan 5, 1894 Died Mr Nieste Wednesday eve. Leaves his aged wife lying close to death with little hopes of recovery. Buried Quincy Friday.

NIESTE, MR - Prairie - Jan 5, 1894 Death Messrs Clarence and Elmer Bowman and wives have been visiting their parents, Mr and Mrs Nieste in Columbus. Mr Nieste died Wednesday night

leaving his aged wife lying close to death with
little hopes of her recovery. Taken to Quincy
for burial Friday.

NOAKES, MRS - Local - Nov 23, 1894 Died Mrs
Noakes, mother of Dr T.V. Noakes died yesterday
A.M. of typhoid fever.

NOAKES, MRS EMMA (HOGSETT) - Local - Apr 20,
1893 The death of Mrs Emma (Hogsett) Noakes
occured at LaPrairie Thursday from consumption
induced by la grippe. Buried York Neck
Cemetery. She was eldest daughter of Mr and
Mrs William Hogsett and the wife of Dr Noakes.

NOAKES, MRS MELISSA - Mrs Melissa Noakes - Dec
4, 1894 Mrs Noakes death notice from LaPrairie
Correspondence of the Augusta Courier: Died,
at her home in Camp Point Thursday A.M. Nov 22,
1894 at 7:30 P.M., Mrs Melissa Noakes, mother
of T.V. Noakes formerly of this place. Melissa
Herron born June 1823 married T.J. Noakes 1845.
Husband died 1851. Was a widow 43 years.
Leaves only 2 children. Was 72 years old.
Remains taken to Henryville, Ind. for burial as
per her request.

NOAKES, MRS T.A. - Ancient History - Apr 22,
1903 - Apr 13-20, 1893 Mrs T.A. Noakes died at
LaPrairie.

NOBLE, MRS HARRIET M. - Obituary - nov 25, 1896
Died Mrs Harriet M. Noble died Nov 18, 1896
early A.M. at her home in Camp Point. Harriet
M. Danforth born Jun 13, 1825 in Sodus, N.Y.
where she lived till after her marriage in 1850
to Ormond Noble. Lived Camp Point 40 years.
No children, 2 foster children Miss Mary Alter
and Mrs Mattie (Merrick) Ward. Mr Noble died
Sep 30, 1893. Services at the family home last
Thursday at 2 P.M. by pastor R.H. Edwards.
Buried immediately after services.

NOBLE, HARRIET M. - Probate Notice - Dec 2,
1896 Harriet M. Noble, deceased 1st Monday of
Feb 1897 (1st) Mary L. Alter, Ex.

NOBLE, MRS HARRIET M. - Recent Deaths - Nov 18, 1896 Died Mrs Harriet M. Noble died this A.M. after a protracted illness. Funeral from the home tomorrow at 2 P.M.

NOBLE, ORMOND - Obituary - Oct 5, 1893 Died on the 30th ult at his home in this village Ormond Noble. He was stricken with paralysis some 3 years ago and since has been confined to bed. Born Sodus, Wayne Co. N.Y. Mar 29, 1827 and spent his early years in that county. Dec 11, 1850 he married Harriet M. Danforth, who survives him. In fall of 1856 they came west stopping in the winter of 1856-57 in Beloit, Wisc. In spring of 1857 they came to Camp Point where he was engaged for some years in the milling business in connection with the Eagle Mills afterwards he and others erected the Casco Mills. Buried Sunday Oct 1st.

NOBLE, ORMOND - Probate Notice - Feb 23, 1894 Ormond Noble, deceased   1st Monday of April 1894   Harriet M. Noble, adm.

NOBLE, ORMOND - Ancient History - Oct 21, 1903 October 1893 Ormond Noble died Sept 30th.

NOFTZ, CHARLES F. - Clayton - May 18, 1894   Mr Charles F. Noftz a well known citizen of Kellerville died at 1 A.M. Tuesday. Leaves a wife and 5 grown children.

NOLAN, MILES - Killed in Runaway - Nov 10, 1897 "Whig" - Miles Nolan, an inmate of the county farm was killed in a runaway at Paloma Thursday afternoon while helping get the winter's supply of coal at the Paloma depot. Was thrown from the wagon and hit his head. Died within a few minutes. Will Pilcher was also thrown, but not hurt. Nolan was 55 years old and had been an inmate of the county home off and on for 20 years. He was feeble minded, but a good worker if told what to do.

NORRIS, MR AND MRS D.S. - Columbus - Nov 6, 1894 Died infant daughter of Mr and Mrs D.S. Norris died Tuesday and buried in village cemetery Wednesday.

NORRIS, EDITH LILLIAN - Death of Mr and Mrs
D.S. Norris's Babe - Nov 6, 1894 Died Edith
Lillian, daughter of D.S. and Katie Norris died
Oct 30th, 1894 age 3 weeks. Services by Rev
A.A. White Wednesday Oct 31st.

NORRIS, WALTER - Quincy - Dec 31, 1902 James
W. Norris has filed a report as adm of the
estate of Walter Norris. He had collected
$10,298.94 and expended $9,046.87 leaving on
hand $1,251.77.

NORTON, MISS ELIZA - Death of Miss E. Norton -
May 6, 1896 Died Miss Eliza Norton in Memphis,
Tenn April 23rd in her 88th year. Lived Camp
Point about 30 years where she had a millinery
store. Last years she lived with a niece, Miss
Mary Clark.

NUTTING, NISS - Stories of the Storm - Jun 28,
1895 Near Loraine Tom Wilson was setting on a
shock of wheat about 2 miles from where Niss
Nutting was killed.

O'BRIEN, DANIEL - Quincy - Mar 6, 1894 Died
Daniel O'Brien age 23 a fireman on the Q road
died after a few weeks sickness with typhoid
fever.

O'FARRELL, ROBERT - Local - Jun 3, 1903 Jacob
T. Myers was appointed last week by probate
court as adm. of the estate of Robert
O'Farrell, deceased.

O'FARRELL, ROBERT - Local - May 6, 1903 Robert
O'Farrell who is well known in this part of the
county is lying dangerously ill with typhoid
fever at Blessing Hospital, Quincy.
Later: Word was received that he died this A.M.
about 4.

O'FARRELL, ROBERT - Dead - May 13, 1903 Robert
O'Farrell died at Blessing hospital, Quincy
last Wednesday A.M. from complications of
diseases in liver and kidneys. Went to

hospital Friday before. Age 58 years. Lived
Adams Co. over 30 years. Was a student of
Maplewood and Chaddock College and taught
school. Had no relatives that he knew of, as a
child he was taken from a foundling home in
Penn. by a man named Brisen, who kept him until
he was grown when he came to the home of an
acquaintance at Payson and spent his life in
the county since. Lived many years with the
late W.W. Norris at Columbus and after Mr
Norris's death lived with J.T. Myers when not
teaching. Services at Columbus Friday
afternoon. Buried Myers grave yard near
Fowler.

OGLE, WILLIAM - Paloma - May 4, 1894 Word
received here by telegram last Friday that
William Ogle of Belgrade, Mont. was shot and
killed last Thursday by burglars. He was
telegraph operator there. He lived here
several years ago.

OGLE, WILLIAM H. - Killed by Burglars - May 11,
1894 Murder of William H. Ogle by burglars at
Belgrade, Mont. Mr Ogle was reared at Paloma
where he has many relatives. Leaves wife and 5
children.

O'HARA, WILLIAM - Ancient History - Apr 21,
1897 - July 1879 William O'Hara, an early
settler at Camp Point died at Bowen.

O'HARE, MRS MARY V. - Recent Deaths - Feb 10,
1897 Died Mrs Mary V. O'Hare died in Burton
Sunday night, 78 years old. Born Virginia.
Came to Ill. 1856 and settled with husband in
Burton twp. Leaves husband and 7 children.

OHNEMUS, CARRIE - Death - Jan 29, 1895 Miss
Carrie Ohnemus died at the home of her brother
in law, Mr William Vanden Boom in Quincy
yesterday of typhoid fever. She was daughter
of Mr C. Ohnemus and lived Camp Point twp. She
had worked out in the city and when taken sick
was removed to home of Mr Vanden Boom.

OHNEMUS, CARRIE - Coatsburg - Feb 1, 1895

Monday last Carrie Ohnemus, a former resident of Coatsburg died in Quincy.

OHNEMUS, CONRAD - Obituary - Mar 26, 1895 Conrad Ohnemus died at his home in Camp Point twp Mar 23rd, age 66 years. Born Germany. Leaves wife, 2 sons and 3 daughters. Remains taken to Quincy for burial.

OHLSCHLAGER, HENRY - Dead - Jul 1, 1903 Henry Ohlschlager, a prominent German-American citizen of Quincy died Friday night of heart disease. Born Cincinnati, but was in grocery business in Quincy many years. Buried Monday with mason honors.

O'KEEFE, JOHN - Local - Feb 15, 1895 The jury in the case of William Simons the murderer of John O'Keefe returned a verdict of manslaughter and fixed punishment at 12 years in penitentiary.

O'KEEFE, JOHN - Quincy - Sep 28, 1894 Adams Co. criminal court case of William Simon of Little Rock, Ark who is charged with the murder of John O'Keefe, in the city on Jul 4, 1894 was continued until Jan. term of court.

OLSON, MISS IDA - West Point - Oct 18, 1895 To many friends of T.A. Olson, of Axtell, NE formerly a resident of this place, are sorry to hear of the death of his daughter, Miss Ida Olson.

OMENT, MISS TILLIE - Quincy - Nov 13, 1894 Died Miss Tillie Oment a student in the Quincy high school died the past week.

OMER, CARROL K. - Local - Feb 9, 1893 Carrol K. Omer died at his home near Kirksville, MO on the 1st inst. Remains brought to R.S. Curry's Friday and taken to Pleasant View Saturday afternoon for burial. Services by Rev Van Dervoort of Clayton. Deceased formerly lived near Clayton and was a brother of Oliver S. Omer, of this village.

OMER, MRS DELILAH - Death - Dec 2, 1903 On
Friday Nov 27th Mrs Delilah Omer, wife of
Daniel Omer died at the old home near Camp
Point. Lived there since 1855. Born in
Jefferson Co. KY and from there she came with
her husband to Camp Point twp. 74 years old.
Buried Pleasant View Cemetery. Services by O.
Dilley and J.M. Lowe. Leaves husband and 5
children - Robert A., Oscar E., J. Edward,
Ellis R. and Mrs Effie Bennett.

OMER, DIXIE - In Memoriam - Jan 19, 1893
Little Dixie, daughter of Mr and Mrs Harry
Omer, who died of scarlet fever at New London,
MO. She was born Jan 19, 1890 and died Dec 24,
1892. Buried Mt Sterling cemetery.

OMER, DIXIE J. - Obituary - Jan 5, 1893 Dixie
J. Omer, little daughter of Mr and Mrs Harry
Omer died at their home near New London, MO Dec
24, 1892, age 23 months 4 days from scarlet
fever. Sick 2 weeks. Buried in cemetery at Mt
Sterling Church, Missouri.

OMER, JAMES S. - Died - Oct 4, 1895 At the
home of his parents in Grove Center, KY Sep 29,
1895 James S., 3rd son of James and Jane
(Seaton) Omer. Sick 75 days with typhoid
fever. Born Camp Point twp Feb 29, 1876.
Leaves father, mother, 3 brothers and 3
sisters.

OMER, MRS P.T. - Additional Locals - Sep 30,
1903 Mrs P.T. Omer was called to Lima last
Wednesday to attend funeral of an aunt.

OMER, REV R.A. - Local - Dec 2, 1903 Rev R.A.
Omer arrived from Kansas City Saturday, called
here by the death of his mother.

OMER, RUBY - Local - Jan 15, 1902 Mrs G.C.
Bobbitt was called to Frankford, MO by the
death of her grandaughter, little Ruby Omer.

OMER, RUBY L. - Death - Jan 15, 1902 Ruby L.
Omer died at the home of her parents near
Frankford, MO Jan 9, age 2 years 9 months 25

days. Was youngest daughter of Mr and Mrs
Harry Omer.

OPIE, ANCIL - West Point - Jan 1, 1895 Died
Dec 28th Ancil, infant son of Mr and Mrs Frank
Opie.

ORCHARDSON, MRS MINERVA MERRICK - Mrs
Orchardson's Will - Jun 29, 1894 Prof. Charles
Orchardson is a rich man. The will of his late
wife, Mrs Minerva Merrick Orchardson was
admitted to probate Monday. Leaves the bulk of
her estate to him, some to a nephew in Michigan
George H. Turner, her niece, Minerva Merrick
Sayles, grandson, James M. Gardner. Mr
Orchardson is exec.

ORCHARDSON, MINERVA MERRICK - Will Case - Dec
24, 1895 The jury set aside Mrs Orchardson's
will, dated Feb 3, 1894 and mentioned in the
bill of complaints, is not the last will and
testament of the said Minerva Merrick-
Orchardson.

ORCHARDSON, MINERVA MERRICK - Quincy - Apr 30,
1895 The hearing of the suit to break the will
of Minerva Merrick Orchardson has been set for
June 1st in Adams Co. circuit court.

ORCHARDSON, MRS MINERVA MERRICK - Quincy - Nov
5, 1895 Judge O.P. Bonney of Adams Co. circuit
court has set Nov 25th for the hearing of the
will case of the late Mrs Minerva Merrick
Orchardson. Case has been in the courts past
year or two.

ORCHARDSON, MRS MINERVA MERRICK - Quincy - Jun
26, 1894 The will of the late Mrs Minerva
Merrick Orchardson has not yet been filed for
probate. She left no children it is thought
her estate has been willed to her husband Prof.
Orchardson.

ORTON, THOMAS - Local - Jan 15, 1902 Rolla
Booth and Mrs Arthur Cate went to Barry Monday
to attend the funeral of Thomas Orton, a
brother in law, who died in St Louis Friday.

Mr Orton formerly lived near Liberty.

OSBORN GEORGE - Eccentric Farmer - Sep 17, 1902
The late George Osborn of Little York the
eccentric individual who prior to his death
revealed where he had hidden $8,400 in gold.
The Oquawka Spectator has this information. Mr
Osborn left a farm of 240 acres also. He was
born 1835 on the place where he lived and died.

OSBORN, H.S. - Death - Dec 3, 1895 H.S. Osborn
died in San Diego, Calif Friday. Born London
Jun 6, 1814 located at Quincy 1846 where he
engaged in milling. Leaves a wife and 2 sons.
Remains temporarily interred in Calif and be
brought to Quincy later.

OSBORN, H.S. - Co. Seat - Jun 17, 1896 Funeral
of the late H.S. Osborn was held at the Vermont
St Baptist Church Monday afternoon. Buried
Woodland cemetery in family vault with Masonic
burial rites.

OSBORN, MRS MARY - Quincy - Jun 1, 1894 Died
Mrs Mary Osborn, age 79 years at Blessing
Hospital after a long illness.

OSWALT, GEO. H. - Local - Aug 13, 1895 Geo. H.
Oswalt of Warsaw was drowned in the river on
the 1st inst while bathing, 19 years old.

OWEN, MRS C.J. - Ancient History - Nov 26, 1902
May 1884 Mrs C.J. Owen (Nellie Farlow) died on
the 27th.

OWEN, MRS NELLIE - Ancient History - Jun 12,
1894 - June 5, 1884 Mrs Nellie Owen died May
29th.

OWEN, STEPHEN - Ancient History - Apr 22, 1903
April 17-24, 1873 Stephen Owen was drowned in
the north fork of Bear Creek returning from
Lima to Chili.

OWEN, STEPHEN - 20 Years Ago - May 4, 1893
Stephen Owen a young man living near Chili, was
drowned while attempting to cross Bear Creek.

PACKARD, MISS MARIA - Obituary - Jul 27, 1893
Miss Maria Packard died at the home of F.W.
Blood in Camp Point Jul 12, 1893. Lived with
the family 24 years. Born New Salem, Mass. Feb
25, 1816. Joined Cong'l Church at age 16
years. Summer of 1875 she united with Christian
Church at Cameron, Ill. Was a teacher in
public schools while her health was good. Was
a sister of Mrs B.F. Snell who was at her
bedside. Services held at 8 A.M. on the 13th
by Rev O. Dilley and remains taken to Delton,
Wisc. in charge of her sister.

PACKARD, MISS MARIA - Local - Jul 13, 1893
Miss Maria Packard died Wednesday eve at the
home of F.W. Blood where she has made her home
for many years, about 78 years old. Remains
taken by her sister, Mrs Snell, to Kilbourne
City, Wisc. for burial.

PAGE, MRS ANNA KORN - Local - Nov 3, 1897
Died, Mrs Anna Korn Page died at Bushnell last
week. She lived many years in Camp Point.

PALMER, JOHN - Local - Oct 1, 1902 John
Palmer, an old Wabash freight conductor was
knocked down and run over by his own train
Saturday A.M. and killed.

PAPE, FREDERICK - Quincy - Oct 25, 1895
Frederick Pape, one of the pioneer millers of
Adams Co. died in Melrose twp Monday, age 75
years.

PAPE, FREDERICK - Old Miller Gone - Oct 25,
1895 Died at noon Monday in Melrose twp,
Frederick Pape, 75 years old. Sick 10 days.
Born Aug 24, 1820 in Hanover, Germany where he
received his education. The he learned the
milling business. In 1847 he came to U.S. and
worked his trade 2 years in Quincy, Dubuque and
other cities. Then settled Payson where he ran
historical old wind mill. Since 1864 he
operated the Melrose Mill. Married Margaret
Aton 1851 she was a native of Scotland and died
Payson 1862, they had 6 children, only Wm H.
Pape is living. In 1878 he married Mrs Jennet

Palmer who survives him. Mrs Henry Meyer of
Quincy and Mrs Christian Crane of Ursa are
sisters. Funeral Thursday at the home in
Melrose 11 A.M. and at the Congregational
Church, Payson 1 P.M.

PARKER, FRANCIS - Local - Dec 27, 1895 Capt
A.S. McDonald, B.W. Bryant and J.L. Staker of
Clayton came down Thursday to the funeral of
Francis Parker.

PARKER, FRANCIS - Quincy - Oct 27, 1897 The
will of Francis Parker leaves all of his estate
to his widow, absolutely and names her as
executix.

PARKER, FRANCIS - Obituary - Jan 2, 1896
Franics Parker, born Troy, MO Dec 8, 1824 came
to Adams Co. when quite young. On Oct 4, 1853
he married Harriet Erving. They had 4
children, only 1 daughter survives him. In
1874 the family came to Camp Point. Died on
the 24th inst. Services at Presbyterian Church
Camp Point at 2 PM Thursday.

PARKER, FRANK - Death - Dec 24, 1895 Mr Frank
Parker died this A.M. after a lingering illness
of several months. Funeral will probably be
Thursday afternoon.

PARKER, MISS LULU - Ancient History - Nov 11,
1903 - November 1883 Miss Lulu Parker died
October 31st.

PARKER, MISS LULU - 10 Years Ago - Nov 16, 1893
Miss Lulu Parker died after a protracted
illness.

PARKER, MRS S.P. - Quincy - Oct 29, 1895 Mrs
S.P. Parker, a former well known resident of
this city died the past week in Omaha.

PARKS, MISS OLLIE - Suicide - Jun 4, 1902 Miss
Ollie Parks committed suicide in Quincy by
taking Rough on Rats. Was daughter of Mrs
Eudora Parks, who was a daughter of John
Porter, formerly a resident of Camp Point and

later Springfield.   She was a cousin of Mrs
E.B.O. Dean.

PARKS, OSCAR - Local - May 18, 1894 Mrs Belle
Craig went to Quincy Thursday to attend the
funeral of little Oscar Parks who was drowned
Tuesday.

PARKS, OSCAR H. - Local - May 18, 1894
Drowned, Oscar H. Parks, 13 year old son of
Harry O. Parks was drowned in Quincy bay
Tuesday afternoon while swimming.

PARKS, PORTER - Youthful Suicide - Aug 25, 1897
Porter Parks age 13 years committed suicide in
Quincy Thursday A.M. by hanging himself. He
was son of Harry Parks a well known commercial
traveler. His mother was the daughter of the
late John Porter, a former resident of Camp
Point. Mr and Mrs Parks are divorced. Mrs
Parks keeping the children. His younger
brother found him dead in his room about 10:30.
He was born Apr 10, 1884 at Springfield, Ill
and attended the Franklin School and was in
room 9. Mrs Parks lost a son Oscar H. Jr., 13
years of age, 3 years ago, the boy was drowned
in the bay while bathing.

PARKS, MRS TOM - Local - Sep 28, 1894 Mrs Tom
Parks, the Clayton woman who disappeared from
her home in Quincy 2 months ago and everyone
thought had committed suicide appeared in
Clayton Thursday.

PARRICK, MRS JOHN - Death - Mar 4, 1903 Mrs
John Parrick who lived at Wolf Ridge about 6
miles south of Camp Point, died Friday night of
heart disease. Had started for Rock school
house with her husband, Rev Parrick when
attacked by a stroke of heart disease. Moved
there about 10 years ago. He is pastor of
Union Church.

PARROTT, ELLEN - Local - May 21, 1895 Ellen
Parrott, an aged inmate of the county alms
house a sufferer for years with epilepsy died
Sunday.

PARVIN, WILLIAM - Ancient History - Nov 12, 1895 - November 1881 William Parvin of Liberty committed suicide.

PARVIN, WILLIAM - Ancient History - Nov 2, 1894 Nov 3, 1894 William Parvin of Liberty committed suicide by hanging.

PATCH, EVA - Died - Dec 7, 1894 Died in Cleveland, Ohio Dec 3rd, Eva, daughter of Rev O.D. and Emma Patch and a grandaughter of Mrs J.B. Christie.

PATTERSON, MRS LILLIE PEABODY - Ancient History Feb 9, 1893 Mrs Lillie Peabody Patterson died in Riverside twp on the 1st.

PEARCE, JOSHUA - Coatsburg - Feb 5, 1895 Joshua Pearce, an inmate of the poor farm died Saturday A.M. about 78 years old. Was an old resident of the northern part of the county. Remains taken away by friends for burial.

PEARCE, THOMAS D. - Quincy - Jan 8, 1902 Will of Thomas D. Pearce leaves 240 acres of land in Hancock and Adams Co. and the family homestead to his widow. To his brother John C. Pearce and sisters, Mary Ann and Elizabeth Lawless 1/4 each of the residue of the estate and to his nieces, Mary Anderson and Louisa Hall and his nephews David and John Yeargain each 1/16 of the residue. John C. Pearce appointed executor. Methodist Church at Camp Point received $500.00

PEARCE, THOMAS D. - Probate Notice - Jan 29, 1902 Thomas D,. Pearce, deceased 1st Monday of April 1902 (7th) John C. Pearce, exec.

PEARCE, THOMAS D. - Death - Jan 1, 1902 Thomas D. Pearce, son of David and Elizabeth Pearce was born in Butler Co. Ohio Dec 3, 1836. Came with parents to Adams Co. 1848. Lived on father's home place 30 years. Married Rachel Henry Dec 29, 1881. Retired from active life 1894 and moved to Camp Point. Died Dec 28th, 1901 being 65 years 25 days old. Leaves a wife, 1 brother, John C. Pearce of Bowen and 2 sisters, Mrs Mary A. Lawless of Gilmer twp and Mrs Elizabeth S. Lawless of Columbus twp. Services at ME Church Camp Point 11 A.M. Dec 30th, 1901. Buried Camp Point cemetery.

PEARL, JAMES - Quincy - Oct 21, 1903 Harry Dickinson named adm of James Pearl estate who with his wife was run over and killed by a street car in Quincy. Suit was filed for damages.

PEARL, SARAH L. - Quincy - Oct 21, 1903 Rhoda F. May was named adm of estate of Sarah L. Pearl estate.

PEASE, ROBERT E. - Killed at Omaha - Jul 29, 1896 Robert E. Pease, a former business man of Quincy was killed at Omaha Saturday night when thrown from his horse. Remains brought to Quincy Tuesday for burial.

PEDDICORD, EUGENE - Local - Jul 22, 1903 Eugene Peddicord, while working a quarry near Loraine Tuesday was caught by a premature blast and dreadfully injured. Both eyes destroyed and his skull fractured, no hopes for his recovery. Was about 55 years old and has a family.

PENDERGRAST, PATRICK - Quincy - Nov 10, 1897 Patrick Pendergrast, an employee of the Quincy Gas Co. mysteriously disappeared the past week.

PENN, JAMES - Local - Dec 21, 1893 James Penn, an old pauper of many years experience at the poor farm died Saturday. He was at one time an engineer on a steamboat. Whiskey was his worst enemy.

PENNY, WILLIAM W. - Quincy - Nov 26, 1902 William W. Penny, of this city, disappeared from his home last Sunday. Not heard from since.

PERRY, W.D. - Death of W.D. Perry - Feb 19, 1896 Died W.D. Perry, editor of the Payson

News yesterday at 1 P.M. in his home in Payson. Funeral tomorrow (Thursday) at 2 P.M. at the Cong. Church in Payson.

PERRY, WILLIAM D. - Co. Seat - Mar 6, 1896 Mrs Clara F. Perry had been appointed adm of the estate of William D. Perry.

PETERS, MRS CHRISTINA - Death - Sep 24, 1902 Died, Christina, wife of Fred Peters, at their home 5 miles north of Coatsburg, Sep 11, 1902. She was daughter of Charles Felsman. Leaves husband and 2 small children. Was 23 years old. Sick 6 months. Services at Christian Church at Coatsburg Sep 12, 1902 by O. Dilley of Camp Point. Buried Coatsburg Cemetery.

PEVEHOUSE, LOUISA J. - Death - Sep 30, 1903 Louisa J. Pevehouse was born Adams Co. Ill Apr 7, 1846. Married Dec 24, 1863 to Jonathon Smallwood who died Apr 29, 1889. Mrs Smallwood moved to Pekin, Ill where she was struck by a train on the 13th and died of injuries that eve. Brought to Camp Point and taken to Byler Cemetery in Honey Creek twp for burial on the 18th. She leaves 4 sons, 3 daughters, a number of grandchildren, 1 brother, James W. Pevehouse of Colusa, Col., 2 sisters, Miss Laura of this village and Miss Nannie of Chicago, her aged father, Isaac N. Pevehouse of Camp Point and her stepmother.

PEVEHOUSE, SAMUEL L. - Fell 30 Feet - Feb 10, 1897 Last Wednesday in Quincy Samuel L. Pevehouse a lineman fell 30 feet from a pole. Was about 28 years old. Married, lived at 1415 Spring St. No Children. Son of Isaac N. Pevehouse of Camp Point. Buried Coatsburg Thursday. Services by Rev Kleene. Leaves wife, parents and sister.

PFEIFFER, CHARLES - Quincy - Apr 14, 1897 Charles Pfeiffer, a former resident of St Louis died at the German Old Folks home on Friday, age 71 years.

PFEIFFER, PROF. GEO. R. - Local - Jun 9, 1897

Died-Prof Geo. R. Pfeiffer, formerly of Quincy and widely known in musical circles, died May 29th at the Insane Hospital, Jacksonville.

PFEIFFER, PROF GEORGE R. - Quincy - Jun 9, 1897 Prof. George R. Pfeiffer, formerly a prominent music teacher in this city, died last week in the insane asylum at Jacksonville.

PIEPER, HENRY G. - Death - Feb 19, 1902 Died at the home of F.J. Pieper, Columbus twp Tuesday Feb 11th, Henry G. Pieper age 43 years 6 months 1 day. Born in Quincy Aug 10, 1858. Services at German Lutheran Church by Rev Brandfelt. Preceded in death by his mother and 2 sisters. Leaves father and 1 sister.

PIERCE, EDWIN B. - Golden - Jul 24, 1894 Edwin B. Pierce a former resident of this twp, but now of Wyaconda, MO accompanied the remains of his brother which were buried at York Neck last week.

PIERCE, ELIZABETH J. - Death Record - Aug 4, 1897 Elizabeth J. Pierce born in East Tenn. Jan 17, 1839. Died at her home in Camp Point Jul 29, 1897. Came to Adams Co. with her parents. Married Jan 4, 1855 to Walter Cate to whom she lived 42 years. They had 12 children, 6 sons, 6 daughters- 11 are still living, one son died in infancy. Also leaves 4 brothers and 3 sisters. Had been ill for more than 20 years. Services at the house Friday 8:30 A.M. by Rev W.W. Reed. Buried Columbus Cemetery. Card of Thanks under this from Walter Cate and family.

PIERCE, MRS ELIZABETH THEMAS - Obituary - May 4, 1893 Died at her home in Knox Co. MO April 19th Mrs Elizabeth Themas Pierce, age 75 years 8 months. Leaves 3 sons and aged companion. Was an old time resident of York Neck.

PIERCE, EUSEBIUS O. - Death of E.O. Pierce - Oct 13, 1897 Eusebius O. Pierce died at Leon, KS Saturday Oct 19th after a protracted illness. Remains arrived at Golden Monday A.M.

where services were held at the home of Samuel
R. McAnulty. Buried York Neck cemetery. Born
Houston twp and was about 54 years old and
lived there until a few years ago when he moved
to Butler Co. Kansas. Married Nancy M.
Strickler over 30 years ago who with several
children survive him.

PIERCE, ISAAC - Funeral of Isaac Pierce - Jul
17, 1894 Died-Isaac Pierce at his home in Knox
Co. MO Saturday about 75 years old. Lived
about 30 years in Houston twp at the York Neck
Church. Moved to MO a little over 20 years
ago. Leaves 5 sons, 2 daughters, Mrs S.R.
McAnulty being the elder. Buried York Neck
Cemetery Monday.

PIERCE, MARY ANN - Obituary - Jun 3, 1896 Mary
Ann Pierce born Gilmer twp, Adams Co. Feb 6,
1862 died in Lewis Co. MO May 23, 1896 with
consumption. Married Daniel Boyle Dec 1, 1881.
Was daughter of Joseph and Susan Pierce who
survive her also a husband, 5 children, 2
sisters, 5 brothers. Buried Woodland cemetery
in Quincy.

PIERCE, WILLIAM - Ancient History - Mar 26,
1895 - March 1880 William Pierce died at his
home in Camp Point twp.

PIERSON, DR DANIEL - Ancient History - Nov 12,
1895 - November 1878 Dr Daniel Pierson of
Augusta was assassinated.

PIERSON, DR DANIEL - Indicted for an old Crime
Oct 12, 1893 Carthage, Ill Oct 7 Hancock Co.
grand jury returned an indictment against
Theodore Hetrick, of Ferris for the murder of
Dr Daniel Pierson of Augusta in this county 14
years ago. Theodore Hetrick is a brother of
Marion Hetrick.

PILGER, MARTHA - Quincy -Sep 3, 1902 Martha
Pilger, formerly an assistant in the public
library in this city, died recently in Jos,
California.

PITTMAN, DR J.H. - Local - Feb 18, 1903 Dr
J.H. Pittman was called to Good Hope last
Wednesday by serious illness of his sister, who
died later. He returned home Monday.

PLOWMAN, CHARLES - Death - Jun 30, 1897 Died
Charles Plowman at his home 4 miles east of
Columbus Jun 20th 1897 of diseases contracted
in rebel prisons. He enlisted July 1862 in Co.
F. 78th Ill. Inf. and in Sept 1863 was taken
prisoner near Chattanooga and held till spring
of "65". Was 58 years 7 months 20 days old.
Married America J. Thompson Oct 24, 1869. Had
11 children all present except Frank who lives
Oklahoma. Buried at Harden graveyard near
Woodville.

PLOWMAN, CHAS. - Columbus - Jun 30, 1897 Died,
Chas Plowman from consumption.

POLAND, MINNIE BELLE - Brother Kills Sister
Oct 26, 1894 At Clayton, Minnie Belle Poland
age 18 was killed by Leonard Poland, age 21,
crippled. Parents were Mr and Mrs Bruce Poland.
Was accidently shot while she was attending his
target. Poland farm is a mile south of
Clayton.

POLLOCK, JOSEPH - Deaths - Oct 29, 1895 Joseph
Pollock, an old resident of Honey Creek twp
died Saturday, age 81 years. Leaves a wife and
7 children.

POLLOCK, MR AND MRS MAX - Card of Thanks - Jun
22, 1893 We wish to return our sincere thanks
to our many friends for their sympathy and
kindness shown us during the sickness and death
of our dear mother.   Mr and Mrs Max Pollock

POLLOCK, MRS SUSAN - Oakwood - Dec 2, 1896
Died Mrs Susan Pollock, wife of the deceased
J.S. Pollock, died Sunday the 21st ult.
Funeral by Rev Herzog of the German ME Church
in the ME Church at Columbus. Leaves 4 sons, 2
daughters.

POLLOCK, SUSAN E. - Co. Seat - Feb 10, 1897

H.G. Henry has been appointed adm of the estate of Susan E. Pollock.

POND, AUGUSTA M. - Gone to Her Reward - Feb 19, 1895 Augusta M. Harrington was born in Smithville, N.Y. Nov 2, 1820. Came to Ill 1831. Married Dr George O. Pond Nov 14, 1839. Lived Camp Point last 26 years. Died Feb 16, 1895. Leaves her aged husband of more than 55 years and a sister, her only child, Mrs Lida Cree of Griggsville died some months age. Services at Presbytrian Church Monday at 1 P.M. by Rv E.M. Miner and Rev's L. Royce and A.N. Simmons. Buried village cemetery.

POND, GEORGE O. - Executor's Sale of Real Estate - Aug 5, 1903 George O. Pond, deceased real estate sale, Saturday Sept 5th, 1903 Ephraim E.B. Sawyer, Ex.

PONTIUS, BRYON - Death - Apr 8, 1903 Bryon Pontius a prominent lawyer and Democratic politician of Macomb died Friday, age 52 years. Leaves a wife and family.

POPE, JOSEPH ALLEN - Sudden Death - Oct 29, 1902 Sunday eve about 5 Joseph Pope was taken ill with neuralgia of the heart and died in a couple hours. Joseph Allen Pope was born in Camden, Tenn Nov 29, 1851, was 51 years old. Married Miss Julia Ann Branch Mar 24, 1870 and the following spring they came to Columbus to live. Stayed 24 years and moved to Camp Point Aug 6, 1896. Leeaves wife, 4 sons and 4 daughters of whom 1 son and 1 daughter are at home. Services at the home Tuesday P.M. by Rev C.F. Stecker. Buried village cemetery.

PORTER, GLYDE SORINA - Death Record - Dec 1, 1897 Glyde Sorina, infant daughter of Rev and Mrs W.S. Porter died at Victoria, Ill Wednesday Nov 24th age 11 months 15 days. Remains brought to Camp Point to the home of its grandparents, Mr and Mrs H.W. Childs where services were held Friday P.M. by Rev T.M. Dillion and Rev W.M. Reed and buried in village cemetery.

PORTER, MAJ. HARRY - Quincy - Dec 15, 1897
Maj. Harry Porter, one of the best known
inmates of the State Soldiers Home died
Thursday eve, age 65 years. He was adjutant of
the 13th Ill Inf. and at one time a merchant in
Chicago.

POTTER, URIAH - 10 Years Ago - Nov 16, 1893
Uriah Potter died in Columbus twp.

POUNDER, CLARA - Local - May 25, 1893 Clara, 7
year old daughter of Mr and Mrs Oscar Pounder
of Spring Station was accidently drowned in the
back water Thursday afternoon. She and her
brother were playing when she fell in.
"Versailles Enterprise"

POWELL, DRUSILLA - Quincy - Aug 27, 1902 Anna
Brown home for the aged has received a bequest
of $300 from the estate of Drusilla Powell.

POWELL, GEO. - Obituary - Sep 1, 1897 Died at
Excelsior Springs, Geo. Powell, son of John
Powell one of Ellington twp pioneer settlers.
Geo. moved from Adams Co. 12 years ago and
bought a farm near Hester, MO. He was 45 years
old. Leaves a wife and 6 children. He has a
brother and 4 sisters living in this county and
other relatives.

POWELL, MRS HENRIETTA - Child Burned to Death
Nov 15, 1895 At Clayton yesterday A.M. - death
of 4 year old daughter of Mrs Henrietta Powell
(colored), while her mother was washing in back
yard the girl and her older sister were in the
house when her clothes caught fire.

POWELL, JOSEPH - Co Seat - Dec 9, 1896 Joseph
Powell, a prominent farmer of Ellington twp was
killed near 8th and Broadway Wednesday night
being thrown from his wagon by a collision with
a fence while his team was running away. The
team took fright near 13th St. and turned and
ran back down Broadway. At 8th they turned
onto the walk at the site of the Presy. Church
and the collision with the fence occured a
moment later. Mr Powell's neck was broken by

the fall. He was unmarried and lived on a farm with a widowed sister.

POWELL, RICHARD - Local - Jan 22, 1896 Shot, died, a son of Richard Powell of near Philadelphia.

POWERS, W.B. - Quincy - Sep 20, 1895 Will of W.B. Powers admitted to probate in Adams Co. court. All his life ins. and chattel property left to his widow, his son W.C. Powers of Newton, KS, his gold watch and $500.00. A niece Mary A. Powers of Allegheny City, Penn. $250, grandchildren William Powers and Katherine Powers a store building in Quincy. The residue of estate to be divided between widow, his son William C. Powers and his daughter Mary E. Powers. These 3 appointed as executors.

POWERS, WILLIAM B. - Death of a Pioneer - Aug 27, 1895 Mr William B. Powers of Quincy died at his home on N. 5th St. 5 A.M. Saturday. Lived Quincy nearly 60 years coming here in 1838. Born Temple. N.H. 1810. Went with parents to Bakersfield, VT at age 7. Father died when he was 10 leaving 3 daughters and 5 sons. Wm B. being next to youngest son, 1st went to Lowell and then Boston. 1838 to Quincy. Married 1844 to Mary T. Johnson of Calaia, Maine who survives him and one son William C. Powers of Newton, KS and Miss Emma Powers of this city. Son arrived from west few hours before he died. Owned lot in Woodland cemetery.

POWERS, WILLIAM C. - Great Fire in Quincy - May 12, 1897 The building owned by the estate of William C. Powers at corner of Maine and 6th Sts Quincy burned Tuesday A.M.

PRENTISS, HARRISON TYLER - Quincy - Apr 28, 1897 Died, Harrison Tyler Prentiss of this city who was famous as a drummer in the late war died at the home of his father Gen. B.M. Prentiss in Bethany, MO, age 57 years.

PRENTISS, HARRISON TYLER - Tip Prentiss Dead -

Apr 28, 1897   Died, Harrison Tyler Prentiss
last Wednesday at Bethany, MO.   Was oldest son
of Gen. B.M. Prentiss and was 56 years old.
"Tip" was a drummer and served during the war
of the rebellion.   Married twice his first wife
was Miss Torrence and second Miss Whitney.

PRENTISS, HENRY CLAY - Co Seat - Feb 12, 1896
Died, Henry Clay Prentiss, a brother of Gen
Prentiss and at one time a well known resident
of Quincy died on his farm 2 miles south of
Hurdland, MO. during the past week.   Was about
70 years old.   Leaves a wife and 4 children, 2
sons 2 daughters.   When young he lived Quincy
and operated rope - walks near 18th and Vine
and near 10th and Broadway.

PRESTON, J.M. - Local - Nov 6, 1894   A litle
son of J.M. Preston, living near LaCrosse was
fatally injured while at play last week.

PRETTYMAN, FRANK - Death - Feb 11, 1903   Letter
received here from Mrs Prettyman telling of the
death of Frank Prettyman at Abbeville, LA Jan
28, of pneumonia.   He was born and reared in
Camp Point and married Effie Seaton in 1882.   A
few years later he went to Holden, MO and
followed his trade of plasterer at many places
in the the west and south.   Was 48 years old.

PRETTYMAN, ISAAC - Soldiers buried in Camp
Point Cemetery - May 4, 1893   Listed in Co. F,
25th Iowa Infantry.

PREWITT, EDWARD - Quincy - Jun 28, 1895   George
Coward, the crippled colored man who shot and
killed Edward Prewit is still at large.

PREWITT, EDWARD J. - Local - Jun 25, 1895
George Coward shot and killed Edward J. Prewitt
on Zimmerman Hill, Quincy Friday night about 11
P.M.   Both are colored.   Coward escaped.

PRICE, MRS - Events of 1878 - Jan 19, 1893   Mrs
Price of Pittsfield died in Quincy and Dr Parks
and Springer have been arrested and charged
with murder.

PRICE, MRS MARY R. - Death of Mrs Price - May 29, 1894 Died, Mrs Mary R. Price at her home 304 S. 12th St., Quincy shortly after 7 P.M. Monday, 72 years old had been an invalid last 18 years. Lived Burton for many years moved Quincy 4 or 5 years ago. Leaves 7 children- William of Salina, Kan., Mrs Scarborough of Quincy, Mrs J.W. Rice of Salina, Wickliffe of Minneapolis, Seymour of Oklahoma and Anna of Quincy.

PRICE, WILL E. - Local - Sep 17, 1902 Will E. Price died at Salina, Kan. last week and was buried Sun. He was reared near Newtown and was a member of the well known Price family there.

PRYOR, HENRY - Quincy - Jan 22, 1902 Henry Pryor a carpenter who has been living in a house boat in Quincy bay has received word that he is among heirs to a fortune of $2,000,000 at Elizabeth, N.J. Estimates his share at $16,400.

PRYOR, TIMOTHY - Crushed by a Log - Feb 15, 1895 Timothy Pryor, a well known farmer living 3-1/2 miles NW of Loraine was crushed to death by a log Wednesday. Was 50 years old and leaves a family. His son was formerly ass't janitor at the court house.

PRYOR, WASHINGTON - Died at 104 - Mar 10, 1897 Died in Quincy Wednesday, Washington Pryor, a colored man. He and his wife Nicy had lived Quincy since 1865. Best records obtainable place his age at about 104.

PULLMAN, MRS ALBERT - Local - Mar 6, 1894 Died, Mrs Albert Pullman of Burton died Monday of typhoid pneumonia. Funeral at Presby. Church, Burton today.

PULLMAN, ROY - A Sad Drowning - Feb 26, 1896 In Burton twp on a farm north of the village Friday eve, Mrs Howard Pullman went to the cistern for water with her little 7 year old son, Roy, he lost his footing and fell in. She could not rescue him. He was a partial cripple.   "Herald"

PURCELL, RICHARD - Quincy - Jun 9, 1897 Mary
T. Connely has been appointed adm of the estate
of Richard Purcell.

PYNE, WILLIAM - Local - Feb 8, 1895 William
Pyne a well known old citizen of Kingston died
Tuesday.

QUINBY, MRS MARY A.R. - Local - Jan 2, 1894
Mrs Mary A.R. Quinby of Carthage, a daughter of
the late Maj. Alex Simpson and widow of the
late J.B. Quinby was found dying at 9:15 Sunday
night. Her little grandaughter was taken sick
and she was hurrying for the doctor when she
broke a blood vesel. 62 years old.

QUINN, JOSEPH - Local - Aug 23, 1895 Joseph
Quinn, 72 years old and a veteran employee of
the Wabash Railroad at Mt Sterling dropped dead
Wednesday of heart disease.

RAILEY, GEORGE W. - Local - Sep 8, 1897 Died
George W. Railey, of Concord twp Tuesday from
cholera morbus after a few hours illness.
Funeral today.

RALPH, MRS HENRY - Primrose -Aug 6, 1902 Mrs
Geo. Ralph went to Quincy Saturday to attend
the funeral of Mrs Henry Ralph at Rock Creek.

RANKIN, REV JOHN G. - Rev J.G. Rankin - May 13,
1896 Funeral at the Presybterian Church Quincy
for Rev John G. Rankin at 10:30 A.M. Sunday,
preached 50 years. A long cortege followed the
remains to their resting place.

RANKIN, REV DR JOHN G. - Co Seat - May 13, 1896
Died Rev Dr John G. Rankin, a presbyterian
minister died Thursday A.M., age 85 years.
Born Tenn. His first charge in Ill. was
Warsaw. Later Godfrey, Centralia and
Carrollton. Last 5 years in Ellington twp.

RANKIN, SAMUEL - Local - Jan 26, 1893
According to the Fort Madison papers the body

of Samuel Rankin was stolen from his grave in
the city cemetery, presumably for the
dissecting table in some medical college.
Rankin was a drunkard who took the Keeley cure
and died suddenly a few days ago.

REARICK, JOHN - 10 Years Ago - Feb 23, 1893
John Rearick committed suicide in Cottrells
store, Quincy with a revolver he asked to see.

REARICK, JOHN - Ancient History - Feb 25, 1903
Feb 22, 1883 John Rearick committed suicide in
Cottrell's Hardware store in Quincy.

RECORD, MRS KATE MEAD - Quincy - Nov 6, 1894
Died Mrs Kate Mead Record, a former resident of
this city died during the past week at
Nelsonville, MO.

REDFIELD, MRS M.C. - Local - Nov 9, 1894 Mrs
M.C. Redfield, widow of the late Rev H.S.
Redfield is visiting her sister, Mrs Rev E.B.
Miner.

REECE, ALONZO - Perry Murder - Jan 26, 1894
Alonzo Reece a farmer living within a mile or
two of Perry, Pike Co, 31 years old, given to
drinking killed his 19 year old wife and their
only child, a babe and killed himself within
the hour.

REECE, ALONZO - Local - Jan 26, 1894 Alonzo
Reece living near Perry, Pike Co. murdered his
wife and child Tuesday has fled. Not captured
yet.

REED, F.P. - Accidently Killed - Sep 14, 1894
F.P. Reed, the new proprietor of the mill at
Coatsburg was killed Wednesday eve. Came to
Coatsburg only a short time ago from Colorado.
Leaves a wife and 5 or 6 children from 24 years
old down to a child in arms.

REED, F.P. - Obituary - Sep 18, 1894 Died Sep
12th at Coatsburg F.P. Reed age 41 years 5
months 2 days. Born Massilion, Ohio Jul 10,
1853. Three years later family moved to

Fairfield, Iowa. There on Nov 14, 1874 he
married Miss Isaphrene Law of that place. Had
5 children, 4 living, oldest is a son 18 years
others 13, 11 and 1 year. Mr Reed was son of
Dr Reed, now of Denver, Colo. and a brother of
Rev Elmer E. Reed, pastor of Presybterian
Church of Griswold, Iowa. Funeral Saturday
Sept 15th at Desciples Church at Coatsburg,
younger brother was at funeral. Services by
Rev E.B. Miner of Camp Point. Buried cemetery
at Coatsburg.

REED, GEORGE - Quincy - Nov 24, 1897 The will
of George Reed gives $100 to each of his 3
sons, James, George and Samuel and a like
amount to each grandchild.

REED, GEORGE - Death Record - Sep 29, 1897
George Reed born at Wheeling, W. Virginia Nov
8, 1809 and died at the home of his daughter,
Mrs Charles W. Kessler, Camp Point twp Sep 24,
1897. Married Jan 1, 1833 to Miss Rachel
McHenry who died about 24 years ago. Nine
children were born to them - James of Bates Co.
MO, Geo. and Robert L. of Adams Co., Samuel of
Cawker City, Kan., Mrs C.W. Kessler and Mrs
D.C. McGuire of Camp Point survive him. Mr
Reed and family came to Cass Co. Ill. 1850 for
3 years then to Adams Co. since then. Services
at York Neck Church Sunday 11 A.M. by Rev Frank
Peyton of Warsaw and Rev F.P. Bonnefor of
Quincy.

REED, HARRY - Passed Away - Dec 15, 1897 Little
Harry Reed died Tuesday the 14th inst of
catarrhol fever, age 22 months. Was son of Mr
and Mrs Henry T. Reed. Services tomorrow.

REED, HARRY HULL - Death Record - Dec 22, 1897
Harry Hull Reed, youngest son of Henry T. and
Ruth H. Reed was born Feb 10, 1896, died Dec
14, 1897. Services by Rev T.M. Dillon at his
parents home Thursday Dec 16th at 2 P.M.
Buried our cemetery.

REED, MRS MARY - Quincy - Jul 24, 1894 Died
Mrs Mary Reed, age 50. Died from the effects

of a tumor at Blessing Hospital Monday A.M.

REED, ROBERT - Local - Jun 5, 1894 Died Mr
Robert Reed age 88 years died Friday afternoon
at 5 at his home in Burton twp of old age.
Born Ireland came to this country and settled
Philadelphia when quite young and from there to
Ill. settling in Burton twp where he lived the
last 40 years.

REED, REV W.M. - Obituary - Aug 13, 1902
Washington Maley Reed was born Hamilton Co.
Ohio Sep 4, 1825. Married 1st to Eliza Jane
Burdick on Sep 4, 1846 and they had 5 children,
4 still living. 5 or 6 years later they came
to Ill. and settled near Perry, Pike Co.
Married second Jan 1860 to Mrs E.H. Hamilton of
Barry, Ill and they had 1 son. He died early
Saturday A.M. Aug 2nd, 1902. Services at M.E.
Church Camp Point on Sunday Aug 3rd, 3 P.M.
Buried Camp Point cemetery.

REED, REV W.M. - Local - Aug 6, 1902 RevL.A.
Powell of Bowen was in town Friday and returned
Sunday to attend the funeral of Rev W.M. Reed.

REED, REV W.M. - Death - Aug 6, 1902 "Father"
Reed died early Saturday A.M. Aug 2nd at the
home of his daughter, Mrs S.G. Sparks. Services
Sunday 3 P.M. from Methodist Church by Rev W.T.
Beadles of Quincy district. (We were unable to
obtain a reliable bio. sketch of Rev W.M. Reed
in time, but it will appear later.)

REINKE, FREDERICK W. - Quincy - Oct 22, 1902
Frederick W. Reinke, age 64 years, an inmate of
the state soldiers home, died from heart attack
while sitting in a chair on Tuesday eve. He
entered the home from Chester.

RENFROW, JEFF - Our Neighbors - Aug 26, 1896
Jeff Renfrow, for 40 years a prominent citizen
of Quincy died recently at Chicago.

RENKEN, HENRY - Death - Jan 14, 1903 Henry
Renken, an old and respected German citizen of
Honey Creek died Wednesday the 7th last of

pneumonia. Leaves wife and 5 children in comfortable circumstances. Was a successful farmer and several years a director of the Adams Co. fair.

RENNER, CHARLES P. - Death of C.P. Renner - Jun 16, 1897 Charles P. Renner, prop. of the Farmers Home Quincy died at 6:30 A.M. Wednesday from heart trouble. Born in Liberty twp 46 years ago where his mother, Mrs Jane Graff now lives. Leaves a wife and 7 children all in Quincy except 1 son, Edward who is in South Dakota. Has run the Farmers home for past 4 years. He also run the Quincy and Beverly Stage route for 4 years. Member of Modern Woodman.

RENSCHEL, GEORGE - Local - Feb 5, 1902 George Renschel, of Northeast twp died Sunday night in Blessing hospital, Quincy of cancer of the stomach. Remains shipped to Golden Monday, 21 years old.

REUSCHEL, MISS BERTHA - Death - Jul 8, 1903 Miss Bertha Reuschel, age 30, died at the home of her parents, Mr and Mrs Valentine Reuschel, 2-1/2 miles north of Coatsburg Saturday of consumption. Survived by 2 sisters and 2 brothers.

REYNOLDS, MRS - Local - Mar 31, 1897 Died Ed Reynolds went to Eldora, Iowa Thursday to visit his mother, Mrs Reynolds died Friday.

REYNOLDS, CHARLES C. - Death of Charles Reynolds - May 13, 1896 Died Charles C. Reynolds, a former resident of Camp Point Apr 30th in western Kansas where he moved a few years ago. Over 70 years old. Born Conn. came to Ill as a young man with parents. Spent youth in Houston, then Mendon and 30 years in Camp Point. Leaves a wife, 2 sons and a daughter.

REYNOLDS, MRS D.E. - Local - Mar 5, 1895 Mrs D.E. Reynolds was called to Litchfield, Conn. last week by the illness of her aged parents.

She arrived at home a few hours after the death
of her father. The mother died Monday eve and
the father Tuesday A.M. He was 89 years old.

REYNOLDS, MRS DELIA STODDARD - Obituary - Apr
7, 1897 - Died Mrs Delia Stoddard Reynolds at
the home of her daughter, Mrs J.D. Newcomer of
Eldora, Iowa March 26, 1897, had been confined
to her bed about 16 months. She was born in
Oneida, N.Y. 1833, Delia E. McCall. Later went
to Litchfield, Conn and there married Albert
Stoddard, they had 3 children - Mrs J.D.
Newcomer of Eldora, IA, Charles Stoddard of
Mont. and Albert Stoddard of Duluth, MN. The
family came west 1854, located in Iowa. In
1870 Mr Stoddard died. In 1875 Mrs Stoddard
married James W. Reynolds of Camp Point who
preceded his wife in death in 1892. Mr
Reynolds family consisted of John H., J.E.,
L.A., W.O. and Elizabeth Reynolds who survive
her and George H. who died Mar 1, 1895. Her
home has been in Camp Point since, till October
1895 when she went to visit her daughter, Mrs
Newcomer. In Oct 1887 she took from Woodland
Home of Quincy a girl 7 years old, Minnie E.
Eisenlohr, to whom she performed a true mothers
part. Funeral by Rev Kent of the Cong'l Church
at 7:30 Saturday A.M. at the home of her
daughter in Eldora. Body taken to Toledo, IA
and buried in Toledo cemetery.

REYNOLDS, GEORGE - Death - Mar 5, 1895 J.E.
Reynolds received telegram Saturday telling of
the death of his brother, George, at Cripple
Creek, Colo. from pneumonia. Remains shipped
here arriving this A.M. Born in Camp Point in
1860 lived here until 1879 when he went to
Colo. Leaves a wife, no children. Funeral
this P.M. at the Methodist Church.

REYNOLDS, GEORGE H. - Obituary - Mar 8, 1895
George H. Reynolds died at Cripple Creek, Colo.
Saturday March 2nd. Born and raised Camp
Point. Left here when about 19 years old in
1878 for Colorado to work for railroad.
Requested to be buried at Camp Point. Brother
Will brought remains back Tuesday A.M.

Services at M.E. Church by Rev A.N. Simmons
same day at 2 P.M. Leaves 4 brothers John H.,
Lincoln A., William O. all in Colorado, J.
Edgar at Camp Point and 1 sister Lizzie in
Milford, Conn.

REYNOLDS, HORACE - Ancient History - Feb 11,
1903 - Feb 8, 1883 Horace Reynolds died at his
home in Houston, age 93 years. He located
there in 1835. Was one of the first
abolitionists who were not in much favor in
that day.

RHEA, GEORGE HENRY - Death - May 14, 1902
George Henry Rhea died Thursday A.M. May 8th at
the home of his mother, Mrs Thomas Bailey of
paralysis of which he has suffered many years.
Was son of the late George Rhea and born Gilmer
twp Jan 9, 1852. Came with father's family to
Camp Point in fall of 1869 stayed till he
became of age then went to Kansas. Later
Colorado, but sickness came and he returned to
his mother's home. Never married. Leaves
mother, 2 brothers, 3 sisters. Funeral
Saturday afternoon at the home of mother by Rev
E.B. Miner. Buried village cemetery.

RHEA, GEORGE HENRY - Local - May 21, 1902
CORRECTION Two errors in obituary of
GeorgeHenry Rhea. He was born in 1862 NOT 1852
and he leaves 4 brothers and 4 sisters instead
of 2 brothers and 2 sisters.

RHEA, MRS HARRIET - Local - May 11, 1893 Mrs
Harriet Rhea, wife of James Rhea, of Colusa
died on the 29th. She formerly lived near
Columbus.

RHODEHOUSE, COLIN - Our Neighbors - Jun 25,
1895 The 2 year old son of Colin Rhodehouse of
Monmouth fell into a cistern and drowned.

RHODES, WILLIAM - Ancient History - Jan 15,
1895 - January 1877 William Rhodes, a
photographer was killed in his studio in
Quincy.

RICE, JOHN - Death - Oct 7, 1903 John Rice, an
old resident of Houston twp died Saturday eve
from old age, was 78 years old. Native of
Pennsylvania. Came to Houston twp in early
50's and lived there since and farmed. Wife
and family survives him. Buried Monday
afternoon in York Neck Cemetery.

RICE, JOHN - Primrose - Oct 7, 1903 John Rice
a farmer of Houston twp died Saturday eve Oct
3rd of dropsy. Services at York Neck Church
Monday 2 P.M. by Rev King. Buried York Neck
Cemetery.

RICE, JOHN - Local - Oct 14, 1903 Ed
Strickler, of Skidmore, MO was called here last
week by the death of his father in law, John
Rice.

RICE, JOHN - Additional Locals - Oct 21, 1903
John Rice, the veteran hotel proprietor died in
Quincy Sunday. He conducted the Franklin house
for many years and was well known in Adams Co.

RICHARDS, MISS EVA - Northeast Burton - Jan 5,
1893 Funeral of Miss Eva Richards, daughter of
Mr and Mrs Townsend Richards, took place at
Burton last Sunday.

RICHARDS, MISS EVA - Prairie - Jan 12, 1893
Shocked at death of Miss Eva Richards.

RICHARDS, FRANK - Quincy - Jun 18, 1902 Frank
Richards, one of the early settlers of Adams
Co. died at his home in Burton twp on Thursday,
age 83 years.

RICHARDS, GEORGE LEE - Death Record - Mar 31,
1897 Died George Lee Richards born near
Newton, Ill. Sep 1, 1855 died at Omaha, NE Mar
21, 1897 age 41 years 6 months 20 days. In
November 1881 he and 3 brothers went to Nebr.
settling near Ashland. Died following an
operation on Mar 19th in Omaha. Never married.
Leaves a mother, Mrs Quill Vickers of Adams,
Ill; 3 brothers Clinton T., Otis C. and Earl W.
of Ashland; 3 sisters Mrs Ellen Keller, Mrs

Lucy Workman also of Ashland and Miss Addie
Vickers of Adams, Ill.

RICHARDS, JAMES - Ancient History - May 27,
1903 - May 1873 A stranger committed suicide at
the Mensendike House. His name was supposed to
be James Richards.

RICHARDSON, C.W. - Co Seat - Dec 2, 1896 An
inventory of the estate of C.W. Richardson, who
committed suicide in Beverly twp shows he owned
160 acres of land, $1,500 in cash and personal
property, $600 in notes.

RICHARDSON, CHARLES M. - Suicide at Beverly -
Nov 4, 1896 Charles M. Richardson, 3rd son of
Hon James J. Richardson Sr, the Beverly
pioneer, killed himself Saturday on the
Richardson farm 1 mile NE of Beverly village.
He lived there with his 2nd wife, 3 sons and 2
daughters. A brother committed suicide many
years ago in New York .

RICHARDSON, GEORGE J. - Ancient History - Apr
26, 1895 - April 1876 George J. Richardson died
in Quincy.

RICHARDSON, MISS LIZZIE - Quincy - Nov 1, 1895
Miss Lizzie Richardson, a former well known
resident of this city recently died in Wichita,
Kansas.

RICHARDSON, SUSAN J. - Death - Dec 17, 1895
Susan J. Richardson, nee Cleveland, was born in
Jasper Co. MO and died at the home of Dr W.E.
Miller, Columbus Dec 11th age 34 years. Came
to Columbus 2 years ago. Brother George J.
Cleveland is her only survivor from a family of
12. Services at Methodist Church, Columbus by
Rev A.A. White and Rev W.K. Herzog. Remains
buried in Columbus cemetery.

RICHARDSON, MRS SUSIE - Columbus - Dec 20, 1895
Died Wednesday A.M. at 2, Mrs Susie Richardson.
Services by Rev's White and Herzog at 10 A.M.
Thursday. Buried village cemetery.

RICHARDSON, COL. W.A. - Ancient History - Dec 10, 1895 - December 1875 Col. W.A. Richardson died in Quincy.

RICHARDSON, COL. W.A. - Ancient History - Dec 18, 1894 - December 1875 Died, Col. W.A. Richardson died in Quincy.

RICKART, JOHN - Apr 15, 1896 Died- John Rickart in Richfield twp week before last in his 84th year. Came to Ill. from Ohio in 1838 and engaged in mercantile business in Jacksonville, Quincy and then in Kingston.

RICKEY, DR JOHN C. - Dr Rickey's Death - Mar 3, 1897 Mt Sterling, Ill Feb 26th Dr John C. Rickey, mayor of Mt Sterling died at his home yesterday. Sick 2 weeks, pneumonia. Born near Athens, Ohio Feb 21, 1841 and grew up there. Enlisted in 97th Ohio for 3 months and was 2nd man in Athens Co. to enlist. Attended Ohio Medical School at Cincinnati, Ohio graduated in 1867. Also graduated from Bellevue Medical Hospital of New York 1877 and took a post grad course at N.Y. Polytechnic College in 1881. Came here 16 years ago. Elected mayor 1889 for first time.

RIDDER, MRS DOROTHEA - Quincy - Jul 1, 1896 Died Mrs Dorothea Ridder, wife of H. Ridder died Wednesday, age 64 years from the result of a stroke of paralysis. Had lived in the city since 1857.

RIDDLE, ORVILLE - Local - Oct 11, 1895 Orville Riddle, a wealthy farmer of Ursa was found dead in his bed Monday A.M., 64 years old. Leaves a widow and 1 son.

RIGGS, MISS NORAH - Primrose - Feb 3, 1897 Died Miss Norah Riggs of Texas neighborhood died of consumption Sunday. Buried Woodville cemetery Tuesday, 19 years old.

RILEY, MRS MARY E. - Obituary - Jun 15, 1893 Mrs Mary E. Riley died Thursday at her home in Galesburg, age 40 years. Born Mar 30, 1853 in

Camp Point, daughter of Mr and Mrs H.M. Sears.
Married 1873 to George Lisco who died 1881. In
1884 she married B.F. Riley. Her husband and 3
children survive her. Funeral Saturday.

RILEY, MR AND MRS ROLLO - Local - Oct 7, 1903
A son was born to Mr and Mrs Rollo Riley
Saturday A.M. and died Sunday eve.

RINGWALD, SOPHIA - Burned to Death - Jul 6,
1893 About 7 A.M. Sunday, Sophia Ringwald, 28
years old of Quincy started to get breakfast
for the family of Mr Gleichmann where she was
employed when she was engulfed in flame from a
gasoline stove. Died at 2 P.M. that day at St
Mary's Hospital. She had come from Effingham
only 3 months ago where her mother is living.

RIPPLETOE, MRS ROBERT - Local - Jul 31, 1894
Robert Rippletoe and wife of Rushville were
poisoned while eating dinner Sunday. Mrs
Rippletoe died about 4 P.M. Mr Rippletoe will
recover.

RIST, CHRISTIAN - Death - Feb 22, 1895
Christian Rist, one of the early settlers in
Adams Co. died at Bowen Wednesday age 79 years
of pneumonia.

RITCHIE, REV ROBERT - Quincy - Nov 26, 1902
News received here of the death of Rev Robert
Ritchie at Oakland, Calif. He was a brother of
Mrs R.F. Newcomb and was once rector of the
Cathedral of St John in this city.

RITCHOT, JOE - Joe Ritchot Killed - Jan 1, 1896
Joe Ritchot was hit by the train #68, 3 miles
west of Camp Point Thursday. Train took him to
Golden where he died Friday A.M. He had lived
Golden 2 years. His home in Aurora where his
wife lived. Had a daughter at Aurora and at
Chicago.

RITTER, H.D. - Local - Jun 1, 1893 H.D.
Ritter, of Brown Co. was found dead near
Versailes, Ill. He was probably drowned, as he
was found within 5 feet of a creek and the

water had been over him, but had receded. He
was an ex-sheriff and ex-coroner of Brown Co.

RITTER, JOHN - Local - Nov 20, 1894 Died John
Ritter, postmaster of Fargo, Brown Co. died
Thursday night of malarial fever. 35 years
old. Leaves a wife and 2 children.

ROACH, JOHN - Coatsburg - Apr 22, 1903 Prof
C.M. Wilson of Golden came to attend the
funeral of his friend John Roach who died at
the poor farm on Friday A.M. from some sequel
of the measles. Remains taken to Pleasant
Grove, M.E. Church in Burton twp for funeral,
buried cemetery there. Mr Roach was one of he
employees at the farm.

ROACH, JOHN - Local - Dec 14, 1893 An old
woman known as "Grandma" Elliott died on the
5th inst at the poor farm age 73 years. John
Roach, of Libety an insane inmate, died on the
3rd.

ROBBINS, BILLY - Golden - Aug 20, 1895 Uncle
Billy Robbins died Sunday A.M. at 2, sick
several months. He was one of the old
pioneers.

ROBBINS, MRS JOSEPH - Ancient History - Mar 26,
1895 - March 1876 Mrs Joseph Robbins died in
Quincy.

ROBBINS, MRS JOSEPH - Ancient History - Mar 30,
1894 - March 24, 1876 Mrs Joseph Robbins died
in Quincy.

ROBBINS, WILLIAM - Obituary - Aug 23, 1895
Died William Robbins at his home in Elm Grove
neighborhood last Sunday A.M. after sickness of
several months, 77 years old lacking 1 day.
Lived here since coming with parents from
Guilford Co. N.C. where he was born. Married
Dec 1, 1842 to Miss Mary Dorsett, 5 sons born,
2 dead, John and Jared. Wife and 3 sons
survive- Alix, Jason and William McKendrie.
Services at Elm Grove M.E. Church by Rev W.H.
McDonald Monday A.M. Buried Horeb cemetery.

ROBBINS, WM - Elm Grove - Oct 11, 1895
Porperty sold well at the adm sale of effects
of the late Wm Robbins.

ROBERTS, MRS WINIFRED - Died - Mar 25, 1896
Died at the home of her daughter, Mrs G.A.
Cline Tuesday A.M. the 24th inst, Mrs Winifred
Roberts. Funeral from the home of Mrs Cline at
3 P.M. by Elder E.J. Lampton, Louisiana, MO.

ROBERTS, MRS WINIFRED - Obituary - Apr 8, 1896
Mrs Winifred (Wheeler) Roberts born Kentucky in
1893. Married John Roberts 1841 about 10 years
later Mr Roberts died leaving her with 2 sons
and a daughter who now survive her. She
brought her family to Ill. right after husband
died. Died Tuesday A.M. after illness of 4
months.

ROBERTSON, ALBERT G. - Obituary - Mar 29, 1895
Albert G. Robertson born in Adams Co. Ill Mar
4, 1877 died Mar 22, 1895. Services at Hebron
Church. He was son of John C. and Lovella
Robertson. Was second son of John C. and wife
to died within a year. Both are buried side by
side in Hebron cemetery.

ROBERTSON, ALBERT G. - Obituary - Mar 26, 1895
Albert G. Robertson, son of Mr and Mrs John C.
Robertson of Camp Point twp died Friday the
22nd inst, age 18 years 18 days. Services at
Hebron Church Sunday A.M.

ROBERTSON, CHARLES - Death of Charles Robertson
Jun 5, 1894 Died Charles Robertson, son of Mr
and Mrs John C. Robertson died Saturday June
2nd, 1894 age 19 years. Had been an invalid
for a long time. Services at Hebron Church
Sunday by Rev A. Sears. Buried church
cemetery.

ROBERTSON, GEORGE - Ancient History - May 22,
1894 - May 25, 1877 George Robertson and
William Ketchum of Augusta were drowned in
Crooked Creek.

ROBERTSON, JAMES - Local - Jan 28, 1903 Amos

R. Robertson, of Bentley was in town Saturday, called here by the death of his brother, James.

ROBERTSON, MRS JAMES F. - Ancient History - Sep 11, 1894 - Sep 6, 1883 Mrs James F. Robertson died August 30th.

ROBERTSON, JAMES F. - Local - Feb 4, 1903 John B. Works of Cincinnati, Ohio attended the funeral of his brother in law, James F. Robertson.

ROBERTSON, JAMES F. - Probate Notice - Mar 4, 1903 James F. Robertson, deceased 1st Monday of April 1903 (6th) James R. Guthrie, Ex.

ROBERTSON, JAMES F. - Finished his Journey - Jan 28, 1903 James F. Robertson died Friday night after illness of about 4 years. Services at Christian Church Sunday P.M. by Elder E.J. Lampton of Bowling Green, MO who was pastor of the church in the 80's. Born in Camp Point twp Jun 26, 1846, Died Jan 23, 1903, Was 56 years 6 months 27 days old. Was son of James and Elizabeth (Booth) Robertson. His father located here in the 30's and was one of the early settlers of the twp. James attended school at Maplewood and became agent for Wabash Railroad for about 20 years. Married Sallie Francis Jan 12, 1873. She died Aug 30, 1884 leaving him with one son, Charles F. and daughter Edith. Married second Dec 5, 1899 to Miss Lillian M. Works who survives him along with 3 children. Leaves 1 brother A.R. Robertson of Bentley and 4 sisters Mrs William I. Bates of Camp Point, Mrs J. O'Hara and Mrs Jas. McAnulty of Carthage and Sallie C. Burnett of Camp Point.

ROBERTSON, JAS. F. - Local - Jan 28, 1903 Mrs J.W. O'Hara, A.W. O'Hara and Miss Emma McAnulty of Carthage came down Saturday to attend the funeral of Jas. F. Robertson.

ROBERTSON, JAS. F. - Local - Feb 4, 1903 Will of Jas. F. Robertson was filed last week. James R. Guthrie appointed executor. Widow

received his interest in Mendon Bank and
remainder of property divided under statute.
Executor to hold real estate for 5 years, then
sell it.

ROBERTSON, REV WILLIAM H. - Death - Oct 8, 1895
Rev William H. Robertson died Sept 30th at
Sheridan, LaSalle Co. Was brother of Mrs
Elizabeth Downing and in his youth in the 30's
resided in Camp Point twp, 76 years old.

ROBINSON, CLADE - Local - Jun 5, 1894 Died
Clade Robinson, little son of John F. Robenson
of Abingdon, Ill died Wednesday night from
drinking gasoline.

ROBINSON, EDWARD - Local - Sep 7, 1894 Died
Edward Robinson, the boy who fell under the
cars a couple weeks ago died at St Mary's
hospital Monday eve from lockjaw.

ROBINSON, EDWARD - Crushed by a Freight Train -
Aug 24, 1894 Edward Robinson, son of Andrew
Robinson, 133 S. 7th St., Quincy about 13 years
old was found lying crushed on the tracks
Tuesday forenoon. His left leg was crushed
from knee to ankle and was amputated at the
knee. The left arm had a compound fracture.
Boys parents came and took him to Quincy
Wednesday.

ROBINSON, HENRY - Clayton - Jul 19, 1895 Henry
Robinson of Mounds was killed at Forest while
on the way with cattle to Chicago Monday night.
Was oldest son of James N. Robinson lately
deceased and was about 43 years old. Fell from
train it is thought. Buried at Fargo
Wednesday. Leaves a wife, who was the daughter
of Mrs Capt Mumford of Mounds and a family.
For many years Henry and wife lived in Pike Co.

ROBINSON, JAMES - Ax Slipped - Jan 29, 1895
Jacksonville, Ill Jan 26th This A.M. an
accident in western part of this county James
Robinson who lives near Perry was visiting his
brother in law William Powers who was erecting
a small log house and while on the corners the

ax slipped hitting Mr Robinson in the jugular
vein, almost instant death.

ROBINSON, JAMES N. - Drank Bottled Beer - May
17, 1895   J.N. Robinson of Brown Co. became
sick after drinking a bottle of beer and died
8:15 P.M. last Thursday.   James N. Robinson was
born in Huntingdon Co. Penn. Nov 22, 1823.
Came to Ill. 1837 and located in Pike Co. from
there to Adams Co. In 1847 located in Brown Co.
Leaves a widow and 8 children. He was one of
Brown Co.'s wealthiest citizens and the largest
land owner. Estate is estimated at $100,000 to
$150,000. Mr Mayfield helped dig the grave and
drank from another beer bottle and died also.
Was son of Seborn Mayfield. He was a poor man
and leaves a family in destitute circumstances.

ROCKWELL, CHARLES B. - Quincy - Sep 17, 1902
Charles B. Rockwell, age 28 years, formerly of
this vicinity died in Kansas City, on
Wednesday.

RODEFER, EMMET - Quincy - Dec 24, 1902 Remains
of Emmet Rodefer who was killed by falling
between the cars on Tuesday were taken to
Lewiston, MO for burial.

RODGERS, JOSEPH - 10 Years Ago - Oct 19, 1893
Joseph Rodgers, an "Indian Doctor" killed his
wife and then himself in Quincy.

RODMAN, BENJAMIN H. - Decapitated by the Cars -
Sep 23, 1896 Late Sunday afternoon Benjamin H.
Rodman, foreman of the logging gang at the Gem
City saw mills bent over in front of a switch
engine and it cut the top of his head off. 53
years old. Lived Quincy 4 years, came to
Quincy from LaCrosse, Wisc. Within the past 10
days had moved his family here, consisting of a
wife and daughter.

ROGERS, JOSEPH - Ancient History - Oct 16, 1894
Oct 11, 1883 Joseph Rogers the "Indian Doctor"
killed his wife in Quincy.

ROGERS, LORENA - Co. Seat - Nov 25, 1896

Friday eve Lorena, 3 year old daughter of Mr
and Mrs George Rogers was playing with her
little cousin, who struck her in the head with
a knitting needle, died from paralysis Saturday
A.M.

ROGERS, RICHARD - Local - Jan 2, 1896 Richard,
the 16 year old son of Thad M. Rogers was
drowned in Quincy Bay Tuesday A.M. while
skating.

ROGERS, WILLIAM T. - Ancient History - Apr 26,
1895 - April 1880 William T. Rogers, mayor of
Quincy died.

ROLF, MALACHI - Coatsburg - Aug 20, 1902 On
the eve of the 12th inst at his home, 2 miles
north of Coatsburg, Malachi Rolf an old
Germancitizen died. Mr Rolf was 78 years old,
had been in U.S. 37 years. Leaves aged wife, 1
son and 2 daughters. Son, George lives at
Denver, Colo. Mrs Ben Ohnemus in Quincy and Mrs
Pauline Dittmer of this vicinity. Also leaves
a brother, a twin brother of Pea Ridge, Brown
Co., this brother and 2 daughters were at his
bedside when he died. Remains taken to Quincy
and buried in one of the cemeteries there on
Saturday.

ROLLIN, MRS MARY - West Point - May 3, 1895 Mr
and Mrs William Hicks attended the funeral of
Mrs Mary Rollin of Chili Saturday.

ROONEY, DR MICHAEL - Quincy - Sep 15, 1897
Died Dr Michael Rooney, one of the leading
physicians of this city died Friday P.M.
Native of New York and graduated from Miami
Medical College of Cincinnati, Ohio 1866. Came
to Quincy 1871.

ROOT, HENRY - Quincy - Apr 19, 1895 Will of
the late Henry Root was filed for probate
Wednesday. He left an estate of $196,000, the
bulk left to his descendants.

ROOT, MRS J.A. - Quincy - Mar 12, 1902 Mrs
J.A. Root, age 55 years was stricken with

apoplexy and dropped dead in her yard on
Wednesday A.M.

ROSEBURY, MRS SALLIE - Coatsburg - Sep 7, 1893
Remains of Mrs Sallie Rosebury (nee Young) of
Monmouth, I think, was brought thru Coatsburg
this P.M. to be buried beside the remains of
her father in cemetery at Columbus. Cause was
consumption. She formerly lived Paloma
vicinity.

ROSENTHAL, JOSEPH S. - Quincy - Oct 19, 1894
Died Joseph S. Rossenthal, a native of Yazoo
City, Miss., later of Memphis, Tenn. and for
many years a business man of Quincy died Sunday
age 55 years.

ROSS, CHARLEY - Ancient History - Apr 21, 1897
August 1879 Charley Ross was shot by James A.
Frink on Hampshire St., Quincy and was
instantly killed.

ROSS, CHARLEY - Ancient History - Aug 9, 1895
August 1879 Charley Ross was killed in Quincy
by James A. Frink.

ROSS, GEO. E. - Golden - Jan 26, 1893 Geo. E.
Ross has gone back to Ind. to look after his
father's estate.

ROSS, JAMES - Ancient History - Feb 22, 1895
February 1876 James Ross committed suicide at
LaPrairie by jumping into a well.

ROSS, JAMES R. - Death - Nov 26, 1895 Elder
James R. Ross died Nov 10th at the home of his
daughter in Brunswick, MO age 86 years 10
months 19 days. Born Ohio but preached
Kentucky, Ind., Ill., MO., Iowa and Nebr.
Lived many years in Camp Point where he married
Mrs Bernetta Booth who died 20 years ago.
Buried Brunswick.

ROSS, JAS. - Ancient History - Jun 24, 1896
February 1876 Jas. Ross committed suicide by
jumping in a well at LaPrairie.

ROSS, JOSEPH - Local - May 17, 1895 Joseph
Ross, aged about 40 years one of the prominent
farmers living between Prairie City and Avon
mysteriously disappeared Wednesday last and
cannot to this date be found.

ROSS, SAMUEL H. - Clayton - Dec 13, 1895 Mrs
S.A. Harding received word of the death of her
father, Mr Samuel H. Ross last Monday. Lived
Texas many years, but was in Indian Terr. at
the time of his death. Almost 4 score years
old, being 79 years of age. Leaves a wife and
6 children. About 20 years ago the family
lived in Concord twp near Colpitt's school
house. His disease was chronic diarrhea.

ROSS, WILLIAM C. - Ancient History - May 26,
1897 December 1879 Died, William C. Ross.

ROTH, JOHN - Elm Grove - Jul 6, 1893 John
Roth, grandson of Mr Rumple on Pea Ridge twp,
Brown Co. was drowned Monday eve of last week
in a deep water hole in the north fork of
Missouri Creek. Leaves wife. Was about 22
years old. Also leaves a child.

ROTH, JOHN A. - Ancient History - Oct 12, 1894
Oct 8, 1875 John A. Roth, one of the first
merchants of Camp Point died October 1st.

ROTH, MARGARET A. - Ancient History - Nov 27,
1894 - Nov 27, 1874 Mrs Margaret A. Roth died
on the 12th.

ROTHGEB, WILLIAM - Quincy - Jan 29, 1895
William Rothgeb, age 34 of this city died
Wednesday in Los Vegas, N.M. Buried here
Saturday.

ROUTH, ROBERT H. - Local - Jun 3, 1896 Died
Robert H. Routh at Augusta Monday. Buried
today. Livd many years in Camp Point. Leaves 1
daughter Mrs Etta Young of Augusta. He was a
brother in law of James J. Earl.

ROUTH, THEODORE - Local - Jan 4, 1895 Theodore
Routh died at Augusta Monday night age 45 from

erysipelas.   Lived Camp Point in his youth.

ROWLAND, MAJOR JOSEPH G. - Dead - Aug 12, 1903
Major Joseph G. Rowland, the Supt of the
Soldiers Home at Leavenworth, Kan. died at that
place on the 5th inst., age 73 years. He was a
real estate dealer in Quincy when the war broke
out and served in the 10th Ill. Inf. Some time
after 1887 he moved to Quincy.

ROYER, MISS MELINDA - Elm Grove - Aug 19, 1896
Died Miss Melinda Royer, age 51 years at the
home of R.J. Alexander last Thursday from
paralysis. Funeral by Rev Carpenter at the
Alexander home. Buried at the Sims cemetery.

RUDDELL, MRS JOHN M. - Local - Apr 29, 1896
Died Mrs John M. Ruddell at Ursa, Friday, age
84 years. This is one of the couple of whom
mention was made recently having been married
64 years. Leaves husband, 2 sons and 2
daughters. Funeral Sunday.

RUDDELL, JOHN M. - Obituary - Sep 2, 1896 Died
John M. Ruddell, said to be the oldest resident
farmer in Adams Co. was buried in Old Stone
Church Cemetery at Ursa Sunday. Mrs Ruddell
died about 4 months ago. Mr Ruddell was born
Bourbon Co. KY Sep 28, 1812. Came to Adams Co.
Nov 20, 1829 . Married Miss Martha Dunlap
1832. At time of his death he lived near
Marcelline. They had 11 children, 4 still
living. Served in Philip Martins Co. during
the Black Hawk War. Services by A.C. Ament of
Marcelline.

RUDOLPH, JUSTICE - Local - Jan 12, 1894 Died
Justice Rudolph, for many years a justice of
peace in Quincy died Monday in his 7oth year.

RUNKLE, WILLIAM - Suicide - Feb 23, 1893
William Runkle, a farmer about 40 years old
hung himself in his barn in Industry twp last
Saturday afternoon. Wife found him. Lived all
his life in that vicinity. Was son of Darius
Runkle one of the earliest citizens of that
locality and one of the wealthiest men in

McDonough Co.   Leaves a wife and number of
children.   "Macomb Journal"

RUSSELL, ABSOLOM - Forgery - Feb 16, 1894
George F. Russell was arrested at Bushnell
Saturday on the charge of forgery.   Russell is
wanted in Oregon.   He is Co. Supt. of Schools
in Linn Co. Oregon.   Was a former resident of
Sciota.   Was called to McDonough Co. to look
after real estate left him by his father,
Absolom Russell who died 20 years ago.   "Macomb
Bystander"

RUSSELL, JAMES - Local - Mar 9, 1893 Tuesday
of last week, James Russell, a farmer living
near Barry was fatally injured when he was
hitching his sled.   Lingered a few days and
died.

RUSSELL, ROB'T - Local - Sep 4, 1894 Died
Rob't Russell an old time printer died in
Quincy last week and buried Sunday.   Worked
Quincy 50 years.

RUSSELL, WAKEFIELD - Death of W. Russell - Dec
29, 1897 Died - Dec 23, 1897 at Galva, Kan.,
Wakefield Russell born in Shelby Co. KY Dec 4,
1826.   Married 1848 to Catherine A. Rhea,
sister of the late George Rhea of Camp Point.
Moved to Ill. spring of 1859.   Settled in
Gilmer twp 1 mile west of Columbus where he
farmed and did blacksmithing.   Wife died 1876.
He moved to Galva, Kan. 1884.   Body arrived
Camp Point Saturday A.M.   Buried in Columbus
beside his wife.   He was a good husband and
kind father.

RYAN, PATRICK - Quincy - Mar 26, 1895 Patrick
Ryan, age 50 an insane tramp was arrested here
and sent to the Adams Co. Alms House, died
there from starvation, for 17 days he refused
to eat.   Left no trace as to his former home or
associations.

SAHLAND, HENRY - Obituary - Sep 7, 1893 Died,
Henry Sahland Sep 2nd at his parents home, Mr
and Mrs A. Sahland.   He was 19 years 11 months

24 days old.   Servics by Rev Klemm in Lutheran
Church in Coatsburg.   Buried Coatsburg
cemetery.

SAHLAND, HENRY - Coatsburg - Sep 7, 1893 Died,
Friday night at his home 1 mile NW of
Coatsburg, Henry Sahland after a very painful
illness of 1 week. Born and raised and received
his education here.   Was 18 or 19 years old.

SALMON, MRS EDWIN C. - Quincy - Jun 21, 1895
Mrs Edwin C. Salmon, living at 1336 N. 4th St.
died at Hannibal Tuesday where she was visiting
her mother.   Had been ill with consumption for
some time.   Husband is a printer for Volk,
Jones and McMein.

SAMMIS, MRS HELEN - Quincy - Dec 10, 1902
Third trial of Mrs Helen Sammis vs C.B. & Q
Railroad for $10,000 damages for the death of
her husband who was killed in a railroad
accident.   Fourth trial to be heard next
session.

SAMMONS, ARTIE - Death - May 5, 1897 Artie
Sammons, daughter of Mr and Mrs Wesley Sammons,
died at the parental home in Columbus twp
Monday age 16 years.   Services at Pleasant View
today 11 A.M.

SAMMONS, ARTIE H. - Obituary - May 12, 1897
Artie H. Sammons born near Camp Point Oct 16,
1880 and died May 3, 1897 age 16 years 6 months
17 days.   She leaves her parents, 2 sisters, 4
brothers. Services at Pleasant View Church last
Wednesday 11 A.M. by Elder O. Dilley.

SAMMONS, ISAAC - Death of Isaac Sammons - Jun
1, 1894 Died - Isaac Sammons at the home of
his daughter, Mrs Seldon G. Earel in Riverside
twp Tuesday. 86 years old.   Born in Virginia.
Came to Adams Co. 1834 settling on a farm south
of Camp Point.   Leaves 7 daughters -- Mrs
Seldon G. Earel, Mrs W.H. Murphy, Mrs Theo.
Feathergill, Mrs Henry Johnson, Mrs John Curry,
Harrisonville, MO, Mrs Wiseman, Canton MO and
Mrs Jefferson Simmons of Polo, MO.   Lived with

Mrs Earel for past 16 years.   Funeral at
Christian Church in Columbus by Elder O.
Dilley. Buried village cemetery.

SAMUEL, CUMBERLAND G. - C.G. Samuel Killed -
Feb 19, 1896 "Feb 15th" C.M. Swain received
word Saturday that Cumberland G. Samuel at
Brookfield, Mo was shot in the head yesterday,
about 50 years old.   Married and 3 grown
children.   Had lived many years near Paloma.
Was brother of Hon. A.M. Samuel now a resident
of Texas and Mrs C.M. Swain of Camp Point.   His
wife was a daughter of the late Alex Collings
of Gilmer twp.   Mrs E.L. Downing of Pomona,
Cal. is a daughter.

SAWYER, CHARLES - Local - Dec 23, 1903 Charles
Sawyer died at Stillwell, Hancock Co.   Coroners
jury brought in verdict that death was due to
alcoholism.   76 empty lemon extract bottles and
61 - 1/2 gallon whiskey jugs were found in his
workshop.

SAWYER, MRS E.E.B. - Local - Jun 4, 1902
Thomas Prentiss, who with his family lost their
lives by the destruction of St Pierre in the
eruption of Mr Pelee and was U.S. Consul.
there, was a cousin of Mrs E.E.B. Sawyer of
Camp Point.

SAWYER, E.E.B. - Ancient History - Jul 14, 1897
December 1880 An obituary for E.E.B. Sawyer
appeared in the Payson News.   Sawyer didn't
believe it.

SAWYER, MRS ESTHER - Ancient History - Aug 9,
1895   August 1878 Mrs Esther Sawyer died.

SAWYER, MRS ESTHER - Ancient History - Jan 27,
1897   August 1878 Mrs Esther Sawyer died July
27th.

SAWYER, GEORGE - Local - Apr 9, 1902 Died-
E.E.B. Sawyer received news last week of the
death of his brother, George Sawyer, in Nevada.
George spent some time in Camp Point back in
the 60's and taught school east of town.

SAWYER, IRVIN B. - Quincy - Nov 12, 1902 Will
of Irvin B. Sawyer leaves his personal property
and real estate to his widow, at her death the
real estate will go to his half sister, Amanda
L. Phillips of Alexander, Ark. and to her son
at her death.

SAWYER, CAPT JAMES T. - Quincy - Apr 7, 1897
Died, Capt James T. Sawyer one of the pioneers
of this city Friday night age 80 years. Born
Hopkinsville, KY and never married and had no
relatives here.

SCHAEFER, WILLIAM - Quincy - Jun 11, 1902 The
will of William Schaefer, who recently died in
Fall Creek twp divides 680 acres of land and
nearly $70,000 in cash among his 2 sons and 7
daughters.

SCHERD, MR AND MRS - York Neck - Feb 16, 1893
Died, on the 10th inst at the home of R. Crows,
an infant child of Mr and Mrs Scherds, of
Houston twp. Child took sick while they were
on their way home from Fowler where they were
visiting and lived but a few hours.

SCHLAGG, MRS - Co Seat - Jul 29, 1896 Mother
of Chief Schlagg, of the fire dept, was buried
July 28th.

SCHLEMMER, HENRY - Local - Dec 4, 1894 Trial
of Willis Morgan a young man who assaulted and
kicked to death an elderly man named Henry
Schlemmer last June was concluded in Pike Co.
Circuit Court Saturday. He received 15 years
in penitentiary.

SCHLINKMAN, EDWARD & WM - Quincy - Jun 4, 1902
Tuesday afternoon Edward Schlinkman aimed a gun
at his brother, Wm Schlinkman and pulled the
trigger, but the cartridge failed to explode.
Trouble between them over father's estate. Wm
was named executor of it. Edward is eluding
arrest.

SCHMIEDESKAMP, JOHN - Coatsburg - Sep 24, 1895
Died, on the 17th inst, John Schmiedeskamp an

insane inmate of the county asylum.   Buried
Quincy.

SCHMIDT, AUGUST - Clayton - Feb 15, 1895 Nine
members of the family of August Schmidt of
Concord were sick last week.   One of the
children, a babe of 10 days died.   Others are
improving.

SCHMIDT, JOHN - Bauman Gabbles - Apr 24, 1894
W. Buskirk attended the funeral of John Schmidt
Thursday at 4 P.M.

SCHMIDT, TOM - A Horrible Accident - Jun 15,
1894 Killed August Schmidt a well to do
German farmer living 5 or 6 miles SE of Camp
Point in Concord twp had his son Tom remove a
limb from in front of the wagon.   Startled the
horses and cycle run over him (Tom).   Thomas
was about 12 years old.

SCHMITT, LEONARD - Local - May 20, 1903
Leonard Schmitt was killed by lightning during
the storm in Quincy Monday.   A boy was trying
to turn on the lights and was severly shocked.
Schmitt caught the boy and the current passed
into his body, killing him. The boy will
recover.

SCHMITT, LEONARD - Quincy - Oct 21, 1903
Emilie Schmitt, adm of the estate of Leonard
Schmitt, filed a suit against Quincy Gas &
Light Co. for $5,000.   Mr Schmitt was killed by
an electric wire.

SCHMITT, WILLIAM A. - Death - Dec 2, 1903 Gen.
William A. Schmitt died in Chicago Nov. 26th,
age 62 years.   Born in Quincy and served 4
years in army during the rebellion, rising from
private to brigadier general.   Worked several
years in Chicago Post Office. Leaves wife and 2
daughters.

SCHOLZ, JOSEPH - Local - Aug 27, 1895 Joseph
Scholz, while attempting to mount a Maine St
motor car in Quincy Sunday afternoon fell and
was run over by the trailer and killed.   61

years old and a laborer.

SCHRAAGE, FREDERICK - Quincy - Jan 4, 1895 The will of Frederick Schraage was admitted to probate Monday. Bulk of his property goes to his daughter, Mrs Adam Fick.

SCHROEDER, BERTHA LOUISA - Local - Aug 2, 1895 Bertha Louisa, one of the twin daughters of Mr and Mrs Louis C.H. Schroeder died Wed. A.M., age 7 months 24 days of cholera infamtum. Funeral Thursday at York Neck Cemetery.

SCHUHARDT, AMOS ARTHUR - Death - Dec 3, 1902 Last Wed. J.F. Schuhardt who lived 2 miles west of town received word a young man named Amos Stuart had died at Springfield from poison and it was probably his son. Fred Schuhardt Jr. went to Springfield and identified the body and brought remains back Thursday A.M. From Springfield papers it is gleamed that Amos registered at the Silas Hotel as Ed Salt, Carthage, Ill. He had left school at Quincy about Nov 1st his brother thought a love affair was partially responsible for his leaving. Funeral at Camp Point Methodist Church by Rev's E.A. Hedges and C.F. Stecher. Obituary reads: Amos Arthur, youngest son of J. Frederick and Margaret Schuhardt born Jun 11, 1884 in the house from which the remains were taken to Church. Was youngest child. He left home in August to attend Gem City Business College. Died Nov 25th age 18 years 5 months 14 days. Leaves father, mother, 3 brothers and 4 sisters. Buried village cemetery.

SCHULTEN, MRS ELIZABETH - Quincy - Dec 18, 1894 Died Mrs Elizabeth Schulten age 56 died of pleurisy of the heart in Burton and buried from St Boniface Church, this city.

SCHULTZ, LELIA AND GROVER - Drowned - Jul 5, 1895 Lelia and Grover Schultz were drowned in Bear Creek near Marcelline Tuesday eve. Grover was about 9 and Lelia 11. Grover was bathing in the creek and got out to deep, Lelia went to help him. Both drowned.

SCHWARTZ, FRANK - Quincy - Oct 12, 1894 Died
Frank Schwartz died Sunday eve, age 59 years.

SCHWARTZ, JACOB - Local - Apr 1, 1896 Died
Jacob Schwartz, an old citizen of Liberty twp
died March 21st, age 85 years. Buried in Old
Nation's graveyard and services by Rev William
Lierly of the Dunkard denomination.

SCHWARTZ, JOHN G. - Obituary - May 26, 1897
John G. Schwartz eldest son of George and Mary
Schwartz born Feb 17, 1841. Married to Martha
J. O'Neal Mar 10, 1864, had 13 children, 6
sons, 7 daughters, 5 proceeded their father in
death. He had been a teacher, soldier and
farmer. Entered in 1861 Co. B of the 28th Reg.
of Ill. Vol. where he served 9 months. After
marriage they moved to a farm near Barry, Ill.
for 2 years. Came to Golden spring of "66"
where they lived since. Died May 16th, 1897.
Funeral from the ME Church Golden, Ill. by Rev
P. Slagle. Services by Masons at his home
afterwards.

SCHWARTZ, JOHN G. - Quincy - Jun 2, 1897 Mrs
Martha J. Schwartz has been appointed adm of
the estate of John G. Schwartz.

SCHWARTZ, JOHN G. - Death of J.G.Schwartz - May
19, 1897 Died John G. Schwartz at his home
near Golden Sunday afternoon from cancer of the
stomach. Leaves a wife and 8 children. Buried
Hebron Cemetery Tuesday afternoon by the Masons
of LaPrairie Lodge of which he was a member.

SCHWARTZ, JOHN G. - Golden - May 26, 1897 John
and Sam Kern of Shelbina, MO attended the
funeral of John G. Schwartz last week.

SCHWARTZ, JOHN G. - Golden - May 26, 1897 Mrs
Laura Huff has been appointed adm of the John
G. Schwartz estate and Mrs Mattie J. Schwartz
guardian for the minor heirs.

SCHWERER, ANNA - Burned to Death - Jun 7, 1895
Anna Schwerer, daughter of Lewis Schwerer an
old resident of the county living 4 miles NE of

Fountain Green died a horrible death Saturday night. She awoke and wrapped a sheet around her and set fire to it. Funeral Monday. Carthage Republican.

SCOGGAN, MARIUS - Marius Scoggan - May 11, 1894 Died, Marius Scoggan an old resident of Concord twp died at the home of Miss Fannie Scoggan at 9 P.M. Monday, age 75 years. His disease was dropsical. He was a soldier in the rebellion and was buried by members of G.A.R. Wednesday.

SCOTT - Local - Mar 9, 1893 An old lady named Scott, living near Augusta, was found dead in her bed one day last week, apoplexy probably the cause. Search of premises revealed $600 in cash and sone notes hid about the house and $100 tucked away in a box containing nails.

SCOTT, MRS HALLIE ISABELLE - Death of Mrs C.W. Scott - Feb 3, 1897 Died Mrs Hallie Isabelle Scott, wife of Mr C. Warren Scott of the Chicago Stock Yards. Died Thursday A.M. at the family home on Garfield Blvd., daughter of D.B. Lowry of Aurora, Ill. Funeral Friday 2 P.M. at 737 Garfield Blvd. Burial at Oakwoods. 29 years 7 months 4 days old.

SCOTT, JOHN - Quincy - Oct 22, 1895 About 30 days ago John Scott, of near Seehorn was shot and killed by Edward Tilby, a brother of Scott's wife. Found to be self defense later. Thursday Tilby came to Quincy with a girl named Effie Brown and they were married. Friday Mrs Fannie Scott, widow of the man that was shot and killed came to the court house here and was married to John Belts, of Seehorn. She is 37 and he is a lank country stripling of 22 years.

SCOTT, WALTER LINN - Drowned in the Sni - Aug 30, 1895 Walter Linn Scott, 19 years old, son of Edward Scott of Payson drowned in the Sni Tuesday eve with John Mann, George Thompson and Carl Wharton, neighbors of about his age. He lived about 1 mile from Payson and graduated Payson high school last spring.

SEALS, WILLIAM - Quincy - Apr 7, 1897 The will
of William Seals leaves all of his property to
his widow for use during her life. At her
death it is to go to his daughter, Amanda
Murphy.

SEARS, MRS J.B. - Obituary - Jan 19, 1894 Died
Mrs Jennie Sears wife of John B. Sears and
daughter of Samuel and Nancy Crippin at her
home in Chicago Jan 13th. Born Oct 11, 1864 in
Hancock Co.. Married Oct 17, 1886 to John B.
Sears of Buffalo, N.Y. Leaves husband, widowed
mother, 3 brothers and 2 sisters. Services at
her old home Jan 15th by Elder O. Dilley.
Buried Camp Point cemetery.

SEARS, MRS JENNIE - Local - Jan 16, 1894 Died
Mrs Jennie Sears in Chicago Saturday. Brought
here for burial Monday P.M. she was 2nd
daughter of Mrs Nancy Crippin and had lived
Chicago several years.

SEATON, MRS CHARLES - Columbus - Nov 9, 1893
Body of Mrs Charles Seaton was buried in our
cemetery Thursday, Nov 2nd. Lived Columbus
many years ago. Was 90 years old.

SEATON, MRS CHAS. D. - Death - Nov 2, 1893 Mrs
Elizabeth Payne Seaton died in Elvaston Oct
31st aged 90 years. Native of Virginia and
married Chas. D. Seaton in 1827. Came to Ill.
1844 and settled near Columbus. Her husband
died 1872 and she since lived with her
children, Geo. D. Seaton of Golden, Jas. A. of
Marion, IA, Mrs Sarah Thomas of Linneus, MO,
Mrs Jane Kelley of Frederick, KS, Mrs Mary Felt
of Laclide, MO. Remains taken to Camp
PointChristian Church last Thursday for
services by Elder O. Dilley and later taken to
Columbus for burial beside her husband.

SEATON, ELIZA ANNE - Death - Dec 23, 1903 Mrs
Eliza Anne Seaton died at the home of her son,
William H. Seaton, Quincy, Thursday A.M.
Remains brought to Camp Point Friday and taken
to Pleasant View Cemetery for burial. Mrs
Seaton, nee Smith was born near Columbus 72

years ago.   Married George D. Seaton 1851.
Leaves only 1 son, William H. the well known
bridge carpenter of the C.B. & Q

SEATON, ELDER J. - Local - Nov 9, 1893 Elder
J. Seaton of Marion, Iowa was called to this
county by the death of his mother last week and
he renewed acquaintances of 40 years ago.

SEATON, JANE - A Pioneer Reunion - Sep 8, 1897
62 years ago this fall there came from
Jefferson Co. Kentucky a colony of 16 people
who settled in what is now known as Camp Point,
They were: Jane Seaton; Richard Seaton, his
wife, Elinor and children Margaret (Wallace)
Kenner, Rebecca (Bailey), John S. and James M.;
Peter B. Garrett and his wife, Elizabeth and
children Silas and Mary (Miller); Daniel H.
Peden, his wife Martha and children, Albert and
Morgan of this number only 5 are living--Mrs
Elizabeth Garrett and John S. Seaton of Camp
Point, Silas Garrett of Iowa, Mrs Mary Miller
of Missouri and Albert Peden of California, all
but Mr Peden were at the reunion.

SEATON, RICHARD - 20 Years Ago - May 4, 1893
Richard Seaton died at the home of Thomas
Bailey aged 83 years.

SEATON, RICHARD - Soldiers Buried in Pleasant
View Cemetery - May 26, 1897 Listed as being
in War of 1812   U.S.A.

SEATON, RICHARD - Ancient History - Apr 22,
1903 - April 17-24, 1873 Richard Seaton, one
of the pioneers of Adams Co. died on the 21st.

SECKMAN, JONATHAN & NANCY P. - Local - Jun 30,
1897 Nancy P., relict of Jonathan Seckman was
stricken with paralysis of the right side at
the old homestead about 6 miles east of this
city in Cooperstown twp last Monday eve.
Little Hope of recovery. She is about 85 years
old.   "Mt Sterling Examiner"

SECRESE, ANDREW J. - Ancient History - Jun 12,

1894 - June 9, 1881 Andrew J. Secrese was
killed at Clayton by a train.

SEELIG, MRS H. - Ancient History - Sep 23, 1896
September 1877 Deaths reported were Mrs H.
Seelig and Vixen P. Gay.

SEELIG, HIRAM - Probate Notice - Oct 6, 1897
Hiram Seelig, deceased   1st Monday of Dec 1897
(6th)   Mary Seelig, adm.

SEELIG, MRS HIRAM - Ancient History - Sep 20,
1895 - September 1877 Mrs Hiram Seelig died on
the 17th.

SEELIG, HIRAM - Dead - Jul 7, 1897 Hiram
Seelig died Saturday July 3rd of malarial
fever. Born Chilicothe, Ohio 1822. Came to
Ill. 1847 and located at Payson until 1854 when
he came to Camp Point. Married Ellen Kamp
1856. She died 1877 leaving him a daughter,
Mrs Fletcher Seelig and a son Frank. Funeral
Sunday by Elder O. Dilley and Rev C.F. Stecker.
Buried village cemetery.

SEELY, MRS RHODA - Ancient History - Sep 25,
1894 - Sep 21, 1877 Died Mrs Rhoda Seely died
on the 19th.

SEGER, CHARLES E. - Quincy - Feb 12, 1902   Mary
Emma Seger, has been appointed adm of the
estate of Charles E. Seger.

SELBY, MR AND MRS SENECA - Golden - May 8, 1894
Funeral - Mr and Mrs Seneca Selby attended the
funeral of Mrs Selby's stepmother at Camp Point
last Sunday.

SELBY, WILLIAM T. - Obituary - Jan 26, 1894
Died William T. Selby at his home near Thayer,
NE Sunday Jan 21st age about 50 years. Spent
boyhood in Houston twp. Was son of Wilson
Selby and brother of H.E. Selby of Golden.
Married a daughter of Joseph Robertson, his
wife dying a couple years since. Leaves
several children.

SELLERS, JOHN - Local - Oct 26, 1894 John
Sellers a half witted young man from Bluffs was
hit by a train Wednesday near Meredosia and
killed.

SEWARD, W.H. - Ancient History - Sep 11, 1894
Sept. 7, 1882 W.H. Seward, of Augusta was
caught in the machinery of the mill and killed.

SHANK, MR AND MRS CHAS. - Local - Jun 9, 1897
Born, Monday A.M. to Mr and Mrs Chas. Shank,
Clayton, a son, which soon ended it brief life.

SHANK, SAMUEL - Bowen's Big Fire - May 31, 1895
Samuel Shank lost his life in the fire Thursday
between 1 A.M. and 2 A.M. Shank was of Mt
Sterling.

SHAPLEY, NEWELL - Quincy - Oct 27, 1897 Newell
Shapley, the old veteran who cut his throat
with a razor last week died Friday eve. The
woman Kittie McKnight whom he cut with his
razor is improving.

SHARP, EDWARD - Ancient History - Jul 24, 1894
July 24, 1874 Edward Sharp died at his home in
Concord twp.

SHARP, MR AND MRS J.F. - Local - Dec 7, 1894
Mr and Mrs J.F. Sharp of Purcell, I.T. arrived
via the Wabash last night with the remains of
their father and went to the home of Dr A.D.
Bates. Baxter Sharp was in Arizona and does
not know of his fathers death.

SHARP, JAMES - Deaths Doings - Dec 11, 1894
Died James Sharp at Purcell, Indian Territory,
Tuesday Dec 4th age 72 years. Was member of
Camp Point Methodist Church 20 years from which
the funeral was held. Born Londonderry,
Ireland in 1822. His father died in his
childhood and his mother came to America with
her family, of whom Mrs Margaret McClintock of
Golden is the sole survivor. Lived Penn. and
Ohio and on to Camp Point twp where he married
Permelia J. Bates Apr 22, 1864 she died Jul 25,
1882. They had 4 sons, 2 dead, survivors are

J. Fletcher Sharp of Purcell and Baxter who is
now in Arizona. Remains arrived in Camp Point
Thursday night. Funeral Methodist Church
Friday by Rev A.N. Simmons.

SHARP, JUDGE THOMAS C. - An Old Pioneer Gone -
Apr 10, 1894 Died Judge Thomas C. Sharp,
editor and prop. of the Carthage Gazette died
at his home in that city Tuesday night from
paralysis. Born Mt Holly, N.Y. Sep 25, 1818,
was 76 years old. His father was Rev Solomon
Sharp. Thomas came to Quincy Aug 11, 1840.
Son, Will O. Sharp now runs the newspaper.
Leaves a widow (his 2nd wife), an adopted
daughter and 2 other children survive him.
Funeral Wednesday.

SHEA, MRS T. JEREMIAH - Quincy - Jun 1, 1894
Died Mrs T. Jeremiah Shea died Monday night
after a sickness of several weeks.

SHEFFIELD, DAVID M. - Soldiers Buried in Camp
Point Cemetery - May 26, 1897 Listed in Co. B,
137th Ill Infantry.

SHEPHERD, AUSTIN L. - Ancient History - Nov 26,
1902 - May 1884 Austin L. Shepherd died in
Columbus April 25th.

SHEPHERD, HENRY - Local - Dec 15, 1897 Died,
Henry Shepherd who was injured at Clayton last
week by falling from a trestle, died at the
home of his brother Friday at 4 P.M. Funeral
from Poe school house Sunday by Elder Crawford.

SHEPHERD, JAS. R. - Suicide in California - Dec
23, 1896 Lodi, Calif. Dec 21st James R.
Shepherd charged with embezzlement of $800 from
a bank in Quincy, Ill was located on his
brothers place near here where he killed
himself when arrested. Shepherd came here 2
months ago to live with his brother. Was 25
years old and unmarried. Shepherd was wanted
here and in Hancock county for embezzlement.
His mother and 3 brothers live at Loraine. He
was 25 years old.

SHEPHERD, JOHN - Local - Jul 20, 1893 Mr John
Shepherd, of Mendon, Ill died very suddenly
Sunday eve of a paralytic stroke, was 70 years
old. Leaves wife and 6 children, they are
Alonzo, S.A., Mrs D.C. Laughlin, Mrs D.F.
McNay, Mrs G. Laughlin and Mrs G.W. Groves, all
grown. Lived county over 40 years. "Quincy
Journal"

SHEPHERD, MRS MARY H.R. - Obituary - Jan 13,
1897 Died Mrs Mary H.R. Shepherd at her home
in Columbus Jan 5h age 78 years. Mary H.R.
Swain born Bedford Co. Virginia Mar 26, 1818.
Married Austin L. Shepherd Nov 24, 1838. They
came to Ill. settled at Columbus about 40 years
ago. They had 9 children, 5 sons and 4
daughters. The husband, 2 sons and 1 daughter
died before her. Services at Christian Church
by Elder J.A. Shoptaugh and Rev W.K. Herzog.
Remains were borne to rest by her 3 sons and 3
son inlaws.

SHERMAN, EDWARD - Deaths Latest Doings - Apr 1,
1896 Edward Sherman born May 13, 1816 in
Plumstard, Norfolk Co. England died at his home
in Camp Point Mar 28th 1896. At age 21 he
married Elizabeth Mortimer at Wickhampton,
England and they had 9 children, 5 boys 4
girls. The family came to U.S. in 1855 and
settled in Columbus, Adams Co. where his wife
died 5 years later. In 1865 he married Miss
Mary Taylor and they had 1 daughter, now Mrs
William Earthman, who was the only one of the
children close enough to see their sick father.
Leaves wife and 5 children: John Sherman in
Colorado, George Sherman in Kansas, Mary Alps
and Ellen Ferris, one in east and one in west
and Emma Earthman of Camp Point. Funeral at 2
P.M. at Methodist Church today.

SHERMAN, MRS ELIZABETH A. - Death - Apr 9, 1895
Mrs Elizabeth A. Sherman, wife of John W.
Sherman, died at her home in Golden, Colo.
April 2nd, age 55 years. Services at Methodist
Church on the 4th. Elizabeth A. Johnston
wastwice married. First to Dr F.D. Ward and
lived many years in Camp Point. 1877 they went
to

Colo. where he died.   In October 1881 she
married John W. Sherman who survives her.   Was
a sister of James Johnston of Camp Point.

SHERRICK, MRS J.D. - Ancient History - Jul 24,
1894 - July 19, 1878 Mrs J.D. Sherrick of
Houston died on the 13th.

SHERRICK, MARTIN - Ancient History - Jan 15,
1895 - January 1875 Martin Sherrick a prominent
farmer of Houston died in Keokuk on the 10th.

SHEWARD - MRS J.T. - Suicide in Pacific Ocean
Dec 9, 1903 Mrs J.T. Sheward of Los Angeles,
Calif., formerly Miss Lou Zeiger of this county
was found on the beach at Santa Monica Nov
27th.   Disappeared on the 25th and it is
supposed she cast herself into the ocean.
Leaves a husband and a 5 year old son and a 5
month old babe.   She was a niece of Henry
Zeiger of Camp Point

SHIELDS, GEN. JAMES - Ancient History - Jun 12,
1894 - June 6, 1879 Gen. James Shields died at
Ottumwa June 2nd.

SHINN, C.W. - Quincy - Apr 30, 1895 - In
Justice Morehead's court C.W. Shinn of Melrose
was placed under $800 bond to keep the peace,
and defaulting has been placed in jail.   At the
funeral of his wife he made an attempt to kill
2 or 3 persons.   Thought at first to be insane
but the trial developed a different state of
things.

SHRADER, HIRAM - Primrose - Apr 30, 1902 Mrs
Frank Achelpohl of Kansas and Mrs E. Riley of
Oklahoma, were called here by the death of
their father, Hiram Shrader.

SHRADER, HIRAM - York Neck - May 14, 1902 Mrs
E. Riley, of the Indian nation was called here
to attend her father, Hiram Schrader's,
funeral.   Returned home Thursday.

SHRADER, HIRAM - Death - Apr 30, 1902 Hiram
Shrader, a pioneer of Adams Co. died suddenly

at his home in Honey Creek twp Apr 25, age 79
years 8 months 2 days. Had been working in the
fields and came to the house about 11 A.M. and
sat down and talking to his wife when he fell
backwards from apoplexy. Born Westmoreland Co.
Penn. in 1822. Came to Ill. 1847. Married
Matilda Lippincott Dec 29, 1849. He improved a
farm on north line of Honey Creek twp what is
known as "Lower York Neck" and lived there
since. Had 9 children, 5 survive: 2 sons John
and Elmer of that vicinity, 3 daughters Mrs E.
Riley of Indian Terr., Mrs F. Achepohl of
Kansas and Mrs E.H. Reynolds of Houston.
Services at York Neck Church Monday 11 A.M. by
Rev L.A. Powell of Bowen. Buried in church
cemetery.

SHRADER, MRS MARY - "From the Necks" - Jul 28,
1897 Died Thurday eve July 22nd Mrs Mary
Shrader (nee Hunter). Mary Hunter was born Apr
19, 1850 in Penn. Came with parents to Ill.
1856. Leaves husband and 6 children, 5
brothers and 2 sisters. Services by Rev Rose
at Union Church and buried Curless Cemetery.
Present for funeral from a distance were: Mrs
Martha Hunter and son Joe of Quincy, Aunt and
cousin of the deceased also her brothers Tom
Hunter from Stronghurst and John Hunter from
Adrain.

SHUHARDT, FRED - Ancient History - May 24, 1895
May 1879 A little son of Fred Shuhardt was hurt
at school and died.

SHULTZ, ARTHUR - Arthur Shultz - Nov 27, 1894
Died, Arthur Shultz at the home of his father,
Henry Shultz in Columbus twp Nov 22, 1894, 21
years old from typhoid fever. Leaves parents.

SHULTZ, ARTHUR E. - Gone to Rest - Dec 4, 1894
Died-Arthur E. son of Mr and Mrs H. Shultz Nov
23, 1894, age 21 years 1 month 28 days.
Services by Rev Parrick at the Union Church.
Leaves father, mother, 4 sisters and 2
brothers.

SHULTZ, HENRY - Probate Notice - Mar 25, 1903

Henry Shultz, deceased   1st Monday of June
1903   George H. Shultz, adm.

SHULTZ, HENRY - Death - Feb 25, 1903 Henry
Shultz died Friday night Feb 21st. Services at
Christian Church, Columbus twp near his home
Monday 1 P.M. He was born in Germany June 19,
1819. Was 83 years 8 months 2 days old. Came
to U.S. in 1835 and settled at Meredosia, Ill
until 1865 when he came to Adams Co. to farm in
Concord twp. Married 1851 to Katherine Kruse
who lived but a few years. Married second to
Margaret Kinker on June 17, 1856 who with 3
sons and 4 daughters survive him.

SHUMAR, MRS HENRIETTA E. - Ancient History -
Jul 24, 1894 - July 23, 1875 Mrs Henrieta E.
Shumar died on the 21st.

SHUPE, MRS MARY - Quincy - Jan 7, 1903 Mrs
Mary Shupe, a resident of Adams Co. since 1840
died from a stoke of apoplexy at her home in
Mendon on Thursday, 84 years old.

SHURTLEFF, J.V.G. - Quincy - May 25, 1894 Died
J.V.G. Shurtleff, one of the oldest clerks in
the railway mail service died at the home of
his daughter in East Saginaw, Mich. Funeral in
this city Tuesday afternoon.

SIBLEY, JUDGE JOSEPH - Judge Sibley Dead - Jun
23, 1897 Judge Joseph Sibley died at his home
in Quincy Friday A.M. Born in Hampden Co.
Mass. 1818. Father was Aaron Sibley. 1846
came to Nauvoo, Ill. Moved to Warsaw in 1853.
Moved to Quincy in 1866. Married 1849 to Miss
Maria Brackett, daughter of Dr Brackett of East
St Louis who survives him with 2 children, Miss
Julia L. of Quincy and Joseph J. of Scotland
Co. Missouri. (this is a long article, this is
a condensed version.)

SIBLEY, JOSEPH I. - Quincy - Jun 30, 1897 The
will of Judge Joseph I. Sibley gives $2,000 to
his son Jarrett J. Sibley and the rest to his
widow for her use during her life and at her
death to go to the daughter Julia I. Sibley.

SIGSBEE, A.J. - Co. Seat - Jan 22, 1896   A.J.
Sigsbee was a member of Ill. Ancient Order
United Workman and a post office employee.
Several years ago he moved to Peoria and on eve
of July 10, 1887 he disappeared. No trace of
him since. His wife trying to collect his
insurance.

SIGSBEE, ARTHUR J. - Co. Seat - Dec 16, 1896
Arthur J. Sigsbee of this city disappeared from
his home and family on July 10, 1887 at that
time he was a member in good standing in
ancient order of united workmen. His wife
believing him dead is trying to collect
insurance.

SIMMONS, FLORA - Fatal Gasoline Accident - Feb
11, 1903 Flora Simmons, age 31 years in
starting a fire Friday A.M. in Quincy was using
gasoline which she mistook for kerosene oil and
it exploded setting fire to Mis Simmons
clothing. Was taken to St Mary's Hospital
where she died in the afternoon.

SIMMONS, ELIAS - Quincy - Dec 22, 1897 Elias
Simmons, an old resident of Adams Co. died in
Mendon, age 79 years.

SIMMONS, MACK - West Point - Aug 23, 1895
Died, last Wednesday August 14th little Mack,
son of Mr and Mrs Curtis Simmons of cholera
infantum. Services by Rev Miller in ME Church
Thursday 10 A.M. Buried West Point cemetery.
(Was their oldest son)

SIMON, WM - Coatsburg - Jun 10, 1896 Died Wm
Simon, an old settler of this vicinity died
Sunday A.M. after an illness of 3 or 4 years.
He was a German about 70 years old. Father of
a large family.

SIMONS, MRS MARY - Quincy - Sep 11, 1894 Died
Mrs Mary Simons age 50 of Fall Creek died from
dropsy at St Mary's Hospital Wednesday A.M.

SIMPSON, OBED - Quincy - Mar 3, 1897 W.R. Mock
has been appointed adm of the estate of Obed

Simpson.

SIMPSON, OBADIAH - Local - Feb 10, 1897
Obadiah Simpson died at his home in LaPrairie
Monday the 1st inst age 72 years. Long
resident of that neighborhood.

SIMS, NORA - A Fatal Accident - May 24, 1895 A
family named Sims living in the Indian Grove
district Ursa twp when going to church Sunday
had their horse run away upsetting the buggy.
Nora Sims a 9 year old girl struck her head and
died Monday afternoon.

SINGLETON, MISS IDA - Our Neighbors - Jun 25,
1895 Miss Ida Singleton, of Canton was fatally
burned on Monday when her clothes caught fire.
Lived only 4 hours.

SINGLETON, MRS JAS. W. - Local - Mar 5, 1902
Mrs Jas. W. Singleton died in West Virginia
last Friday. Was widow of Gen. Singleton and
78 years old.

SITES, DAVID - Local - Aug 5, 1896 A son of
David Sites age 25 years was drowned last week
in Ellis Co. Kansas. Mr Sites is a brother of
J.F. Sites of Columbus and formerly lived here.

SIVERTSON, MRS MARCIA - Coatsburg - Jan 9, 1894
Died, Mrs Marcia Sivertson at her home near the
center of Honey Creek twp last Saturday night.
Was among the oldest settlers of Adams Co. Was
relict of the late C.F. Sivertson and lived twp
over 50 years. About 70 years old. Leaves 2
sons, William F. and Edwin. Buried Coatsburg
Cemetery Monday beside her husband.

SIVERTSON, MARCIA L. - Obituary - Jan 12, 1894
Died at the home of her son near Paloma Jan 7th
Mrs Marcia Larkin Sivertson relict of the late
C.F. Sivertson age 77 years 11 months 6 days.
Miss Marcia Larkin born White Hall, N.Y. Feb 1,
1816. Married Mr Sivertson Oct 22, 1840. They
had 4 children, 2 are dead. Joined the Presby.
Church in Ohio at age 20 years. Later in 1840
she joined Presby. Church in Columbus and later

Free Will Baptist Church in Paloma.

SIX, DR ALEXANDER D. - Local - Dec 8, 1897 Dr
Alexander D. Six died at Mt Sterling on Tuesday
of last week. Born in Morgan Co. in 1828 and
was taken to Brown Co. when an infant and lived
there since.

SKAATS, JAMES H. - 15 Years Ago - Feb 13, 1894
James H. Skaats age 60 years died at his home
in Camp Point.

SKAATS, JAS. H. - Ancient History - Jan 15,
1895 - January 1879 Jas. H. Skaats died on the
27th.

SKINNER, JUDGE O.C. - Ancient History - Feb 22,
1895 - February 1877 Judge O.C. Skinner died
in Quincy.

SKINNER, JUDGE O.C. - Ancient History - Jul 15,
1896 March 1877 Judge O.C. Skinner died at his
home in Quincy.

SKINNER, ORRIN W. - Orrin Skinner Dead - Sep
23, 1896 News received that Orrin W. Skinner,
formerly of Quincy died in the Auburn, N.Y.
penitentiary where he was serving time for
grand larceny. Married the daughter of the
last Hon. O.H. Browning and lived at 16th and
Maine Sts, Quincy. Has spent much of his time
since leaving Quincy in prisons.

SLADE, ABRAHAM - Quincy - Feb 18, 1903 The
will of Abraham Slade divides his estate among
his children.

SLADE, ABRAHAM - Local - Feb 11, 1903 Will of
the late Abraham Slade was admitted to probate
Tuesday.

SLADE, ABRAHAM - Probate Notice - Mar 18, 1903
Abraham Slade, deceased 1st Monday of May,
1903 (4th) Geo. R. Stewart and Seldon O.
Slade, executors.

SLADE, MRS AMANDA - Death Record - Apr 21, 1897

Amanda M. Lytle born Mar 31, 1833 in Baltimore,
MD died at her home in Camp Point Apr 15th,
1897 age 64 years 15 days. Married A. Slade in
Maryland 1855 and following year they came to
Adams Co. near Pleasant Grove Church for 3
years ago when they moved to Camp Point. She
leaves her husband, 5 daughters and 1 son-Mrs
George R. Stewart, Mrs J.E. Simmonds, Mrs
George C. Dean, Mrs James W. Limb, Miss Ella
Slade and Seldon O. Slade. Three children died
before her, 2 in infancy and Mrs Lida W. Dean
in 1887. Also leaves 3 brothers and 5 sisters
all living in the east except a brother, J.O.
Lytle of Burton twp. Services at the family
home Saturday A.M. and Methodist Church,
Columbus at 2 P.M. and buried Columbus
Cemetery.

SLADE, MRS AMANDA - Columbus - Apr 21, 1897
Funeral of Mrs Amanda Slade here, Saturday
April 17th by Rev Simmons, White and Reed.
Buried our cemetery by the side of her
daughter, Mrs Deah, who died 10 years ago.

SLOAN, JOHN JR. - Obituary - Apr 3, 1894 Died
John Sloan, son of John and Lucinda Sloan at
the home of his mother in Coatsburg Mar 24,
1894 born in that vicinity Nov 13, 1870 being
23 years 4 months 11 days old. Leaves father,
mother, 3 sisters, 3 brothers. Services at
Christian Church Coatsburg March 26th by Elder
O. Dilley. Buried village cemetery.

SLOAN, COL. ROBERT - Quincy - Feb 5, 1895 Col.
Robert Sloan, who committed suicide at Rockford
was buried here Saturday under the auspices of
the Knights of Pythias.

SLONEKER, ADAM W. - Ancient History - Dec 16,
1896 - October 1877 Adam W. Sloneker of Camp
Point twp died on the 12th.

SLUSHER, MR AND MRS FREDERICK - Quincy - Dec
22, 1897 The baby daughter of Mr and Mrs
Frederick Slusher, weighing 1 ounce less than a
pound, died Thursday A.M. age 6 days. Special
casket was made 8" deep and 12" long.

SMITH, MRS ALEX - Columbus - Dec 28, 1893 The
body of Mrs Alex Smith was laid to rest in our
cemetery on Thursday, the 21st.

SMITH, ALEXANDER M. - Local - Oct 19, 1894
Will of the late Alexander M. Smith was filed
for probate Wednesday . F.D. Smith appointed
executor.

SMITH, ALEXANDER M. - Deah of Alexander M.
Smith - Oct 16, 1894 Died Alexander M. Smith
at his home in Columbus twp Oct 14th 1894 age
73 years. Born Jefferson Co. KY May 21, 1821.
Came to Ill. when 16 years with parents and
settled on farm where he died. Married Dec 4,
1845 Eliza A. Turner who died 1861 leaving 2
children Ellen A. and Winfield S. Married
second in February 1862 to Rebecca J. Turner
who died Dec 19, 1883 leaving 1 son, F. Delano.
His 2 sons W.S. and F.D. survive him. Services
will be at Methodist Church in Columbus this
afternoon.

SMITH, ALEXANDER M. - Probate Notice - Oct 19,
1894 Alexander M. Smith, deceased   1st Monday
of December 1894   Francis D. Smith, Ex.

SMITH, MISS BELLE - Elm Grove - Nov 23, 1893
The death of Miss Belle Smith occured the
latter part of last week after an illness of
several months. Formerly taught school. Was
daughter of Mr and Mrs Wm Smith who lives in
Huntsville twp near Pine Grove P.O. Burial at
cemetery near Shiloh Church last Sunday.

SMITH, CATHERINE H. - Died - Dec 14, 1893
Catherine H. Smith died Saturday Nov 25th, 1893
at the home of her son in law John
Meatheringham near Polo, MO. Catherine H.
Bogle, age 74 years 8 months 16 days. Born in
Washington Co. Ind. Mar 9, 1819. Married
Christopher A. Smith Aug 31, 1843. United with
Methodist Episcopal Church at age 17 years.
Leaves 3 daughters--Mrs John Meatheringham and
Mrs William Bowman of Polo, MO and Mrs Samuel
Farlow of Camp Point.

SMITH, CLARENCE - Death Record - Jun 9, 1897
Died-Clarence, the son of Mr and Mrs Ed P.
Smith June 2nd age 7 years.

SMITH, MR AND MRS ED - Local - Nov 23, 1893 Mr
and Mrs Ed Smith's babe died Saturday night of
typhoid fever. Taken Monday to Bloomfield for
burial.

SMITH, MISS ELLEN A. - Obituary - Jan 9, 1894
Died-Miss Ellen A. Smith at the home of her
brother, W. Scott Smith Sunday A.M., 42 years
old. Daughter of Alexander M. Smith of
Columbus twp. Services at Christian Church by
Elder O. Dilley.

SMITH, ELLEN A. - Probate Notice - Feb 9, 1894
Ellen A. Smith, deceased   1st Monday of April
1894   W. Scott Smith, adm.

SMITH, MISS ELLEN A. - Obituary - Jan 9, 1894
Miss Ellen A. Smith, died at the home of her
brother, W. Scott Smith Sunday A.M. after a
severe attack of pleuro pneumonia, age 42
years. Was daughter of Alexander M. Smith of
Columbus twp. Services at Christian Church by
Elder O. Dilley.

SMITH, ELLEN ANN - Obituary - Jan 12, 1894
Died, Ellen Ann Smith born Columbus twp Adams
Co. Mar 7, 1850 died Jan 7, 1894 age 43 years 6
months. Mother died 1861. Father, Alexander
Smith, brother, Scott Smith and one 1/2 brother
survive her. Services January 8th. Buried
Camp Point cemetery.

SMITH, EMANUEL - Local - Jun 10, 1903 Mrs A.P.
Gay was called to Abingdon Sunday by the death
of her brother in law Emanuel Smith.

SMITH, EMANUEL - Death - Jun 10, 1903 Emanuel
Smith died at Abingdon Sunday A.M. after
illness of consumption for a couple of years.
He came to Camp Point about 10 years ago as
agent of the C.B. & Q until last summer when
his health became so poor and moved to Abingdon
to be outdoors. Leaves a wife, a son and 2

daughters.   Funeral at Methodist Church
Abingdon, Monday P.M.

SMITH, FLOYD - Local - Feb 23, 1893 Floyd, the
little 4 month old babe of Mr and Mrs W.D.
Smith died Saturday afternoon. Funeral at the
home Sunday afternoon by Elder O. Dilley.

SMITH, HARRY - Local - Oct 4, 1895 Harry
Smith, a young man crazed by the use of
morphine committed suicide at Pittsfield last
Sunday. He was son of respected parents and
was himself an intelligent and cultured young
man until he began the use of the terrible drug
and blighted his life.

SMITH, MR AND MRS HENRY - Columbus - Jan 22,
1902 Infant child of Mr and Mrs Henry Smith
was buried Sunday Jan 19th. Services at 11
A.M. at home of Rev F.E. Meader's buried
village cemetery.   .

SMITH, HENRY C. - Local - Jan 1, 1902 Henry C.
Smith was brought home from Oklahoma a couple
of weeks ago very low with consumption. He
died Saturday. Funeral Monday at the Christian
Church.

SMITH, HENRY C. - Death - Jan 8, 1902 Henry C.
Smith born Adams Co. Ill. Mar 15, 1849 died at
his home in Camp Point, Ill. Dec 28, 1901 age
52 years 9 months 13 days. Married Sep 28,
1872 to Miss Belle Taylor who with 7 children
survive him. He had been in the west for 2 or
3 years up to about 2 weeks before his death
when he was brought home. Member of Christian
Church. Funeral services from Christian Church
Dec 30th by Elder O. Dilley and Rev C.N. Cain
of the ME Church. Buried village cemetery.

SMITH, MR JAMES - Local - Nov 2, 1893 Hez
Henry was called to LaHarpe Saturday by the
death of his wife's father, Mr James Smith, an
aged citizen of that place.

SMITH, JAMES - Exec. Sale of Real Estate - Jun
15, 1893 James Smith, deceased, Thomas C.

Smith exec. Sale July 15th at 2 P.M. at the
front door of Post Office in Camp Point.
Hamilton and Woods, attorneys.

SMITH, JAMES C. - Local - May 11, 1893 Will of
the late James C. Smith was admitted to probate
Tuesday dated Oct 12, 1885 and witnessed by
B.A. Curry and Richard Seaton. Farm is left to
the widow, Mrs Mary Smith and rest divided
among the children. After death of widow the
farm is to be divided.

SMITH, JAMES C. - Obituary - May 4, 1893 James
C. Smith died Wednesday eve May 3rd after
illness of several years, 73 years old. Born
Kentucky. Came to Ill 1836 and lived Adams Co.
since. Lived many years in Clayton twp but
came to Camp Point a few years ago. Leaves a
widow, 5 sons and 4 daughters.

SMITH, JAMES C. - Ancient History - May 13,
1903 - May 4-11, 1893 James C. Smith died on
the 3rd.

SMITH, JAMES H. - Killed by Lightning - Jun 23,
1897 Two farmers named James H. Smith and
Samuel Hickman were struck by lightning and
killed about 5:30 A.M. Saturday on Mrs
Jasretts' farm about 1 mile east of Taylor, MO
and 5 miles west of Quincy. Smith occupied the
home on the farm and Hickman boarded with him.
Women heard the lightning but couldn't get
Hickman body out so he burn with the barn, but
they did pull Smith out. Hickman was about 60
years old, a widower with 7 grown children, one
is William Hickman the Camppoint liveryman
wholeft Saturday to take charge of the remains.

SMITH, MR AND MRS JESSE JR - Columbus - Feb 19,
1902 Only son of Mr and Mrs Jesse Smith Jr was
buried Saturday Feb 15th, age 2 years 6 months.

SMITH, JOHN - Obituary - Apr 27, 1894 Died
John Smith, son of George Smith deceased and
step son of Mrs Mary J. Smith of Camp Point.
Died at his home 6 miles SW of Camp Point April
18th of pneumonia. Born Columbus Oct 10, 1857

and married Sep 19, 1892 to Miss Isabella
Railey who with 1 sister, 2 half brothers, 2
half sisters and step mother survive him.
Funeral at Union Christian Church April 19th by
Elder Dilley and buried by the church.

SMITH, JOHN - Local - Apr 17, 1894 John Smith,
living in Concord twp died Wed. Leaves a wife,
(a daughter of George W. Bailey) but no
children. He was son of Mrs Mary J. Smith of
Camp Point.

SMITH, JOHN K. - Ancient History - May 26, 1897
May 1880 John K. Smith died at Clayton.

SMITH, MRS LETITIA - Ancient History - May 8,
1894 - May 9, 1879 Mrs Letitia Smith died at
Adrain and was buried in Camp Point cemetery.

SMITH, MRS MARGARET - Elm Grove - Aug 25, 1897
Death of Mrs Margaret Smith occured last Friday
at her home not far from Horeb Church, 62 years
old. Born in Russell Co. Virg. and came with
parents, William and Mary Alexander to here at
a tender age. At adult age she married D.A.
Smith, who demise occured several years ago.
She had 3 sons and 1 daughter to survive her-Wm
L., Andrew J., Robert and Mrs Matilda J. Storer
all living near by here. Services by Rev W.H.
McDonald at Horeb Church on Friday afternoon,
burial in cemetery nearby.

SMITH, MRS MARGARET - Death - Aug 10, 1893 Mrs
Margaret Smith, wife of Patrick Smith and
mother of Ed P. Smith of Camp Point, died at
Bloomfield Friday. Born Ireland 60 years ago
and came to this country as a child. Leaves
husband and 7 children, Ed, Tom, Barney,
William, Andrew, Mrs J.R. Williamson of Liberty
and Mrs Berdel of Quincy.

SMITH, MRS MARGARET - Elm Grove - Aug 25, 1897
Wm L. Alexander, of Galesburg attended the
funeral of his sister, Mrs Margaret Smith last
Friday.

SMITH, MRS MARGARET - Died - Aug 9, 1895 Mrs

Margaret A. Smith died at Santa Rosa,
Calif.July 18th at the home of her daughter,
Mrs Thomas Hood, 78 years old. Was widow of
Jacob Smith and went to Calif. with him during
the summer of 1854 from Columbus. Margaret
Rhea born Kentucky. Came to Ill. in her youth
and settled Columbus twp where she married
Jacob Smith. Lived Santa Rosa 40 years where
her family lives. Had many relatives here in
Adams Co.

SMITH, MRS MARY - Obituary - Nov 4, 1896 Mary
Curry born Jeffersontown, KY Sept 18, 1826 came
with parents to Ill. 1838. Parents are Thomas
and Malinda Curry. Married Nov 7, 1844 to
James C. Smith and settled on farm in Camp
point twp. Later moved Clayton where they
lived till 1886. Came to Camp Point. Mr Smith
died May 3, 1892 since then she lived with
daughter (eldest) Mrs John Bellew. Mother of
11 children--Thomas C., George W., Sarah E.
(Bellew), Celestia A. (McCarty), Harriet E.
(Bennett) Malinda I. (Omer), A. Lincoln, James
H., Ida M., and William all surviving except
Ida M. who died at age 17 years. All reside
this vicinity except Geo. W. who lives at
McKerson, KS and William M. at Mason City, Ill.
Mrs Smith died November 3rd. Services at 2
o'clock this P.M. at Christian Church.

SMITH, MAUD - Obituary - Feb 26, 1896 Died,
Maud, only daughter of Jeremiah and Amanda
Smith and wife of Hez G. Henry died in Camp
Point Feb 15, 1896. Born LaHarpe June 14,
1869. Married Hez G. Henry Oct 2, 1889, had 3
children - Riva B., James S., Maud Helen.

SMITH, MILES - Sensation at Bowen - Jan 8, 1895
Miles Smith, a young man who is said to have
shot and killed William Petit at Hibernia a
small town near Charlestown, Ind. has been in
hiding at the home of his uncle G.B. Gant who
lives 2 miles east of Bowen since December
15th. Escaped!   "Carthage Journal"

SMITH, MORRIS - Local - Dec 11, 1894 Died,
Morris Smith, who was killed in the Washington

Street tunnel accident in Chicago Tuesday eve was son of Jacob M. Smith who was widely known as a pork packer of Quincy and elected mayor of Quincy in 1875.

SMITH, NELLIE - Local - Sep 24, 1895 Nellie Smith an 18 year old girl at Columbus died Saturday from a spider bite. Funeral by Elder G.F. Booth on Sunday.

SMITH, NELLIE M. - Columbus - Sep 24, 1895 Died at her home in Columbus Saturday Sep 21st of blood poisoning Nellie M. Smith age 18 years 1 month 19 days. Services by Elder Booth at 3 P.M. Sunday from Christian Church of which she was a member, having united with it last May.

SMITH, OWEN A. - Mar 16, 1893 Owen A. Smith of Quincy died Sunday. He was at one time a member of the board of supervisors.

SMITH, PETER - Local - Jun 8, 1893 Peter Smith, at one time county surveyor died in Quincy Monday, age 77 years. Was a native of Ireland. Coming to the U.S. in 1849.

SMITH, PORTER - Ancient History - Jul 17, 1894 July 12, 1878 Porter Smith died in Quincy.

SMITH, PORTER - Ancient History - Jul 16, 1895 July 1878 Porter Smith, a prominent citizen of Quincy died.

SMITH, COL. R.F. - Death - Apr 27, 1893 Col. R.F. Smith died at his home in Hamilton, Ill. on Monday A.M. age 86 years. Was commanding officer of the 16th Reg. Ill. Inf. which was part of Gen. Morgan's brigade.

SMITH, R.M. - Quincy - Apr 7, 1897 Died, R.M. Smith a prominent resident of Bushnell was found dead in Blessing Hospital with the bed spread around his neck. 76 years old.

SMITH, RATICLIFF - Local - May 4, 1893 Raticliff Smith, formerly of Elm Grove died April 17th at the home of his son in Brown Co.

Buried at cemetery near Elm Grove Church where
the funeral was preached by Rev J.J. Thompson
on the 18th. Mr Smith was 83 years old.

SMITH, MRS REBECCA J. - Late Deaths - Dec 21,
1893 Mrs Rebecca J. Smith, wife of Alexander
M. Smith, died Tuesday afternoon. Funeral from
the family home in Columbus twp this afternoon
at 2.

SMITH, MRS REBECCA J. - Ancient History - Dec
9, 1903 - December 1893 Mrs Rebecca J. Smith,
mother of F.D. Smith, died on the 19th.

SMITH, MRS SARAH - Quincy - Jul 19, 1902 Mrs
Sarah Smith age 80 years was run over and
killed near Tennessee, McDonough Co. by a
special train that was bringing Christian
Endeavores to this city on Thursday.

SMITH, THOMAS S. - Obituary - Apr 2, 1902
Thomas S. Smith died at the home of A.M. Earel
Columbus Twp Friday March 28th, 79 years old.
Born Tennessee Aug 22, 1824. Leaves 2
daughters and 3 sons. Remains taken to Ursa
for burial on Saturday. Services by Elder O.
Dilley at the Ursa Christian Church and Rev
E.E. Reed. Buried cemetery north of Ursa.

SMITH, WILL - Local - May 11, 1893 Will Smith
who was called home last week to the funeral of
his father returned to Mason City Monday eve.

SMITH, WILLIAM B. - Clayton - Mar 16, 1894
William B. Smith died about 3 P.M. Wednesday.

SMITH, WILLIAM T. - Local - Dec 11, 1894
Funeral - James A. Smith of Clayton was in town
Saturday and tells us of the death of his
brother, William T. in Quincy that A.M. of
typhoid fever.

SMITH, WILLIAM T. - The Late Wm T. Smith - Dec
11, 1894 Died, William T. Smith born Clayton,
Ill. August 1852 lived there till 1879 when he
moved to Denver, Ill. 1880 moved to Carthage
and about 5 years ago moved to Quincy. Married

March 30, 1880 to Lillian Fielding, a step
daughter of R.H. Hardy. Leaves a child a few
months old. Services Sunday P.M. and on Monday
taken to Clayton for burial by Masonic lodge.

SMITH, WILLIE A. - Local - Mar 16, 1893 Willie
A. Smith, a boy age 10 years who lives with his
father at Reed City was run over by a T.P. & W.
freight train in that village Tuesday A.M. died
later at the home of his parents.

SNYDER, ELIZA A. - Probate Notice - Apr 1, 1903
Eliza A. Snyder, deceased   1st Monday of May
1903 Lulu P. Holstein, adm.

SNYDER, MRS ELIZA E. - Death - Mar 4, 1903 Mrs
Eliza E. Snyder died Saturday afternoon Feb
28th of pneumonia. Eliza Gallemore was born in
N. Carolina Jan 27, 1834 and came to Lima twp
with parents in 1835. Moved to Camp Point
1895. Married William Carney at age 16 years
bore him 3 children, one still living, he died
1858 and in 1860 she married second to Philip
Snyder and bore him 4 children, 2 of whom
survive her. Services held at family home
Monday A.M. by Geo. F. Booth. Buried Lima
Tuesday.

SNYDER, PETER - Bauman Gabbles - Apr 10, 1894
Died, Uncle Peter Snyder, an old and respected
resident of this neighborhood died at the home
of his niece, Mrs L. Phillips last Tuesday
night. Buried Walker cemetery.

SONTAG, MRS JOHANNA - Quincy - Jan 23, 1894
Died, Mrs Johanna Sontag age 76 years, a
resident of Quincy 48 years died Tuesday.

SORRELS, LEWIS - Local - Jun 10, 1896 Lewis
Sorrels, a young man working for a farmer near
Industry was killed by lightning Saturday eve
while unhitching his team.

SOWERS, ALBERT - Local - Sep 20, 1895 Albert
Sowers left Monday for Pennsylvania to look
after an estate which is coming to him. He
returned Wednesday night.

SOWERS, PERRY - Local - Jul 13, 1893 Perry
Sowers, who died recently in Penn. left a large
fortune in real estate and money, all of which
is inherited by his 8 brothers and sisters, one
of whom was the late William Sowers, who died
in Camp Point last year. Albert Sowers, the
only living child of William inherits his
fathers share which will probably be $25,000 to
$30,000.

SPANGLER, MRS MARIA - Local - Dec 7, 1893 Mrs
Maria Spangler, of Macomb twp was burned to
death Friday by her clothes catching fire at
the stove. She lived until Monday.

SPARKS, FLORA E. - Gone - Mar 30, 1893 Flora
E. wife of Henry Sparks and daughter of W.D.
and Mary E. DeMoss died Monday eve March 20th,
1893 after illness of 10 days. Born Columbus
twp Adams Co. Jan 24, 1864 was 29 years 1 month
24 days old. Member of Christian Church 14
years. Leaves husband, little daughter,
father, mother and 2 sisters.

SPARKS, MRS FLORA E. - Ancient History - Apr 1,
1903 - March 30, 1893 Mrs Flora E. Sparks died
on the 20th.

SPARKS, MR AND MRS HENRY - Local - Mar 16, 1893
The infant child of Mr and Mrs Henry Sparks
died Monday of this week and was buried the
next morning at 11 at Pleasant View cemetery.
Services by Elder Orin Dilley.

SPARKS, MRS HENRY - Local - Mar 23, 1893 Mrs
Henry Sparks, a daughter of W.D. DeMoss died
Tuesday. An obituary of her babe appears in
todays Journal.

SPARKS, MRS THOMAS - Local - Aug 7, 1894 Mrs
Thomas Sparks of Quincy left a note that she
was going to kill herself and disappeared (ill
health).

SPENCER, LEWIS G. - Quincy - Mar 2, 1894 Died
Lewis G. Spencer, steward of the Quincy
Commercial Club died from pleurisy Sun. night.

SPICER, MRS A.N. - Death Record - Mar 3, 1897
Died Mrs A.N. Spicer at her home near Loraine
Tuesday Feb 16th in her 52nd year. Funeral
Thursday in the Methodist Church at Loraine.
Leaves husband and 6 children.

SPIKER, W.J. - Blandinsville Tragedy - Jul 15,
1896 Killing of W.J. Spiker by Charles Collins
of Blandinsville twp McDonough Co. at home of
Edward Dodd 4 miles NW of town of
Blandinsville. The 2 men were cousins.
Collins was engaged to Spiker's sister. Spiker
was 21 years old and weighed 200 pounds.
Collins about same age but not as big, feelings
are with Collins.

SPRENN, FREDERICK - Quincy - Mar 8, 1895
Frederick Sprenn, formerly of this city who
died at Atchison, Kansas was buried here
Sunday.

STABLER, LILLIAN - Local - Jul 2, 1895 Little
Lillian, daughter of Mr and Mrs W.S.Stabler
died Sunday eve, 18 months old.

STABLER, OSCAR - Local - Jul 23, 1895 Mrs Sam
Stabler of Fremont, Neb. who has been visiting
her brothers G.M. and J.W. Stabler received
word of the death of her son Oscar age 21
years. Taken ill very suddenly with
inflammation of the bowels and died at 4 A.M.
Sunday. "McPherson, Kansas Republican"

STABLER, W.S. - Local - Dec 11, 1894 W.S.
Stabler received a letter Tuesday telling of
the death of his mother at Stablesville, MD on
December 5th.

STARK, GEORGE - Local - May 4, 1893 George
Stark, one of the pioneer citizens and
merchants of Augusta died in that village April
24th, age 71 years.. Native of Scotland and
came to Augusta in 1834.

STARRETT, MRS MARTHA - Quincy - Feb 16, 1894
Died, Mrs Martha Starrett, one of the pioneers
of Adams Co. died at Payson age 83 years.

STATON, MRS HELEN - Death of Mrs Helen Staton -
Mar 16, 1894 Died, Mrs Helen Staton at her
home in Albany, MO Feb 24th, 1894 age 36 years
10 days. Helen Asher born Adams Co. Feb 14,
1858 youngest daughter of Presley Asher and a
sister of Mrs Ophelia Omer and Mrs Florence
Adams. Went to Missouri with father in 1871
where she married W.R. Staton who with 2
daughters survive her. Since 1876 she has
resided in Trenton. Was member of Methodist
Church. Funeral by her pastor.

STAUTERMAN, EMMA PEARL - Obituary - May 11,
1894 Died, near Renick, Missouri March 18,
1894 7 year old daughter of Mr and Mrs Jacob
Stauterman, Emma Pearl. Buried from the ME
Church at New Hope Cemetery March 20th.
Services by Rev Diggs. Pallbearers were Misses
Mary Hancock, Emma Hancock, Lorena Freeman and
Flora Ess.

STEARNS, STEPHEN A. - "Stephen A. Stearns Hangs
Himself" - May 25, 1894 Stephen A. Stearns of
LaHarpe committed suicide in his room at the
poor house some time Tuesday night of last
week. Taken to LaHarpe for funeral Thursday,
about 55 years old.   "Carthage Republican"

STECHER, C.F. - Local - Sep 22, 1897   C.F.
Stecher was called to Bethel, Missouri by the
death of his nephew.

STEED, REV R.L. - Elm Grove - Apr 27, 1894
Died, the little child of Rev R.L. Steed died
on Saturday eve and buried at Horeb Cemetery on
Monday eve. Services at the home of Mrs Steed
and services at the grave by Rev A.A. Hartrick.

STEERS, ELDER WILLIAM - Killed - Jan 29, 1902
Accidental death of Elder Wm Steers near
Louisiana, MO last Saturday eve an old and
familiar citizen of Pike Co. when walking on
the R.R. track. Taken to Pittsfield on Sunday.
Funeral Monday. Was 81 years old. "Barry
Adage"

STEFFEN, W.H. - Quincy - Jul 6, 1894 W.H.

Steffen age 73 died at the German home for the aged Friday A.M.

STEFFENS, MRS ADAM - Quincy - Dec 22, 1897   Mrs Adam Steffens of Steffenville, MO who has been here 2 months for medical treatment died at the Missouri House Wednesday A.M. age 42 years.

STENBECK, WILLIAM B. - Power of Attorney - Feb 19, 1896   Public notice given to all persons having claims against estate of William B. Stenbeck, deceased.   C.C. Sparks

STEVENS, ALEXANDER H. - Ancient History - Mar 11, 1903 - Mar 8, 1883   Alexander H. Stevens died at Atlanta, Georgia.

STEVENS, MISS ALTA - Elm Grove - Mar 2, 1894 Miss Alta Stevens will live with Mrs L. Smith. Miss Stevens is a daughter of Abel Stevens, deceased, late of Marshall Co. Kansas and a former resident of this locality.

STEVENS, EARL - Killed by a Cow - Apr 29, 1896 Colchester was shocked Wednesday A.M. Earl Stevens, the 11 year old son of W.O. Stevens was drug by a milk cow died 1/2 hour later.

STEVENS, H.H. - Local - Nov 2, 1893   H.H. Stevens, a well known newspaper writer & editor, died at Colchester October 22nd.

STEVENS, MRS MARY - Death of Mrs Stevens - Mar 2, 1894   Died, Mrs Mary Stevens, widow of the late Dr A.F. Stevens died suddenly Wednesday. Born New York.   Came to Ill. when young where she married Dr Stevens.   They located Camp Point 1855 where she lived since.   Funeral from Presby. Church today at 10, about 75 years old.

STEVENS, MRS MARY CURTIS - "Died" - Mar 6, 1894 Died at her home here Feb 28th, 1894, Mrs Mary Curtis Stevens, age 74 years 8 months 22 days. Mary Curtis born in Elbridge, New York June 6, 1816.   With her father Deacon S.R. Curtis in 1856 she moved to Woodville, Ill.   In 1854 she married Augustus F. Stevens and they moved to

Camp Point. Her sister Miss Louisa Curtis of
Chicago was at funeral. She had 4 children all
died early in childhood. Husband was dead
also.

STEVENS, PHEBE FLETCHER - Obituary - Oct 21,
1896 Phebe Fletcher Stevens, nee Patch born
Litchfield, Mass. July 9, 1816 married Thomas
G. Stevens in Lowell, Mass July 9, 1836 on her
21st birthday. Had 6 children Charles L. born
Sep 23, 1839, Lucinda A. born Nov 8, 1842,
Solon A. born Oct 9, 1845, Annie born Dec 19,
1848, Chauncey T. born Aug 5, 1853, Newell born
Oct 23, 1863. Leaves all children except
Charles who died in early infancy and her
husband. Moved with husband to Columbus, Ill
1838. She died Oct 8, 1896 at age 80 years 3
months.

STEWART, ENOS T. - Local - Mar 30, 1893 Enos
T. Stewart, a former resident of Clayton &
Golden and a brother of W.S. Stewart of this
twp, died recently at LaCygne, Kansas. He was
born in vicinity of Fowler. He had kept hotels
in various localities.

STEWART, MARTIN - Ancient History - May 26,
1897 - December 1879 died, Martin Stewart.

STEWART, ROBERT - Co. Seat - Nov 11, 1896
Robert Stewart, age 70 years and John Altmix,
age 71 years both residents of this city died
Tuesday afternoon.

STOCKTON, W.L. - Quincy - Sep 10, 1902 W.L.
Stockton died in Augusta age 85 years.

STOCKWELL, GEORGE - Quincy - Jun 1, 1894
George Stockwell, formerly in the livestock
business in Quincy died in Atchinson, Kansas
and was buried here Tuesday.

STOKES, W.C. - Death of W.C. Stokes - Apr 1,
1896 We learn from Craig, MO. newspaper that
William C. Stokes died in that city March 4th.
Born Ind. 1821 came to Ill. 1847. Lived Morgan
and Schuyler Co.'s and lived several years at

Camp Point, then Kansas and Missouri. Leaves a wife and 2 children.

STOLTE, MRS HENRY - Local - Nov 15, 1895 Mrs Henry Stolte of Burton twp died Tuesday, age 60. Mother of 16 children, 11 of them and husband survive her.

STORMER, MRS GOTLIEB H. - Quincy - Feb 27, 1894 Died, Mrs Gotlieb H. Stormer, age 44 years, Friday eve from cancer of the stomach.

STORMER, JOHN W. - In Memoriam - Jan 18, 1895 By LaPrairie Lodge #267 A.F. and A.M. relative to the death of brother John W. Stormer, Dec 24, 1894. His late home in Augusta. Leaves widow.

STORMER, JOHN W. - Local - Dec 28, 1894 Died, John W. Stormer died at Augusta Thursday age 65 years. Formerly lived at LaPrairie and was well known here.

STOUT, James - Child Burned to Death - May 1, 1894 Mt Sterling, Ill April 30th A 6 year old daughter of James Stout of Ripley was burned to death Saturday. Parents lost another child about 2 years ago when it fell from a gate, breaking its neck.

STRAUB, ALBERT B. - Death Record - Jun 9, 1897 Died at the Illinois Soldiers and Sailors home, Quincy, Ill June 6th, 1897. Albert B. Straub. Was member of 50th Ill. Inf. and lived many years at Fowler. Moved to Galesburg 1880 and worked for C.B. & Q Railroad as a brakeman for 5 years and then depot master at Galesburg 10 years. Two years ago he left the company and since then has been unable to work.

STRICKLER, MRS ANNA - Ancient History - Jul 14, 1897 - December 1880 Mrs Anna Strickler died on the 29th age 77 years.

STRICKLER, MRS ANNA - Ancient History - Aug 25, 1897 December 1880 Mrs Anna Strickler died in Augusta.

STRICKLER, MRS CATHERINE - Death Record - May
20, 1896 Catherine Strickler, daughter of
Joseph and Elizabeth Kern born Westmoreland Co.
Penn. Apr 11, 1824. Came to Ill. with parents
1840 to Houston twp where she married Wesley
Strickler Nov 16, 1843. Lived there 40 years
then went to Atchison Co. MO. Returned to Camp
Point 1882 where Mr Strickler died Nov 1894.
Mother of 7 children, 6 survive her Valentine,
Charles, Harry, and Guy who live in N.W. MO,
Mrs Anna E.Gay of Camp Point and Mrs Emma C.
Whitford of Fairfax, MO. Died May 12, 1896.
Services at family home on the 14th by Elder O.
Dilley. Buried village cemetery.

STRICKLER, MRS CATHERINE - Death of Mrs
Strickler - May 13, 1896 Died Mrs Catherine
Strickler, widow of the late Wesley Strickler
died Tuesday night, age 72 years. Funeral
Thursday at 3 P.M.

STRICKLER, MRS CHRISTIANA - Death - Jun 29,
1893 Mrs Christiana Strickler, wife of Lewis
Strickler died at Thayer, NE June 23rd of
cancer of the stomach, age 53 years about. Was
daughter of the late Peter and Elizabeth Brewer
and born in Ohio. Parents brought her to Ill.
and settled Camp Point twp about 1856 where she
married. The remainder of her life was spent
in Houston twp and Camp Point until last fall
when she and her husband moved to NE to be with
her children who had homes there. Leaves
husband, son and daughter. Funeral near their
home Sunday when the frail body was laid to
rest.

STRICKLER, CLARK - Obituary - Mar 29, 1895
Clark Strickler died at his home in Mendon
Thursday March 28th 1895 in his 61st year.
Born in Penn. Nov 15, 1833. Came with parents
to Ill. 1837 and lived Adams Co. since.
Married Julia A. Sprout Aug 28, 1862 who died
several years ago. Leaves 2 sons, 1 daughter,
3 brothers, and 3 sisters. Funeral at Mendon
Sunday 2 P.M.

STRICKLER, CLARK - Quincy - Apr 19, 1895 An

inventory of the estate of the late Clark Strickler, of Mendon was filed in county court Wednesday consisted of 305 acres of land, $9,500 in notes and $215 in cash. Inventory of the firm of Strickler and Son show $5,000 in accounts, $8,000 in notes, $1,900 in cash.

STRICKLER, DAVID - Local - Nov 27, 1894 David Strickler of Maryville, MO arrived to attend funeral of his brother, Wesley Strickler.

STRICKLER, MRS E.R. - Local - Jan 22, 1902 Ray Strickler of Maryville, MO came Friday to attend funeral of his sister in law, Mrs E.R. Strickler and visited relatives in Camp Point.

STRICKLER, MRS EDGAR R. - Deaths - Jan 22, 1902 Mrs Edgar R. Strickler of Marysville, MO was called to Houston twp couple of weeks ago by the illness of her father, John Rice. Few days after arrival she became sick (on the 10th) died on the 16th inst. Britomarte Strickler was youngest daughter of John Rice and born in Houston twp Nov 7, 1865. Married Edgar R. Strickler Nov 26, 1885 and next spring moved to Marysville, MO. Leaves 4 daughters from 15 to 2-1/2 years beside her husband. Services at York Neck Cemetery by Rev J.B. King. Burial in adjacent cemetery.

STRICKLER, MRS ELSPY SCOTT - Obituary - Nov 2, 1893 Elspy Scott Strickler was born May 4, 1828 in New Salem, Fayette Co. Penn. and died Oct 27, 1893 at 3 A.M. near LaPrairie, Ill. Married Uniontown, Penn Feb 17, 1848 to J.L. Strickler and 1854 they came to Ill. Joined Presby. church 22 years ago. Leaves husband some years her senior, 3 daughters, 4 sons, 21 grandchildren, an aged mother in her 94th year, 2 sisters and 1 brother and a large number of relatives and friends. Services by Rev R.A. Hartrick and Rev W.D. Atkinson, buried York Neck Cemetery.

STRICKLER, FRANK - Local - Mar 4, 1903 Information received by friends Saturday of the death of Frank Strickler at Skidmore, MO Friday

night the 27th ult. He was 2nd son of David
Strickler and was about 35 years old. Leaves a
wife, formerly Miss Leone Bottorff of Golden,
but no children.

STRICKLER, FRANK W. - Obituary - Mar 18, 1903
Frank W. Strickler was born in Adams Co. Ill.
Oct 19, 1863. In fall of 1886 he moved to
Atchison Co. Missouri and settled on a farm,
his parents moved to Nodaway Co. S.W. of
Maryville the spring before. He lived there 2
years and moved to a farm NE of Skidmore. 1894
moved to Skidmore and employed in the
mercantile business with his sister, Mrs
Wright. Three years ago he went into drug
business. Married Jan 24, 1884 to Miss Leona
Bottorff of Adams Co. who survives him. A year
ago they took into their home the 2 year old
daughter, Mildred, of Mr Strickler's brother
who mother died while on a visit to Ill. Child
is ill with same disease Mr Strickler died of.
Leaves 2 brothers, Ed R. and Ray Strickler
ofMaryville and a sister, Mrs Cora Wright of St
Joseph. Funeral at the home Sunday March 1st
by pastor of ME Church South, Rev C.B.
Campbell.   "Maryville Democrat"

STRICKLER, JOHN R. - Death - Apr 9, 1902 John
R. Strickler died last Wednesday the 2nd inst.
after a protracted illness, 17 years old.
Services Thursday afternoon at the home of his
mother, Mrs Sarah L. Strickler. Buried village
cemetery. Leaves widowed mother and 2 sisters.

STRICKLER, MARY J. - Death's Doings - Dec 11,
1894 Died Mary J. Strickler Saturday Dec 8th
age 66 years was the daughter of Isaac and Jane
Strickler who came to Ill. about 1840 and
located in York Neck where Mr Strickler died.
The family then returned to Penn. She returned
in 1854. Her mother and 5 brother and 1 sister
are dead, only 1 surviver of the family left,
Isaac Strickler of Kansas City. Services by
Elder O. Dilley at the Christian Church Monday
P.M. Buried village cemetery.

STRICKLER, OSCAR B. - Death of Oscar Strickler -

Jul 13, 1894 Died A telegram from Galesburg
Wed. tells of the death of Oscar B. Strickler
from consumption. Worked as a brakeman on the
Q. Was raised in Camp Point. About 33 years
old and unmarried. Funeral in Galesburg by
Masonic fraternity.

STRICKLER, OSCAR B. - Funeral of Oscar B.
Strickler - Jul 17, 1894 Funeral of the late
Oscar B. Strickler were at the home of his
brother, R.R. Strickler in Galesburg at 3 PM
Friday by Rev Dr Bodgett of the First ME
Church. Burial in Hope Cemetery and rites by
Masonic fraternity.

STRICKLER, STEWART - Ancient History - Apr 26,
1895 Stewart Strickler died at the home of his
mother in Camp Point.

STRICKLER, WESLEY - Local - Nov 27, 1894
Funeral -- Mrs Maria A. Thomas of Augusta came
down Friday A.M. and remained with relatives
over Sunday and attended the funeral of her
brother, Wesley Strickler.

STRICKLER, WESLEY - Death of Wesley Strickler -
Nov 27, 1894 Died Wesley Strickler died
Friday Nov 23rd, 1894 in his 74th year. Has
been an invalid several years. Born
Pennsylvania. Came to Ill. with his parents in
1837. They settled in Houston twp. Married
Catherine Kern 1843 they had 4 sons, 2
daughters. Wife and 6 children survive him.
Funeral Sunday P.M. buried village cemetery.

STRICKLER, WILL R. - Ancient History - Mar 30,
1894 - March 29, 1883 Will R. Strickler died at
Galesburg on the 22nd.

STRICKLER, WILL R. - Ancient History - Apr 1,
1903 - March 29, 1883 Will R. Strickler, a
Camp Point railroad boy died on the 22nd.

STRICKLER, WILL R. - 10 Years Ago - Apr 6, 1893
Will R. Strickler, a Camp Point brakeman on the
Q, died at Galesburg.

STUFFLEBEAN, DELLA - Local - Jan 22, 1895
Della Stufflebean, a woman of the town, making
her home in Quincy committed suicide Sunday
night from jealousy. She took a dose of
laudanum.

STUHRENBERG, FRED - Obituary - Sep 7, 1893
Fred Stuhrenberg, son of August Stuhrenberg, of
Camp Point twp died August 30th age 17 years
after an illness of about 6 months. Born
Germany. Funeral at the Lutheran Church of
Coatsburg where he was buried. Pallbearers
being 6 school mates from Primrose school.

STUMP, MRS F.M. - Local - Apr 6, 1893 Mrs F.M.
Stump, of Big Neck died Tuesday at noon.

STUMP, MRS F.M. - Ancient History - Apr 22,
1903 - April 13-20, 1893 - Mrs F.M. Stump died
at her home in Big Neck on the 4th.

STUMP, HANNAH V. - Obituary - Apr 13, 1893
Hannah V. Stump, wife of F.M. Stump died at her
home in Big Neck Apr 4, 1893, 53 years 17 days
old. Born Bourbon Co. KY Mar 18, 1840.
Married F.M. Stump Jul 1, 1858. Had 2 sons.
Buried Ebenezer Cemetery. Services by Rev J.B.
King.

STUMP, PRESLEY - Columbus - Feb 2, 1893
Presley Stump buried their baby Saturday,
January 21st.

STURGISS, EDWIN - Local - Mar 13, 1894 Died
Edwin Sturgiss son of the late Dr S.M. Sturgiss
of Quincy committed suicide Sunday by shooting
himself at Spokane, Washington. Heavy drinking
was the cause.

STURGISS, EDWIN K. - Quincy - Jul 6, 1894 The
will of the late Edwin K. Strugiss who
committed suicide at Spokane, Wash. has been
admitted to probate in Adams Co. He leaves all
his estate, valued at $10,000 to his brother,
Wilbur R. Sturgiss of this city.

SULLIVAN, MAYOR H.V. - Ancient History - Nov 2,
1894 - November 1, 1883 Mayor H.V. Sullivan
died in Quincy.

SULLIVAN, HENRY V. - 10 Years Ago - Nov 16,
1893 Mayor Henry V. Sullivan died in Quincy.

SULLIVAN, JOHN - Horrible Accident - Feb 20,
1894 Killed John Sullivan, Saturday, on the
J.T. Nelson farm in Lima Lake levee district
opposite, Canton, MO in a portable sawmill when
he fell on a whirling blade. He was a tramp,
had been on the road 11 years, former home was
Petersbora, Ind.

SUMMER, MISS ABBIE - 20 Years Ago - Mar 16,
1893 Trial of Andros Coe for the murder of
Miss Abbie Summers was in progress at Palmyra.

SURMEYER, MISS IDA - Quincy - Dec 18, 1894
Died, Miss Ida Surmeyer who died last Thursday
in Los Vegas, N.M. Will be buried here Tuesday
A.M.

SUTER, MRS EVA A. - Death of Mrs Suter - Jan 8,
1895 Mrs Eva A. Suter, wife of John Suter died
at her home in Houston twp Jan 7th, 77 years
old. Born Butler Co. Ohio where she married Mr
John Suter who survives her. Came to Adams Co.
1847 and to Houston twp 1865. Had 4 sons, 5
daughters living here, Kansas, Nebr. and Calif.
Funeral from Ebenezer Church Houston Wednesday
11 A.M.

SUTER, JOHN - Local - Sep 17, 1895 John Suter,
an aged citizen of Houston twp died Friday
afternoon 83 years old. Lived Houston twp
about 30 years. Wife died a few months ago.
Funeral at Ebenezer Church Sunday A.M.

SUTER, JOHN - Local - Oct 18, 1895 Jacob
Groves was appointed adm. Wednesday of the
estate of John Suter.

SUTER, JOHN - Death - Sep 17, 1895 John Suter,
born October 1812 in Virginia and moved to
Butler Co. Ohio until 1847 when he came to

Adams Co. and lived since. Died Sep 13, 1895
at age 82 years 10 months 25 days. Services at
Ebenezer Church Sunday 11 A.M. buried beside
his aged companion who died a few months ago.

SUTER, JOHN - Probate Notice - Nov 1, 1895
John Suter, deceased 1st Monday of December
1895 Jacob Groves, adm.

SWAN, CHAS. W. - Local - Sep 16, 1903 Mrs
Angeline Swan and daughter Carrie and Miss
Myrtle Swan of Abingdon and Charles W. Purdum,
cashier in the Burlington Route freight office
at Red Oak, Iowa was here last week to attend
funeral of their brother in law and uncle,
Chas. W. Swan.

SWAN, CHARLES WILLIAM - Death - Sep 9, 1903
Charles William Swan was born Sep 26, 1821.
Died at the home of his daughter, Mrs H.S. Hahn
in Camp Point Sep 8, 1903. Came with parents
to Belmont Co. Ohio when 18 years old. Married
Jul 4, 1842 to Elizabeth Keene of Belmont Co.
They had 4 children, 1 son and 3 daughters.
The son and 1 daughter died in early childhood.
Mrs Swan died Sep 8, 1879 after her death Mr
Swan lived with his youngest brother, Rev Jas.
M. Swan a methodist minister of Allegheny City,
Penn. and his youngest child Dora, came to Ill.
to live with her sister. She died of typhoid
fever August 1882. Jan 1887 Mr Swan came to
Camp Point to live. He is survived by his
daughter, Mrs H.S. Hahn, 1 sister Mrs Caroline
Purdman of Red Oak, IA, 2 brothers Melvin Swan
of Abingdon and John of Paris, Edgar Co. Ill.
and 2 grandchildren Harry Swan Hahn and Mrs
Fred Seaton of Camp Point. Services at the
home this P.M. by Rev E.A. Hedges. Buried Camp
Point cemetery.

SWAN, GEORGE W. - Local - Nov 17, 1897 Charles
W. Swan was called to Abingdon last week by the
death of his brother, George W. Swan a
prominent business man of that city. Funeral
was held Friday P.M.

SWEAT, ELNORA E. - Died - Jul 26, 1895 Died

Elnora E., daughter of Harvey and Mary Sweat age 13 months. Died July 21st of erysipelas. Services at the home 3 miles west of Camp Point on the 22nd by Elder O. Dilley. Buried Coatsburg cemetery.

SWEAT, HARVEY AND MARY - Coatsburg - Jul 23, 1895 This morning at 4 at the old homestead in Camp Point twp the little 1 year old daughter of Harvey and Mary Sweat died. Was an only child.

SWEAT, MRS LULU (W.T.) - Obituary - Oct 5, 1894 Died Mrs Lulu (Gray) Sweat born Coatsburg, Ill. Jul 2, 1873. Married W.T. Sweat Sep 8, 1892, had 1 child, Ona Vivan 5 months old who with the father survives. Funeral October 3rd at the Christian Church by Rev O. Dilley of the Christian Church, Camp Point.

SWEAT, ORSON - Local - Jan 16, 1894 Died Orson Sweat, living midway between Camp Point and Coatsburg died suddenly Thursday. Funeral Saturday.

SWEAT, ORSON G. - Local - Feb 20, 1894 William T. Sweat as adm will sell the personal property of the late Orson G. Sweat at auction at his late residence 2 miles east of Coatsburg Tuesday March 13th.

SWEAT, ORSON G. - Obituary - Jan 19, 1894 Died Orson G. Sweat Jan 11th, 1894 of heart disease while at work. Born Vermont June 25, 1837. Lived Adams Co. about 55 years. Married twice. Buried his second Dec 19, 1891. Leaves 1 child by 1st marriage, Mrs Mary Felsman and 4 by the second marriage William F., John D., Harvey J. and Orson G. the youngest being 14 years old. Services at Christian Church in Coatsburg Jan 15th by Elder O. Dilley. Buried village cemetery.

TACKE, WILLIAM F. - Quincy - Jun 25, 1902 The trial of John Schanz charged with murdering William F. Tacke has been continued until June 30th.

TANDY, EVERETT - Killed at Kingston - Nov 17,
1897 Everett Tandy, 17 year old son of Dr T.S.
Tandy of Kingston was killed near that village
Friday P.M. by the accidental discharge of a
shotgun. Was with Will McVey. Will had gone
to a farm house to buy some turkeys when the
gun went off.

TATE, MRS J.M. - Quincy - Dec 13, 1895 Mrs
J.M. Tate, dropped dead Tuesday A.M. at the
front gate of her home on N. 5th St. from heart
disease, 22 years old.

TATHAM, GEORGE M. - Death - May 25, 1893 A
telegram to the editor of this paper telling of
the death Sunday of George M. Tatham, editor of
the Greenville Advocate and for 16 years Treas.
of the Ill. Press Assoc. Leaves widow and a
son.

TAYLOR, MRS ELIZABETH - Quincy - Mar 29, 1895
Mrs Elizabeth Taylor, mother of Fred P. Taylor,
of the Journal of Industry died Wednesday
afternoon at the home of her daughter, Mrs
Hedges, Riverside twp. Born England. Came to
Quincy 1848. Leaves 6 children.

TAYLOR, MR AND MRS FRANK - Local - Jul 29, 1896
An infant child of Mr and Mrs Frank Taylor,
Columbus twp died Sunday from convulsions.

TAYLOR, REV FREDERICK W. - Local - Apr 29, 1903
Rev Frederick W. Taylor, Episcopal Bishop of
Quincy diocese died at Kenosha, Wisc. Sunday
night, age 50 years. Was a sufferer from
Brights disease and was stricken down, Easter
in Quincy, while conducting services in the
Cathedral.

TAYLOR, MRS M.B. - Local - Jan 16, 1894 Died
Mrs M.B. Taylor at Maywood, MO Saturday. Was
daughter of the late Paris T. Judy and a sister
of J.M. Judy of Camp Point.

TAYLOR, W.H. - A Veteran Insurance Man Gone -
Dec 30, 1896 Died W.H. Taylor. Mr Taylor
established the Hartford Ageny in Camp Point 25

years ago.

TAYLOR, W.R. - Quincy - Dec 4, 1894 Died W.R. Taylor, a former resident of this city and a brother of Fred P. Taylor died at Fort Scott, Kansas Thursday of paralysis. 43 years old.

TAYLOR, WASHINGTON C. - Quincy - Jan 20, 1897 Thomas S. Elliott has been appointed adm of the estate of Washington C. Taylor.

TAYLOR, MR AND MRS WILLIAM - Local - Feb 3, 1897 Died the baby daughter of Mr and Mrs William Taylor died Sunday. Buried Monday at Pleasant View.

TENHOUSE, HENRY - Northeast Burton - Mar 5, 1902 Mrs Gilbert of Coatsburg is keeping house for Henry Tenhouse since the recent death of his wife.

TERRILL, EDMUND - An Old Settler Gone - Jul 26, 1895 Edmund Terrill, an old settler of Reno Co. and an old veteran died at his home on W. 6th St. at 6:30 PM last eve of flux. Lived Reno Co. for about 20 years. Served with Co. G, 3rd Ill. Cavalry. At one time owned 3 sections of land in Reno Co. near Partridge. Was comparatively poor at the time of his death. Remains to be taken to Partridge tomorrow at 7:30 where they will be buried by Joe Hooker Post. Formerly lived Concord twp and well known here 20 years ago.

TERRY, JOHN - Probate Notice - Jan 15, 1902 John Terry, deceased   1st Monday of March 1902 (3rd)   Anna Terry, adm.

TERWISCHE, GEORGE HENRY - Co. Seat - Jan 22, 1896 Will of George Henry Terwische left all the money he had in the bank and invested be divided equally among his widow and 6 children, all realty left to widow and she was named exec.

THAYER, MRS CHAS. - Obituary - Oct 28, 1903 Mrs Charles Thayer died suddenly at her home in

Macomb Friday afternoon. She was out driving
with her husband and her daughter who was
visiting from Kansas and she started feeling
badly. Alice Thayer was daughter of James
Tomlinson and was born 66 years ago in this
county. Married Charles Thayer who with one
son and 2 daughters survive her. Family came
to Camp Point a few years ago and stayed a
couple of years and moved to Macomb to permit
their younger daughter, Lillie to attend the
new normal school. Remains brought here Monday
at 1 P.M. and buried village cemetery beside
her father who died many years before her.
Services by Rev E.H. Fuller at the grave. Miss
Lillie Thayer is very ill and was unable to
attend the funeral.

THAYER, REV F.A. - Ancient History - Mar 30,
1894 - March 29, 1883 Rev F.A. Thayer pastor of
the Quincy Cong. Church died on the 25th.

THAYER, REV FREDERICK A. - Ancient History -
Apr 1, 1903 - March 29, 1883 Rev Frederick A.
Thayer, pastor of the Cong. Church Quincy died
on the 26th.

THAYER, MRS HANNAH A. (HORACE) - Death Record -
Jul 14, 1897 Died Mrs Hannah A. Thayer in
Kansas City July 2nd at the Medical Hospital.
Lived Severance, Doniphan Co. Kansas. Born
Wheeling, W. Virginia Aug 9, 1831. Married
Horace Thayer Dec 18, 1851. Had 10 children, 4
boys and 3 girls survive her. Husband only
expected to live a few days.

THAYER, SARAH JUSTENIE - Obituary - Feb 8, 1895
Sarah Justenie Thayer, daughter of Charles and
Alice J. Thayer born Honey Creek twp Adams Co.
Ill Apr 23, 1868. Died at her home in Columbus
twp Jan 22, 1895. Married Wilbur W. Frost of
Fowler, Ill Mar 2, 1887. Had 3 children, 2
boys and a girl 17 days old. Also leaves her
husband. Funeral by Rev A.A. White in the ME
Church at Paloma. Remains buried in the home
cemetery at Fowler. All 3 children survive her.

THIEMAN, WILLIAM - Quincy - Nov 26, 1902

William Thieman, a resident of Quincy for a half century died Tuesday A.M. age 77 years.

THOLEN, GERHART - Quincy - Jul 23, 1902   On Tuesday afternoon Gerhart Tholen age 12 years fell off of the ferry landing, where he was playing and drowned.

THOMAS, MRS E.P. - Golden - Sep 7, 1893 Mrs E.P. Thomas received telegram last Saturday saying her sister and sisters daughter were seriously burned by a gasoline explosion at Kirksville, MO that A.M. The daughter died from her injuries that night.

THOMAS ELI R. - Sudden Death - Feb 6, 1894 Died Eli R. Thomas of Clayton twp 2 miles south of Golden found dead in barnyard Friday eve by his wife. Lived here since boyhood. Funeral from Hebron Church Sunday. Leaves a wife and 3 sons.

THOMAS, MRS EMILY (DAVID) - Obituary - Feb 16, 1893 Mrs Emily Thomas, relict of the late David Thomas of Camp Point twp died Wednesday Feb 8th at the home of her daughter, Mrs S.V. Brewer, Shelbina, MO age 73 years. She lived nearly 50 years in this vicinity. Leaves 2 sons and 2 daughters.

THOMAS, MICHAEL - Ancient History - Sep 18, 1894 - Sep 12, 1879 Michael Thomas, a former resident of Clayton was killed at Louisiana, MO when a gravel bank caved in on him.

THOMAS, PETER - Ancient History - Mar 24, 1897 March 1879 Peter Thomas, an early settler in Camp Point twp died in Augusta.

THOMAS, MRS WHITMER A. - Death of Mrs W.A. Thomas - Aug 4, 1897 - Died Mrs Whitmer A. Thomas July 31st at her home near Fairfax, Mo. Buried at Paloma on Monday, at her old home. Leaves husband alone.

THOMASMEYER, FRED W. - Co Seat - Jan 22, 1896 Died Friday afternoon about 2, Ald. Fred W.

Thomasmeyer at his home 830 Kentucky Street
from typhoid fever.   Funeral Monday afternoon.

THOMASMEYER, FREDERICK C. - Co. Seat - Feb 26,
1896   Will of the late Frederick C. Thomasmeyer
leaves all his real estate and personal
property to his widow.

THOMPSON, CULBERTSON - Local - Dec 28, 1893
Culbertson Thompson, a son of the late Joseph
C. Thompson, postmaster at Quincy committed
suicide Thursday afternoon.   Had suffered from
grippe and his mind was probably impaired.
Shot himself in the presence of his mother.

THOMPSON, MRS ELIZABETH - Death - Sep 30, 1903
Mrs Elizabeth Thompson age 73 years died Wed.
A.M. at her home in Quincy.   Lived county 50
years.   Was widow of the late Samuel Thompson
who died 12 years ago.   Leaves 5 children-2
sons, Alex and S.H. Thompson of Gilmer twp--3
daughters, Mrs Henry Baker of Augusta and
Misses Annie and Mary at home.   Member of
Methodist Church.

THOMPSON, MRS ELIZABETH - Quincy - Jun 11, 1902
Mrs Elizabeth Thompson, a resident of Adams Co.
since 1831 died at her home near Payson, age 74
years.

THOMPSON, ELIZABETH - Probate Notice - Oct 14,
1903   Elizabeth Thompson, deceased   1st Monday
of Dec. 1903 (7th)   Alexander Thompson, adm.

THOMPSON, ENOCH - Local - Jul 1, 1896   Died,
Enoch Thompson, an aged citizen of Columbus
twp, died Monday night.

THOMPSON, MR J.L. - Local - Sep 28, 1894
During a charavari Monday Night in the country
25 miles NE of Mila, MO, J.L. Thompson, the
bridegroom was shot thru the heart with a rifle
and killed.   He had only been married 24 hours.
It is supposed the person firing the gun
thought it was not loaded.

THOMPSON, JAS. - Elm Grove - Dec 14, 1893

Intelligence of the death of Jas. Thompson was received by letter. He was a brother of Lester C. Thompson, deceased and John M. Thompson who lives near Elm Grove post office.

THOMPSON, JAMES - Death - Jan 29, 1895 James Thompson died last week in El Paso, Texas of consumption. Returned to El Paso from Camp Point about Christmas time. Was eldest son of the late William Thompson who died about 30 years ago at his home west of Camp Point. El Paso Herald says: Died at Lindell Hotel of consumption Jan 20th at 4 P.M. James Thompson, age 48 years. Was a brother of William Thompson, formerly of the firm of Smith & Thompson for which firm he worked several years. He was a locomotive engineer and several years ago went to work for National Road in Mexico. While there he contracted a cold which ran into consumption. Funeral today at Emerson and Berrien by Rev Hoffman.

THOMPSON, JOSEPH C. - Ancient History - Aug 12, 1903 - August 1893 Joseph C. Thompson, postmaster at Quincy died on the 19th.

THOMPSON, JOSEPH C. - Death - Aug 13, 1893 Joseph C. Thompson, postmaster at Quincy died Sunday, age 66 years. Born Penn. Came to Ill. in 1847 and to Macomb in 1856. 1868 he settled in Quincy. Leaves wife and 2 sons. Funeral Tuesday.

THOMPSON, MARIA - Quincy - Jan 28, 1903 Maria Thompson died in Payson on Tuesday, age 78 years. Born in Maine and had lived in Adams Co. since 1833.

THOMPSON, PHILO E. - Local - Apr 20, 1893 Philo E. Thompson, one of the old citizens of Adams Co. dropped dead in the streets of Payson, Saturday afternoon, from apoplexy. Was a native of Connecticut and located at Payson 1835.

THOMPSON, R.F. - Killed by the Cars - Oct 13, 1897 The 4 year old son of R.F. Thompson of

Colchester was killed by a freight train Friday afternoon.

THOMPSON, SAMUEL - Corpse Came to Life - Jan 4, 1895 Bowen, Ill Jan 2 -- A case of the dead coming to life is reported from Denver, this county, last week. Samuel Thompson, a school teacher in that vicinity had an operation by Doctor's at Keokuk and died Thursday A.M. or so they thought. Watchers seen corpse breathe Tuesday A.M. No funeral.

THOMPSON, SAMUEL C. - Events of 1883 - Jan 19, 1893 Samuel C. Thompson, a former well known citizen died at Junction City, Kansas.

THOMPSON, THOS. J. - Primrose - Mar 12, 1895 Thos. J. Thompson who lived across the county line in Hancock Co. was buried at Ebenezer Sunday at 2 P.M. His wife is very low and not expected to live. Mr Thompson was about 60 years old.

THOMPSON, WALTER - Kills Himself - Jul 1, 1896 Walter Thompson, a wealthy stock dealer shot and instantly killed himself at his home at Burnside, a small town 12 miles West of LaHarpe at 9 A.M. Sunday.

THOMPSON, WILLIAM - Quincy - Jan 16, 1894 Died William Thompson age 60 years. A member of Co. B, 50th Ill. Inf. Died at St Marys Hospital Tuesday. Cause was traced to wounds received at the battle of Shiloh.

THOMPSON, WILLIAM H. - W.H. Thompson Dead - Apr 9, 1895 William H. Thompson died at the home of his daughter, Mrs Lelia Gentry in Galesburg, Thursday afternopon age 65 years. After about a weeks illness with heart trouble. William H. Thompson was born in Jacksonville in 1830 and was son of Elijah Thompson who settled at an early day in the east end of Burton twp. Mr Thompson spent the greater part of his life in that vicinity, where he obtained a reputation as a practical horticulturist. Funeral Sunday in Galesburg.

THORNTON, BART - Local - Jan 8, 1895 Horrible
accident at Augusta, Thursday, a miner named
Bart Thornton lost his life working in Sam
Jones mine when he was crushed by a heavy piece
of soapstone falling in the wheel way at 9 A.M.
Died 7:15 P.M.

THORP, JOHN H. - Killed by the Wabash - Feb
17, 1897 John H. Thorp, a farmer of Pike Co.
Ill. was struck by a Wabash passenger train at
11 A.M. Saturday at Aladdin, 2 miles East of
Shepherd, Ill. and almost instantly killed. He
was intoxicated. Leaves a large family.

THORPE, MISS ROSA - Elm Grove - Jun 14, 1895
Miss Rosa Thorpe died Tuesday A.M. about 15
years old. She was working at the hotel in
Golden when taken sick with Bilous and typhoid
fever 3 weeks ago. Went to her parents home
near Franzen's wind mill. Services by Rev
McDonald at the ME church, Golden Wednesday
A.M. Buried cemetery near Loraine in P.M.

THRUSH, GEORGE - Local - Oct 29, 1902 George
Thrush, well known in Camp Point died at his
home in Quincy suddenly Monday night. Was
veteran of Civil War. John Wimer of Camp Point
is an uncle, brother of Thrush's mother.

THRUSH, GEORGE H. - Death - Nov 5, 1902 George
H. Thursh, prominent in grand army and secret
society circles, well known in every part of
the county, died of heart disease 4 A.M.
Tuesday at his home , 730 N. 11th St., Quincy,
where he lived 23 years. Wife survives him.
Served during war in Co. A of 10th Missouri
Inf. and the 34th Ill. Born Morgan Co. Ohio 61
years ago. His mother died last Jan. Shortly
afterwards he married Mrs Lillian Smith who
survives him also leaves 3 sisters and a
brother.   "Whig"

TODD, WILLIAM - Local - Aug 16, 1895 William
Todd who at one time lived Camp Point was
killed by a train at Davenport, Iowa Tuesday
night. He was a fireman. Body will be brought
to Camp Point.

TODD, WM - From the Necks - Mar 31, 1897 Wm
Todd and family attended the funeral of his
sister near Bowen Saturday.

TODD, WM - Death - Aug 20, 1895 Fridays paper
mentions death of Wm Todd on the Rock Island
line. Later news states that Todd was sick in
hospital with typhoid fever and while delirous
he jumped from second story window and ran to
th railroad yards where he was run over.
Remains brought to Camp Point and left at
Earl's Undertaking rooms until Saturday when
they were taken to the cemetery at Union
Church. Leaves a wife, the daughter of J.G.
Akers and an infant child.

TOETTNER, A. - Killed by a Train - Jul 6, 1893
A man thought to be A. Toettner was run over by
a train Thursday by the Sny bridge. Thought to
be about 50 years old. Toettner was in the
employ of Camp and Phillips, a musical
instrument Co. of Jacksonville, Ill. "Barry
Adage"

TOMLINSON, MRS JAMES - Local - Apr 6, 1894 Mrs
James Tomlinson died at the home of her
daughter, Mrs Thayer, north of Paloma Tuesday.
Buried Camp Point cemetery Thursday. 80 years
old and widow of James Tomlinson who died 10
years ago. They lived in Camp Point from 1855
till in the 70's.

TORRENCE, MRS SARAH - Quincy - Mar 19, 1895
Mrs Sarah Torrence, wife of Dr John Torrence
died at the home of her daughter, Mrs Jas. H.
Richardson Wednesday, age 74 years. 40 years
ago she and her husband lived in Columbus,
where they stayed till 1861. Leaves 3
daughters Mrs Richardson, Mrs C.H. Nance and
Mrs J.H. Crump and one son Dr L.P. Torrence.

TOTTEN, MISS MARIA - Ancient History - Sep 4,
1894 - August 31, 1882 Miss Maria Totten, for
many years a teacher in Maplewood died in
Schuyler County.

TOUT, WILLIAM SHEPHARD - Died in California -

Jun 9, 1897 News from Dinuba, Calif.--Died
William S. Tout who lived here many years on
the north line of Honey Creek twp and went to
Calif. a few years ago. William Shephard Tout
born Boone Co. KY Oct 20, 1812, died May 22,
1897. Married Danville, Ind. April 1834 to
Miss Loveina Garl with whom he lived 59 years 3
months when she died Aug 8, 1893. They had 16
children - 5 sons, 6 daughters still living.

TOUZALIN, ANTHONY - Local - Dec 24, 1902
Anthony Touzalin who was a merchant in Adams
Co. 50 years ago died in Chicago Thursday.
Brought to Quincy and buried Saturday. Mr
Touzalin kept a general store in Columbus in
the early 50's and later in Quincy and Paloma.

TOUZALIN, ANTHONY - Quincy - Dec 24, 1902
Anthony Touzalin, a former resident of Quincy
died in Chicago Thursday age 84 years. Remains
brought to Quincy for burial.

TRIPLETT, BARBARA - Golden - Feb 2, 1893 J.B.
Thomas sold a tombstone to be put up over the
grave of Barbara Triplett, of Hancock Co. at
her death she was the oldest woman in Hancock
Co. being 96 years 2 months 16 days old.

TROGDON, JOHN - Ancient History - Oct 26, 1894
Oct 23, 1884 John Trogdon, a former resident
of Camp Point died at Ladona, Missouri.

TROGDON, JOHN D. - Soldiers buried in Hebron
Cemetery - May 26, 1897 - Listed in Co. D,
10th Missouri Infantry.

TROTTER, DR OTIS - Local - Apr 21, 1897 Dr
Otis Trotter was called to Fairhaven Vernon Co.
Missouri by the accidental death of his father
last Thursday night.

TROTTER, DR W.C. - Death Record - Apr 21, 1897
Dr W.C. Trotter, for 10 years a physician of
Fairhaven, MO was killed when he was thrown
from a buggy by a runaway team Thursday.
Leaves a wife, a son and daughter. Son is Dr
Otis Trotter of Camp Point. Daughter is

married and lives at Fairhaven. Dr was reared
in Richfield and practiced there many years.
His wife is daughter of Hon. Ira Tyler of
Richfield.

TROUT, MR AND MRS JAMES - Local - Mar 25, 1896
An 18 month old babe of Mr and Mrs James Trout
died last Wednesday of measles.

TROUT, MRS JAS. - Death - Nov 12, 1902 Mrs
Jas. Trout died Wed. night at St Mary's
Hospital Quincy from a cancer. Was about 49
years old. Raised at Columbus. Maiden name
was Elizabeth Smith, daughter of Jesse Smith.
Husband and 8 children survive her.

TURNER, FRED C. - Local - Apr 6, 1893 Fred C.
Turner a farmer of Mendon twp, died Friday of
apoplexy. Funeral Sunday under direction of
Masonic fraternity of Mendon of which he was a
member. Was reared in this county, being a son
of the late Joseph Turner.

TURNER, FRED C. - Ancient History - Apr 8, 1903
March 6, 1893 Fred C. Turner, a prominent
farmer of Mendon died suddenly of apoplexy.

TURNER, HOUSTON ALEXANDER - Died - Jul 7, 1897
Died Houston Alexander Turner died at his home
near Alva, Oklahoma June 26th in his 46th year.
Born Honey Creek twp Adams Co. Ill. Oct 16,
1851. Married Mary D. Thompson Oct. 1876 had 4
children, 2 boys, 2 girls. Moved to Kansas
1885 and 1894 to Oklahoma. Leaves a wife and 3
children. Buried Partridge, KS beside his
little son who died a few years ago.

TURNER, JOHN F. - Obituary - Aug 17, 1893 John
F. Turner was born in Indiana Apr 11, 1830 and
came to Adams Co. by his parents in 1835.
Married Isabel Smith 1859 and settled on the
farm adjoining the one occupied by his parents.
Where he lived until Feb. when he moved to Camp
Point. Stricken with paralysis in June 1892
losing the use of his right side. Suffered a
2nd attack from which he died Aug 11, 1893.
Leaves wife and 2 sons. Funeral at Methodist

Church Saturday A.M. Remains taken to Columbus
for burial.

TURNER, JOHN F. - Probate Notice - Aug 31, 1893
John F. Turner, deceased 1st Monday of
November 1893 (6th) William E. Turner, Exec.

TURNER, JOHN F. - Ancient History - Aug 12,
1903 - August 1893 John F. Turner died on the
11th.

TURNER, JOSEPH - Ancient History - Mar 30, 1894
March 24, 1876 Joseph Turner a prominent
citizen of the county died at Mendon on the
16th.

TURNER, MRS MARY - Quincy - Dec 30, 1896 Died
Mrs Mary Turner for several years a teacher in
the Quincy Schools died in Canon City, Colo on
last Tuesday.

TURNER, RALPH - Quincy - Jun 21, 1895 Ralph,
little son of Mr and Mrs Arthur W. Turner, 1453
Hampshire St. accidently hung himself while
playing in the attic of the family home.

TURNER, REBECCA J. - Obituary - Dec 28, 1893
Rebecca J. Turner was born in Clark Co. Ind.
Sep 28, 1825 and died Columbus Dec 19, 1893.
Was 68 years 2 months 21 days old. When 10
years old came with her father's family to
Adams Co. Ill. settling on Section 17 in
Columbus twp where she lived until her marriage
to Alexander M. Smith Feb 25, 1862. Leaves her
husband, 1 son, Francis Delano Smith and 1
grandson.

TURNER, SUSAN E. - Obituary - Nov 23, 1893
Susan E. Turner, youngest child of Francis and
Elizabeth Turner was born in Adams Co. Ill. Dec
21, 1836 and died Nov 19, 1893. Married James
Banton Aug 27, 1857. They had 3 sons, William
Oliver, Robert and James. The husband and
father died in service of his country June
1863. The oldest son died in the winter of
1865. Two sons survive her. Funeral at
Pleasant View Church Monday, Nov 20th by Elder

O. Dilley.   Buried in the Church burying
ground.

TUSHAUS, J.H. - Quincy - Nov 20, 1894 Died
J.H. Tushaus, age 64, for many years a grocery
merchant died Friday night.

TYLER, HARVEY - Local - Jan 26, 1893 Harvey
Tyler, of Kentucky arrived on the 13th to visit
L.G. Hoke's and Jas. E. Funk's. Friday he
received a telegram telling of the death of his
wife and departed for home.

TYNER, CO. N.N. - Death - Nov 25, 1903 Col.
N.N. Tyner died Saturday A.M. at his home in
Augusta. Leaving a wife, but no children. Was
veteran from Civil War from, Indiana, but lived
Augusta many years.

UNDERWOOD, PETER - Death - Jul 2, 1902 Peter
Underwood of Camp Point died suddenly Friday
eve June 27th of heart failure. He had been to
town Thursday with his daughter, Mrs Buck.
Services Sunday P.M. at Christian Church by Rev
A. McGaw. Born in Virginia Jul 4, 1830 and as
a child went to Missouri where he followed
blacksmithing. Married Jun 28, 1868 to Sylvia
Gillespie who with 3 daughters survive him.
Came to Camp Point and went into grocery
business.

URBAN, ANDREW - Quincy - Jan 21, 1903 Andrew
Urban, a resident of the city for nearly a
quarter of a century died Wednesday, age 73
years.

VANCE, MRS ELIZA - Death - Sep 10, 1902 Mrs
Eliza Vance, wife of Moses Vance, died at her
home in Camp Point twp Tues. Sep 2, 1902, 74
years old. Sick 3 weeks. Funeral at Hebron
Church Wed. afternoon by Rev R.A. Omer. Buried
in cemetery near church. Eliza McClintock born
in Ireland 1829. Came to U.S.A. as a child.
Parents located in Camp Point 1835. She spent
remainder of her life here. Married Moses
Vance May 5, 1859, had 2 son, 2 daughters, both
daughters died in childhood. Surviving her is

aged husband and 2 sons John and Charles. Also
2 sisters, Mrs Doran of Quincy and Mrs Crow of
Oregon, left of her fathers family.

VANCE, RICHARD - Death Record - Nov 3, 1897
Died, Richard Vance Oct 30th at the home of his
brother, Moses Vance near Camp Point age 64
years 10 months 12 days. Born Penn. lived last
10 years with his brother. Was unmarried and
leaves no other relatives. Services Sunday
P.M. at Hebron by Elder Laycock.

VANCIL, MRS ISOM - Local - Dec 28, 1893 Mrs
Isom Vancil died at her home 2 miles north of
Liberty, Sunday. She was afflicted with
softening of the brain. Was 73 years old and
lived near Liberty with her husband many years.

VANCIL, WILLIAM - Suicide - Sep 21, 1893
William Vancil of Liberty committed suicide
Saturday by shooting himself, had suffered
Brights disease. He was about 70 years old and
lived many years on a farm in Liberty twp.
Leaves wife, 2 sons and 2 unmarried daughters.
Sheriff Vancil of Quincy is one of the sons.

VANCIL, MRS WM - Local Nov 30, 1893 Mrs Wm
Vancil, mother of Sheriff John W. Vancil, died
at Liberty Saturday. 68 years old. Native of
France, being brought to Liberty in childhood
where she spent the remainder of her life.

VANDENBOOM, BERNARD - Quincy - Jan 18, 1895
Bernard Vandenboom was drowned in Quincy Bay
Tuesday eve. He was skating on the bay and
went on the ice where ice cutting had been
done, breaking through. Body was recovered,
age 18 years.

VANDEN BOOM, MARY ELIZABETH - Quincy - Apr 14,
1897 The will of Mary Elizabeth Vanden Boom
gives $260 to St Francis Church and addition
$50 to it societies, $5 to St Mary's Hospital,
daughter, Mrs Frances Mast received all
personal property and grand children $5 each
and rest divided between son, Joseph V. Vanden
Boom and Mrs Mast.

VANDEN BOOM - HENRY - Co Seat - Mar 6, 1896
Died Henry Vanden Boom, a well known German
chair maker, died Saturday eve.

VAN ETTEN, C.C. - Local - Sep 22, 1897 C.C.
Van Etten died in Chicago Sunday age 40 years.
Was husband of Clara Patton who taught school
in Maplewood high school about 13 years ago.

VANHOLT, HARRY - Prairie - Aug 3, 1893 A
brother of Harry Vanholt came out Thursday from
Quincy to inform him of his uncle's death.

VAN HORN, S.W. - Fun followed by Death - May 6,
1896 Friends of Mr and Mrs G.L. Van Horn,
Kearney, MO were pained to hear of the sad
death of their son S.W. Van Horn 20 years 2
months old on Saturday April 26th. Leaves
family and sisters.

VAN METER, ELDER I.N. - Local - Dec 25, 1894
Elder I.N. Van Meter, probably the most widely
known minister in McDonough Co. and adjoining
counties died at his home 6 miles NE of Macomb
on the 13th inst. in his 80th year. Was
Baptist minister over 50 years.

VAN PELT, DR - Local - Jul 12, 1895 Dr Van
Pelt of Good Hope, McDonough Co. was gored
Wednesday by a Jersey bull and died. Was about
80 years old.

VAN VALER, MRS FRANK - Coatsburg - Sep 24, 1895
A.S. Van Valer and wife attended the funeral
Saturday in Galesburg of their son Frank's
wife.

VAN WAY, JOHN - Elm Grove - Nov 30, 1894 Died
John Van Way, living about 2 miles NE of Elm
Grove Church died with malarial fever. Buried
last Sunday.

VARNER, ROBERT A. - Quincy - Oct 11, 1895 Will
of Robert A. Varner gives his widow the
household furniture and 1/3 of property, his
daughters, Anna M. Weigland $1,000, Mary E. Roy
$1,200, Daisy Varner $300, Sarah Varner $500,

rest of estate to his son R.E. Varner, and he
and Daniel Corrigan were appointed adm's.

VIAR, MRS ELIZABETH - Local - Nov 8, 1895 Mrs
Elizabeth Viar died Tuesday at the home of her
son Thomas Viar in Liberty twp. Funeral
Wednesday at Union Church.

VIAR, MICAJAH - Brush Prairie - Mar 23, 1893
Infant daughter of Micajah Viar was buried at
Union Church cemetery.

VICKERS, MRS HOWARD J. - Quincy - Jul 23, 1902
Mrs Howard J. Vickers died at her home in
Burton twp, age 50 years.

VICKERS, JOHN W. - Ancient History - Nov 2,
1894 - Nov 3, 1876 John W. Vickers,
democratic candidate for sheriff died at his
home in Payson.

VICKERS, JOHN W. - Ancient History - Nov 12,
1895 - November 1876 John W. Vickers of Payson,
democratic candidate for sheriff died Oct 29th
just before election.

VICKERS, LUCY A. - Obituary - Mar 18, 1896
Lucy A. Vickers, daughter of H.J. and Ann R.
Vickers was born Aug 12, 1854 died at San
Antonia, Texas Mar 2, 1896 age 41 years 6
months 20 days. In Autumn of 1875 she went to
Grant Co. West Virginia and while there married
G.T. Lewis in October 1877 then returned to
Adams Co. in Feb 1878. Moved with her family
to San Antonio Oct 1894 in hopes of helping her
lung trouble. Was mother of 3 children, of
which one died in infancy and another at age 13
years. She was the last of her father's 4
children to die. Funeral Monday March 9 at
Burton Church by Rev William Stewart and Rev
A.A. White. Buried Burton cemetery.

VONHOLT, MISS HANNAH - Brush Prairie - Mar 23,
1893 Buried at Union Church cemetery, Miss
Hannah Vonholt, daughter of Henry Vonholt. Two
days later a younger daughter age 12 years
died.

WADDELL, EDWARD - Columbus - Mar 23, 1894   Mr
Edward Waddell of Neb. came to attend the
funeral of his father.

WADDELL, J.O. - Death of J.O. Waddell - Mar 20,
1894   Died J.O. Waddell of Gilmer twp Sunday
eve at 6 o'clock from paralysis.   71 years old.
Funeral at Columbus at 2 P.M. Tuesday.

WADDELL, JAMES O. - Probate Notice - Apr 6,
1894   James O. Waddell, deceased   1st Monday
of June 1894   Lucinda Waddell, adm

WADDELL, JAMES OLIVER - Obituary - Mar 23, 1894
Died James Oliver Waddell an old citizen of
Gilmer twp at his home Sunday eve March 18th at
6 P.M. of paralysis.   Born near Jacksonville,
Ill Nov 8, 1822.   Came to Adams Co. June 1829.
Married Lucinda Ogle Nov 4, 1851.   Leaves a
widow, 1 sister, 4 children, 3 grand children.
Funeral by Rev A.A. White at Columbus and
buried in the cemetery at that place on the
20th inst.

WADDELL, OLIVER - Prairie Picking - Mar 27,
1894   Death of Mr Oliver Waddell was quite a
shock.   Suffered from paralysis which ended his
life.   Funeral at Columbus Tuesday at 2 P.M.
Buried Columbus cemetery.

WAGNER, IRA - Quincy - Dec 21, 1894   Died Ira
Wagner, a student in the business college died
suddenly Sunday eve from heart trouble.

WAGY, JAMES OSCAR - Suicide Near Plainville -
Mar 10, 1897   James Oscar Wagy, a son of John
Wagy committed suicide at the home of his
parents about 2 miles west of Plainville Sunday
eve by shooting himself.   Was 25 years old.

WAGY, OSCAR - Quincy - Jun 4, 1902   Oscar Wagy,
a resident of Adams Co. since 1832 died at his
home in Plainville, age 76 years.

WALKER, ALFRED - Co. Seat - Apr 22, 1896   Will
of Alfred Walker has been admitted to probate--
leaves 100 acres to widow and 40 acres to

daughter, Sarah Arnold. At widows death her
share goes to son, Charles.

WALKER, MRS MARIA - Elm Grove - Feb 8, 1895
Death of Mrs Maria Walker, wife of J.B. Walker
last Monday night after a short illness.
Services at Elm Grove Church and burial at the
Walker cemetery in the locality. Leaves a
husband, 1 son, Virgil A. Walker of Dodge City,
KS and a daughter, Mrs E.F. Baldwin.

WALKER, MRS SARAH E. - Obituary - Apr 3, 1894
Died Mrs Sarah E. Walker at the home of her son
Samuel Walker March 24th A.M. Cause paralysis.
Funeral by Rev I.M. Johnson and Rev R.A.
Hartick. Born 1826 in state of New York and
with parents came to Brooklyn, Schuyler Co.
Ill. at an early date. Married Alexander
Walker 1849, who died in 1859. Four sons and
their families survive-Roswell N., James R.,
Samuel and Charles N. all of this vicinity.
Elm Grove March 29, 1894

WALLACE, ALLEN - Ancient History - Jun 22, 1894
June 18, 1875 Allen Wallace died.

WALLACE, ALLEN - Ancient History - Jun 25, 1895
June 1875 Allen Wallace died at age 65 years.

WALLACE, MISS ELIZABETH R. - Obituary - May 6,
1903 Miss Elizabeth R. Wallace, daughter of
Thos S. Wallace was born in Wallace home in
vicinity of Clayton Sep 6, 1856 and died
Chicago, Apr 23, 1903. Week before she died
she went to Chicago for a surgical operation.
Remains brought to family home and funeral by
her minister Rev T.A. McKernon. Buried Wallace
cemetery.

WALLACE, FRED E. - Quincy - Jul 5, 1895 Fred
E. Wallace died in St Mary's Hospital Wednesday
from an overdose of morphine. It is unknown
whether he intended suicide. He was a
confirmed drunkard.

WALLACE, FULLER - Local - Oct 26, 1894 Fuller
Wallace age 38 was run over by a train (after

drinking) at LaGrange Monday eve.

WALLACE, MRS ISABELLA - Death - Mar 19, 1902
Mrs Isabella Wallace, widow of the late Jason
Wallace, died in Clayton on the 7th., 84 years
old. Was sister of A.R. Wallace, of Camp Point
twp. Lived in house where she died 52 years.
Leaves 1 daughter, Mrs Isabella Moffett.

WALLACE, JAMES A. - Probate Notice - May 13,
1896 James A. Wallace, deceased   1st Monday
of July 1896 (6th) John M. Wallace, adm.

WALLACE, JAMES A. - Adm's Sale of Real Estate
Feb 5, 1902 January term--Adm sale of the
estate of James A. Wallace, deceased against
Mary P. Wallace and others, I will on 15th of
Feb 1902 at 2 P.M. sell at public vendue.
Walter B. Wallace, adm.

WALLACE, JAMES A. JR. - Obituary - Apr 8, 1896
Died James A. Wallace Jr. Tuesday A.M. at his
home 3 miles north of Camp Point of pneumonia.
Was son of the late Mason Wallace and a nephew
of James A. and A.R. Wallace. 60 years old
(about). Spent most of his life in this
vicinity. Leaves a wife, 4 sons and 1
daughter. Funeral from the family home at 9:30
A.M. Thursday and buried at the family burying
ground on Jas. A. Wallace's premises.

WALLACE, JAMES ANDERSON - Obituary - Apr 22,
1896 Died on evening of the 6th inst at his
home 3 miles north of Camp Point of pneumonia,
James Anderson Wallace age 59 years 14 days.
Born at old homestead 2 miles south of Golden
on the farm now occupied by Mr Mason Wallace on
March 22, 1837. On March 26, 1863 he married
Miss Martha Jane Millen who still lives. They
had 4 sons and 2 daughters, eldest daughter
died when quite young, rest survive him.

WALLACE, JASON I. - Ancient History - May 26,
1897 - February 1880 Jason I. Wallace died at
his home near Golden.

WALLACE, MISS JENNIE - Died in Tennessee - Sep

15, 1897 Miss Jennie Wallace, the younger
daughter of Mr and Mrs Thos. S. Wallace of
Concord twp. She went to Missouri a few weeks
ago to visit and then to visit her brother Reid
at Idaville, Tenn. where she was taken down
with typhoid fever. She died Thursday eve of
last week. Remains arrived here Tuesday and
funeral at 11 A.M. Monday at the family home in
Concord twp by Rev M.W. Lorimer. Buried
Wallace graveyard nearby. Was 23 years 1 month
15 days old. "Clayton Enterprise"

WALLACE, MRS MARY E. - Death of Mrs Wallace -
Mar 18, 1896 Died Mrs Mary E. Wallace, widow
of the late Allen Wallace in Quincy at the home
of her sister, Mrs John Cranston on the 11th
inst of paralysis of the brain. She was
daughter of the late Rev Jesse Cromwell a
resident of Clayton twp many years. Married in
1859 to Allen Wallace who died in 1876. In her
71st year. Remains brought to Camp Point and
taken to Hebron cemetery Thursday for burial.
Four brothers and 3 sisters survive her.

WALLACE, REV PETER - Death Record - Mar 3, 1897
Died Rev Peter Wallace in Chicago Sunday night,
the 2st ult in his 84th year. Had been a
methodist minister over 60 years. Leaves a
wife and 2 daughters, Mrs J.H. Clark and Mrs
Frank Arrowsmith, both of Quincy.

WALLACE, MRS WM - Ancient History - Jul 14,
1897 - September 1880 Mrs Wm Wallace died on
the 19th.

WALLACE, MRS WILLIAM - Ancient History - Oct
16, 1894 - October 14, 1880 Mrs William Wallace
died on Sept. 19th.

WALLEY, MRS MARY - Local - Feb 4, 1903 Mrs
Mary Walley died at Hattiesburg, Miss., Friday
Jan 30th about 60 years old. She was sister of
Mrs M.C. Chase who was with her 2 or 3 weeks
before her death.

WALLIN, MRS MARIE J. - Co. Cullings - Dec 21,
1893 Quincy Mrs Marie J. Wallin, age 48 died

at Blessing Hospital Sunday after a weeks
illness with bronchial asthma.   Native of
France and had lived this city many years.   Was
widow of the late James H. Wallin, a life long
newspaper reporter.

WALTERS, MRS CHRISTINE - Local - Apr 9, 1902
Mr and Mrs Geo. C. Bartells were called to
Bushnell Tuesday A.M. by the death of Mrs
Bartells mother, Mrs Christine Walters, 82
years old.   Was mother of 10 children, 8 of
whom and aged husband survives her.   Husband is
2 years her senior.

WALTZ, FREDERICK - Quincy - May 21, 1902
Frederick Waltz, a former well known young
resident of this city, died in the hospital at
El Paso, Texas on Thursday.

WARD, MRS DORA - Local - Dec 24, 1895   Mrs Dora
Ward, wife of William T. Ward died in
Georgetown, Colo. November 27th age 29 years.
She was Miss Dora Hartman and was married in
Georgetown.

WARD, DR F.D. - Ancient History - Mar 23, 1894
March 21, 1879 Dr F.D. Ward who went from Camp
Point to Golden, Colo. fell into a basement and
was killed.

WARD, O.B. - 10 Years Ago - Sep 28, 1893   O.B.
Ward and Charley Johnson were poisoned by
drinking bitters and both died.

WARMKER, CHARLES H. - Quincy - Jan 20, 1897
Charles H. Warmker, an old resident of the city
died Wednesday night age 80 years.

WARMKER, CHARLES H. - Co. Seat - Feb 3, 1897
The will of Charles H. Warmker divides the
estate equally among his 6 children share and
share alike.   Appoints Mary C. Warmker, ex.

WARREN, ANSEL - 10 Years Ago - Feb 13, 1894
Ansel Warren died at the home of his niece, Mrs
J.F. Linn in his 85th year.   He was one of the
old time printers.

WARREN, ANSEL - Ancient History - Feb 5, 1902
February 1884 Ansel Warren, an old printer died
on the 2nd in his 85th year.

WARREN, CALVIN A. - Ancient History - Aug 25,
1897 February 1881 Calvin A. Warren, a
prominent attorney of Quincy died.

WARREN, CHARLES A. - Quincy - Nov 20, 1894
Charles A. Warren age 20 a student died
Thursday. Remains sent to the family home in
Armstrong, Vermillion Co.

WARTICK, SIMON - Death Record - Dec 1, 1897
Simon Wartick died at his home in Sect 5 Camp
Point twp Monday the 29th ult of dropsy. Was
about 55 years old. Leaves a wife and several
children. Buried Coatsburg Cemetery Tuesday
P.M.

WATERS, ISAAC - Quincy - Jul 5, 1895 Will of
Isaac Waters admitted to probate. Leaves 250
acre home farm and his farm in Pike Co. to his
widow and income to be used to support herself
and a daughter Mary. At the death of Mrs
Waters the income to be used to support Mary.
At Mary's death to be divided among other 4
children share and share alike.

WATSON, D.K. - Death Record - Mar 3, 1897 Died
D.K. Watson, an old citizen died Saturday A.M.
Feb 19th at the home of Judson Davis, 4 miles
east of Clayton, about 80 years old. Leaves 2
son, Albert and Mark and 1 daughter Mrs Judson
Davis at whose home he died. Wife died some
years ago and he was buried beside her in
Mounds cemetery on the 22nd.

WATSON, DR LOUIS - Quincy - Sep 28, 1894 Dr
Louis Watson, an old resident of this city, who
died in Ellis, KS was buried here yesterday
under the auspices of Bodley Lodge A.F. and
A.M.

WATTMAN, FRANK - Local - Jan 2, 1894 Frank
Wattman, son of a farmer living north of Quincy
was thrown from a horse Thursday and fatally

injured.

WATTMAN, FRANK - Local - Jan 2, 1894 Frank
Wattman son of a farmer living north of Quincy
was thrown from a horse and drug, skull
fractured.

WEAR, D.C. - Paloma - Sep 2, 1896   D.C. Wear
and family attended the funeral of his brother,
near Liberty, Sunday.

WEBB, KATIE - Columbus - May 28, 1895 Died
Katie, daughter of Mr and Mrs James Webb of
brain trouble Sat. A.M. age 3 years 2 months.

WEBB, KATIE - Columbus - May 28, 1895 Died
early Saturday A.M. May 25th Katie, only
daughter of Isaac and Susan Webb age 3 years.
Services at the home on Sunday at 2 P.M. by Rev
F. Booth.

WEBBER, ALBERT - Quincy - Apr 3, 1894 Albert
Webber a molder at the Smith-Hill Foundry
received a letter from the Swiss Consul. that
he will come into the possession of a
considerable fortune thru the death of a
relative in Switzerland.

WEBBER, FREDERICK - Quincy - Oct 7, 1903
Arthur C. Webber, adm of the estate of
Frederick Webber has filed suit against C.B. &
Q. railroad for $10,000 damages for killing of
Frederick Webber at a railroad crossing near
Quincy several months ago.

WEBER, MRS BERTHA - Quincy - Feb 26, 1902 Will
of Mrs Bertha Weber gives to Carrie Worth,
Helen and Margaret Heuer, Mary Wehmeyer and the
children of deceased sister, Mrs Regina
Wehmeyer. E.H. Osborn, executor   Estate
valued at $70,000 to $80,000.

WEBER, BERTHA - Quincy - Oct 22, 1902 In Adams
Co. court Wednesday it was ordered that E.H.
Osborn, as adm. of the estate of Bertha Weber,
should file an additional $80,000 bond before
making the sale of the Tremont Hotel.

WEBER, FREDERICK S. - Killed by Train - Jul 22,
1903 Frederick S. Weber, a prosperous farmer
living 5 miles west of Ursa was killed near
Quincy by the afternoon passenger train. Weber
was driving a pair of horses to a buggy and was
caught on the crossing.

WEBER, MRS HERMAN - Local - Aug 3, 1893 Mrs
Herman Weber, nee Lizzie Seaton, died at her
home in Quincy Sunday. She was daughter of the
late Kenner Seaton of Camp Point. An internal
cancer caused her death. Buried Woodland
cemetery Monday afternoon.

WEBSTER, MRS - Primrose - Oct 11, 1895 Mrs
J.S. Laront was called to Colchester Friday to
attend the funeral of her mother, Mrs Webster.

WEBSTER, JACK - Primrose - Feb 8, 1895 Jack
Webster whose suicide was reported in Tuesday's
journal was a brother of Mrs J.S. Laront of
York Neck. Mrs Laront attended the funeral at
Colchester.

WEBSTER, JOHN N. - Suicide a Galesburg - Feb 5,
1895 John N. Webster for many years conductor
on the Q. committed suicide Sunday A.M. by
shooting himself in the head. Ill health from
an accident the probable cause.

WEBSTER, MRS MAHALA - Death - Mar 12, 1902 Mrs
Mahala Webster died Saturday A.M. from attack
of appendicitis, grippe and pneumonia at the
home of her parents, Mr and Mrs John Wimer.
Born Ind. Nov 1, 1858. Came to Ill. as a
child. Lived Camp Point many years. Married
twice, 1st to Charles Holden and 2nd to John W.
Webster in Oct 1900. Funeral at parents home
Sunday 3 P.M. by Rev C.N. Cain. Buried village
cemetery.

WEBSTER, MRS MAY - Local - Mar 12, 1902 Mrs
Sarah Thrush of Quincy came Saturday and
remained over Sunday to attend the funeral of
her cousin, Mrs May Webster.

WEERTS, W.J. - Local - Nov 1, 1895   W.J.

Weerts, a German farmer of Columbus twp died
Wednesday eve after a brief illness. About 54
years old. Leaves a wife, daughter and 5 sons.
Funeral at Coatsburg today.

WEIDENHAMMER, JOHN C. - Quincy - Aug 13, 1902
John C. Weidenhammer, a resident conductor
formerly of this city, died in Galesburg age 54
years.

WEIER, JOHN - Co. Seat - May 13, 1896 Died
John Weier a resident of this city for nearly a
half century died Tuesday night of last week.
age 78 years.

WEIHL, CATHERINE - Quincy - Aug 20, 1902 Will
of Catherine Weihl of Columbus left her entire
estate to A.M. Earel.

WEIS, MRS CHRIS - Quincy - Jan 12, 1894 Died
Mrs Chris Weis age 34 Sunday A.M.

WEISHEIT, CHRISTIAN T. - Probate Notice - Jan
19, 1894 Christian T. Weisheit, deceased 1st
Monday of March 1894 John W. Weisheit, adm.

WELLS, SENATOR ALBERT W. - Death Record - Mar
10, 1897 Died Friday Senator Albert W. Wells
at his home in Quincy. Born S. Woodstock,
Conn. May 9, 1841. Came to Quincy 1870.
Funeral Sunday at Cong'l Church.

WELLS, MISS MAGGIE - She Took Strychnine - May
20, 1896 Miss Maggie Wells lived with her
parents on what is known as the Persley farm
between Pittsfield and Barry. Left a note to
her brother that she had committed suicide by
taking strychnine because her parents didn't
treat her right.

WELLS, MRS MARY B. - Local - Mar 30, 1894 Died
Mrs Mary B. Wells, widow of the late Edward
Wells dropped dead in her home in Quincy
Tuesday in her 75th year.

WELSH, MRS GEORGE - Local - Jul 6, 1893 Mrs
George Welsh died at Cameron, MO June 24th.

She was a sister of Mrs Wm Haley of Camp Point.
Leaves husband and 9 children.

WELSH, MRS JAMES G. - Local - Jul 27, 1894
Died Mrs James G. Welsh died Thursday about 78
years old. Leaves aged husband, 4 sons and 4
daughters. Funeral at the family home at 4
P.M. this afternoon.

WELSH, JAMES G. - Obituary - Sep 2, 1896 Died
James G. Welsh died Monday Aug 31st. Sick
several weeks at his residence in Camp Point.
Services Tuesday from his home buried beside
his wife who died nearly 2 years ago. Born
Jefferson Co. KY June 25, 1811. Was eldest son
of Robert and Mary Welsh. Married Sarah Booth
Aug 14, 1834 and soon came to Ill. Settled
Camp Point twp 1836. They had 4 sons and 4
daughters all were at his bedside.

WELSH, JAMES G. - Probate Notice - Oct 7, 1896
James G. Welsh, deceased 1st Monday of
December 1896 (7th) R.W. Garrett, Ex.

WELSH, JOHN M.C. - Death - Jan 14, 1903 John
M.C. Welsh born in Camp Point Jan 29, 1849 and
died in Quincy Jan 8, 1903. His wife died May
17, 1890 and left him 4 little children.
Services at home of his sister, Mrs Geo. C.
Bobbitt, Camp Point Saturday P.M. by Rev F.A.
McGaw.

WELSH, WILLIAM - Ancient History - Apr 6, 1894
April 6, 1882 William Welsh was killed by a
train at Bluffs.

WERTZ, MR - Columbus - Nov 8, 1895 Mr Wertz
died at his home in Columbus twp from injuries
received when thrown from his wagon 2 weeks
ago. Funeral at Coatsburg the 1st. Buried in
that cemetery. He was 54 years old. Leaves a
wife, 4 sons and 1 daughter.

WESHON, AARON - North Houston - Aug 26, 1896
The infant child of Aaron Weshon was buried at
the Ebenezer cemetery last Tuesday.

WESKINS, H.H. - Quincy - Dec 18, 1894 Died
H.H. Weskins, an old resident of the city died
Tuesday eve, age 73 years.

WESSELS, FRED - 10 Years Ago - Jan 16, 1894
Fred Wessels of Golden committed suicide.

WEST, MRS HENRY - Local - Apr 27, 1893 Mrs
Henry West died Tuesday afternoon from
consumption resulting from an atack of the
grippe. Leaves husband and 4 children. Her
maiden name was Kesting and she was reared in
Concord twp.

WEST, MR AND MRS LAFE - Child Burned to Death
Mar 10, 1897 2 year old son of Mr and Mrs Lafe
West, of Big Neck was burned Friday. Died a
few hours later. It appears he was playing
with matches. Father runs a general store and
is postmaster of Big Neck. Buried Ebenezer
cemetery Saturday A.M.

WEST, MRS MARY E. - Died - Apr 27, 1893 Died
of consumption April 24th at her home in Camp
Point, Mrs Mary E. West, wife of Henry West
whom she leaves with 4 children, 35 years old.
Been poor health a year or more. Came to Camp
Point with her husband and children from
Missouri December 1892. Funeral from her home
on Jefferson St. Wednesday April 26th by Elder
O. Dilley. Buried Ausmus cemetery.

WETTSTEIN, HENRY - Quincy - Mar 2, 1894 Died
one of the Franciscan brethren died at the
monks monastery Sunday eve. His former name
was Henry Wettstein and he lived in Alton
before entering the monastery.

WETZEL, ANDREW - Quincy - Dec 14, 1894 Died
Andrew Wetzel a former citizen of Quincy died
at the insane asylum at Jacksonville and buried
here Tuesday.

WHALEN, JOHN - Local - Dec 27, 1895 John
Whalen was killed Sat. at Colchester by a train
while attempting to cross in front of it. Was
24 years old. On the same day George Hixon was

killed at Abingdon. He was deaf and did not
hear the train.

WHEAT, ALMERON - Almeron Wheat Dead - Jul 19,
1895 Almeron Wheat died Tuesday A.M. at his
home in Quincy, age 82 years. Born near
Auburn, N.Y. Mar 7, 1813. When 14 years old he
left home and became a country school teacher.
Later attended Low academy near Auburn.
Settled Quincy 1839 and married shortly after.
Lived 47 years on 8th St. where they celebrated
their golden wedding. Leaves a wife and 4
children. Children are: Mrs E.M. Miller,
Almeron Wheat Jr. and Hiram R. Wheat of Quincy
and Mrs W.M. Whittlesey of Rochester, N.Y.
Services at the house P.M. Friday.

WHEAT, MRS JOSEPHINE - Quincy - Dec 17, 1902
Mrs Josephine Wheat, a well known Quincy lady,
who died in Chicago on Tuesday was buried here
Friday.

WHEELER, MRS ELIZABETH - Livingston - Jun 15,
1893 The mortal remains of Elizabeth, widow of
the late Ferdinand Wheeler passed thru this
nieghborhood at noon Thursday. She was buried
in Burton cemetery.

WHEELER, GEORGE - Quincy - Oct 1, 1902 George
Wheeler, age 42 years formerly a farmer living
near Newtown left here on Sunday eve for Raton,
N.M. for his health. Died there Wednesday A.M.
Remains brought to Quincy for burial.

WHEELER, MR AND MRS J.A. - Card of Thanks - Jan
12, 1893 Thanks to friends and neighbors for
help during sickness and death of our babe.
Mr and Mrs J.A. Wheeler.

WHEELER, J. FRANK - Local - Mar 12, 1902 J.
Frank Wheeler, son of John Wheeler, of Quincy
died in New York City Sat. night, 59 years old.

WHEELER, MRS J.O. - Death - Jan 22, 1902 Lou
Alva Ward born near Mound, Brown Co. Ill. Aug
20, 1873. Came with parents to Camp Point.
Married oct 10, 1890 to J.O. Wheeler, had 5

children. She died Jan 19th at her home in
Camp Point, age 28 years 5 months lacking 1
day. Leaves husband, 5 children, father, mother
and 4 brothers. Funeral at the home by Elder
J. Thos. Webb and Rev C.N. Cain of the
Methodist. Buried village cemetery. Signed
J.O. Wheeler and Mr and Mrs J.W. Ward.

WHEELER, THEODORE - Deaths - Sep 17, 1902
Theodore Wheeler died in Columbus Thursday eve
the 11th inst, age 79 years. Leaves 3 sons,
Joel A. and Jesse of Camp Point, William of
Columbus and 2 daughters, Mrs Emma Pilcher and
Mrs Anna McCann. Services at Columbus
Saturday.

WHIPPLE, MRS W.W. - 10 Years Ago - Feb 2, 1894
Mrs W.W. Whipple died in her 70th year.

WHITE, DICKEY, - From the Necks - Jun 9, 1897
Messrs A.D. Allen and Hez Henry were out Wed.
looking up the estate of Dickey White.

WHITE, UNCLE DICKY - From the Necks - Feb 24,
1897 Died old Uncle Dicky White, an old
resident of Honey Creek and Keene twps died Feb
19th at 1 P.M. at Mrs Polly Asher's, his niece.
 Born Mississippi. Moved with parents to
Alabama when about 5 years. Was 82 years 1
month old. Buried Coatsburg cemetery Feb 21st.

WHITE, MR AND MRS DOUGLAS - Elm Grove - Jan 26,
1894 Douglas White and wife attended the
funeral of a brother of Mrs White's last week,
who lived near Coatsburg.

WHITE, MRS ELIZABETH - Local - Apr 6, 1893 Mrs
Elizabeth White, widow of the late John A.
White died at the family home in Honey Creek,
Friday, March 31st, age 72 years. Born Tenn.
Came to Adams Co. about 60 years ago. Buried
beside her husband in Coatsburg cemetery Sunday
afternoon.

WHITE, GEORGE W. - Co. Seat - Dec 167, 1896
The will of George W. White gives the homestead
to his stepson, Herbert Ferrell, providing he

pay ex fee of $3,000, rest to be devided between the 2 children Louis White and Mary Miller.

WHITE, HUGH A. - Death of Hugh A. White - Mar 27, 1894 Died Hugh A. White, a wealthy Chicago lawyer at his home in Evanston Saturday age 64 years. Born in Adams Co. in 1830. Both parents died when he was small, taken in by an uncle, Moses Guthrie living near Columbus. Leaves a wife had no children.

WHITE, JACKSON - From the Necks - Nov 18, 1896 Jackson White age 91 years was buried at Coatsburg cemetery Saturday. Deceased was the oldest man in Keene twp.

WHITE, JASPER & WILL - Local - Apr 6, 1893 Jasper White of Austin, Texas and Joel White of Cass Co. MO were called to Coatsburg by the death of their mother.

WHITE, THOMAS - Deaths This Week - Apr 8, 1896 Died Thomas White at his home in Quincy Monday afternoon. Been sick a long time. Born Scotland. Came to Quincy 45 years ago to work as a pattern maker in Comstocks Stone Foundry. Later manufactured his own stones. Services this afternoon under charge of Masonic fraternity.

WHITFORD, MR AND MRS DAN - Local - Sep 3, 1895 A little daughter of Mr and Mrs Dan Whitford died Sunday. Buried Monday in Hebron Cemetery.

WHITFORD, MRS GEORGE - Columbus - Feb 19, 1902 Three funerals here last week: Mrs George Whitford of Cliola buried from Christian Church Tuesday Feb 11th. Mrs Elizabeth Judy, widow of the late Phillip S. Judy was buried from Methodist Church Wednesday Feb 12th. Little Thomas Smith on the 15th.

WHITFORD, HENRY S. - Probate Notice - Jun 10, 1896 Henry S. Whitford, deceased 1st Monday of August (3rd) Dora A. Whitford, Ex.

WHITFORD, HENRY S. - Local - May 13, 1896
Henry S. Whitford continues in a critical
condition, all his children except John are
with him. Miss Kate arrived last week from
Philadelphia, James T., Ed C. and Mrs A. Peden
from Fairfax, MO and Mrs John S. Wallace of
Eldorado, KS came also.

WHITFORD, HENRY S. - Local - Jun 3, 1896 Died
Henry S. Whitford Tuesday afternoon about 5:30.
Funeral will be at the residence Thursday at 2
P.M. Burial in Hebron cemetery later.

WHITFORD, HENRY S. - Obituary - Jun 10, 1896
Henry S. Whitford born Rhode Island Dec 6,
1808. Boyhood he was apprenticed to a tailor
in Providence where he worked 9 years. Then to
Ill. 1833 and Clayton twp where he stayed 63
years. Married 3 times, 1st Mary James Oct 20,
1829 who had their 1 daughter, Mary C. Second
to Miss Sarah A. Downing Jan 16, 1840, they had
9 children Albert R., Edward C., John S., James
T., Lydia A. (Peden), Harriet E., Charles G.
and Nancy M. of whom Albert, Lydia, Charles,
Harriet and Nancy are dead. Mrs Whitford died
May 6, 1856. Third he married Miss Myra C.
Clark Feb 7, 1861 who survives him with 5
children: Henry B., Alice E. (Wallace), Dora A,
Fannie C. (Downing) and Daniel W. Funeral at
family home Thursday 2 P.M. by Rev Peter
Slagel. Buried Heron Cemetery.

WHITHOUSE, AUGUST - Run Over by a Train - May
28, 1902 August Whithouse of Troy, Mo age 35,
employed as a laborer on the C.B. & Q was
killed by the cars near LaPrairie 6:20 P.M.
Saturday. Had been drinking and layed down on
the track and fell asleep. Train passed over
the body. Remains taken to Quincy awaiting
disposition from relatives who live at Troy,
MO. He was married, but not living with his
wife. Leaves 2 children, 2 brothers and a
sister. Died May 24th at 6:20 P.M. "Herald"

WHITING, DR - Local - May 4, 1893 Mr and Mrs
George W. Butler went to Canton last week to
attend funeral of their old friend and pastor,

Dr Whiting.

WHITLOCK, MR AND MRS - Columbus - Feb 2, 1894
One of Mr and Mrs Whitlock's twins were buried
here Friday the 26th.

WHITLOCK, MRS D. - Local - Dec 2, 1896 Mrs D.
Whitlock died at her home in Columbus Sunday,
after illness of several weeks.

WHITLOCK, MRS DERRICK - Oakwood - Dec 2, 1896
Died Mrs Derrick Whitlock of Columbus died
Sunday eve at Paloma. Funeral from Columbus ME
Church and buried beside her husband in the
village cemetery.

WHITLOCK, MRS GEORGE - Columbus - Jan 30, 1894
One of the twin babies of Mr and Mrs George
Whitlock of Cliola died Wednesday and buried
here Thursday.

WIEL, HENRY - Quincy - Aug 4, 1897 Henry Wiel,
formerly of Beardstown died at St Vincent's
home Friday, age 87 years.

WIER, DR W.A. - Local - Sep 28, 1893 Dr W.A.
Wier, who practiced medicine in Camp Point 10
years ago died at Carthage on the 15th inst of
consumption. Wife and 2 children survive him.
He spent some time in New Mexico in hopes of
regaining his health, but with out effect.

WIGLE, SOLOMON - Ancient History - Nov 2, 1894
October 31, 1879 Solomon Wigle died at Clayton.

WILCOX, DANIEL - Ancient History - Jan 27, 1897
May 1878 Daniel Wilcox prop. of the Quincy
Whig died.

WILCOX, MESHA_ - Ancient History - Jun 25, 1895
June 1880 Mesha_ Wilcox was found dead in his
bed.

WILCOX, MESHAC - Ancient History - Jun 23, 1897
June 1880 Meshac Wilcox was found dead in his
bed.

WILD, MRS - Local - Jul 30, 1902 Mrs Wild, an aged German woman who has lived many years in Columbus twp died Friday night, 90 years old. Leaves 1 son Fred Wild who is an inmate at the insane dept at the poor farm.

WILD, HENRY - Obituary - Apr 3, 1894 Died, Henry Wild born Jan 6, 1848 at New Orleans. Married Miss Angeline Viar 1873 and died at his home 6 miles SE of Camp Point Mar 29, 1894. Leaves a wife and his aged mother and dependant brother. Funeral at Union Church Saturday March 31 by Elder O. Dilley. Buried in small cemetery by the church.

WILD, HENRY - Death of Henry Wild - Mar 30, 1894 Died Henry Wild, a well known resident of Columbus twp died Thursday from the effects of an overdose of morphine. Had been a hard drinker for years, being almost always under the influence of liquor, but had a short time ago stopped. Was of German parentage.

WILKE, CHRISTIAN - Local - Feb 16, 1894 Dead, Christian Wilke, a german farmer of Columbus twp was found dead in his bed Monday A.M. Cause-heart disease.

W1LKES, DANIEL - 20 Years Ago - Jun 22, 1893 Daniel Wilkes, one of the pioneers of this neighborhood died at the age of 68 years.

WILKES, DANIEL - Ancient History - Jun 10, 1903 June 1873 Daniel Wilkes died on the 22nd. He was one of the earliest settlers of Camp Point twp.

WILKES, JAMES - Local - Dec 21, 1894 Died James Wilkes, a son of John Wilkes died Wednesday night. Funeral today at 10.

WILKES, JAMES - Columbus - Dec 28, 1894 James Wilkes of Camp Point was buried in village cemetery Friday.

WILKINSON, FRED - Local - May 13, 1903 Fred Wilkinson of St Joseph, MO was called to

Coatsburg last week by the death of his father.

WILKINSON, LEWIS - Ancient History - Aug 12, 1903 - August 1893 Lewis Wilkinson, age 18 years was killed by falling between 2 coal cars while a train was switching.

WILKINSON, LEWIS - Killed at Coatsburg - Aug 17, 1893 Dave Webster's way freight killed Lewis Wilkinson, a youth of 18 years at Coatsurg Wednesday A.M. He was son of Moses Wilkinson, section foreman from Coatsburg to Paloma. He was run over by the train and died within a few minutes.

WILKINSON, LEWIS E. - Under the Wheels - Aug 13, 1893 Wednesday A.M. about 8, Lewis E. Wilkinson, eldest son of Mr and Mrs Wilkinson was killed at this place by an east bound freight train. Lewis was on top doing some switching when he fell between the cars and instantly killed. Was 19 years old. Services by Rev Miner of Camp Point at Christian Church Thursday 3 P.M. Buried in village cemetery. Article dated August 21st.

WILKINSON, MOSES - Local - May 6, 1903 Moses Wilkinson, liveryman at Coatsburg, died suddenly Saturday night from apoplexy.

WILKINSON, MOSES -Full of Years - May 6, 1903 Moses Wilkinson, the well known Coatsburg liveryman died of apoplexy at his home about 7 A.M. Sunday. Was about 55 years old. Leaves a wife and family.

WILLARD, MR - West Point - May 3, 1895 Mrs J.H. Wolf and Mrs William Ward attended the funeral of their uncle, Mr Willard, of Camp Point Sunday.

WILLARD, MISS AMANDA - Fairview - Apr 15, 1903 Bert Willard was called to LaHarpe last week on account of the death of French Butler. Mrs Butler was formerly Miss Amanda Willard.

WILLARD, MRS EDWIN - Local - Mar 5, 1902 Mr

and Mrs Charles Connor of New Philadelphia,
McDonough Co. came down Saturday to attend
funeral of Mrs Edwin Willard at Ebenezer
Church, Houston. Mrs Conner and Mrs Willard
were sisters.

WILLARD, MRS JOHN - Death of Mrs John Willard
Mar 16, 1894 Died, Rebecca Ann McFarland born
Green Co. Ohio Jul 21, 1817 died at the home of
her son James H. Willard, Houston twp Mar 13,
1894 age 76 years 6 months 20 days. Came to
Camp Point twp with parents, Capt John and
Rebecca McFarland Oct 8, 1832. Married John
Willard Dec 29, 1836. Married John Willard Dec
29, 1836. Mr Willard died in Houston twp about
4 years ago. Two sons, William M. and James H.
of Houston twp and Mrs R.A. Crum of Camp Point,
and one dead daughter were her children. Two
brothers and 1 sister left, William M.
McFarland of Houston, Daniel G. McFarland and
Mrs Priscilla Powers of Camp Point. Joined
Methodist Church at Hebron and baptized in Bear
Creek north of the church. Funeral at Ebenezer
Church Houston twp and buried beside her
husband.

WILLARD, MADISON - Adm Sale - Aug 28, 1894
Sept 25th at the late home of Madison Willard,
deceased on the NE 1/4 of Sect 10 Houston twp
Adams Co. his personal property. Almira W.
Miller, adm.

WILLARD, MADISON - Local - Aug 10, 1894 Word
received Thursday at Camp Point that Madison
Willard fell dead while harrowing on his farm
in Houston twp Thursday A.M. from heart
disease, 72 years old. Spent about 60 years of
his life in Houston. Wife dead many years.
Leaves 1 daughter Mrs L.W. Miller.

WILLARD, MADISON - Funeral of Madison Willard
Aug 14, 1894 Funeral of Madison Willard was
from his home in Houston twp Saturday at 11
A.M. by Elder O. Dilley buried Ebenezer
cemetery. Born in Clay Co. MO Nov 25, 1820.
Came to Ill. with his parents when a lad and
settled Houston. Married 1855 to Miss Lucinda

Taylor of New York who died 10 years later.
They had 1 daughter, Mrs Lawrence W. Miller who
survives him.

WILLARD, MADISON - Probate Notice - Aug 17,
1894 Madison Willard, deceased 1st Monday of
October, 1894 Almira W. Miller, adm.

WILLARD, REBECCA A. - Probate Notice - Aug 7,
1894 Rebecca A. Willard, deceased 1st Monday
of October, 1894 W.M. Willard, adm.

WILLARD, SAMANTHA SUMMERS - Obituary - Mar 17,
1897 Died Samantha Summers Willard, born in
Tenn. Jul 12, 1827 died Hannibal, MO Mar 2,
1897 age 69 years 7 months 20 days. Her family
moved to Adams Co. 1832. Married Dec 28, 1848
to Albert Hoyt, had 7 children, 4 of these and
her husband survive her. She was the youngest
of 9 children, 5 dying before her. Her
father's house was the regular stopping place
of the Methodist preachers who visited the
community. Services at Ebenezer Church Adams
Co. Ill. and buried there.

WILLARD, MRS SALOMA S. - Death - Mar 5, 1902
Saloma S., wife of Edwin Willard and daughter
of Andrew Decker born Sep 6, 1866 at Camp
Dennison, Hamilton Co. Ohio and came with
parents to Ill. 1872 to Camp Point twp.
Married Edwin Willard Nov 8, 1893 at Carthage.
After 8 years of married life she had a little
girl, but was not permitted to live and enjoy
her. Babe 4 weeks old at her death which
occured on Feb 28th, 1902 age 35 years 5 months
22 days. Leaves husband, 4 brothers, 3
sisters, father and infant daughter. Services
at Ebenezer Church, Houston twp Sunday 11 A.M.
by Rev C.F. Stecher of Camp Point and Rev L.A.
Powell, of Bowen.

WILLARD, MRS WILLIAM - Death of Mrs Willard -
Jan 22, 1895 Mrs William Willard died Friday
A.M. at her home in Houston twp where she lived
for nearly 60 years. Funeral from Ebenezer
Church Sunday 11 A.M. Leaves aged husband and
2 children - William H. Williard and Mrs

Virginia Eckles, both of Houston twp.

WILLARD, MRS WILLIAM - Local - Jan 22, 1895
Sam Woods of Quincy came up Saturday eve and
attended the funeral of Mrs William Willard at
Ebenezer Sunday.

WILLARD, WILLIAM - A Pioneer Gone - Apr 30,
1895 William Willard, one of the oldest
residents of Houston twp died on the 27th inst
in his 84th year. Came to Adams Co. as a young
man with parents from Tenn. and settled Houston
twp 1832 lived there since. He leaves a son,
William H. and a daughter Mrs Virginia Eckles,
his wife died last winter. Lived on farm where
he died about 60 years. Of his father's family
2 brothers remain, Samuel and Thomas both of
Houston, Mrs J.H. McFarland of Camp Point and
Mrs Albert Hoyt of Oklahoma. Services at
Ebenezer Church Sunday afternoon.

WILLARD, WILLIAM - Will of William Willard -
May 3, 1895 The last will of the late William
Willard of Houston, who died April 27th was
probated Wednesday. He leaves all his personal
and chattel property to his wife absolutely and
the use of his real estate for life. At her
death it is to be devided between her son
William H. Willard and his daughter, Mrs W.F.
Eckles. The will was made March 15th, 1886 and
witnessed by H.H. Emminga and William Hanna.

WILLIAMS, ELI - Died - Oct 22, 1895 Died at
Carthage, Ill last week, Eli Williams 82 years
old. Dropped dead while walking in his yard.
For more than 40 years he was the village
tailor and lived same cottage for more than 50
years. His wife died many years ago and he
never spoke of his early life. Never received
one letter in his 50 years here. Leaves 1
daughter who went mad soon after her mother
died.

WILLIAMS, FRANCIS MARION - Death - Apr 9, 1902
Francis Marion Williams died March 29th at 10
P.M. very suddenly of rheumatism of the heart,

72 years old. Had spent evening with son,
Warren. Born near Rock Creek, Adams Co. Oct
24, 1830. Married Jane Dayton of Liberty twp
and lived that twp till the early 70's when he
moved to Camp Point. Then went to Quincy until
fall of 1892 when he moved to Lordsburg, Calif.
Leaves his widow and 2 sons, Hobart and Warren,
brothers and sisters in Ill., Missouri and
Nebraska. Services Tuesday April 1st.

WILLIAMS, FRANK - Quincy - Jun 8, 1894 Frank
Williams, the Quincy painter who was killed by
an accident in St Louis, was buried here
Tuesday.

WILLIAMS, FRANK M. - Local - Apr 2, 1902
Telegram received Sunday by David Allen of the
sudden death Saturday of Frank M. Williams at
Lordsburg, Calif. Mr Williams formerly lived
in the J.E. Funk farm east of town and was
reared in vicinity of Liberty. Was nearly 70
years old. Leaves a wife and 2 sons.

WILLIAMS, MRS HARRIET SAWINS - Death - Sep 3,
1895 Died at the home of her son at Nebo,
Ill., P.M. of Aug 14th Mrs Harriet Sawins
Williams, of Newtown, Ill. 78 years old. Had
been an invalid several years. Buried in
little hillside cemetery near where she died.
Four children survive her: Dr W.T. Williams of
Nebo at whose home she died, Miss Martha
Williams of Chicago, Mrs John C. Collett of
Callao, MO, Mrs Jos. F. Slipper of Liberty,
Ill.

WILLIAMS, JOHN - Murder - Feb 2, 1893 John
Williams was a few years ago a prominent figure
in Quincy. He was a boilermaker, growing rich,
had a happy family. Business reversed and he
started drinking and left Quincy. The St Louis
Globe Democrat of Monday says he was killed by
2 sandbaggers there Sunday night. He was a
saloon keeper and had closed for the night.
Died Monday A.M. at 2:15 in the hospital. Was
born in Ireland. Came to Quincy 1855. Wife
was Miss Eliza Redmond, a daughter of a
prominent Irish family.

WILLIAMS, MISS OLLIE - Ancient History - Feb 22, 1895 - February 1878 Miss Ollie Williams died on the 2nd.

WILLIAMS, PETER - Death - Jan 29, 1895 Peter Williams died at the home of his son in law B. Boren, Liberty twp Friday night, 85 years old. Settled Liberty 1840.

WILLIAMS, DR RICHARD - Local - Apr 27, 1893 Dr Richard Williams died at Marcelline Thursday. Had lived Adams Co. 50 years. Was about 70 years old.

WILLIAMS, STANTON MCCOY - Local - Oct 28, 1903 Stanton McCoy Williams, little son of Mr and Mrs Hobart M. Williams died at Lordsburg, Calif. Oct 20th from the effects of the poisoning from eating green figs.

WILLIAMSON, JAMES - Killed by Cars - May 7, 1902 James Williamson, a young man whose home was at Clayton, was killed between Bardolph and Macomb Monday night of last week by falling between the cars while riding on the front end of the mail car. Remains were brought to Clayton Wednesday for burial.

WILLIAMSON, JOHN R. - Death - Mar 5, 1895 John R. Williamson died at his home in Liberty twp Sunday March 3rd of consumption, age 40 years. Lived Liberty twp nearly his whole life. Leaves a wife and 3 children. Funeral will be at Catholic Church in Liberty today.

WILSON, COL. - Deeds Must be Delivered - Nov 8, 1895 Col. Wilson about 4 years prior to his death deeded his large farm in Bethel twp McDonough Co. to his daughter Lizzie and his sons Ed and Samuel. Col. Wilson died at Colchester Nov 30, 1893. Some other children protested will and had it thrown out. Farm divided equally by court.

WILSON, DR - Local - Apr 27, 1894 Dr Wilson of Quincy committed suicide Wednesday by taking morphine.

WILSON, MRS DARLEY - Quincy - Nov 8, 1895 Mrs
Darley Wilson, one of the early settlers of
Adams Co. died at Loraine, age 75 years.

WILSON, DAVID B. - Death Record - Aug 18, 1897
David B. Wilson died at Clayton last Wednesday
the 11th inst age 60 years. Lived Clayton last
8 years. Previous to that he had been a
railroad conductor. Services Thursday
afternoon. Remains brought to Camp Point to be
taken to East Dubuque for burial.

WILSON, JOHN G. - Comm. Sale of Real Estate -
Mar 30, 1893 March term of Adams Co. Circuit
Court Mary Huddleston, David J. Huddleston,
Ida Ratiff and Ira Ratiff as complainants vs
Ruth Wilson, Andrew J. Wilson, Rhoda Wilson,
Douglas Wilson and Andrew J. Wilson, as adm of
the estate of John G. Wilson, deceased #4417
partition.

WlLSON, WILLIAM - Ancient History - Apr 21,
1897 - Sep. 1879 William Wilson of North East
killed his step father, Samuel Hinkson in a
quarrel, by striking him in the head with an
ax.

WIMP, JESSE - Killed at Colusa - Nov 29, 1895
Jesse Wimp, a prominent stockman and farmer of
Colusa was killed Thursday A.M. by the Carthage
train at a crossing near his home. 55 years
old and quite wealthy.

WING, MRS THEODORE - Clayton - Sep 28, 1894
Died, Mrs Theodore Wing at the family home in
this twp Saturday A.M. of typhoid fever.

WINGET, MRS ZENOS - Recent Death - Oct 14, 1896
Mrs Zenos Winget of Burton twp died Monday
night during confinement. She was a sister of
Mrs D. Hunsaker and at one time lived in Camp
Point. Was mother of 10 children.

WINKELMAN, CHARLES H. - Quincy - Jul 19, 1895
Remains of Charles H. Winkleman formerly of
Quincy who died suddenly while camping out near
Meredosia. Was buried here Tuesday.

WINTER, SOUVNOUR - Local - Oct 2, 1894 Died
Sunday Sept 16th Souvnour Winter, son of Judge
J.S. Winter of Lewiston from a accidental gun
shot wound at Table Grove. "Rushville Citizen"

WINTERS, WILLIAM H. - Quincy - Feb 11, 1903
William H. Winters, who recently returned to
Quincy from Denver, after an absence of 20
years was stricken with paralysis on Thursday
and died following day, age 63 years.

WISDOM, JOHN R. - Quincy - Aug 12, 1903 1500
employees of the lumber co. at Mount Cloud,
Calif. have asked for the privilege of erecting
a monument to the memory of it late Supt. John
R. Wisdom, who was buried here.

WISDOM, JOHN R. - Local - Jul 29, 1903 John R.
Wisdom died in California Monday of typhoid
fever. He was former manager of the Quincy
sawmill and went to Calif. last year.

WISEHART, EDWARD C. - Reviewing Ancient History
May 26, 1897 - October 1879 Edward C. Wisehart
died.

WISEHART, ELIZA - Obituary - Aug 17, 1893
Eliza (Curry) Wisehart was born in Jefferson
Co. KY Dec 11, 1810 and died Camp Point Aug 12,
1893. Came to Columbus with her parent in 1834
and married James Wisehart July 1835. Was
mother of 9 children of whom 7 survive her, all
being with her at death. Member 26 years of
Christian Church. Funeral at Pleasant View
Church Sunday Aug 13th by Rev O. Dilley and
buried in Pleasant View cemetery.

WISEHART, MRS ELIZA - Ancient History - Aug 12,
1903 August 1893 Mrs Eliza Wisehart died on
the 12th.

WISEHART, MRS ELIZA - Local - Aug 17, 1893
John Curry, of Hamilton, spent a few days here
last week having been called to the bedside of
his sister, Mrs Eliza Wisehart, who died
Saturday.

WISEHART, ELIZA C. - Local - Sep 28, 1893 W.N.
Wisehart, as agent for the heirs, will sell the
property of the late Eliza C. Wisehart at
public sale on Thursday Oct 5th at her late
residence.

WISEHART, JAMES - Ancient History - Aug 25,
1897 - February 1881 James Wisehart, an old
settler living near town died.

WISHERD, MISS - Local - Feb 2, 1893 The body
of Miss Wisherd 45 years old was found in a
garrett in Bushnell about noon Friday, frozen
stiff. It was discovered by her brother in an
old back room where she had been living alone.
She was simple minded and preferred to live
alone, rather than the poorhouse. Relatives
missed her 5 or 6 weeks ago and had been
looking for her and thought she left town.

WITT, JACKSON - Local - Jan 20, 1897 Died
Jackson Witt died at his home in Houston twp
recently. He was a son of one of the earliest
settlers in Houston and was the last, but one
of several brothers who were well known
citizens of Keene and Houston.

WITT, JACKSON - North Houston - Feb 3, 1897
Died Jackson Witt died Tuesday Jan 5th. buried
Thursday at York Neck cemetery. Services by
Rice Harris. Leaves a wife, 3 children and
many relatives, all his children are married.

WITT, JOHN J. - Probate Notice - Feb 3, 1897
John J. Witt, deceased 1st Monday of April
1897 D.H. Carlin, adm.

WITT, MARY A. - Card of Thanks - Mar 23, 1893
-- during the recent illness of loss of our
mother. signed Mary A. Witt

WITT, SAMUEL - Local - Jun 29, 1894 Died
Samuel Witt of Big Neck died on Tuesday of this
week, of cancer of the face. Buried York Neck
cemetery Thursday. Was one of the old settlers
of Adams Co.

WITT, SAMUEL - Will of Samuel Witt - Jul 3,
1894 Will of Samuel Witt who died in Keene twp
June 27th was probated last Saturday. Leaves
all his property to his wife at her death, $300
to go to Salena Herring, $300 to Samuel Witt
Jr., $3.00 to Alpha Witt and $100 to Albert
Downing rest divided to his brothers and
sisters.

WITT, SAMUEL - Primrose - Jul 3, 1894 Samuel
Witt was buried at York Neck cemetery Thursday,
64 years old, had lived on one farm in Big Neck
45 years. Services by Rev Rose.

WITT, SAMUEL B. - Probate Notice - Jaul 10,
1894 Samuel B. Witt, deceased   1st Monday of
September 1894 Samuel O. Witt, adm.

WITTY, MISS DORA B. - Death - Nov 12, 1902
Miss Dora B. Witty born in Cass Co. Ill Aug 22,
1871 died Brown Co. Nov 4th, 1902 age 31 years
2 months 12 days. Moved with parents about 10
years ago from Cass Co. to Brown Co. Married
Feb 6, 1895 to Samuel W. McClintock and lived
with him on a farm. Few years ago they moved
to Camp Point. Died at the home of mother and
father. Was eldest of 8 children, 4 boys 4
girls, the other 7 survive her. Services at ME
Chruch Mt Sterling Thursday P.M. Nov 6th 2 P.M.
by Rev N.M. Rigg and Rev C.E. Fulton of Fargo.
Buried city cemetery.

WOLF, WILLIAM - Local - May 10, 1895 Addison
W. Moore received telegram of the death of
William Wolf, his wife's brother in Colorado.
Wolf was a former resident of Kingston, this
county. Was unmarried.

WOLFE, REV DAVID - Ancient History - May 26,
1897 - October 1879 Rev David Wolfe died at
Liberty.

WOOD, MRS CATHERINE - Died - Jan 26, 1893 Mrs
Catherine Wood died Friday the 20th inst after
a short illness. Was widow of James Wood who
died here a few years ago. Funeral at
Presbyterian Church Sunday afternoon by her

pastor Rev E.B. Miner.   Left no children.
Property left will go to the Presbyterian
Church.

WOOD, MRS CATHERINE - Local - Jan 26, 1893   Mr
and Mrs H. Byington of Quincy attended the
funeral of Mrs Catherine Wood, Sunday.

WOOD, CHARLEY - Ancient History - Jun 12, 1894
June 8, 1877 Charley Wood, a former resident of
Camp Point was killed in a railroad yards at
Aurora while working as a brakeman.

WOOD, CHARLEY - Ancient History - Oct 7, 1896
June 1877 Charley Wood, a brakeman on the Q
fell from the train while switching at Rochelle
and was killed. He had lived in Camp Point.

WOOD, CHARLEY - Ancient History - Jun 25, 1895
June 1877 Charley Wood, a Q brakeman was
killed in the Aurora yards.

WOOD, MRS JOSHUA - Quincy - Oct 18, 1895 Mrs
Joshua Wood, a former resident to the city,
died in Galena, KS Friday and was buried here
Sunday.

WOOD, LEWIS - Local - Feb 5, 1902 Miss Zada
Boyle went to Fowler Saturday to attend the
funeral of Lewis Wood which was held Sunday in
Ellington twp.

WOOD, LOUIS E. - Died of his Wound - Feb 5,
1902 Louis E. Wood, the young man who shot
himself at his boarding house in Quincy Jan
17th died Friday in St Mary's Hospital where he
was taken when he made the attempt on his life.
His brother committed suicide in Quincy several
years ago. Was son of Charles Wood a farmer of
Ellington twp and was 23 years of age.

WOODS, CATHERINE - Probate Notice - Feb 23,
1893 Catherine, deceased   1st Monday of May
1893 (1st) Geo. C. Bartells, Executor.

WOODS, CHARLEY - Ancient History - Jul 15, 1896
June 1877 Charley Woods a brakeman on the C.B.

& Q was killed at Rochelle by falling across
the rail and being run over. He was a Camp
Point boy.

WOODS, MRS JAMES - Local - Mar 16, 1893
Remember the executor sale, Friday, March 17th
at the home of the late Mrs James Woods.

WOODS, WILLIAM J. - 20 Years Ago - Aug 31, 1893
William J. Woods died at his home in Houston
twp.

WORDEN, REV HORACE - Quincy - Feb 22, 1895 Rev
Horace Worden for many years a Baptist
clergyman in this city died in Minneapolis last
week 83 years old.

WORTH, CARRIE M. - Quincy - Sep 3, 1902 Carrie
M. Worth, a well known milliner, died on
Friday, age 44 years.

WRIGHT, MRS CHARITY - Sept 24, 1895 Canton,
Ill Sept 20th Mrs Charity Wright died at her
home in Banner twp Wednesday 8 P.M. Was 106
years 7 months 26 days old. Surviving her are
4 children all over 70 years.

WRIGHT, DR CHARLES W. - Quincy - Dec 29, 1897
Dr Charles W. Wright an inmate of the Soldiers
Home died Tuesday night. Remains taken to St
Louis to be cremated.

WYLE, JOHN - Ancient History - Jun 25, 1895
June 1877 John Wyle died age 66.

WYLE, JOHN - Ancient History - Oct 7, 1896
June 1877 John Wyle died.

XANDER, DAVID - Obituary - Sep 15, 1897 David
Xander born in Lehigh Co. Penn Jan 20, 1812
died near Liberty Sep 11, 1897 age 85 years 7
months 22 days. Married Hannah Blank Dec 30,
1832 and came to Ill. 1834 and settled Adams
Co. Had 10 children, 4 sons and 2 daughters
still living - Edward and Josiah of Missouri,
Aaron and Mrs Susan Fry of Liberty, David of
Quincy and Mrs Elizabeth Getts of Camp Point.

Wife died Jun 19, 1894 at age 80 years.   Member
of Lutheran Church at Liberty.   Services held
there Monday afternoon and buried Lutheran
cemetery.

YACKLEY, PHILIP - Quincy - Sep 3, 1902 Philip
Yackley, a well known resident of this city,
died at Colorado Springs, Colo. on Wednesday,
age 78 years.

YANCEY, DR CHARLES H. - Local - Jul 30, 1902
Dr Charles H. Yancey who practiced medicine in
Camp Point about 20 years ago died in Salt Lake
City Saturday afternoon.   He had started for
Calif. for his health and stopped at Salt Lake
City.   For many years he was local surgeon a
Hannibal of M.K. & T. and Wabash railroads.

YEARGAIN, EDWARD - Columbus - Jul 5, 1895
Edward Yeargain, an old resident of this
vicinity died at his home in Quincy July 1st.
Funeral at Mt Pleasant Wednesday 11 A.M.

YEARGAIN, EDWARD A. - Quincy - Jul 2, 1895
Edward A. Yeargain died at his home on Kentucky
St. Monday afternoon age 65 years.   Born
Kentucky and settled Gilmer twp with his
parents in early childhood about 11 years ago
he moved to Quincy.   Leaves a wife and 7
children.

YEARGAIN, ELMER THORNTON - Recent Deaths - Feb
10, 1897 Died, Elmer Thornton Yeargain, son of
William A. Yeargain and wife.   Born near Camp
Point Dec 16, 1893 died Camp Point Jan 31st of
croup.   Services at the house.   Buried Mt
Pleasant cemetery.

YEARGAIN, FLOYD WALTER - Obituary - Aug 13,
1893 Floyd Walter, son of William and Kate
Yeargain, died at their home, near Columbus,
Ill Sunday Aug 13, 1893 age 14 months.
Services at Mt Pleasant Church.

YEARGAIN, WILLIAM A. - Local - Feb 3, 1897 A
little son of Mr and Mrs William A. Yeargain
died Sunday A.M. of croup.   Remains taken

Monday to Pleasant Grove for burial, age 3
years 1 month 15 days.

YOUNG, MRS - Paloma - Sep 30, 1903 Mrs Young
died at the home of her daughter, Mrs
Hendricks, Saturday A.M.

YOUNG, HARVEY - Found Dead - Oct 23, 1894
Springfield, Ill October 22nd A dying man
found on the Wabash track at New Berlin with a
revolver in his hand. A bullet hole in his
temple. From papers it is supposed he is
Harvey Young of Kinderhook, Ill.

YOUNG, LUDWIG - Local - Jun 15, 1893 Jury in
the case of the state vs Adam Young, charged
with murder of his father, Ludwig Young, near
Benbow, MO on trial at special term of the
Marion Co. Circuit Court at Palmyra returned
verdict at 11 P.M. Friday of murder in the 1st
degree. Adam Young was a student at Gem City
College at Quincy.

YOUNG, MRS MARY - Quincy - Jun 1, 1894 Died
Mrs Mary Young, one of the early settlers of
this city died in Wichita, Sunday, age 85
years. Funeral here Tuesday.

YOUNG, MRS POLLY - Mrs Polly Young - Jan 6,
1897 Mrs Polly Young, widow of Capt Young,
died at the home of her sister, Mrs Chauncey
Cook near Newtown Dec 30th. She formerly lived
in Richfield twp and many years in Quincy.

YOUNG, MRS SAMUEL - Local - Jun 19, 1894
Killed, Mrs Samuel Young of Macomb was killed
by the train Saturday eve.

ZAHN, LOUIS J. - Legal Notice - Sep 3, 1902
Mary Zahn as adm of the estate of Louis J. Zahn
deceased petitioner vs to sell real estate to
pay debts Bernhard J. Zahn, Theodore Zahn,
Colin Zahn, Anna Conrad, Louise Collins, Helen
Giese, Julius Zahn, William J. Sagehorn, Julius
W. Sagehorn, Emma Sagehorn, Martha Schwab,
Frieda King and Henry W. Cordsiemon,
defendants.   J.R. Pierce, Co. clerk.

ZEIGER, WILLIAM - Local - Aug 25, 1897 Died
William Zeiger died at his home in Concord
Monday age 80 years. He was a German who lived
there many years and respected by all who knew
him.

ZEIGER, WILLIAM - Obituary - Sep 1, 1897
William Zeiger born Prussia 1816. Married
Louisa Kohnert 1840. Came to America 1858.
First locating in Quincy for 1 year. Then
settled about 4 miles south of Camp Point where
he stayed till death on the 23rd inst at the
home of his daughter, Mrs Louis Steiner where
he had lived many years. Leaves 2 daughters
and 3 brothers. Services on the 24th (Tuesday)
by Elder O. Dilley. Buried on private cemetery
on the farm of Louis Steiner.

ZIEGLER, LORENTZ - Ancient History - Jul 16,
1895 - July 1879 Lorentz Ziegler died, age 68.

ZIEGLER, LORENTZ - Ancient History - Apr 21,
1897 - July 1879 Lorentz Ziegler, an old
German resident died.

ZIMMERMAN, MR AND MRS JOSEPH - Quincy - Nov 26,
1902 The 4 month old boy of Mr and Mrs Joseph
Zimmerman, who was scalded by hot coffee a few
days ago died from his injuries Friday.

ZIMMERMAN, VALENTINE - Quincy - Dec 3, 1902
Valentine Zimmerman, one of the pioneers of
Adams Co. died at his home near Fall Creek on
Tuesday, age 83 years.

ZINN, SAMUEL - Death - Oct 29, 1895 Samuel
Zinn, age 90 years died at his home near
Stillwell Sunday. Had gone to the barn to
hitch up a horse when he fell to the ground and
died instantly. Was a pioneer settler of
Hancock Co. coming from Virginia when a young
man. Leaves a wife, a hopeless invalid and a
large family of children, of whom Mrs H.E.
Selby of Golden is one and Mrs C.F. McKown is
another.

Heritage Books by
Mrs. Joseph J. Beals, Sr. and Mrs. Sandra Kirchner:

Births and Related Items Abstracted from The Camp Point Journal
of Camp Point, Adams County, Illinois, 1873–1903

Deaths Abstracted from The Camp Point Journal, *1873–1882,
Camp Point, Adams County, Illinois*

Deaths Abstracted from The Camp Point Journal, *1883–1892,
Camp Point, Adams County, Illinois*

Deaths Abstracted from The Camp Point Journal, *1893–1903,
Camp Point, Adams County, Illinois*

*Marriages (1895–1905) and Deaths (1895–1900) and Related Items Abstracted
from the* Golden New Era *of Golden, Adams County, Illinois*

Marriages and Related Items Abstracted from The Clayton Enterprise
Newspaper of Clayton, Adams County, Illinois, 1879–1900

Marriages and Related Items Abstracted from the Mendon Dispatch
of Mendon, Adams County, Illinois, 1877–1905

Obituaries and Death Related Items Abstracted from Clayton Enterprise
Newspaper of Clayton, Adams County Illinois, 1879–1900, Volume 1

Obituaries and Death Related Items Abstracted from the Hendon Dispatch
of Mendon, Adams County, Illinois, 1877–1905

CD: Births and Deaths Abstracted from The Camp Point Journal,
Camp Point, Adams County, Illinois, 1873–1903

CD: Marriages and Related Items Abstracts from the Golden New Era
Newspaper of Golden, Adam County, Illinois, 1895–1905

CD: Marriages and Related Items Abstracts from the Mendon Dispatch
of Mendon, Adams County, Illinois, 1877–1905

CD: Obituaries and Death Related Items Abstracts from the Golden New Era
Newspaper of Golden, Adam County, Illinois, 1895–1900

CD: Obituaries and Death Related Items Abstracts from the Mendon Dispatch
of Mendon, Adams County, Illinois, 1877–1905